WORD POWER

A Dictionary of Fascinating and Learned Words and Phrases for Vocabulary Enrichment

---

John Fleming

D1378131

University Press of America,® Inc.
Lanham · Boulder · New York · Toronto · Plymouth, UK

Copyright © 2007 by
University Press of America,® Inc.
4501 Forbes Boulevard
Suite 200
Lanham, Maryland 20706
UPA Acquisitions Department (301) 459-3366

Estover Road
Plymouth PL6 7PY
United Kingdom

Library of Congress Control Number: 2007925511
ISBN-13: 978-0-7618-3804-3 (paperback : alk. paper)
ISBN-10: 0-7618-3804-X (paperback : alk. paper)

♾™ The paper used in this publication meets the minimum
requirements of American National Standard for Information
Sciences—Permanence of Paper for Printed Library Materials,
ANSI Z39.48—1984

For Timothy and Jeanne,

Who did well in raising a family despite difficult circumstances

Table of Contents

Preface

It would have been impossible to use a phonetic, true system of pronunciation for a work like this; hence, the pronunciation for each word is an approximation, with the reader's prior knowledge being used to fill in the gaps in the pronunciation shorthand. The normal alphabet has been used here for pronunciation, which is given in brackets. *The syllable in capital letters is stressed.* For example, in the pronunciation of *contumely* [konTOOmulee], the second syllable [TOO] is stressed (receives the emphasis).

An ellipsis in a pronunciation indicates that the pronunciation of the entry is obvious and so is omitted. An *h* after the vowel *i* or *o* indicates that it is long, like [SIHmunee] for the entry *simony*, the *ih* denoting the sound of *i* in *kite*. And the letters *oh* in a pronunciation indicate the sound of *o* in *snow*.

A few abbreviations are used in the text: Syn.=synonym or synonyms; Ant.=antonym or antonyms; esp.=especially. Synonyms and antonyms are given in alphabetical order. A synonym given in the definition of an entry is not repeated under Syn. Thus, if it were used in the definition of *acerbic*, the word "harsh" would not be given as a synonym. Some entries logically have no synonym or antonym—for example, *melting pot*.

Most of the entries—as a defined word or phrase is called—have a few examples of usage; in other words, the entry is used in a sentence to show how it can be applied. However, the usage may contain a form of the word rather than the exact word itself; for example, under *acerbity* may be a sentence with "acerbic." This method allows greater freedom to compose or think up a sample sentence.

Word Power is in dictionary form, with the entries being in alphabetical order. Each term—of which there are about 2,000—is defined, given a pronunciation and then given usually four examples of usage. Synonyms and antonyms, where possible, are listed at the end of each term.

Terms were chosen based on a reading of the dictionary and on my own notation over the years of remarkable words and phrases. For example, the former include *contumely*, *pulchritude* and *vilify*. The entries are thus in a sense intermediate—neither too common nor too rare, neither too familiar nor too unusual. This was an important consideration in writing the book, since in a capacious language like English the number of defined terms could go on and on. The inclusion of too many terms would have made the book little different from an ordinary desk dictionary. Consider the term *bacchanal*. This word is rather infrequent and therefore possibly unknown to a casual reader. By reading *Word Power*, one immediately gets a definition and an understanding of *bacchanal* that might otherwise have required years of reading. The reader sees that it means a "riotous celebration," sees the pronunciation (an aid to remembering) and how it can be used. The synonyms and antonyms further clarify the meaning, and, where relevant, the etymology (origin) of the term is given.

In addition, perusal of a dictionary of slang was used to provide some colorful terms, such as *munchasaurus* and *zulued*. Some terms from foreign languages are included, especially from French and Latin, but also from German, Italian, Spanish and Russian. The result is intended to be an informative guide to English vocabulary for the student, scholar or layman.

John Fleming
St. Louis, MO
January, 2007

A

ab initio [AB iNISHeeoh] (Latin) from the beginning. "When their house was destroyed by fire, the family had to rebuild *ab initio*." "He forgot everything he had learned about Russian and had to learn *ab initio*." "When another boy arrived, the children started their kickball game *ab initio*." "The trial of the accused was redone *ab initio* after a procedural error."

abjure [abJOOR] to renounce. "Immigrants to America *abjured* the Old World culture and language." "He *abjured* gluttony and tried to stop overeating." "He *abjured* Christianity and took up atheism." "The man *abjured* his 'heresy' after being questioned by the Inquisition." Syn. disown, forswear, renounce, repudiate, retract. Ant.: maintain.

ablution [abLOOshun] a cleansing with water, especially as a religious ritual. "They went to the river for an *ablution*." "The *ablution* took place in the morning." "The emperor received *ablution* by priests." "The *ablution* felt good to the woman."

abrogate [ABrugayt] to annul. "The Russo-German pact of 1941 was *abrogated* by the German invasion of Russia." "Their marriage was *abrogated* in divorce proceedings." "He *abrogated* his previous agreement." "Signing the deal *abrogated* the previous contract." Syn.: abolish, cancel, negate, nullify, repeal, revoke.

abrosia [uBROHzhu] fasting. "The ballerina did not know how dangerous *abrosia* was." "He found *abrosia* easy." "She practiced *abrosia* for half a day." "The monk practiced *abrosia* for a religious reason." This is an uncommon word reminiscent of *ambrosia*.

abstemious [abSTEEmeeus] eating and drinking in moderation. "He was anything but *abstemious*, weighing 300 pounds." "*Abstemiousness* is virtuous." "Working in a cafeteria with delicious food made being *abstemious* hard." "The fat man tried hard to be *abstemious*." Syn.: forbearing, moderate, temperate.

abstruse [abSTROOS] difficult to understand. "Many students find quantum mechanics *abstruse*." "His field of learning was *abstruse*." "The mathematical equation was *abstruse*." "The theory was *abstruse*." Syn.: esoteric, incomprehensible, recondite. Ant.: self-evident.

Acapulco gold [ahkuPOLko GOLD] marijuana grown in Mexico, supposedly having a superior quality. "They were in the habit of getting a 'buzz' from *Acapulco gold* after dinner." "The grass they bought was not premium *Acapulco gold*." "They rolled up several joints using *Acapulco gold*." (Spears; see bibliography.)

accident [AKsidunt] a bastard. "He was reputed to be a so-called '*accident*,' though these days the stigma is not so great." "He was an *accident*, a love child." "The *accident* went from one orphanage and institution to another." "The *accident* became a problem child." Syn.: avetrol, bar steward, blankard, momzer, whore's kitling. (Spears.)

accolade [AKulayd] acclaim or an award. "The movie *Heaven's Gate* did not exactly receive *accolades*." "The *accolade* for the book said it was 'undeniably brilliant.'" "The *accolade* came with $10,000." "*Accolades* in the form of passing grades were available for all who showed up for class." "The opera of Ruggiero Leoncavallo (1858-1919) received much *accolade*." Syn.: honor, laurels. Ant.: demerit.

accouterments [uKOOturmunts] trappings; the external features by which something may be identified. "The vast *accouterments* of the American presidency include the White House, Air Force One and the Secret Service." "The *accouterments* of baseball are a ball and glove." "He was chasing the *accouterments* of happiness instead of happiness itself." "One of the *accouterments* of fame is money."

A.C.-D.C. [AYSEE DEESEE] bisexual. "His friend said the guy was '*A.C.-D.C.*,' but what he meant by that did not become apparent until later." "The bright girl was *A.C.-D.C.*" "He was not straight, but *A.C.-D.C.*" "The man appeared *A.C.-D.C.* but was more gay than heterosexual." (Spears.)

acerbate [ASurbayt] to annoy. "His brother's drum playing *acerbated* him to no end." "It *acerbated* him to know that she probably told others about the altercation." "His *acerbation* was complete when she returned the car with the gas tank on empty." "He unintentionally *acerbated* his room mate." Syn.: bother, irk, irritate, molest. Ant.: please.

acerbity [uSERbitee] severity; harshness. "The dictator's speech was full of *acerbity*." "The singer's personality was *acerbic*." "He had a nasty *acerbic* temper." "Her punishment was *acerbic*." Syn.: ferocity, rigorousness, roughness. Ant.: gentleness.

acid [ASid] LSD. "He experimented with *acid* in order to try to expand his understanding of reality, but concluded that the drug was not very helpful in that respect." "The high-school student sold *acid* part-time." "He was afraid to take *acid*, which his friends were doing." "He experienced a flashback due to having taken *acid*." Syn.: blue cheer, lucy in the sky with diamonds, mellow-yellow, owsley, pearly gates, purple microdots. (Spears.)

acidulous [uSIJulus] caustic. "His *acidulous* comments at the post-game press conference gave him a reputation as a radical." "He was *acidulous* in evaluating the beauty of his wife, who was 44." "She was *acidulous* with her mother." "His reply to his opponent was *acidulous*." Syn.: biting. Ant.: laudatory.

acquiesce man [akweeES MAN] a sycophant (a variant of the term "yes man"). "He was derided as an *acquiesce man*, though he did make good contributions to the business." "The *acquiesce man* did exactly as he was told." "The *acquiesce man* did not criticize the others." "The *acquiesce man* was not promoted." Syn.: ass-kisser, boot lick, catch-fart, spaniel, toad-eater, truckler. (Spears.)

acrimony [AKrimohnee] enmity or rancor. "Mention of compulsory busing caused an *acrimonious* debate at the school board meeting." "There was *acrimony* between whites and blacks in the city." "His arrival at the meeting sent one faction streaming out the doors in an *acrimonious* huff." "He was *acrimonious* toward his son." Syn.: acerbity, bitterness, irascibility, malevolence. Ant.: amiability, civility.

acumen [AKyoomun] quick discernment; shrewdness. "His social *acumen* was amazing." "Her *acumen* could really size up a person." "Little escaped the teacher's *acumen*." "He had *acumen* for buying and selling securities." Syn.: astuteness, incisiveness, perspicacity, understanding. Ant.: obtuseness, stupidity.

Adam and Eve it [ADum AND EEV IT] to have sex. "They were told in polite terms that the couple was *Adam and Eving it* on the bed when they came in." "To *Adam and Eve it* on the first date was not her style." "She did not wish to *Adam and Eve it* with him." "The couple put off *Adam and Eving it* until marriage." (Spears.)

adamantine [aduMANteen] unyielding in attitude or opinion. "He was *adamantine* that the student failed her class." "The loan shark was *adamantine* that the loan be repaid." "The referee was *adamantine* about his call." "He was *adamantine* that the show would go on."

ad crumenam [AD KRUmenum] pertaining to an argument of fallacious reasoning whereby one takes a position based on what he has to gain financially. "Outrageous *ad crumenam* positions are taken in Congress without being criticized." "He was guilty of the *ad crumenam* argument." "'Don't kill music, America,' said the songwriter *ad crumenam*." "His justification for selling out was *ad crumenam*."

addle [ADul] to confuse. "The fact that celebrities are overpaid is *addled* in the public mind by constant portrayal of them on television as worthy aristocracy." "All the champagne he imbibed *addled* his mind." "He was *addled* by geometry." "The blow to the head *addled* his senses." Syn.: bewilder, muddle. Ant.: clarify.

ad hoc [AD HAUK] (Latin) for a specific purpose. "The *ad hoc* anti-war group protested the use of the horrifying weapon Napalm." "The *ad hoc* committee on medicine held a hearing to investigate the restriction on medical school enrollment." "The *ad hoc* government agency did its job poorly." "The *ad hoc* association campaigned for gun control."

ad hominem [AD HOMinum] appealing to emotion or bias rather than to reason. "Her argument was guilty of the *ad hominem* fallacy, since she was actually only referring to her opponent's obesity." "His argument contained the *ad hominem* and straw man fallacies." "He proceeded to use the *ad hominem* during the whole debate." "The dialogue of rival political candidates is full of *ad hominem* attacks."

adjure [uJOOR] to entreat or enjoin. "Some commentators maintain that only cowardice *adjured* President Ford to pardon Nixon." "The essay *adjured* readers to think about propaganda on television." "The letter *adjured* the family to move to another city." Syn.: beseech, implore, supplicate. Ant.: demand.

ad libitum [AD LIBitum] at one's pleasure. "The president spoke *ad libitum* without being interrupted." "He had access to her checking account *ad libitum*." "He used the phrase *ad libitum*, as often as he wished." "He ate her cookies *ad libitum*."

ad majorem Dei gloriam [AD muJORum DEEe GLOReeum] (Latin) "to the greater glory of God." "Heretics were sometimes ritually executed in the Middle Ages with the idea *ad majorem Dei gloriam.*" "The cathedral was dedicated *ad majorem Dei gloriam.*" "The priest said a mass *ad majorem Dei gloriam.*" "The sun's rising every morning occurs *ad majorem Dei gloriam.*"

Adonis [uDONis] a beautiful boy or man. "The *Adonis* had several girls to choose from." "The *Adonis* was, as they say in French, *beau et grand à la fois.*" "The *Adonis* lost his handsomeness in middle age." "The *Adonis* played basketball well." This word comes from Greek mythology.

ad rem [AD REM] pertinent; in a straightforward manner. "The lawyer's citation was *ad rem.*" "The child answered the question *ad rem.*" "The judge's remark was *ad rem.*" "The suspect did not speak to police *ad rem.*"

adscititious [adsiTISHus] unnecessary. "The radicals of the 60s found the war to be *adscititious.*" "Washing your own car is *adscititious* when you are rich." "Cleaning the carpet, he thought, was expensive and *adscititious.*" "Washing your hands seems to be *adscititious* after a certain point." Syn.: superfluous. Ant.: vital.

adumbrate [ADumbrayt] to foreshadow. "The dark clouds *adumbrated* the storm that ruined the picnic." "*Es lag in der Luft*' is German for 'it was foretold' or 'it was in the air, as if *adumbrated.*'" "The man *adumbrated* his future action at the meeting." "The rain *adumbrated* the flood."

ad valorum [AD vuLORum] (Latin) according to the value. "With expensive jewelry, for example, the tax climbs *ad valorum*, but is not progressive and hits the poor hard." "The cost of participation was fixed *ad valorum* to potential winnings." "They each chipped in *ad valorum*, depending on how much they stood to gain." "The tax was levied *ad valorum.*"

aegis [EEjis] protection, sponsorship. "Under the *aegis* of his foster parents, the boy developed into a self-assured, successful man." "Artists flourished under the *aegis* of aristocratic families." "He attended college under the *aegis* of his father." "Alexandria became a great city under the *aegis* of a foreign power."

affaire d'interet [ahFER danTRE] self-interest; having a financial stake. "The *affaire d'interet* of American politicians should be more closely scrutinized." "The councilman had an *affaire d'interet* in the sale of the building." "The governor's wife had an *affaire d'interet* in the development of the property." "The *affaire d'interet* was ownership of some stock." "Public opinion attributed no *affaire d'interet* to the woman, extremely wealthy though she was."

affiance [AFeeans] to betroth in marriage. "The lovely woman was *affianced* at an early age." "She was *affianced* to a dentist." "She became *affianced* at age 17." "He was *affianced* to a doctor."

affray [uFRAY] a public fight; disturbance of the peace. "An *affray* of snowball fights interrupted the football game." "The *affray* was an ugly fight." "The *affray* between the police and partygoers led to a law suit." "The *affray* took place in the quadrangle of the university." Syn.: battle, clash, fistfight, quarrel, scuffle, struggle.

a fortiori [AY fauteeORee] all the more reason. *"A fortiori* should he be restrained, argued the lawyer in court." "Because of the love of power, people *a fortiori* should be wary of politicians." "Because blue-collar jobs are a grind, one ought, *a fortiori* to plan for a specific career while in college." "Because life is short *a fortiori* should you live for the day."

Afro-Saxon [AFro SAKsun] a black person who tries to behave like whites. "Noone in the class said he was familiar with the term *'Afro-Saxon.'*" "He was an *'Afro-Saxon'* and an Uncle Tom." "The *Afro-Saxon* was not ambitious." "The *Afro-Saxon* wanted to be an accountant." (Spears.)

agape [uGAYP] in a gaping state. "His eyes were *agape* as he watched the woman undress." "The gaze of the school principal was *agape* as the unruly boys filed past." "His face was *agape* at the clothing-optional beach." "The man was *agape* as he watched the scene through binoculars."

agent provocateur [ahZHAN provakaTEUR] a person hired to incite political activists to engage in a crime for which they can be prosecuted. "The stand-up comedian made a very amusing joke about an *'agent provocateurr'*" "The *agent provocateur* was hired by the employer to disrupt the union." "Have you ever met an *agent provocateur*?" "The corporation had an *agent provocateur* in the labor union."

agitprop [AJitprop] agitation and propaganda, especially as engaged in by communists. *"Agitprop* is not found solely in communist countries, but is part of the West as well." "The television station engaged in *agitprop*." "The *agitprop* attacked imperialism." "The radical asserted that *agitprop* should be judged by how it affects inequality."

agnostic [agNOStik] pertaining to the idea that whether there is a God cannot be known; a person believing in such an idea. "Taking a middle course between atheism and Christianity, the man declared himself an *agnostic,* but that did not place him above controversy." "The pessimist went from being an *agnostic* to a confirmed atheist." "He referred to himself as a 'born-again *agnostic.'*" "The *agnostic* thought he had good reason for not believing in God."

agonal [AGunul] pertaining to suffering or the throes of death. This is the adjectival form of *agony.* "Francis Bacon (1561-1626), in 'Of Death,' dismissed the idea that death caused *agonal* pain, and maintained that for many it would come as a relief, or release from a difficult life, saying that a man may look forward to the conclusion of life as one of nature's blessings." "The cancer patient felt *agonal* pain." "Her *agonal* cries were heard up and down the corridor." "He suffered *agonal* pain before dying."

agora [AGuru] a marketplace, especially one in ancient Greece. This word is used to form *agoraphobia* (dread of open places). "The city's *agora* bustles with activity." "They found the *agora* a pleasant place." "The *agora* was located in the town's Altstadt." "The *agora* was a pleasant place."

agrestic [uGREStik] rural or unrefined. *"Agrestic* families are often looked down upon by their suburban neighbors, especially if their house is a mess." *"Agrestic* life can be lonesome." *"Agrestic* scenery can be lovely." "The woman did not like *agrestic* life." Syn.: boorish, crude, hoosierish, parochial, philistine, provincial, redneck, rustic.

ajax [AYjaks] a privy. Syn.: can, chapel of ease, hoosegow, leak-house, Quaker's burying ground, Sir Henry, spice island, stool of ease. "The *ajax* was filthy and in poor condition." "Coming from the *ajax* was a horrendous stink." "He hated to use the *ajax* because he thought it disgusting." (Spears.)

a la belle etoile [AH LAH BEL eTWAL] (French) "under the stars," in the open air. "They had a gazebo for eating lunch *a la belle etoile.*" "They dined al fresco, *a la belle etoile.*" "The couple took a walk *a la belle etoile.*"

alacrity [uLAKritee] eagerness. "Tocqueville noted the *alacrity* with which Americans pursued material wealth." "The magistrate attended the porno-graphic film screenings with *alacrity.*" "The children opened their Christmas presents with joyful *alacrity.*" "He played tennis with *alacrity.*"

a la francaise [AH LAH franSEZ] (French) "in the French manner." "When in Paris it is only fitting that you act *a la francaise.*" "They spoke French and acted *a la francaise.*" "The students' artwork was *a la francaise.*" "They frequented a cafe *a la francaise.*"

alcalde [alKAHLday] the mayor of a town. "The *alcalde* of San Juan was young." "The woman *alcalde* was re-elected." "The *alcalde* opened the town's fiesta." "The *alcalde* was honest and fair."

alchy [ALkee] an alcoholic. "The *alchy* engineer was fired from his job after repeated breaches of duty." "The *alchy* attended the AA meetings." "The *alchy* lost his wife because of his drinking." "The *alchy* was guilty of driving drunk." Syn.: bar-fly, bib-all-night, boozeheister, bubber, crock, dipso, ken-nurd, love-pot, lush, pretzel-bender, slush hog, sot, wassailer, winebibber. (Spears.)

aleatory [AYleeutoree] pertaining to chance or gambling. "The *aleatory* habits of silver and gold diggers in Nevada paved the way for the state's gambling industry." "She loved *aleatory* contests like bingo and the slots." "He bet on the ponies whenever he had an extra buck for his *aleatory* squander of money." "His *aleatory* habit was a vice."

alembic [uLEMbik] something that transforms or purifies. "The man hoped for an emotional *alembic* to change his life." "Their vacation was very relaxing and worked like an *alembic.*" "Money can be like an *alembic* when show-ered on a poor person." "An *alembic* was needed to revamp the quality of education."

allegory [ALugoree] an artistic or literary work that symbolically depicts ideas through material representation. "In the *allegorical* novel *Moby Dick* a great white whale represents evil." "The *allegory* in Kafka is not easy to under-stand." "He wrote an *allegorical* short story in which good and evil were represented by the main character." "The *allegory* explored the life of a woman who strove for celebrity fame merely because her parents otherwise withheld their approval."

altar [ALtur] a toilet, chamber pot. "Their father's references to the '*altar*' and the throne always amused them." "The prince's *altar* was tended by a ser-vant." "She had to go to the *altar* often." (Spears.)

amantes, amentes [amANtes aMENtes] (Latin) "lovers are mad." "He quoted

Terence, '*amantes, amentes,*' to the effect that love transports one to madness." "The idea *amantes, amentes* is frequently not part of romance novels." "Remembering the quote *amantes, amentes,* he tried to avoid extremes of passion in his relationship." "Francis Bacon (1561-1626) wrote of the idea *amantes, amentes.*"

amaranthine [amuRANthin] eternally beautiful; everlasting. "He poetically told his sweetheart that his love for her was *amaranthine.*" "The stars in the sky are *amaranthine.*" "He thought that the beautiful memory was *amaranthine.*" "In her mind the Christmas of 1965 was *amaranthine.*"

amazon [AMuzan] a warlike woman of Greek mythology; a big aggressive woman. "'We don't stand a chance up against these *amazons,*' he said at the volleyball game, referring to a few players on the opposite team who were pretty big for women." "The athletic woman, an *amazon,* was big and tall." "She was sort of a mix between a man and a woman, sort of an *amazon.*" Syn.: androgyne, beldame, bull bitch, virago.

ambient [AMbeeunt] completely surrounding; circulating. "The animal was cooler than the *ambient* air." "The *ambience* of the room was pleasant and relaxing." "The *ambience* of the stream was too hot for much life." "The *ambient* desert air was dry."

ambisextrous [ambiSEKStrus] pertaining to bisexuality. "She bitterly repeated a term she had heard that applied to her husband, she found out late—*ambisextrous.*" "The *ambisextrous* man died at age 30." "She was *ambisextrous,* but preferred women." This is a humorous pun on "ambidextrous." (Spears; see bibliography.)

ambrosia [amBROHzhu] something especially delicious. "The meal was like *ambrosia.*" "The pizza tasted to him like *ambrosia.*" "Chocolate was like *ambrosia* when he was a child." "Food must be fresh and preservative-free to be *ambrosia.*"

ament [AYmunt] an insane person. From Latin *a,* "out of," and *mens,* "mind." "The *ament* was committed to an institution." "The *ament* was affected by the moon." "The *ament* was taking a neuroleptic (antipsychotic)." "The *ament* needed 'help.'" Syn.: lunatic, madman, schizophrenic.

âme perdue [AHM perDUE] (French) a desperate person; literally, a "lost soul." "His emotional crisis made of him an *âme perdue.*" "The *âme perdue* thought too much." "The *âme perdue* was alone much of the time." "The *âme perdue* sometimes lost his nerve in social situations."

amok [uMUK] (also *amuck*) in a wild frenzy to do violence; losing self-control. "The children ran *amok,* and the parents claimed they were helpless to discipline them." "He ran *amok* after being fired and went looking for an outlet for his rage." "The children ran *amok* on the playground." "The crowd ran *amok* after their team lost." *Amok* was originally a Malay term.

amortize [uMORtihz] to pay off a debt. "Unable to *amortize* his debts, he was hounded by creditors." "Their house was *amortized,* was free-and-clear." "The bank told him he had to *amortize* his bills before he could receive a loan." "He never *amortized* his obligations."

amour-propre [ahMOOR PROPRE] (French) self-respect. "He had no *amour-*

propre, and thus his hatred for others." "He taught his son *amour-propre.*"
"He was dignified and had *amour-propre* in full." "Lack of *amour-propre*
prevents normal interaction with others."

amp [AMP] a dose of amphetamine. "He took an *amp* to keep on going through
the night." "The trucker used *amps.*" "The drug addict would use downers to
balance the *amps* he took." Syn.: bam, black mollies, road dope, thrusters,
West-Coast turnarounds. (Spears.)

Amy-John [AYmee JON] a masculine homosexual woman. "She had the reputation of being an *Amy-John,* an aggressive lesbian, on campus." "The *Amy-
John* took a lover in prison." "The *Amy-John* had a passive lover." (Spears.)

anachronism [uNAKrunizm] something that has lasted beyond its useful period.
"The stars of an earlier decade can easily become an *anachronism* in American culture." "The unknown mogul who governs behind the scenes is an
anachronism in American society." "He became an *anachronism* in his own
lifetime." "The wooden tennis racket is an *anachronism.*" *Khronos,* Greek
for time, forms part of this word.

anal avenger [AYnul uVENjur] a pederast. "They labeled him an '*anal avenger*'
without really knowing much about the homosexual man." "He was not in
fact an *anal avenger.*" "The *anal avenger* disgusted him." Syn.: bum hole
engineer, gentleman of the back door, inspector of manholes, Prussian, sau-
sage jockey, turd burglar. (Spears.)

analects [ANulekts] (plural) selected passages from an author or authors. "It was
an excellent book of *analects.*" "*The Faber Book of America* is an excellent
collection of *analects.*" "The *analects* were written by preRaphaelites." "The
anthology contained *analects* by 19th century American authors."

analogue [ANulog] something analogous to another thing; the word also has a
biological and chemical meaning. "The human penis and clitoris are biological *analogues.*" "He made an *analogy* between his running speed and a jack
rabbit." "The writer claimed that there was a relationship, an *analogy,* there."
"The model plane was an *analogue* of the real one."

anathema [uNATHemu] a disliked person or thing. "He felt *anathema* in his
own house." "In no other country is it more of an *anathema* to be aged."
"The soldier was *anathema* in the village." "He was *anathema* on the football field."

anchorite [ANGkuriht] a religious recluse. "The widow vowed spinsterhood and
became an *anchorite.*" "The *anchorite* lived in the monastery." "The *anchorite* taught math at the seminary." "The monastery harbored a number of *an-
chorites.*"

ancien régime [anSYE reZHIM] (French) the previous political order; the old
order. "The *ancien régime* of the American South is that region prior to
1860." "France's *ancien régime* went bankrupt." "In the Tennis Court Oath,
the nobles of the *ancien régime* renounced their class privilege." "The *ancien régime* tried to reassert power."

angst [AHNGST] anxiety. "Supposedly the modern world is full of *angst.*"
"*Angst*-ridden teenage years is not a cultural universal, is not found everywhere." "The groom was full of *angst* on the day of the wedding." "She tried

to relieve her *angst* with diazepam (a benzodiazepine minor tranquilizer)." Syn.: apprehensiveness. Ant.: tranquility.

animadversion [anumadVURzhun] forceful criticism. "The right wing's *animadversion* of feminism and the whole 'liberal-left' was unrealistic and overblown." "The radical's *animadversion* of inequality was persuasive." "His team's *animadversion* of the other team was a disgrace." "He lived to regret his *animadversion* of the president." "The historian believed that *animadversion* of the boycotted country is undeserved."

annus luctus [ANus LUKtus] a year of mourning. (In German, *Trauerjahr*.) During this year a widow or widower is forbidden to remarry; that way, the paternity of an as yet unborn child is made certain. "An *annus luctus* tradition apparently was never established in America." "Due to the custom of *annus luctus*, he could not immediately remarry." "The church supported *annus luctus*." "After a proper *annus luctus*, the widow remarried."

annus mirabilis [ANus miraBILis] (Latin) a remarkable year. "The year 1975 was an *annus mirabilis* in his life as far as happiness is concerned." "His best friend helped to make it an *annus mirabilis*." "The year he got married was an *annus mirabilis*." "Since their team won the championship that year, 1979 was an *annus mirabilis*."

anodyne [ANudihn] soothing; trite. "The politician's speech was full of *anodyne* glittering generalizations about alleged greatness that bored the audience." "Vitamins transformed his life, made it *anodyne*." "Fluoxetine, an antidepressant well-known by its trade name, can be *anodyne* for a depressed, jaded life." "Scrubbing toilets at minimum wage is not exactly an *anodyne*."

anomie [ANumee] social chaos. "The country's defeat and the approach of the enemy army brought about *anomie*, including looting and desperate attempts to flee." "Lack of parental guidance can cause *anomie*." "*Anomie* reigned in the country, and noone wanted to show compassion for others." "The sociologist studied *anomie*."

ante bellum [ANtee BELum] (Latin) before the war. "They visited an *ante bellum* mansion in Mississippi." "The museum exhibited *ante bellum* photographs." "The *ante bellum* book was worth a few hundred dollars as an antique." "The *ante bellum* submarine was obsolete."

antedate [ANtudayt] to precede in time. "The loss of empire by Britain *antedates* its economic problems." "His alcoholism *antedates* the death of his wife." "The Boston Tea Party *antedated* the American Revolution."

antediluvian [anteediLOOveeun] antiquated or primitive; (noun) a very old or old-fashioned person. "His beliefs about the place of women were *antediluvian*." "The navy ship was *antediluvian*." "The Ford car was *antediluvian*." "Their black-and-white television set was *antediluvian*."

anthropomorphism [anthrupuMORFizum] the attribution of human characteristics to a thing or event. "To say that the tree cried when cut down is an example of *anthropomorphism*." "The country was enlivened by the election, it can be asserted using *anthropomorphism*." "The grammarian said that *anthropomorphism* would not be out of place in that context." "The poet used much *anthropomorphism*."

antipathy [anTIPuthee] revulsion. "Ancient Rome showed *antipathy* toward Carthage." "The teacher felt *antipathy* toward one of his sixth-grade students." "She showed no *antipathy* toward him in court." "He actually felt no *antipathy* toward the woman who insulted him." The roots of this word are *anti,* against, and *pathos,* feeling. Syn.: antagonism, enmity, hatred, hostility. Ant.: sympathy.

antiquated [ANtikwaytid] out of date. "Many *antiquated* state laws governing sex still exist." "Making automobiles *antiquated* several years after they were made is a means of renewing profit." "Planned obsolescence involves *antiquated* products." "The man drove up to the school in an *antiquated* jalopy."

antithesis [anTITHesis] the direct opposite; contrasting ideas of a phrase in parallel form. In dialectic philosophy, an antithesis is opposed to a thesis, and their resolution is the synthesis, which contains a revised assertion. The dialectic, as this method is called, dealt with ideas in Hegel's philosophy, whereas Marx substituted matter for Hegel's idealism, thus creating dialectic materialism. "Noone wants to be poor (thesis); however, wealth cannot purchase everything (antithesis); it is better to be wealthy than poor (synthesis)." "The imprisoned man was the *antithesis* of a criminal." "The fat woman was the *antithesis* of an athlete." "The politician was the *antithesis* of a humanist." "He gave her the *antithesis* of what she wanted."

apercu [aperSEU] (French) a glimpse; an insight; a summary. "Each of the medical articles had an *apercu.*" "He had *apercu* into the subject of chemistry." "He caught an *apercu* of the woman nude in the shower." "The scientific article she wanted lacked an *apercu.*"

aphorism [AFurizum] a proverb or pithy saying. "One *aphorism* says that the end of folly is the beginning of wisdom." "According to his favorite *aphorism,* 'Magna civitas, magna solitudo': A great city is a great solitude." "He quoted a Japanese *aphorism* to the effect that the salt in our blood comes from the salt of the sea." "The writer collected *aphorisms.*" Syn.: adage, apothegm, byword, dictum, maxim, saw, saying.

aplomb [uPLUM] self-assured poise. "She played the part of shrew with *aplomb.*" "After the humiliation of being exposed as a sexual deviant, it took courage for the man to walk out of the club with *aplomb.*" "He was equable and always acted with *aplomb.*" "The student's *aplomb* amazed the others." Syn.: confidence, self-control.

apocalypse [uPOKulips] a revelation. "The postulated 'World War lll' is sometimes referred to as the *apocalypse.*" "He ran across an *apocalypse* that the social contract is a hoax." "He was dying to see what the *apocalypse* would bring." "The preacher believed that an *apocalypse* was near."

apocryphal [uPOKriful] inauthentic, counterfeit. "The so-called Hitler diary was found to be *apocryphal.*" "Some of the books of the Bible are *apocryphal.*" "The fabricated rumor was *apocryphal.*" "Gossip about his death was *apocryphal.*"

apodictic [apuDIKtik] clearly proven or demonstrated. "The teacher's incompetence was *apodictic.*" "The truth of his claim of harassment was *apodictic.*"

"Evolution is *apodictic*." "The Bible is not *apodictic*."

apogee [APugee] the highest point. "The *apogee* of his career came in the 1960s." "The suicide victim jumped from the bridge at its *apogee*." "He reached an *apogee* of income at an early age." "He reached a physical *apogee* at age 32."

aposiopesis [apusiyuPEEses] the halting of a speaker in the middle of a sentence, as though he could not finish. "Journalists noted that the Defense Secretary was given to *aposiopesis* at news conferences." "The teacher struggled to overcome *aposiopesis*." "*Aposiopesis* can be a big problem for a public speaker." "The teacher suffered from stuttering and *aposiopesis*."

apostasy [uPOStusee] the renunciation of one's former faith, as religion or politics. "Some radicals of the 60s gave in to *apostasy* and in the 80s joined the right-wing." "The minister declared *apostasy* and lived as an atheist." "His *apostasy* involved turning his back on the environmental movement." "The former hippy committed *apostasy*."

a posteriori [A postireeORee] based on actual observation; not independent of experience. "His essay on the subject was mainly *a posteriori*." "*A posteriori* is the method of science." "Her reasoning was inductive, *a posteriori*." "In his dissertation he used *a posteriori* reasoning."

apothegm [APuthem] a maxim. "It is *apothegmatic* that he who goes a-borrowing goes a-sorrowing." "An *apothegm* among workers runs, 'Are you working hard or hardly working?'" "He could recite the *apothegm* but he could not live up to it." "An *apothegm* warns of leaping before you look." Syn.: adage, aphorism, dictum, proverb.

apotheosis [upotheeOHsis] an exulted example. "The dictator was the *apotheosis* of evil." "The prisoner saw all too well damnation, for he was the *apotheosis* of it." "The actor's binge of endorsement deals was the *apotheosis* of greed." "The poor man was the *apotheosis* of virtue."

apparition [apuRISHun] specter; the act of appearing. "His *apparition* in drag at the stag party surprised even his closest friends." "The magician performed the *apparition* of a woman from nowhere." "The *apparition* of a 'ghost' haunted them." "The *apparition* came and went in an instant."

appellation [apuLAYshun] a substitute name. "Her *appellation* sex goddess was no longer deserved." "The dog answered to the *appellation* Molly." "He earned the *appellation* 'Babe' for his ability in baseball." "His *appellation* was Rudy." Syn.: epithet, moniker, nickname, sobriquet.

appendage [uPENdizh] something attached to something else. "Science is but an *appendage* to industry." "The culture portrayed women as merely an *appendage* of men." "The building was an *appendage* of the university." "The center is an *appendage* of the institute."

appetence [APutuns] strong desire; tendency. "The shunned boy had an *appetence* for science that would serve him well later." "He had an *appetence* to play sports at an early age." "The *appetence* of the country was to material gain." "She had an *appetence* for reading." Syn.: inclination, predisposition, propensity.

apposite [APuzit] pertinent; suitable; apt. "Money was *apposite* to his getting a higher education." "Physical health was *apposite* to qualifying for the job." "The boots were *apposite* for hiking." "The film was *apposite* for the occasion." Syn.: apropos. Ant.: irrelevant.

apprise [uPRIHZ] to inform. "President Kennedy was *apprised* of the missiles in Cuba when he met the Soviet diplomats." "Only later was she *apprised* that her husband was dead." "He was not *apprised* of the situation in advance." "She was not *apprised* of his absence."

approbation [apruBAYshun] approval. "The Inquisition had the *approbation* of the reigning Spanish monarchs." "Many of history's greatest crimes had the full *approbation* of the government." "He did not have her *approbation* when they had sex." "Parental *approbation* was required for the trip."

appropriate [uPROpreeayt] to take for oneself. "Poland has a history of being *appropriated* by its stronger neighbors." "The thief *appropriated* the wallet for himself." "The family *appropriated* the stray dog." "The reader *appropriated* the library book."

appurtenance [uPURtenuns] accessory. "Books are an *appurtenance* to learning." "In effect, workers are an *appurtenance* to the leisure class." "Eating hot dogs at a ball game is just an *appurtenance* to taking in the action." "Friends are an *appurtenance* to happiness."

a priori [A priORi] based on analysis; independent of experience. "His reasoning was *a priori,* and not based directly on observed facts." "It is a pseudoscience because it is *a priori.*" "Any psychological science should combine the *a priori* and the *a posteriori.*" "*A priori* deductions are necessarily true."

apropos [ahproPO] pertinent. "Learning the basic stroke by practicing against a wall is *apropos* to playing tennis." "He did not bring the *apropos* material to class." "Biology and chemistry are *apropos* to medicine." "Speed is *apropos* to soccer." Syn. apposite, germane.

arabesque [ayruBESK] pertaining to a complex, ornate design of floral, foliate and geometrical patterns. "*Arabesque* art decorated the sheik's palace." "His painting was *arabesque.*" "The *arabesque* architecture featured geometric patterns." "The *arabesque* furniture sold at auction for $55,000."

arcadian [ahrKAYDeeun] pastoral. "In the 1920s a man wrote a book entitled *Arcadian Adventures of the Idle Rich.*" "The writer loved *arcadian* settings and lodges in the country." "He traveled to the more *arcadian* places of Europe." "He preferred *arcadian* life, but had to seek work in the city." Syn.: agrestic, bucolic, rustic. Ant.: urban.

arcane [ahrKAYN] esoteric; secret. "Many artists prefer to protect the methods of their *arcane* craft from the public." "Specialists and professionals are fortified with *arcane* knowledge." "Her training was in the *arcane* field of astrophysics." "The news of the army's defeat was kept *arcane.*" "Knowledge may be *arcane,* monopolized by an elite and only poorly distributed among the masses." Syn.: cabalistic, mysterious, occult.

arcanum [ahrKAYNum] a deep secret; elixir. "The use of satellite surveillance was an *arcanum* that would have caused scandal." "The fact that the politician was murdered was an *arcanum* unknown to the world." "It was an *arcanum* unknown to even the man's wife." "The development of the atomic bomb was an *arcanum*."

archaic smile [arKAYik...] the human mouth shown with slightly upturned corners, characteristic of Greek sculpture prior to the fifth century B.C. "She had an *archaic smile* in her yearbook picture." "The statue was of a woman with an *archaic smile*." "She gave an *archaic smile* for the camera." "The boy went around school with an *archaic smile*."

ardent [ahrDENT] relating to fond desire; fervent. "The children's love of Christmas and Christmas presents was *ardent*." "He *ardently* wished to make love to the ingénue." "His desire for peaceful coexistence was *ardent* and sincere." "She *ardently* loved her husband." Syn.: amorous, passionate. Ant.: phlegmatic.

ardor [AHRdur] strong enthusiasm. "Ponce de Leon's *ardor* to find the 'fountain of youth' was unsuccessful, but in a way it is carried on today by the cosmetics industry." "He had an *ardor* for hockey in his youth." "He used to have an *ardor* for numismatics (coin collecting)." "She had an *ardor* for dancing." Syn.: fervor, passion, rapture.

arduous [AHRjoous] requiring difficult labor. "The ascent of most peaks in the Cascade Range of the Northwest is not *arduous*." "He conducted an *arduous* campaign for election to the House of Representatives but lost." "It was *arduous* work to clear the yard of debris." "His job was *arduous*." Syn.: laborious, strenuous, toilsome. Ant.: easy.

argot [AHRgo] the specialized vocabulary of a specific group. "The *argot* of the underworld reflected its violence." "Baseball has its own lore and *argot*." "Legal *argot* is involved and requires study to interpret." "In C.I.A. *argot*, to 'terminate with extreme prejudice' meant to murder." Syn.: cant, jargon, lingo, patois, slang.

argumentam ad populum [ARgumentum AD POPulum] a fallacy in reasoning or argument by which one appeals to the selfish interest of others in order to win them to his side. "Roman politicians of the Empire days were no strangers to use of the *argumentam ad populum*, which in fact was the staple of their speeches." "Their political dialogue had degenerated into *argumentam ad populum*." "He committed the *argumentam ad populum* fallacy over and over." "Their politics was full of *argumentam ad populum*."

aria [AHReeu] a tune. "Chopin (1810-49) wrote some beautiful *arias*." "America is represented in classical *arias* by John Phillip Sousa (1854-1932), the march king." "The depressed man could not get certain *arias* out of his head." "He tried but found it hard to write a hit *aria*." Syn.: air, anthem, ballad, ballet, cantata, canticle, carol, composition, dirge, hymn, lay, lullaby, madrigal, march, minuet, nocturne, opus, oratorio, overture, polka, psalm, score, serenade, sonata, strain, suite, waltz.

arid [ARid] dry, as a climate or desert; dull. "The *aridity* of the country put a strain on water resources." "People were required to take along much water when going through an *arid* region." "The Colorado River flows through an *arid* region." "The July day was hot and *arid*."

arm the cannon [ARM THU KANun] to masturbate. "He discovered *arming the cannon* at age 14." "His advice to his son was that it is alright to *arm the* *cannon*, just do not tell anyone about it." "Do not prefer *arming the cannon* to actual sex, was his facetious advice." "The men were laughing about *arming the cannon*." Syn.: choke the chicken, jack off, shoot from the hip, spank the monkey.

arrant [AHRunt] thoroughgoing. "An *arrant* fool would never survive a trek through that desert." "He was stupid, an *arrant* idiot who had an eighth-grade education." "In *The Lone Ranger*, Jay Silverheels must have been portrayed as an *arrant* numbskull, since his name in the show, Tonto, is Spanish for 'stupid.'" "The college instructor was an *arrant* jerk." Syn.: absolute, out-and-out, utter.

arrears [uRIRZ] an unpaid debt; used with *in*. "He was so in *arrears* that he felt as though there were a great burden on his shoulders." "The writer was living in *arrears*, owing people money for various services." "He realized he was in *arrears* but planned to pay his bills before dying, that is, some time in the future." "The working-class woman disliked being in *arrears*."

arrière-pensée [aryer panSAY] (French) a mental reservation; a hidden motive. "He suspected his wife of having an *arrière-pensée*." "He shook the hand of the tramp with an *arrière-pensée*." "He had an *arrière-pensée* for borrowing the money." "She had no idea what his *arrière-pensée* could be."

arriviste [ahreeVEEST] (French) an upstart; a person who has moved up in the world by shady means. "The newly-rich try to enter the upper-class, but as *arrivistes* it is hard." "A wife is usually the more insistent *arriviste*." "*Arrivistes* are especially vulgar, claimed the social critic." "The *arriviste* merely wanted to travel, not break into fashionable society." "The family was rejected by the upper-class as *arriviste*." "The financial *arriviste* kicked down the ladder by which he ascended." This term is from a French word meaning "to arrive." Syn.: pusher, upstart.

arrogate [AHRugayt] to take or assume unjustly. "The servant *arrogated* the mansion upon the death of its owner, his master." "He *arrogated* the main principal of the earnings of his son, a successful child actor." "He *arrogated* the antique from his grandmother's collection for himself." "She *arrogated* as her own the majority of the estate." Syn.: appropriate, usurp.

artichoke [ARTichohk] a debauched hag. "To him the judge was an *artichoke*, unattractive to say the least." "The *artichoke* cursed him as he left." "The *artichoke* was so withered that she looked as old as Methuselah." "The *artichoke* did not have a good reputation."

ascetic [uSETik] a person living very frugally; (adj.) austere. "American televangelists violate the tradition of the religious *ascetic*." "Since he subsisted on a pension, he was forced to live like an *ascetic*." "The college dorm was an *ascetic* place to live." "She was an *ascetic* anchorite."

asinus ad lyram [ASinus AD LIrum] (Latin) "an ass at the harp"; that is, a philistine who has no artistic ability. "The columnist dismissed the actor in the clunker of a movie as an *asinus ad lyram*." "He was gifted musically, not an *asinus ad lyram*." "The family was ill at ease, like an *asinus ad lyram*, at the opera house." "The cracker-barrel philosopher was dismissed as an *asinus ad lyram*."

askance [uSKANS] with implied disapproval. "The white neighbors looked *askance* at the black family that moved in on the block." "The cashier looked *askance* at the boy stealing the candy bar but did not blow the whistle." "They looked *askance* at the sign indicating a nudist colony." "He looked *askance* at the speeding motorist."

asperity [uSPURitee] something with a harsh aspect; irritability. "The woman's screen test was a disaster due to her on-camera *asperity*." "The woman's *asperity* came to a head when the waitress spilled her soda." "His *asperity* was aggravated by his failed career." "He showed *asperity* when he drank."

asperse [uSPERS] to slander. "The politician claimed that she had been *aspersed* by the radio broadcast." "He felt *aspersed* by his fellow students." "It seemed as though the group of people *aspersed* him as he walked past." "The insensitive boy *aspersed* the mentally retarded girl." Syn.: defame, libel.

asseverate [uSEVerayt] to affirm. "Some politicians find it easy to *asseverate* the lie when they are in powerful office and journalists are reluctant to press them." "His boss *asseverated* that he had been canned, been fired." "He *asseverated* that they had called her a 'tub o' lard.'" "The teacher *asseverated* that the student had failed the test." Syn.: allege, assert.

assiduous [uSIDjoous] diligent. "The middle class is *assiduous* in the upkeep of its houses." "He *assiduously* attended to his homework." "The couple *assiduously* denied the rumor." "He *assiduously* avoided scandal." Syn.: industrious, sedulous.

assignation [asigNAYshun] an assignment; tryst. "Shakespeare referred to an unusual means of *assignation* when he wrote 'and waft her love to come again to Carthage.'" "Their romantic *assignation* was at the golf course at midnight." "They planned an *assignation* on the Acropolis in June." "The lovers consummated their forbidden love at their *assignation*."

assonance [ASununs] vowel rhyme. "Musicians often make use of *assonance*." "*Assonance* and alliteration are tools of the lyricist." "The song writer made much use of *assonance*." "The poet weaved *assonance* into his sonnets." "An example of *assonance* is *make* and *day*."

assuage [uSWAYJ] to ease or calm. "All attempts to *assuage* the widow's grief were fruitless." "They attempted to *assuage* his anger before he committed mischief." "He could not *assuage* his wife's guilt after the miscarriage." "The nearby sea *assuaged* the would-be-bitter winter."

asthenic [asTHENik] weak. "The pale boy suffered from *asthenia*." "Poor nutrition made him *asthenic*." "Lack of sleep made her *asthenic*." "Her anemia caused *asthenia*."

as useful as tits on a bull [AZ...] not useful at all. "In between the obscenities he yelled out to his estranged girlfriend, 'you're as useful as tits on a bull.'" "The old automobile, after the transmission gave out, was *as useful as tits on a bull*." "She lashed out at her lazy son, 'you're as useful as tits on a bull.'" "The old house was rickety and *as useful as tits on a bull*." (Spears.)

atone [uTOHN] to make amends. "Not all those who *atone* for their sins are religious." "He meant to *atone* for the shabby way he treated her." "The teacher did not *atone* for wronging the student." "The two friends *atoned* for their fight." Syn.: expiate, propitiate, reclaim, redress, restitute.

a tort et a travers [AH TOR EH AH traVER] (French) randomly, without any rhyme or reason. "The shootings at work took place *a tort et a travers*, as far as anyone could tell." "The F handed out by the teacher was *a tort et a travers*." "In the 1990s there was a rash of school shootings, *a tort et a travers*." "He seemed to denigrate him *a tort et a travers*."

á tout prix [AH TOO PREE] (French) "at any price." "The general sent his cavalry charging recklessly, *a tout prix*." "The hit man was hired *a tout prix*." "The police searched for the killer *a tout prix*." "He wanted relief *a tout prix*."

atrabilious [atruBILyus] melancholic; irritable; sullen. "Abraham Lincoln suffered from *atrabilious* moods." "The patient was diagnosed with depression, and had an *atrabilious* outlook." "He was *atrabilious* and angry about nothing in particular." "He was an *atrabilious* old man who drank and smoked too much." Syn.: dejected, downhearted, peevish, petulant, saddened. Ant.: cheerful.

attic [ATik] (adj.) elegant, witty and incisive. "His speech was marked by *attic* wit." "Her *attic* article debunked the myth of his greatness." "The historian's book was *attic* polemics." "It may not have been *attic*, but his argument was sensible: Everyone deserves a living wage." Attica is an area near Athens in Greece, and is the source of this word.

attitudinize [atiTOODnihz] to put on airs. "To *attitudinize* may from a sociological viewpoint be an attempt to, though temporarily, raise one's status." "He was tempted to *attitudinize* at the party, since he felt contempt for some of the guests." "*Attitudinizing* gets one nowhere." "His *attitudinizing* was pathetic." Syn.: affect, feign, mince, simper.

au courant [AU kooRAHN] up-to-date. "The detective was *au courant* as he spoke to the suspect." "He was *au courant* on the affairs of the world, since he went to the library and read newspapers and magazines every morning." "The people in the newsroom were *au courant*, with the help of a special calendar which listed noteworthy anniversaries, holidays, and so forth." "The gossiper was socially *au courant*."

aude sapere [AWde SAPere] (Latin) "dare to be wise." "The philosopher taught a principle of *aude sapere*, meant as a guide to behavior in troubled times." "*Aude sapere* suggests courage when it is needed the most." "He remembered the proverb *aude sapere* when he went to court." "When the going gets rough, heed *aude sapere*."

au fait [AU FE] well-informed or expert. "She was an *au fait* social worker with a reputation as 'the best' in the business." "He was an *au fait* anthropologist." "He was *au fait* on the subject of horses." "She is *au fait* on the subject of medieval history."

Aufklärung [AUFklayrung] (German) the Enlightenment. "Voltaire (1694-1778) was one great force of the *Aufklärung*." "The *Aufklärung* swept away some religious prejudices." "Ben Franklin was an *Aufklärung* man." "The *Aufklärung* spread knowledge."

augur [AUgur] to foretell through signs. "President Johnson's stance as a 'peace candidate' did not *augur* well as an indication of the coming war." "He had a bad feeling that did not *augur* well for him in the college course." "The resentful look his new neighbor gave him did not *augur* well for happiness in their new home." "His *augury* was incorrect: Greece won the war." "Not a whit we defy augury; there's a special providence in the fall of a sparrow" (Shakespeare). Syn.: divine, presage, prophecy.

au naturel [AU natuREL] nude. "On a certain summer day the family takes a walk *au naturel* in London without being reproached for 'indecent exposure.'" "She walked around *au naturel* at the nudist colony." "They swam *au naturel* at the clothing-optional beach." "The celebrity model was secretly photographed *au naturel*." Syn.: naked. Ant.: clothed.

Aunt Jane [ANT JAYN] a black woman who adopts the attitude of whites. "An *Aunt Jane* would not have been welcome in that group." "They accused her of being an *Aunt Jane*." "The *Aunt Jane* was progressive in politics." "*Aunt Jane* said no to drugs." Patterned on Uncle Tom. (Spears; see bibiliography.)

aurea mediocritas [AUreeah meediOKritus] (Latin) "the golden mean," a central principle of Stoic philosophers which meant avoidance of extremes and adherence to a middle ground of humanity. "*Aurea mediocritas* was his professed faith for life, though his critics said that that was made very easy by his large fortune." "The writer counseled patience and the *aurea mediocritas*." "He had trouble keeping an 'even keel' and needed to discover an *aurea mediocrities*." "*Aurea mediocritas* is not *always* the best course."

auriferous [AUrifurus] containing gold. "Thoreau condemned the rush of the forty-niners to the *auriferous* hills of California." "The jewelry was *auriferous*." "There was a minor gold rush to Cripple Creek, an *auriferous* area of Colorado." "The *auriferous* patina is lovely."

ausgespielt [AUZgushpeelt] (German) played out, spent. "The tennis player lost the match, as his will to win was *ausgespielt*." "The army's morale was *ausgespielt* and it retreated in chaos." "Her $10,000 checking account was *ausgespielt*, so she stopped spending." "The will of the 'West' is supposedly *ausgespielt*." Syn.: exhausted.

auspices [AUspiseez] patronage; a favorable sign. "Martin Luther propounded his beliefs under the *auspices* of powerful princes." "Karl Marx wrote about capitalism under the *auspices* of Friedrich Engels." "Since the morning was sunny the *auspices* for a picnic were good." "The pianist got off to an *auspicious* start in life as a Wunderkind." "Their wedding was *auspicious* of a blissful life to come." Syn.: aegis, backing, sponsorship.

autarchy [AUtarkee] a policy of independence from the aid or resources of other nations. "The American *autarchy* that consisted of using domestic oil made no sense in that buying OPEC oil was a better way to conserve domestic resources for a crisis." "The 'developing' nations accepted aid and did not pursue *autarchy*." "Europe sought *autarchy* but still was dependent on certain outside resources." "The nation was incapable of *autarchy*."

auto-da-fe [AUtoduFAY] the burning at the stake of condemned heretics as provided for by the Inquisition. "The *auto-da-fe* was one of the horrifying products of the Counter Reformation." "Contemporary onlookers of the *auto-da-fe* may have approved of it." "*Auto-da-fe* means 'act of faith' in Portuguese." "A procession preceded the *auto-da-fe*."

avarice [AVuris] greed. "Mark Twain's 'The Man That Corrupted Hadleyburg' is an ironic tale of American *avarice*." "The ministry seemed steeped in *avarice* rather than the Golden Rule." "*Avarice* led to the inheritance." "*Avarice* was involved in the sell out." Syn. avidity, cupidity, rapacity.

avatar [AVutar] an incarnation; an embodiment of some abstract quality. "His ability at the piano was an *avatar* belying his crude appearance." "The writer believed him to be an *avatar* of wrongdoing." "She was an *avatar* of joy." "The dictator was an *avatar* of meanness." The word is from Sanskrit.

aver [uVER] to affirm. "He *averred* that he could play chess with the best of them." "He *averred* that his family was rich." "The nun *averred* her faith in God." "He *averred* that corporal punishment of children was counterproductive." Syn.: assert, asseverate.

azimuth [AZumuth] a geometric figure involving the intersection of a great circle with a celestial position, important in navigation and astronomy. "The *azimuth* was discovered by the Arabs." "The navigator charted the plane's course with the help of the *azimuth*." "The use of the *azimuth* may be hard to understand." "The astronomer used the *azimuth* in his study of the galaxy."

B

Babbitt [BAbit] a smug, narrow-minded American businessman. "The intellectual thought of his own uncle as a *Babbitt*." "The *Babbitt* belonged to several clubs." "The *Babbitt* did not take much part in the life of his family." "The *Babbitt* was devoted to his business." *Babbitt* is the name of a novel by Sinclair Lewis, published in 1920, the most remarkable feature of which is the true-to-life character of the protagonist, a total conformist. Mr. Babbitt could have been just about any male member of the middle class. Some critics, however, remarked that the novel did not point out any means of salvation from cultural damnation.

bacchanal [BAKunul] a riotous party or celebration. "*Bacchanals* frequently evolve from New Year's Eve parties, though they seldom degenerate into orgies in this society." "The *bacchanalia* was attended by 'party animals.'" "At their *bacchanalias* the Romans would use a vomitorium to be able to enjoy further feasting." "Everyone enjoyed the *bacchanal*, which lasted until the next morning." Syn.: bash, blast, shindig.

badass [BADAS] in black slang, a person of overweening or arrogant confidence; a tough man. "He thought of himself as a *badass* who was somehow better than other people." "He played like a *badass* in basketball, doing fancy dribbles and passes." "The *badass* did not seem to notice the persons around him." "The *badass* appeared confident and unconcerned with things that capture other people's attention." Spears explains *badass* as "an elaboration of the intensifier *bad*, which means good."

badinage [badnAHZH] lighthearted banter. "The two supposedly rival politicians engaged in *badinage* that suggested there is only one political party instead of two." "Their *badinage* escalated into bitter recriminations." "Their fight was no mere *badinage*." "In private the two leaders engaged in *badinage*."

bailiwick [BAYluwik] one's special interest or skill. The word derives from *bailiff*, with *wik* being Middle English for "town." "The professor's *bailiwick* is Russia, though he is learned in many disciplines." "Her *bailiwick* is nursing." "His *bailiwick* is Babylonian number theory." "The geologist's *bailiwick* is mineralogy."

balderdash [BOLdurdash] a senseless jumble of words. "What he wrote is vague *balderdash* rather than being a brilliant essay." "His explanation to his brother was *balderdash*." "The *balderdash* did not fool anyone." "The infant was babbling *balderdash*."

baleful [BAYLful] hurtful; ominous. "They escaped the otherwise *baleful* auto accident almost unscathed." "The journey became *baleful* when all their equipment was lost crossing a scream." "Supposedly a black cat is *baleful*." "Doing anything in court is usually *baleful* for the poor." Syn.: baneful, harmful, malignant, pernicious.

ballast [BALust] something that provides stability or balance. "One researcher suggests that serotonin gives *ballast* to the brain and its various neurotransmitters." "His wife provided *ballast* and even ambition to his corporate career." "The drug gave *ballast* to his inner life." "The ship needed *ballast* to weather the waves."

ballyhoo [baleeHOO] clamorous advertising or promotion. "The choice of a vice-presidential running mate was announced with much *ballyhoo*." "The movie made its debut with much *ballyhoo* that was certain to get it some free commercial exposure when passed off on television as news." "The circus was opened with *ballyhoo*." "The *ballyhoo* surrounding the grand opening was soon forgotten."

baloobas [buLOObas] the female bosom. "Her large *baloobas* helped the seventeen-year-old girl be popular with boys." "The model had large *baloobas*." "The woman teased him with her *baloobas*." "The word *baloobas* was casually used." Syn.: diddies, hooters, whammers. (Spears.)

baneful [BAYNful] ruinous; destructive; poisonous. "The *baneful* effects of clear-cutting on a forest are sad to observe." "Poison ivy is *baneful* if you touch it." "Water and wood is a *baneful* combination." "The *baneful* effects of the hurricane were everywhere." Syn.: baleful, harmful, malignant, pernicious.

banns [BANZ] an announcement of marriage intention. "The priest declared the *banns*, and as expected noone in the church objected." "The *banns* was read on a Friday." "The *banns* was read quickly." "Apparently *banns* is not read for all marriages."

Barmecide feast [BARmisihd FEEST] imaginary plenty. "The economist's idea of prosperity was like a *Barmecide feast*." "What the politician suggested was like a *Barmecide feast*." "He ate, in effect, a *Barmecide feast*." "The candidate for president offered the poor a *Barmecide feast*." This term is from *The Arabian Nights*.

barmy [BARmee] a Britishcism for "crazy." "Have you gone completely *barmy?*" "'You must be *barmy* to do that,' he declared." "He was *barmy* to lend her money." "The *barmy* woman grimaced in front of a mirror."

baroque [buROHK] pertaining to a style of art and architecture in Europe from 1550 to 1750, characterized by elaborate and ornate ornamentation; richly ornamented. "Their Palm Beach home was an expensive masterpiece in *Baroque*." "His literary style was richly *Baroque*." "The *Baroque* cathedral was magnificent." "The palace in Würzburg is beautiful *Baroque*."

barratry [BARutree] the offense of inciting arguments; the sale of office in church or state. "*Barratry* and the sale of indulgences did much to weaken the church." "The gangsters were guilty of *barratry*." "The priest engaged in *barratry*."

basilica [buSILiku] an early or medieval Christian church having a nave and apse. "The *basilica* was first a public hall in ancient Rome." "The beautiful *basilica* was destroyed by fire." "They attended mass in the *basilica*." "The *basilica* was in the center of the city."

bastinado [bastuNAYdo] beating with a club, usually on the soles of the feet. "*Bastinado* was practiced in Spain, Spanish America and the Balkans." "She was punished with *bastinado*." "The police interrogators tried to ring a confession out of the subject using *bastinado*." "The soldiers punished the prisoner with *bastinado*."

bate [BAYT] to decrease the strength of; "bated" is an adjectival form of this word. "The spectators waited with *bated* breath for the king to parade past." "The angle of the sun's rays *bates* their warmth in the poles." "The kiss *bated* his breath." "Sleep *bates* breathing."

bathos [BAYthos] excessive sentimentality. "The popular American stage is riddled with *bathos*." "*Bathos* in the arts may sell, but it still ought to be criticized." "The novel was full of *bathos*." "Disneyland, said one writer, features *bathos*."

bawd [BOD] a prostitute; a madam. "The *bawd* was not expected to go to church." "The *bawd* was getting old." "The *bawd* took good care of her girls." "The *bawd* held forth in the house of ill-repute." Syn.: harlot, hooker, whore.

Beat Generation [BEET jenuRAYshun] a group of unconventional people of the 1950s. "The *Beat Generation* adopted new means of self-expression." "The motorcyclists included some persons of the *Beat Generation*." "The *Beat Generation* was a challenge to the conformism of the time." "The *Beat Generation* faded away with the 1960s."

beatific [beeuTIFik] pertaining to exalted joy. "All eyes were on the *beatific*

young bride." "The man remembered his childhood house as *beatific*." "Life-
long continual *beatitude* is rare." "He recalled the tenth year of his life as *beatitude,* when he was genuinely happy."

Beau Brummel [BO BRUMl] a dandy. This term derives from an Englishman
(1778-1840), who after getting to know the King of England, lived lavishly
on borrowed money, cultivating the etiquette of a fop until his luck and
money ran out and his creditors forced him to flee to France, where he died
in obscurity. "Because he had a large expense account and dressed well, in a
way he was a *Beau Brummel*." "The *Beau Brummel*, though a ridiculous fop,
was known all around town." "The *Beau Brummel* used make-up." "The celebrity *Beau Brummel* cultivated fashion for a reason." Syn.: fop.

beau geste [boh ZHEST] (French) a gracious gesture; a fine gesture done only
for an effect. "His *beau geste* did not succeed in appeasing his enemy." "The
man's *beau geste* to the woman was only literary." "His *beau geste* was to
straighten the tie the man was wearing." "The girl did a *beau geste*, pulling
down the hat the boy was wearing."

beau ideal [BOH ihDEEul] (French) an idealized type or model; literally, "ideal
beauty." "One *beau ideal* of the flower children was the novel *Siddhartha* by
Herman Hesse (1877-1962)." "His *beau ideal* of feminine beauty was his
wife." "His *beau ideal* of romanticism was the music of Claude Debussy
(1862-1918)." "The *beau ideal* of the American heroine is zaftig."

beau monde [BOH MOND] (French) the world of rich, fashionable people; high
society. "One critic referred to the 'moral imbecility' of the *beau monde* and
the leisure class." "The *beau monde* is not cut off from the political elite."
"The upper-middle-class family longed to join the *beau monde*." "The *beau
monde* rejected the wealthy social climber because his money was vulgarly-
new." On the one hand, that there is an American leisure class is not surprising given the country's great overall wealth; on the other hand, the public is
not consciously or articulately aware of the existence of the leisure class in a
society with a still-strong work ethic. Discussion of the immorality of the
beau monde is taboo in American society, and the fact that the idle rich inherited their wealth is considered an impolite thought; such is the position of
the American beau monde.

bedizen [biDIHzun] to dress or adorn in a showy, vulgar manner. "The working-
class couple *bedizened* their little house in a pathetic manner." "Their living
room was *bedizened* tastelessly." "The prostitute was *bedizened*." "The car
driven in the parade was *bedizened*."

beldam [BELdum] an ugly old woman. "The *beldam* tried to hide her age with
make-up and hair dye." "He called the dean in disgust a '*beldam*.'" "The
schizoid *beldam* grimaced." "The poor *beldam* lived alone in a small house."
"She was more like a *beldam* but dressed like a young woman." Syn.: hag,
harridan. Ant.: belle.

bel-esprit [beleSPREE] (French) a cultivated, intellectual person. "The university professor was a *bel-esprit* who spoke five languages." "The *bel-esprit*
criticized the stereotyping in his society." "She was a *bel-esprit,* but not a
doctor or Ph.D." "The *bel-esprit* was a graduate of Oxford University." Syn.:

polymath.

belladonna [beluDONu] literally, "beautiful lady" in Italian; a substance derived from *Atropa belladonna*—atropine. Among its other effects, atropine dilates pupils, which women see as enhancing their attractiveness. "Atropine, from *belladonna*, causes an unpleasant slowing sensation in high dosage." "The woman used *belladonna* to dilate her pupils."

belle époque [BEL ePOK] (French) "beautiful period," an ideal time for the flourishing of culture and art. "It would be hard to pin down a *belle époque* in American history, except for specific disciplines such as literature or architecture." "The critics were rather unanimous in declaring the age a *belle époque*." "The 19th century was a *belle époque* for Impressionism." "Literature flourished in the *belle époque*."

belles-lettres [BEL LETr] (French) "fine letters," or literature that is entertaining and not meant to be instructive. "Some of the best American *belles-lettres* are by Poe, Longfellow and Dickinson." "The *belles-lettres* was written in Spanish." "The *belles-lettres* dealt with falling in love." "Poetry is a good example of *belles-lettres*."

bellicose [BELukohs] pugnacious; warlike. "He was *bellicose* and just itching for a fight." "So many countries and tribes have been *bellicose* throughout history that it is remarkable to find one that is peaceable." "She was mean and *bellicose* when she drank." "His stepfather was a *bellicose* jerk." Syn.: belligerent, quarrelsome, truculent.

bellwether [BELwethur] someone or something that goes in the lead. "Dark cumulonimbus clouds are the *bellwether* of a storm." "He was a *bellwether* for organizing the students." "The soldier was the *bellwether* of the platoon." "The *bellwether* of the group of friends had the highest status."

belvedere [BELvideer] a part of a building that affords a good view. "Their hotel in the La Defense area did not furnish a *belvedere* to Paris." "The porch made a great *belvedere*." "They lounged in the *belvedere* enjoying the view." "The *belvedere* afforded a great view of the Pacific Ocean."

benighted [buNITEed] intellectually bankrupt. "The so-called schools of education, where teachers matriculate, are *benighted* places that waste the students' time and money." "The suburban journal was *benighted*." "The social critic declared liberalism *benighted*." "The historian was an apologist, was *benighted*." "The redneck town was *benighted*."

benignant [biNIGnunt] favorable; a variant of benign. "One historian, D.W. Brogan, asserted that American provincialism can be creative and *benignant*." "The antidepressant's side effect profile was *benignant*." "The weather was *benignant* for the game." "The auspices for happiness were *benignant*."

besot [biSOT] to make foolish, as with drink or emotion. "He was *besotted* already by 7 p.m." "The softball players got *besotted* with beer." "He was *besotted* and thrilled when the woman asked to dance with him." "The *besotted*, love-sick youth did not know how to act on his emotion."

bête noir [BET NWAR] (French) an object or person of dislike. "The seven-year-old *bête noir* was detested by his classmates." "She was a brat and *bête* *noir*, and wore the pants in the family." "The room became the teenaged boy's *bête noir.*" "Basketball was his *bête noir.*" "The youth was the man's *bête noir* and scapegoat." This term means "black beast" in French. Syn.: bugbear.

bêtise [beTEEZ] a lack of understanding; stupidity. "Her *bêtise* showed." "The man from the police academy manifested *bêtise.*" "Suddenly at the age of 40 he struggled with *bêtise* where previously he had had no problem." "'What *bêtise!*' declared the piano teacher about his student." Syn.: denseness, doltishness, dumbness, idiocy, obtuseness. Ant.: intelligence.

bibber [BIBur] a drinker. "The *bibber* was intoxicated, Zulued." "The *bibber* walked into the tavern." "The *bibber* enjoyed a cocktail or two after work." "The *bibber* got angry when anyone mentioned that he should not drink so much." Syn.: tippler.

biddy [BIDee] an old woman, especially a fussy one. "The *biddy* could no longer function and had to retire to a nursing home." "At 80 she was no 'old *biddy*,' and was a marvel of age-defiance." "They could not resist a joke at the expense of the *biddy*." "The *biddy* who took vitamins for many years lived to age 96."

Bildungsroman [BILdungzroman] (German) a novel that traces the development of the protagonist. "Goethe's *Die Leiden des Jungen Werthers* is a classic *Bildungsroman.*" "He wrote a bestselling *Bildungsroman.*" "His *Bildungsroman* started with his hero in his teens." "After the failure of her first book she went to work on a *Bildungsroman.*"

bilious [BILyus] ill-tempered; irritating. "The late cult hero Elvis Presley could be *bilious* at times." "Seeing the dentist can be *bilious* and painful." "He had the *bilious* habit of never shutting his mouth." "Some people become *bilious* when administered a protein drink devoid of tryptophan." Syn.: annoying, irksome, vexatious. Ant.: pleasant.

bilk [BILK] to cheat; to avoid payment of. "The poor man without dental insurance *bilked* a dentist for $500." "The system of taxes *bilks* the poor." "The worker *bilked* one business after another, so that many bill collectors were after him." "She *bilked* the hair stylist by not leaving a tip." "The corporation *bilked* consumers by not passing along money saved through technological advances." Syn.: con, defraud, mulct, swindle.

billet-doux [beeyayDOO] (French) a love letter. "She took offense at the *billet-doux* she received." "His *billet-doux* to her was overwrought." "The heiress received multiple *billet-doux*." "She rejected his *billet-doux*." This term literally means "sweet little letter."

billett [BILit] room and board for troops, especially with civilians; a job. "The American colonists angrily complained of *billeting* the king's troops." "His *billett* was as a school janitor—not exactly a glamorous job." "He could find no *billett*, even though he had academic credentials and could do many jobs." "The *billeting* for officers and privates was not on a par."

bindlestiff [BINdulstiff] a hobo. "The *bindlestiff* hopped aboard the train bound for Memphis." "The *bindlestiff* was alone most of the time." "The *bindlestiff* was desperate for a meal." "The *bindlestiff* had no family." Syn.: drifter, tramp, vagabond.

blackguard [BLAGurd] a scoundrel. "The *blackguard* ran off with the young man's entire savings." "The murderous *blackguard* was never caught." "The *blackguard* harbored grudges against certain students." "The *blackguard* came from a good family and was a church-goer." Syn.: knave, rogue, villain.

blarney [BLARnee] flattering or cajoling talk. "He plied the girl with *blarney*, trying to get her to yield to his desire." "'*Blarney* will not get you a passing grade,' said the teacher to the student." "He laid the *blarney* on thick." "Not even *blarney* could have helped in that situation." The word comes from the legend of the Blarney Stone in a castle near Cork, Ireland.

blasphemy [BLASfumee] irreverence with respect to something sacred and religious. "The celebrity professed to be a Christian but her dress and demeanor were *blasphemy*." "The language of the Marquis de Sade (1740-1814) was *blasphemy*." "It would have been *blasphemy* for him to show up in that condition." "The visitor to Teheran was careful not to *blaspheme* Islam." Syn.: desecration, profanity, sacrilege.

blather [BLATHur] foolish talk. "The writings of aides to the presidents of the U.S. show that they are not above *blather* and obscenity in private." "The semiconscious man could get out nothing but *blather*." "The child's *blather* upset his mother." "They engaged in *blather* about buying a restaurant."

blatherskite [BLATHurskiht] someone given to foolish talkativeness. "The family was constantly treating little Mike as a *blatherskite* and reproaching him with 'hush.'" "The girl was a *blatherskite*." "The *blatherskite* was actually no fool." "The *blatherskite* talked about nothing important."

blandish [BLANdish] to cajole. "Many courtiers and associates of powerful persons try to *blandish* favors from them." "He tried to *blandish* her with charm in order to sleep with her." "He tried to *blandish* money from his father." "She did not succumb to his *blandishments*."

blasé [blahZAY] bored from overexposure; "burned-out." "Some songs seem to be too in vogue, do not last and so become *blasé* and seldom played on the radio." "The entertainment provided for the picnic was *blasé*." "The day at the theme park was *blasé*." "The tennis match was *blasé*."

bleeding heart [BLEEding HART] (pejorative) a person who makes a display of excessive concern or pity for others. "The right-winger brought out his usual accusation—*bleeding heart*." "The liberal *bleeding hearts* are mistaken, claimed the conservative." "He felt a *bleeding heart* for oppressed minorities." "The *bleeding heart* was a professional laying claim to the family." "Conservatives claim radicals are *bleeding hearts*, but liberals and right-wingers in effect preserve their respective parties as their main opponents, thus monopolizing political power, the conservatives being tacitly aligned with those they derogate as bleeding hearts."

blithe [BLIHTH] cheerful; casual. "A *blithe* 'perky' attitude does not always mean one is very happy." "She was a *blithe* fun-loving girl." "The teenager was by no means *blithe*." "He sought to be *blithe*, but it was hard."

blither [BLITHur] to talk nonsense. "He was a *blithering* idiot at the trial."

"Drink made him *blither*." "His nerves made him *blither*." "She ran inside *blithering* hysterical nonsense which noone could understand." Syn.: babble, dither, drivel.

blitzkrieg [BLITSkreeg] (also *blitz*) an overwhelming, sudden military offensive. "The Nazi *blitzkrieg* defeated Poland." "The *blitzkrieg* surprised the enemy." "The *blitzkrieg* was accompanied by air support." "A *blitzkrieg* was launched along a 400 mile front." This word literally means in German "lightning war."

blunderbuss [BLUNdurbus] a stupid, ungainly person. "The journalist was accused of '*blunderbuss* incompetence.'" "He was a *blunderbuss*, no athlete." "The *blunderbuss* was in the working-class." "The *blunderbuss* mistakenly tried out for football."

Boeotian [beeOHshun] lacking cultural refinement; (noun) a philistine. "The *Boeotians* of American society are the high school principals." "One characteristic of the *Boeotian* is his lack of awareness of his own dullness." "The *Boeotian* had only a high-school diploma." "The unfortunate '*Boeotian*' was poorly-paid." After Boeotia, a district in ancient Greece. Syn.: lowbrow, rude, uncultured, vulgar. Ant.: refined, urbane.

bohemian [boHEEmeeun] unconventional in behavior or art; a person, especially an artist, who lives an unconventional life. "The transient *bohemian* quarters of American cities are quite unlike London's Soho or Paris' Left Bank." "The *bohemian* sold paintings on the sidewalk." "The woman collected *bohemian* art." "The group of *bohemians* was poor." Syn.: countercultural, nonconformist, offbeat, unorthodox. Ant.: conformist, orthodox, prim.

bon mot [BON MOH] a witticism. "He told the wise *bon mot* that 'while striving to avoid one vice, fools run into its opposite.'" "She got in the last laugh, a *bon mot* referring to his penchant for sleep." "The *bon mot* made the social rounds as a rumor, and was repeated again and again." "His *bon mot* was more obscene than funny."

bon ton [BON TON] (French) a sophisticated style; fashionable society. "Though she tried to join it, the business tycoon's wife was not part of *bon ton*." "Most people of the *bon ton* inherited their money." "The *bon ton* gravitated toward balls, country clubs, polo, horse tracks, villas, mansions and castles." "The lovely model had a *bon ton*." Syn.: beau monde, haut monde, high society.

bon vivant [bonveeVAN] (French) someone people like to be around; an epicure. "The *bon vivant* spent most of his time conversing with a group of friends at their favorite nightclub." "The *bon vivant* was old and jolly." "The former *bon vivant* became a recluse in old age." "The *bon vivant* stayed up until 2 a.m. and woke up at 10 a.m." Syn.: sybarite.

boodle [BOOdul] tainted money, such as that from a bribe. "The *boodle* of national television opportunists is as plentiful as if money grew thickly on trees." "He was shocked when he saw the *boodle*, a paper bag full of cash." "The judge accepted a suitcase of *boodle*." "The *boodle* was never recovered."

boondocks [BOONdoks] the backwoods; a remote rural area. "He never knew life outside of the *boondocks*." "The Ozark *boondocks* was their home." "Propped up on bricks in the front yard of the *boondocks* home was an automobile." "They liked the song 'Down in the Boondocks.'"

boondoggle [BOONdogul] useless work done merely to keep or look busy. "The military's helicopter *boondoggle* was very expensive." "The construction company cooked up a *boondoggle* to repave county roads at a handsome profit." "Congress approves of numerous *boondoggles* each year." "*Boondoggles* can be very wasteful."

bootlicker [BOOTlikur] a servile person. "The prime minister seemed to some the president's *bootlicker*." "The proud man refused to be a *bootlicker*." "She was not the kind to play the *bootlicker*." "The newspaper editor was a *bootlicker* to the paper's owner." Syn.: ass-kisser, brown-nose, truckler, yes-man.

bosh [BOSH[foolish talk; nonsense. "Their *bosh* about robbing the home could very well have gotten them into trouble." "Their talk of starting a business was *bosh*." "His heroic exploits were merely so much *bosh*." "The *bosh* about a 'dream team' was empty." *Bosh* is from a Turkish word. Syn.: balderdash, bunkum, flapdoodle, folderol, jabber, prattle.

boulevardier [boluvarDEER] (French) a man about town. "The multimillionaire was also a *boulevardier*." "The *boulevardier* frequented the city's night clubs." "The *boulevardier* was suave and sophisticated." "The American *boulevardier* may be a vanishing type."

bouleversement [booluversMAN] (French) a reversal; turmoil. "The *bouleversement* was destructive of property." "The coup ended in a *bouleversement*." "The student rebellion of 1968 was a *bouleversement* aimed at the establishment." "The election turned out to be a *bouleversement*." From a French verb meaning to "overturn." Syn.: commotion, disorder, tumult.

bowldlerize [BODluriz] to remove, as from a literary work, material prudishly considered socially unacceptable. Thomas Bowldler (1754-1825), an English editor, published *The Family Shakespeare*, expurgated to his liking, and his name became a word pertaining to censorship. "The title of the poem was *bowldlerized* to remove the word 'whore.'" "The anthology was *bowldlerized* for high school students." "The *bowldlerized* book was a family edition." "Perhaps the days of *bowldlerizing* are over."

bracero [braSEro] a Mexican migrant farm worker in the U.S. "The radical claimed that *braceros* are grossly underpaid." "The *bracero* picked strawberries for pennies a bushel." "The *bracero* had no home." "The *bracero* family wandered the U.S. following the ripening of the crops they harvested."

braggadocio [braguDOseeo] cocky bragging. "The man's *braggadocio* about his sexual prowess earned him a charge of rape." "The little man was full of *braggadocio*." "The behavior of the medical interns suggested *braggadocio*." "The colonel exhibited *braggadocio*."

Brahmin [BRAHmin] a person of high status. The original meaning of *Brahmin* refers to an aristocrat of the caste system of India. "The *Brahmin* carefully deposited a coin in the hand of the woman from the untouchable caste." "The *Brahmin* had money." "The commoners resented *Brahmins*." "The *Brahmin* lived in a large house." Syn.: aristocrat, blueblood, noble.

bravura [bruVOORu] a showy or flashy manner. From the Italian word *bravo*, meaning "fine." "The best athletes exhibit no *bravura*." "He played tennis with *bravura*." "The hammy actor displayed *bravura*." "He was all *bravura* and no skill."

breast-beating [BREST BEEting] a display of self-conscious remorse or emotion. "His *breast-beating* did not save his job." "The boy found himself crying and *breast-beating* in front of his mother." "The convict's *breast-beating* was Pecksniffian." "The man found that sobbing and *breast-beating* did not make him feel better."

brigand [BRIGund] a freebooter; someone who steals without scruples. "Radicals view venture capitalists as *brigands*." "The *brigands* waylaid the convoy." "The *brigands* robbed the train and fled on their horses." "The *brigands* observed honor among thieves." Syn.: highwayman.

Bronx cheer [BRONKS CHEER] a boo in which the fans splutter with the lips and tongue to show contempt. Also called the "raspberry." "The people roared a *Bronx cheer*." "A *Bronx cheer* carried from the stands." "The *Bronx cheer* told the batter he was not liked." "The statesman was greeted in the hall by a *Bronx cheer*." So-called after the New York borough that is home to Yankee stadium.

brouhaha [BROOhaha] an uproar; a tempest in a teapot. "The *brouhaha* over who got the promotion showed the competitiveness of the society." "The *brouhaha* ended quickly when the manager walked in." "The *brouhaha* was a disturbance that brought in the police." "The *brouhaha* concerned the winner of the volleyball game."

browbeat [BRAUbeet] to talk harshly to someone. "Lyndon Johnson had a habit of *browbeating* fellow politicians." "The father *browbeat* the teacher for mistreatment of his son." "The supervisor *browbeat* the dishwashers as a means of encouraging their work." "The driver, being late for work, knew he was in for a *browbeating*."

brown-nose [BROUNnohz] to obsequiously curry favor; (noun) a sycophant. "She *brown-nosed* a promotion from her boss." "He was a *brown-nose* all his life." "The *brown-nose* sought favor from the king." "The *brown-nose* was an egotist." *Brown-nose* refers to the fancied action of kissing the ass of the superior.

brumal [BROOMul] pertaining to winter. "The short *brumal* days depress some people." "A *brumal* storm hit the city." "The dark *brumal* sky was gloomy." "They enjoyed the *brumal* holiday."

brummagem [BRUMujum] a glittering and showy but cheap thing. "The back yard of the working class is often littered with *brummagem*." "The store on Broadway sold *brummagem* knickknacks." "The thrift store had an aisle full of *brummagem*." "In the yard of the worker's house was *brummagem* kitsch." An alteration of Birmingham, England.

brusque [BRUSK] abrupt in manner. "The French woman found the people of New York *brusque*." "He was *brusque* and had no manners." "The *brusque* affair was over in three days." "The wedding consisted of a *brusque* church service." Syn.: discourteous, gruff, impolite. Ant.: mannerly, polite, well-mannered.

bucolic [byooKOLik] pastoral; characteristic of country life. "Some people prefer a *bucolic* home instead of city living." "His *bucolic* ideal took him to Tuscany to live." "He loved a *bucolic* life of wandering meadows in summer." "The woman hated camping but liked beautiful *bucolic* scenery." Syn.: agrestic, Arcadian, rural. Ant.: urban.

buggery [BUGuree] sodomy. "The extent of *buggery*, since it is done discretely, is hard to estimate." "The two men engaged in *buggery*." "*Buggery* was not his style." "Heterosexual oral sex is considered *buggery*."

bumpkin [BUMPkin] an awkward yokel. "The *bumpkin* liked to swill beer all day." "The *bumpkin* started working at nineteen." "The *bumpkin* married at age 20." "The *bumpkin* had a high-school-equivalency (GED)." "The *bumpkin* was unfamiliar with the ways of the city." Syn.: hoosier, oakie, redneck, rube.

bumptious [BUMPshus] awkwardly forward in behavior. "The *bumptious* man was put in his place." "He had a *bumptious* reputation." "The *bumptious* man should have been more diplomatic." "The *bumptious* singer got off to a bad start." "The child's *bumptious* table manners were annoying." "When an abortion doctor died in an automobile accident, a *bumptious* minister said that God had recalled another baby killer; He made a clean getaway too."

bunco [BUNGkoh] a swindle. "The men had set up a *bunco* in the small town." "The *bunco* was broken up by police." "He could hardly believe the *bunco* he had just witnessed." "The *bunco* was not tolerated by the people." Syn.: con, fraud.

bunkum [BUNGkum] empty talk; humbug. "The whole employment interview was *bunkum*." "The presidential candidate drenched his speech in *bunkum*." "His friend's talk of his exploits was *bunkum*." "The prosecutor's swagger was *bunkum*." From a speech early in the 19th century by an American politician. Syn.: bosh, claptrap, nonsense.

burg [BURG] a town or city. "The growth of the provincial *burg* was due to the interstate which ran through it." "The lonesome *burg* featured a drive-in theatre and two banks." "The *burg* was the writer's hometown and very special to him." "The *burg* was known in the state as the site of a notorious prison."

burke [BURK] to kill by suffocation; to cover up. "News of the missing funds was *burked*." "The sordid affair was *burked*, swept under the carpet." "The convicted murderer was *burked*." "The state changed capital punishment from *burking* to lethal injection." "That the people had no compassion was, in effect, *burked* by societal taboo and strictures." Syn.: strangle.

buskin [BUSkin] tragic drama; the art of acting. "They learned *buskin* in high school." "*Buskin* came naturally to the actor." "Ancient Greece is famed for *buskin*." "The thespians excelled in *buskin*."

busman's holiday [BUSmanz...] a vacation in which a person does something similar to what he does at work. "It was a *busman's holiday* for the taxi driver who drove around sight-seeing." "The baker tried to avoid a *busman's* *holiday* by not cooking." "The woman had a *busman's holiday*, going from taking care of kindergarten children to minding her own children." "The *busman's holiday* consisted of carpentry work."

butt-wipe [BUT WIHP] a sycophant. "The radical referred to his opponent as a '*butt-wipe*' who would never dare discuss the distribution of wealth." "He is a '*butt-wipe*' declared the president of his vice-president." "The '*butt-wipe*' refused to go along." "'He's just another *butt-wipe*,' said the admiral of his foe." Syn.: ass-kisser, bootlicker, yes-man.

C

cabal [kuBAHL] a group of conspirators. "The *cabal* which attempted to kill Hitler in 1944 was ruthlessly dealt with." "The *cabal* decided to put its plot into action in May." "The *cabal* discussed and discussed but was too timid to act." "The *cabal* was betrayed by one of its members."

cachinnate [KAKunayt] to laugh loudly. "His *cachinnation* interrupted the movie." "The comedy had many people *cachinnating*." "He was doubled-over and red-faced with *cachinnation*." "Their *cachinnation* was forced."

cackle [KAKul] unusual laughter, like a hen's sound. "If the comedian's jokes receive but few *cackles*, there is always the laugh track as back up." "The amused man let out a *cackle*." "The comedy had many people *cackling*." "He should not have *cackled* at that moment."

cacoethes [kakoEEtheez] a mania. "Poetry, it has been said, is the devil's wine, as it can read like a *cacoethes*." "He suffered from a hand washing *cacoethes*." "She had a *cacoethes* for chocolate." "He had a *cacoethes* of not being able to get certain words out of his mind." Syn.: obsession.

cacophony [kuKOFunee] dissonance; a din. "The child's ability at violin is a horrible *cacophony*." "The *cacophony* from the third-grade music class was awful." "The crowd emitted a *cacophony*." "The good teacher was considered to be one who had no *cacophony* coming from his class." In its Greek root, *cacophony* means "bad voice."

cad [KAD] a man who is impolite with women. "The source of the nature of the *cad* may have been the early death of his mother." "The *cad* used women." "The *cad* never married." "At heart the *cad* hated women." Syn.: bounder, churl.

cadence [KAYDns] a rhythmic flow. "The summer rain was like a heavenly *cadence*." "The *cadence* was harsh and unsettling." "The *cadence* was hard to ignore." "The ticking bore a *cadence*."

cadge [KAJ] to obtain through wheedling. "He *cadged* a promotion from his boss, who found such manipulation hard to resist." "The Congressman *cadged* a $170,000 'consulting fee' from a cable television company." "The CEO *cadged* from the corporation $80 million a year." "His friend *cadged* money from him by allowing him to pay for the both of them." "He *cadged* lunch money from a classmate." "She *cadged* charity donations from her neighbors." Syn.: blandish, cajole, coax, soft-soap.

cajole [kuJOL] to persuade using flattery or falsehood. "He tried to *cajole* the judge into dismissing the heavy fine." "The boy *cajoled* presents from his relatives." "She was *cajoled* into being an accomplice." "The youth was *cajoled* into attending church."

cake whore [KAYK HOHR] a woman with a ton of make-up on. "He was disappointed by the number of *cake whores* he met." "The *cake whore* wished to look young." "The so-called *cake whore* spent much time and money on her appearance." "She was young and no *cake whore*." (Spears; see bibliography.)

callow [KALoh] immature. "The young man was still mentally *callow*." "The teenager trying out for football had narrow, undeveloped shoulders and was physically *callow*." "In 1800 America was *callow*." "The six-month-old puppy was *callow* in every way."

calumniate [kuLUMneeayt] to slander. "The plain woman felt *calumniated* merely by standing next to the beautiful woman." "The politician avoided 'negative' ads but did not escape *calumny*." "Like a true stoic he merely shook off the *calumny*." "The man felt *calumniated* by the newspaper." A related adjective is *calumnious* ("slanderous").

camarilla [kamaRILu] a group of advisers; a cabal. "The *camarilla* advised the president not to hold elections." "The *camarilla* consisted of military men." "The *camarilla* warned the premier about inflation." "The president consulted his *camarilla* on foreign policy."

Camelot [KAmulot] an idyllic place and time. "The administration of President Kennedy was likened by some to *Camelot*, though there was no truth to the idea." "The radical asserted that no mass society has ever qualified as a *Camelot*." "The *Camelot* did not come into being." "The 'Gay 90s' was hardly a *Camelot*." The term comes from the legend of Arthur, king of England in the early Middle Ages, and the Knights of the Round Table, and specifically means the legendary town where the king had his court.

canaille [kuNIY] riffraff. This French word derogates the masses. Other terms are *hoi polloi, rabble,* and from Marxist terminology, *Lumpenproletariat.* "He was born to the *canaille* but rose to the middle class." "The *canaille* filled up the stadium." "The *canaille* loves soccer." "She hid among the *canaille*." Said Horace, "the common crowd is vulgar." The very dregs of society comprise prison inmates, the institutionalized mentally ill, hobos, winos, prostitutes, petty criminals, the homeless, welfare recipients, drug addicts and ghetto squatters. Such people have the lowest status in society and make up the canaille, along with, in some interpretations, the working class.

canard [kuNARD] (literally "duck" or "hoax" in French) a malicious, unfounded report. "The newspaper published a *canard* impeaching the character of the man, but he was powerless to stop it." "The *canard* had the man as dead."

"The mischievous pair crafted a *canard*." "The *canard* said that his wife was unfaithful." A false report can also be referred to as apocryphal.

canon [KANun] a code or body of laws. Religious in origin, canon is like "rules" or "principles" in the phrase "the canons of fashion," or "the canons of fair play." *Canonical* means "orthodox" or "authoritative." "He felt compelled to follow the *canons* of his faith." "The widower was, according to religious *canons,* to wait a year before remarrying." "Social *canons* required deference to the custom." "It was *canonical* that a working-class man marry young."

cant [KANT] whining, affected speech; hypocritically insincere statements; the jargon of a class of people. "Professionals deliberately used *cant* that was incomprehensible to the public." "His *cant* at the hearing was believed by the board of trustees." "Some types of *cant* are hard to understand." "The bad actor's speech sounded like *cant*." Syn.: lingo, patois, slang.

cantankerous [kanTANGkurus] quarrelsome; irritable. "Her *cantankerous* personality made her unsuited to work with customers." "He was *cantankerous* after five or more glasses of wine." "The old woman was *cantankerous* about people touching her possessions." "The man became *cantankerous* when someone changed the television channel." Syn.: ill-natured, peevish.

capacious [kePAYshus] able to contain much; spacious. "His *capacious* intellect was said to be unsurpassed." "The museum had a *capacious* collection of great artists like Rembrandt and Fragonard." "The obese man *capaciously* devoured three whole cakes." "Their mansion had a *capacious* great hall."

capitulate [kePICHyulate] to give up, or surrender a battle or struggle. "Von Paulus was forced to *capitulate* at the Battle of Stalingrad." "She *capitulated* to his demand for sex." "He *capitulated* out of necessity." "Her effort to reform her husband ended in *capitulation*." Syn.: relinquish, submit. Ant.: defy, withstand.

capon [KAYpon] a eunuch. "The *capon* was used to manage the harem." "The *capon* had a high-pitched voice." "He was forcibly made a *capon*." "He hated being a *capon*."

captious [KAPshus] apt to find fault with. "The drill sergeant was stern and *captious*." "Being *captious* is a terrible trait for anyone who judges or grades." "He was fair and never *captious*." "The policeman was *captious*, handing out traffic citations for any minor offense."

careerism [kuREERizum] extreme devotion to professional success. "His *careerism* embraced office politics." "His *careerism* left little time for his family." "She was a *careerist* on the make." "His politics was highly colored by his *careerism*."

carp [KAHRP] to raise trivial objections. "He complained that the critic who reviewed his book was '*carping*, caviling, being captious.'" "The student stung with an F complained that the instructor was *carping*." "She was a niggling, *carping* witch." *Carp* can also refer to "complaining constantly." "The visitor *carped* about the cold weather." Syn.: cavil.

carpetbagger [KARpitbagur] a Northern politician or businessman who went to the South after the Civil War to seek profit; any politician who takes up residence in a locality in order to procure profitable advantages. "The senator from Tennessee angered other candidates by refusing to debate them, and had only taken up residence in the state recently, *carpetbagger*-style." "The Arkansas merchant, originally from another state, was called a *carpetbagger*." "The KKK terrorized black politicians and *carpetbaggers*." "The *carpetbaggers* were apparently doing nothing that Southern businessmen themselves were not doing."

carriage trade [KAYRij...] wealthy patrons. "The 'up-scale' department store got most of the city's *carriage trade*." "Every large American city has some *carriage trade*." "The hotel catered to the *carriage trade*." "The *carriage trade* dominated the district." "While the *carriage trade* dined in splendor homeless and jobless men made do in Hoovervilles." "The *carriage trade* consisted of heirs and heiresses."

carte blanche [KART BLANSH] (French) unconditional authority. "The president gave the general *carte blanche* to wage the war as he saw fit." "He had *carte blanche* in running the factory." "The doyen had *carte blanche* in the criminal gang." "The lawyer had *carte blanche* to deal with the will." "The minister was given *carte blanche* to negotiate a treaty."

Cassandra [kuSANdru] a prophet of doom. "The economist was like a *Cassandra* due to his gloomy economic predictions." "The predictions of the *Cassandra* were not believed." "The *Cassandra* forecast a devastating storm." "The *Cassandra* said the world would be exterminated in a final war." After a Greek myth involving a prophetess condemned never to be believed. Syn.: calamity howler, cynic, gloomy Gus.

caste [KAYST] a class with rigid customs allowing little change. The classic caste system is the Indian, which ranges from the Brahmins at top to the pariahs and "untouchables" at bottom, who accept handouts and wages from higher caste members careful not to be "polluted." "The *caste* system in India condemned many people to a hard-scrabble living." "The South was considered a *caste* system because the slaves and sharecroppers could not break away from wealthy merchants and planters." "Class systems may be more common that *castes*." "The writer condemned the *caste* society." A social class differs from a caste in being more open and less tradition-bound. The ancient Inca empire also had a caste. Also, certain social insects--for example, ants, termites and bees--are said to feature castes.

castigate [KAStigayt] to punish or severely reprimand. "The employees were *castigated* for not working harder." "The disobedient soldier was *castigated*." "The man should never have been *castigated*." "The dog squealed when the man tried to *castigate* him." Like *chastise* and *chasten*, "castigate" bears a reference to purity or "chastity"; somehow punishment is related to sexuality. Apparently one who has been castigated or chastened has thereby been, in a sort of analogy, deprived of sexual pleasure. "The Marquis de Sade was chastened and imprisoned for his sexual violence."

casuistry [KAZHooistree] sophistry. "Far too many instances of *casuistry* are allowed to pass unchallenged on American television." "His reasoning was subtle but guilty of *casuistry*." "His *casuistry* could have turned the Golden Rule into a Gilded Rule of sorts." "He used *casuistry* to wriggle out of the agreement." Much casuistry arises from the confusion of evidence with authority. In logic, the truth of an assertion depends on evidence, not authority. The opinions of experts should carry no weight unless they are accompanied by evidence, which in the final analysis is the sole criterion of truth.

casus belli [KAYsus BELih] (Latin) an argument or justification for war; an event that leads to war. "The assassination of an archduke in 1914 was the *casus belli* of World War l." "The *casus belli* for the Nazi invasion of Poland was Joseph Goebbels propaganda." "The *casus belli* was the failure of diplomatic negotiations." "The *casus belli* of American entry into World War l was mainly U-boat torpedoing of American ships."

catafalque [KATufalk] a raised structure on which a dead body rests in a state funeral. "The president's body lay on the *catafalque* in the rotunda." "The *catafalque* used in Lincoln's funeral was re-used in Kennedy's funeral." "The *catafalque* held the body of the late premier." "The *catafalque* was a simple structure."

catamite [KATumiht] a boy kept for pederasty. "After a few hours of abuse the *catamite* escaped." "The man searched the park for a *catamite*." "The priest had a *catamite*." "The *catamite* had to be coerced."

catechize [KATekihz] to teach through questions and answers; to interrogate. "The detectives *catechized* the defendant for five straight hours, but still the court ruled that the confession was admissible." "Many teachers of French *catechize* their students in the foreign language." "The five-year-old who continually *catechizes* his parents may be underloved." "He *catechized* his unfaithful wife on where she had been." "Boswell was eternally catechizing him on all kinds of subjects" (Thomas Macaulay). The Greek root of catechize means to teach by word of mouth.

catechumen [katiKYOOmun] a student in the creeds of Christianity; any beginning student. "The *catechumen* was awkward." "The *catechumens* lived in the seminary." "She was a *catechumen* at chess." "The *catechumen* had much knowledge to acquire." Syn. amateur, beginner, neophyte, novice, tyro. Ant.: veteran.

caterwaul [KATurwol] to howl or screech; to quarrel like cats. "The five brothers and sisters were often *caterwauling* when young." "He *caterwauled* when struck." "*Caterwauling* in the school was forbidden." "The children were *caterwauling* on the playground with joy."

catharsis [kuTHARsis] in tragic drama, a period of suffering that expiates a sin. "*Catharsis* is not the same as psychological purging." "The protagonist underwent *catharsis*." "The *catharsis* was brutal." "*Catharsis* was not part of the program." In Freudian-oriented therapy, *catharsis* is psychoanalysis that aims to discharge inhibited, socially-unacceptable emotions, though the whole thing is vague and unscientific.

cathexis [kuTHEKsis] the concentration of emotion on something. Its Greek root means to "hold down." "She found an outlet for her hysterical nymphomania through a *cathexis* consisting of consumerism." "The woman's *cathexis* was a substitute for a lost child." "*Cathexis* is a term in the bogus psychoanalysis." "The numb man felt *cathexis* for nothing." This word has no synonym in English.

catnap [KATnap] a short nap; to take a short nap. "Instead of getting good sleep the exhausted soldiers took *catnaps*." "The graveyard shift workers tried to adjust to the hours with *catnapping*." "*Catnapping* proved unsatisfactory as a substitute for sleep." "*Catnaps* and the sleep hormone melatonin were used by the airline pilots for jet lag."

caudillo [koDEEyo] the leader of a Spanish-speaking country. "The *caudillo*—although actually a dictator—was truly beloved by his fellow countrymen." "The *caudillo* was a woman." "The *caudillo* was democratically elected." "The voters elected a socialist *caudillo*."

cause celebre [KOZ seLEBru] a celebrated or notorious issue. The phrase literally means "celebrated case" in French. "The Scopes monkey trial was a *cause celebre* ostensibly involving the existence or nonexistence of God." "The Dreyfus *cause celebre* tested anti-semitism in France about 1895." "The *cause celebre* of Sacco and Vanzetti divided intellectuals along ideological grounds." "The kidnapping became a *cause celebre* reported in the newspapers."

cavalier [kavuLIR] casual; arrogant. This word is derived from Latin *caballus*, meaning "horse." (French and Spanish for horse, *cheval* and *caballo*, reflect the same derivation.) "His *cavalier* disregard for manners offended the whole family." "The bride's demeanor was *cavalier* and relaxed throughout the wedding." "His demeanor was *cavalier*." "He dismissed the warning in a *cavalier* manner." An ironic alteration is given by Lord Byron: "In short, he was a perfect cavaliero, And to his very valet seemed a hero" (*Beppo*).

cavil [KAVul] to quibble; to carp. "He accused his debating opponent of *cavilling*." "He was *cavilling* when he came up with that excuse for having been a draft dodger." "He *cavilled* about the taste of the water at the restaurant." "She *cavilled*, found trivial fault with." *Cavil* comes from a Latin word meaning a "jest."

celerity [suLERitee] swiftness. "The word *celerity* reminded him of the proverb 'hasten slowly.'" "DiMaggio covered centerfield with graceful *celerity*." "*Celerity* may be necessary at times but, as Ben Franklin said, 'drive thy business, let not that drive thee.'" "The job waiting tables requires a certain *celerity*." "The middle-aged softball player had no *celerity*." "They showed *celerity* in the management of the resort." "The customers were shown to their rooms with *celerity*." Syn.: dispatch, expeditiousness, quickness, rapidity, speed. Ant.: sluggishness.

cenobite [SEENubiht] a member of a religious convent or community. "The *cenobites* lived in a modest building next to the church." "The *cenobites* had all the modern conveniences in the convent." "Some of the *cenobites* were teachers." "The *cenobites* all were devoted to God." Syn.: anchorite, monk.

cenotaph [SENutaf] a monument to the dead without the remains. This word's root in Greek literally means "empty tomb." "The *cenotaphs* for the rich in the cemetery were grander than those for the poor." "Her *cenotaph* was the largest in the cemetery." "The *cenotaph* was inscribed with something in Latin." "The *cenotaph* was located next to the mausoleum."

censorious [senSOReeus] harshly critical. "He was *censorious* of his wife's relationship with his partner." "He knew not to be *censorious* with his parents." "The coach was *censorious* of his team." "He was often *censorious* to his younger brother." Syn.: disapproving, stern.

centrifugal [senTRIFyugul] moving outward away from a center. "*Centrifugal* force kept the passengers on the amusement ride from falling out." "The physics student studied *centrifugal* force." "The word *centrifugal* literally means 'center fleeing' in Latin." "*Centrifugal* force spun around the car that was traveling the highway cloverleaf."

centripetal [senTRIPitul] moving toward the center. "*Centripetal* is the opposite of centrifugal." "*Centripetal* force moved the object toward the axis." "The tether ball was affected by *centripetal* force as it twirled around the pole." "*Centripetal* can also mean 'afferent' (a term in biology indicating toward the central nervous system)."

chaff [CHAF] trivial stuff. "She deemed the community newspaper to be full of *chaff*." "To separate the wheat from the *chaff*' means to find the important part among miscellaneous things." "The teacher-preparation course was full of *chaff*." "His reasons are as two grains of wheat, hid in two bushels of chaff" (Shakespeare, *The Merchant of Venice*).

chamberlain [CHAYMburlin] an official who manages a royal household; a treasurer or high official of a royal court. "The *chamberlain* managed the duke's finances." "The *chamberlain* stood accused of embezzling funds." "The *chamberlain* issued the king's decree." "The *chamberlain* was very trustworthy."

chance-medley [CHANSmedlee] a sudden, violent quarrel. "She lost her life in a domestic *chance-medley*." "He was afraid that a gun in the house would lead to a tragic *chance-medley* so he threw it out." "A *chance-medley* interrupted the party." "The *chance-medley*, fortunately, did not lead to injury."

chapfallen [CHAPfolun] dejected. "He was *chapfallen* after his girlfriend left him." "She was *chapfallen* because she thought she was ugly." "The woman was *chapfallen* when her cat died." "He was *chapfallen* after losing his job." Syn.: depressed, despondent, disheartened, downcast, downhearted. Ant.: cheerful, enthused, vivacious.

charlatan [SHARlutun] someone who pretends to have skill or knowledge he does not have. "Although he had no medical license, he was no *charlatan*." "The traveling *charlatan* sold faith-healing medicine." "Psychoanalysts are *charlatans*, since Freudianism is unscientific." "Some people believed him to be a *charlatan*." "The *charlatan*—a heart surgeon—claimed he could prolong patients' lives." "The *charlatan* claimed that God talks to him." Syn.: four-flusher, fraud, impostor, mountebank, quack. Ant.: expert.

charnel [CHARnul] resembling or suggesting death. "Many of Edgar Allen Poe's short stories deal with *charnel* things like premature burial." "On the grounds of the cemetery was a *charnel* house." "The road lined with victims of the pogrom was a *charnel* sight." "Buchenwald was a *charnel* place." Syn.: ghastly, grisly, gruesome, macabre.

chary [CHARee] cautious or shy. "On the subject of his parents' finances he was very *chary*." "She was *chary* around him." "The driver should have been more *chary*." "He was *chary* in rattlesnake country." This word stems from an Old English word meaning "care." It is used more often in Britain than America.

chaste [CHAYST] decent or undefiled; free from obscenity; not having engaged in forbidden sex. "The twenty-year-old bride was as *chaste* as the pure-driven snow." "She swore to her husband that she was *chaste* and had not committed adultery." "The magazine was *chaste*, although it did offer sexual advice." "His letter to her was not entirely *chaste*." Syn.: pure, unstained, virgin.

chasten [CHAYsun] to chastise; to punish for the sake of moral improvement. "The teacher *chastened* the student." "She *chastened* her husband for not having repaired the car." "The radical believed that some groups in society needed *chastening* due to their greed." "The man told his wife that there was no need to *chasten* their daughter."

chastity belt [CHAStitee BELT] a beltlike device worn by women in the Middle Ages to prevent sexual intercourse and intended to assure the fidelity of wives. "The man laughed and exclaimed 'a *chastity belt*—that will keep 'em faithful.'" "Before he left on his journey the man fixed his wife with a *chastity belt*." "The woman found the *chastity belt* uncomfortable." "She could hardly imagine the appearance of a *chastity belt*."

chattel [CHATul] an article of movable property; a slave. "The *chattel* furniture went to their new home." "*Chattel* slavery was finally abolished." "The *chattel* was sold at auction." "The *chattel* was stolen from the property."

chef d'oeuvre [sheDOEvru] (French) a masterpiece. "A *chef d'oeuvre* by Rembrandt was among the paintings stolen from the gallery." "His *chef d'oeuvre* was a novel set in the English civil war." "*The Grapes of Wrath* is the *chef d'oeuvre* of John Steinbeck (1902-68)." "The artist's *chef d'oeuvre* was a church fresco."

chicanery [shiKAYnuree] petty deceitfulness. "The judge had had enough of the defendant's *chicanery*." "The doctor was upset with the patient's alleged *chicanery*." "He knew how to handle his pal's *chicanery*." The related verb *chicane* is little used: "He *chicaned* the old man out of thousands of dollars." Syn.: artifice, ruse, subterfuge, wile.

chiliasm [KILeeazum] the doctrine that Christ will return to reign on earth after 1,000 years. "The *chiliastic* hope for the year 2000 was not fulfilled." "The fervent believers had *chiliastic* hopes." "The couple hopefully awaited a *chiliasm*." "The devout still thought *chiliasm* possible." Syn.: millenialism.

chimera [kiMEERu] a vain fancy; a horrible creation of the imagination. "Her pursuit of happiness was obstructed by a *chimera* that she had to prepare for everything, rather than live spontaneously." "The belief of 60s radicals that revolution was immanent was a *chimera*." "She dwelled on a *chimera* of becoming a rich celebrity." "The radical demonstrated that the American dream was a *chimera* for many."

chivaree [SHIVuree] (also spelled "charivaree") a sham serenade to newlyweds. "He had to insist to his friends that they not stage a *chivaree* after his wedding." "A group of friends stood below the groom's hotel window and delivered a *chivaree*." "The bride had never heard of *chivaree*." "The *chivaree* was noisy and clamorous."

choler [KOLur] anger. "His *choler* showed in the redness of his face." "His eyes narrowed in *choler*." "She showed considerable *choler* when her husband left her." "The *choler* was noticeable in her eyes."

churlishness [CHURlishnes] rudeness; boorishness. "The behavior of the two children was seen as *churlishness* by their aunt." "The hosts thought their guest was *churlish*." "The boy was *churlish* on his birthday." "She was warned not to be *churlish*." *Churl* comes from an Old English word meaning "peasant."

circuitous [surKYOOitus] roundabout. "The *circuitous* path through the forest had many switchbacks." "He took a *circuitous* route home." "The drive leading to the manor was *circuitous*." "Her reply was *circuitous*."

circumspect [SURkumspekt] heedful of a situation. *Circumspect* in its Latin root means to "look around." "The report of landmines in the area made him very *circumspect*." "Being in the inner city made him *circumspect*." "The thief went about his business with *circumspection*." "He was too *circumspect* to be a good actor." Syn.: attentive, careful, cautious. Ant.: insouciant.

clamant [KLAYmunt] clamorous; noisy; urgent. "The all-night party was *clamant*." "The woman entered the house with a *clamant* need to use the phone." "His need for money was *clamant*." "He was *clamant* and obstreperous in resisting arrest." Syn.: rowdy, vociferous. Ant.: quiet.

clambake [KLAMbayk] a party, especially a noisy one. "Unfortunately for them it rained on their *clambake*." "The *clambake* at the beach house became unruly." "His *clambake* was a social success." "The *clambake* was supposed to begin at five but was off to a slow start."

clandestine [klanDEStin] secret or surreptitious. "The *clandestine* domestic activity of the CIA violates the law which created the agency." "*Clandestine* satellite surveillance is not supposed to be going on, but it is." "The government program was *clandestine*." "The affair was kept *clandestine*."

claptrap [KLAPtrap] busybody talk intended only to get attention. "The other guests at the party did not know how to stop his endless *claptrap*." "His friend is a 'motor mouth' full of frantic *claptrap*." "The children were full of *claptrap*." "The parents had learned to ignore their daughter's anxious *claptrap*." The word is derived from an obsolete term for a theatrical stunt.

claque [KLAK] a group of fawning admirers. "The studio audience had been selected and processed so as to give a resounding 'spontaneous' laugh on cue, and was actually a *claque*." "The *claque* adulated the celebrity." "The *claque* guffawed heartily." "The *claque* was wild with enthusiasm."

clarion [KLAReeun] clear and shrill. "The government issued a *clarion* call for volunteer soldiers." "The housewife yelled in a *clarion* voice for her children to come home." "The company paid for *clarion* advertising for its new product." "The television commercial extolled a *clarion* message about the 'revolutionary' toilet brush."

clerisy [KLERisee] the literati or intelligentsia. "The *clerisy* of the period re-

volted against American culture." "The *clerisy* decided that the classless society was the wave of the future." "The *clerisy* was renowned for its articula-
tion of the ills of the establishment." "The young woman joined a part of the
clerisy in the hope of reforming society." "The *clerisy* included many scholars from the universities."

climacteric [klihMAKturik] a critical period; a year of change, as in one's luck
or health. "Women reach a biological *climacteric*, nonfertile menopause, at
about age 45." "The year 1775 was a *climacteric* for the fate of the American
colonies." "The conservative argued that a woman's loss of beauty—an inevitable part of nature—is coincident with her physiological *climacteric*."
"The American teenager experiences an 'awkward' *climacteric*."

clotheshorse [KLOHZhors] a person who is considered to be obsessed with
fashionable dress. "Among her other obsessions, the woman was a *clotheshorse*." "The *clotheshorse* spent much money on clothes." "The *clotheshorse*
very much cared about how she appeared." "The *clotheshorse* received a
number of fashion catalogues in the mail."

cloud nine [KLOUD NIHN] a state of great happiness. "The young couple
seemed to be on *cloud nine*." "Suddenly the high-school student had great
friends, some money in the bank and floated on *cloud nine*." "The woman
never lived on *cloud nine* except when her husband clung to her." "The people, though surely deserving, went off in strange paths in search of *cloud
nine*." Syn.: bliss. Ant.: hell, purgatory.

cloy [KLOI] to surfeit or overindulge in. "Being together constantly can be *cloying* for a husband and wife." "Instead of *cloying* he stopped eating after one
bowl of ice cream." "After the buffet it would have been *cloying* to eat
more." "They stayed in the theatre to watch the movie a second time, but it
was a little *cloying*."

Cockaigne [koKAYN] a fabled land of idle luxury. "The writer retired to his
Cockaigne and the good life in a villa in Hawaii." "He once dreamed of finding a *Cockaigne* on a remote island somewhere." "A true *Cockaigne* of the
21st century must be a chimera." "A *Cockaigne* seems to require much
money." Syn.: Garden of Eden, paradise, Promised Land, Shangri-la.

cockalorum [kokuLORum] a tough-sounding little man; boastful talk. "The
Chamber of Commerce gave out much *cockalorum* about how they go-
getters were going to bring a symphony orchestra to town." "The *cockalorum* tried to bluff people." "The boy gave out *cockalorum* about owning
some sort of valuable painting." "His *cockalorum* was much ado about nothing." Syn.: braggadocio.

cock of the walk [KOK...] the leader of a group, especially a domineering one.
"The 'juvenile delinquents' were led by a *cock of the walk*." "He was the
cock of the walk of the brigade." "The *cock of the walk* died leading his men
into battle." "The *cock of the walk* had his own harem and bodyguards."

coeval [kohEEvul] existing during the same period; contemporary. "Francis
Bacon was *coeval* with Shakespeare." "The furniture was *coeval* with the
circa 1900 house." "The church is *coeval* with the founding of the city."
"Her death was *coeval* with the war."

cognate [KOGnayt] related in source; having a blood relationship; (noun) a word related to another word in a kindred language. "Fiend is a *cognate* of German *Feind* ('enemy')." "Studying foreign languages, an English-speaking person will come across many *cognates* in European languages." "German *Fenster* is a *cognate* of French *fenetre* ('window')." "German *ist* is a *cognate* of *is*." "French *serpent* ('snake') is a *cognate* of English *serpent*."

cognoscenti [konyuSHENtee] those who have a superior understanding of the arts and society. "The French *cognoscenti* rejected the artists' work." "The American *cognoscenti* have often been at odds with society." "The *cognoscenti* opposed the project." "The *cognoscenti* rallied to support the accused man." Syn.: clerisy, intellectuals, literati.

cold light [KOLD LIHT] light produced with little or no heat. "The firefly features *cold light*." "Scientists are striving to generate *cold light*." "*Cold light* is not yet understood." "*Cold light* may be useful in the future."

colleen [koLEEN] (Irish) a girl. "They gave their daughter an Irish name— *Colleen*." "The *colleen* had Irish-American parents." "The *colleen* had a brother and two sisters." "There was only one *colleen* in the class." *Colleen* is actually the diminutive of the Irish word for "girl."

collogue [kuLOHG] to conspire. "He *collogued* to defraud the bank he worked at." "The two men *collogued* to embezzle funds." "The court found the couple guilty of having *collogued*." "She went to prison for having *collogued*."

colloquy [KOLukwee] a dialogue; a conversation. "The *colloquy* took place between husband and wife and so was privileged." "The kibitzer could not hear their *colloquy*." "Their *colloquy* was interrupted by his uncle." "Their *colloquy* was hushed, since they were in a library."

collusion [koLOOzhun] a clandestine agreement to commit some fraudulent activity. "Some consider President Ford's pardon of Nixon to have been the result of *collusion*." "The accountant took part in a *collusion*." "She was convicted of *collusion* in the robbery." "The *collusion* included a man who never meant to commit a crime." Syn.: connivance, intrigue, scheme.

colporteur [KOLportur] one who distributes discount books, especially religious ones. "In his youth he made a bare subsistence as a *colporteur* in the South." "The *colporteur* traveled from town to town." "The *colporteur* sold Bibles but was not religious."

comely [KUMlee] proper; ingratiating. "The attractive teen-aged girl was *comely* and charming." "The college teacher was anything but *comely*." "The French girl's behavior was *comely*." "To behave as others do in a foreign country is *comely*." "The speaking in a perpetual hyperbole is comely in nothing but in love" (Francis Bacon). Syn.: personable, pleasing.

comestible [kuMEStubul] edible; *comestibles*: articles of food. "*Comestible* is reminiscent of Spanish *comer*, 'to eat.'" "The food was stale and not *comestible*." "The boy had several *comestibles* in his backpack." "The dead sparrow was not *comestible*."

comity [KOMitee] politeness. "The group's *comity* recommended it to others." "*Comity* of all the nations in the world is not easy to come by." "He showed women delicate *comity*." "The mean fellow lacked *comity*."

comme il faut [kumeelFOH] (French) as it should be. "According to a well-known phrase, sexual differences are *comme il faut*—and *vive la diffrence!*" "According to the wealthy family, the status quo was *comme il faut*." "The parents believed that their method of child rearing was *comme il faut*." "He regarded his own habits as *comme il faut*." Syn.: proper.

commensal [kuMENsul] pertaining to those who eat at the same table. "The communist government decreed that meals should be *commensal*." "The conservative asserted that *commensal* habits did not promote equality." "The nuns had breakfast and lunch *commensally*." "The commune featured *commensal* meals."

commensurable [kuMENsurubul] able to be measured by the same standard. "The fact that the world's currencies are not strictly *commensurable* creates trade obstacles." "The punishment was not *commensurable* with the crime." "The two systems of drawing were not *commensurable*." "The public good and money are not *commensurable*." Syn.: commensurate.

commination [komuNAYshun] an explicit condemnation. "The Nazi government issued a *commination* against Jews." "The *commination* called for repression of the minority." "The *commination* targeted hated persons." "The woman could hardly believe the *commination* contained in the letter." This word is formed from *minari*, Latin for to "threaten," and the intensifier *com*.

commiserate [kuMIZurayt] to sympathize with. "They *commiserated* at the refreshment stand over their loss on the field." "He was basically incapable of *commiseration* with anyone." "She did not *commiserate* with him." "The two girls found solace in mutual *commiseration*." The synonym *sympathize* literally means to "suffer with," as does its German equivalent, *mitleiden*.

commonweal [KOMunweel] the common welfare. "The politician pretended to promote the *commonweal*." "The *commonweal* is a complex thing." "The *commonweal* requires equality." "The *commonweal* featured economic planning."

commute [kuMYOOT] to exchange for another; to convert into something else; to travel to regularly. "The retiree *commuted* to a beach house on an island across the wine-dark sea." "The governor refused to *commute* the convict's sentence." "The alchemist sought to *commute* base metal into gold." "The radical criticized the inefficiency and waste of *commuting* to work in a car."

compendious [kumPENdeeus] succinct. "The essays of Francis Bacon (1561-1626) are *compendious* and erudite." "The one-volume encyclopedia was *compendious*." "His letter was *compendious*." "The slim book was *compendious*." A *compendium* is a short summary. Syn.: concise, laconic. Ant.: verbose.

comport [kumPORT] to conduct oneself in a certain way; to correspond or agree. "Despite his gauche habits, he *comported* well at the wedding reception." "The two things he was comparing did not *comport*." "Her *comportment* in school was fitting." "The commoner did not know how to *comport* in the noble's home."

compunction [kumPUNGKshun] uneasiness or guilt stemming from an action. "Hitler felt no *compunction* in annexing Austria." "The man felt no *com-*

punction about running over the boy with a car." "The teacher felt no *compunction* in giving the student an F." "The heir had no *compunction* about inheriting 108 million dollars." Syn.: remorse.

Comstockery [KOMstokuree] prudish censorship. "The late 19th century witnessed the height of American *Comstockery*, when even piano legs were covered up because they were felt to be too suggestive." "The writer decried the strictures placed on books as *comstockery*." "*Comstockery* went too far in censoring the arts." "*Comstockery* was part of the Puritanism of the Victorian Age." This word comes from the name of Anthony Comstock (1844-1915), an American "social reformer," so-called.

conation [kohNAYshun] the aspect of mental life having to do with impulse, desire and striving. "The psychology major studied *conation*." "His *conation* was sluggish." "He set his *conation* so that it was neither too strenuous nor too slow." "Her *conation* was mainly taking care of children."

concupiscence [konKYOOpisuns] lust. "The obsessed nymphomaniac found it impossible to expend her hysterical *concupiscence*." "In those years he was always *concupiscent*." "*Concupiscence* must be held in check." "*Concupiscence* led to her downfall." Syn.: lasciviousness.

condescend [kondiSEND] to deign to do something. "He *condescended* to allowing his female hitch-hiker to give him a 'hand job.'" "The *condescension* in the unctuous movie was too much to take." "The president *condescended* to meet the political activist." "He *condescended* to listen to the guy's amusing story." Synonyms of *condescending*: fawning, mealy-mouthed, obsequious, servile, smarmy, toady, unctuous.

condign [kunDIHN] (mainly of punishment) fitting, appropriate. "The governor's pardon was not viewed as *condign* by the victim's family." "Some people who sit on corporate boards think it *condign* to vote themselves a large income!" "The punishment of the teacher was *condign*." "The mother tried to dole out *condign* punishment to keep her children orderly."

confabulate [kunFAByulayt] to chat. "The result of their *confabulation* was nothing he did not already know." "She could *confabulate* on the phone for hours." "He refused to *confabulate* with the poor girl." "'*Confabulation* won't get you to bed with me,' she said to him." Syn.: blab, blather, gab, gossip.

confute [kunFYUHT] to prove wrong. "Lysenko's theory of the inheritance of acquired traits was *confuted* by 20th century biologists." "The idea of no social classes is *confuted* every day by the maldistribution of the wealth." "The sociologist *confuted* their mistaken beliefs about the leisure class." "The theory of the source of profit in underpayment of labor was not *confuted*."

congeries [konJEEReez] an assemblage of things. "Before the boy on Christmas morning was a *congeries* of presents." "The *congeries* of fantastic notions in his mind rather troubled him." "The *congeries* of images in the film noir was bizarre." "The *congeries* of dialogue on the radio program tilted from degenerate to tragic and from comic to contemptible."

congruous [KONgroous] appropriate. "Her words in public were always morally *congruous*." "The sports analyst's remarks were not seen as *congruous*."

"Eying a married woman is not *congruous*." "*Congruously*, he was given a big state funeral." This word is better known in the negative, "incongruous."

conjure [kunJOOR] to appeal to or entreat solemnly. "One writer said that Francis Bacon (1561-1626) was 'one to *conjure* with.'" "The delegate *conjured* with the army's leader to surrender." "Bacon *conjured* men to mix seriousness with jest." "The book *conjured* people to rethink democracy."

connubial [kuNOObeeul] pertaining to marriage; conjugal. "Their *connubial* happiness was an inspiration to the whole family." "Their *connubial* tie did not last." "It was the couple's 50th *connubial* anniversary." "*Connubial* love maketh mankind."

consanguine [konSANGwin] related to by blood. "They did not discover their *consanguinity* until a few years later." "The two children of cousins were *consanguine*." "He and his aunt were not actually *consanguine*." "The law forbade him to marry anyone *consanguine*."

consecrate [KONsikrayt] to make official. "The couple *consecrated* their love for each other with a wedding eleven months after meeting." "The ship was *consecrated* The Enterprise." "She *consecrated* the deal with her signature." "Their engagement was *consecrated* with an advertisement in the newspaper." Syn.: ordain, sanctify.

consign [kunSIYN] to entrust to. "The museum's paintings were temporarily *consigned* to the university's art gallery." "The boy was *consigned* to adoptive parents." "The valuable coins were *consigned* to the bank." "He *consigned* the secret to his friend."

consonance [KONsununs] accord or harmony. "The *consonance* of the bidders at the auction was notable." "The *consonance* of the fifth-grade class of Germans was remarkable." "The *consonance* on the show was affected." "The negotiators could not reach *consonance*." Syn.: congruity, unison. Ant.: dissonance.

constabulary [kunSTAByuleree] a police department marked by military features. "When labor went on a general strike the *constabulary* was summoned to 'keep order.'" "The *constabulary* was called in to help put down the work strike." "The *constabulary* attacked the protesting students." "When constabulary duty's to be done, The policeman's lot is not a happy one" (W.S. Gilbert).

consternate [KONsturnayt] to dismay. "The power outage caused *consternation* across the metropolitan region." "His behavior at dinner caused *consternation*." "The forty-year-old man was *consternated* to learn that he could no longer run well." "She looked in the mirror and was *consternated*."

consubstantial [konsubSTANshul] having the same substance, nature or essence. "The brain and the mind are almost *consubstantial*." "The two chemicals are *consubstantial*." "The two organs are *consubstantial*." "The two kinds of meat were *consubstantial*."

consuetude [KONswitood] custom. "The town *consuetude* was to attend an outdoor concert every Saturday during summer." "The *consuetude* mandated a man's marrying the wife of his late brother (levirate)." "The *consuetude* was to jump from the bank onto the tire swing fastened above the creek."

"Sociologists and anthropologists study *consuetude*."

contemn [kunTEM] to despise. "He secretly *contemned* his neighbor's fancy new below-ground pool." "He that contemneth small things shall fall by little and little" (the Bible). "She *contemned* her family's dog." "He *contemned* his wife's male friend." Syn.: abhor, detest, execrate, loathe. Ant. love.

contemporaneous [kuntempuRAYneeus] happening at the same time. "The writings of Shakespeare and Christopher Marlowe were basically *contemporaneous*." "His death and the financial panic were *contemporaneous*." "His art expressed the *contemporaneous* Impressionism movement." "The murder and his trip abroad were *contemporaneous*."

contiguous [kunTIGyoous] nearby; bordering on. "Detroit is *contiguous* with Canada." "Egypt is *contiguous* with the Red Sea." "The town is *contiguous* with the railroad line." "Kansas City is *contiguous* with the Missouri River."

contrariety [kontruRIHitee] a contrary fact or statement; the quality of being contrary. "The idea that there is no media censorship is a *contrariety*." "The *contrariety* declared there is no justice." "'Phone-sex' sounds like a *contrariety*." "The sociologist declared democracy a *contrariety*." Syn.: contradiction. Ant.: verity.

contravene [kontruVEEN] to come into conflict with; to transgress. "His shifty testimony *contravened* his earlier statement." "The burglar rudely *contravened* their house and property." "He *contravened* the 'line,' they claimed." "The corporation *contravened* common decency." "The conservative asserted that hippies *contravene* good taste and manners." In its Latin root *contravene* means to "come against."

contretemps [kontruTAN] a mishap. Being a French word (with the stress on the last syllable), *contretemps* literally means "against time." "His arrival in the midst of their love-making was a *contretemps* that could have led to trouble." "In a *contretemps*, he let slip the fact that there was a surprise birthday party for her." "The *contretemps* was embarrassing because it suggested a 'badge of the man.'" "Their both throwing parties on the same day was a *contretemps*." Syn.: embarrassment.

contrite [kunTRIYT] feeling regret or remorse. "His father, while reproaching him, told the boy he should be *contrite* for deliberately breaking his toy." "He was *contrite* after losing his job." "The soldier felt *contrite* for killing someone." "Bomber pilots are not supposed to feel *contrite* for victims of bombing." The corresponding noun is *contrition*. Ant.: shameless.

contumacious [kontuMAYshus] disobedient. "Her *contumacious* testimony at the hearing got her into trouble." "His *ad hoc* report seemed to reflect his *contumacious*, less than forthright attitude." "You are not allowed to be *contumacious* in the military." "The *contumacious* children ran wild." Syn.: insubordinate.

contumely [konTOOmulee] insulting behavior or speech. "Some people deem it *contumely* to be ignored by someone, as though you weren't even there." "The cheeky teenager seemed to project *contumely* with his very appearance." In his great "to be or not to be" soliloquy, Shakespeare refers to the "proud man's contumely." "The worker felt his boss' *contumely*."

conundrum [kuNUNdrum] a puzzling riddle; something that baffles. "The Prime Minister believed that Russia was a *conundrum*." "The bashful boy who did not talk much was a *conundrum* to his school mates." "He wished to neither declare himself nor be a social *conundrum*." "American life is a *conundrum* of affability and informality to some foreign visitors." Syn. enigma, mystery.

conurbation [konurBAYshun] an expansive metropolitan area. "The Los Angeles *conurbation* is huge." "The radical criticized the lack of planning in the haphazard *conurbation*." "The county *conurbation* had about 90 incorporated townships of all classes, shapes and sizes." "Some people criticize the suburban *conurbation* as tedious." Syn.: metropolis.

convivial [kunVIVeeul] in a cheerful or festive mood. The Latin origin of this word literally means to "live together." "The atmosphere at Munich's Oktoberfest is quite *convivial, gemütlich*." "Conviviality" might be the best translation for the renowned Bavarian word *Gemütlichkeit*. "The American tourists liked the *conviviality* of Bavaria." "She was a very *convivial* hostess." "The hotel in the national park offered *convivial* accommodations."

convocation [konvuKAYshun] assembly; convoking. "The group of well-to-do men formed a political *convocation* to write a new constitution." "The *convocation* formed around members of the profession." "The *convocation* issued new laws for the revolutionary government." "The *convocation* did not attract many delegates."

cool [KOOL] not uptight; calm and collected; excellent; (noun) composure. "He lost his *cool* and engaged in road rage." "As Francis Bacon advised, do not blow your *cool* when life becomes mean." "It was a *cool* sports car." "Their vacation in the Swiss Alps was *cool*." "Related in a way to the word *cool* is the expression 'are you bad or mad?'" "He won a *cool* $10,000." The word *cool* with the younger generation is virtually an American institution; it is very common, and obviously originated in the black community.

coot [KOOT] a foolish old man. "The pathetic aged man was declared 'crazy as a *coot*.'" "The aged painter had a very keen mind and was no *coot*." "The *coot* was living a second childhood in Shangri-la." "The *coot* lived alone in a cabin in the mountains."

cordon sanitaire [kordon saneeTER] (French) a barricade around a quarantined area; a ring of buffer states established around a hostile country. "The police erected a *cordon sanitaire* at the crime scene." "Poland was used as a *cordon sanitaire*." "A crowd gathered outside the *cordon sanitaire*." "The *cordon sanitaire* kept people out."

Corinthian [kuRINtheeun] luxurious; dissolute with plenty. "The *Corinthian* aristocratic festivals of pre-1789 France prefigured the 'deluge.'" "The *Corinthian* bed featured silk sheets." "The heiress lived in *Corinthian* splendor." "The *Corinthian* party ended in an orgy." Syn.: gold-plated, posh, sumptuous, swank.

cornucopia [kornuKOHpeeu] an abundant supply. "The supermarket featured a *cornucopia* of food and drink." "The heiress' inheritance provided her with a life-long *cornucopia* for which she did not have to work." "Socialism promises a *cornucopia* for all." "The fair had a *cornucopia* of hotdogs, pretzels and cotton candy." "The conservative maintained that the path to *cornucopia* is by hard work and private initiative."

corporeal [korPOReeul] pertaining to the body; tangible. "They received *corporeal* benefits in addition to a pension from their employer." "Living to eat would naturally entail *corporeal* expansion." "The *corporeal*, the thing of the flesh, sometimes has a mind of its own." "He was a glutton who overindulged in *corporeal* pleasure."

corrigible [KORigubul] capable of being reformed. "His vice of overspending proved *corrigible*." "The psychologist taught that most unwanted behavior is *corrigible*." "The schizophrenic's voices seemed not to be *corrigible*." "The children's teasing fits proved *corrigible*." Syn.: redeemable. Ant.: incorrigible, intractable, irreclaimable.

corsair [KORsayr] a pirate ship; a pirate. "All the pirates on the captured *corsair* were hanged except two." "The *corsairs* founded 'treasure island.'" "The *corsair* defeated a British frigate." "The *corsairs* engaged in a musket and sword fight with the sailors."

cortege [korTEZH] a ceremonial procession. "At places the *cortege* of celebrities, called a parade, outnumbered the spectators." "The school picnic *cortege* made a circle around the block and returned to the school." "The *cortege* of antiwar demonstrators was impressive." "The *cortege* of overpaid celebrities entered the building on a red carpet."

cosmology [kozMOLujee] the philosophy of the universe and of the laws of space, time and cause and effect. "He loved pursuing *cosmology*." "The students at Stanford University found the *cosmology* course fascinating." "The radical believed that *cosmology* ought to explain universal social hierarchy." "Immanuel Kant (1724-1804) was a great *cosmologist*."

Cossack [KOSak] a Slavic warrior of southeast Russia, formerly one of an elite corps of horsemen in czarist Russia. "The *Cossacks* attacked Napoleon's retreating army." "The *Cossacks* rode into battle at a strategic moment." "The boy was eager to become a *Cossack* like his father." "The *Cossacks* held firm in face of the enemy attack."

cosset [KOSit] to coddle; to treat as a pet. "She was *cosseted* by her mother, the object of maternal overprotection." "The collie was *cosseting* her puppies." "The mother *cosseted* her baby." "The girl *cosseted* her sister." *Cosset* has a root that is related to "kiss."

coterie [KOturee] a group of friends. "The young *coterie* had a favorite café a few blocks from the cathedral." "The *coterie* commuted daily to college together." "The *coterie* consisted of two boys and three girls." "The *coterie* formed two baseball teams." Syn.: clique.

coup de main [koo du MAN] (French) a surprise attack or manouver. "The French army made a *coup de main* by feigning an attack on the center while sending the bulk of its force against the enemy's left flank." "The general's *coup de main* failed." "The *coup de main* was supposed to turn the war around." "The *coup de main* was preceded by a bombardment."

coup de théatre [koo du tayAHtru] (French) a surprising and dramatic turnaround. "The general's refusal to go along with the Putsch amounted to a *coup de théatre.*" "The lawyer's *coup de théatre* won the case." "He presented a *coup de théatre* by showing up at the party in a tuxedo." "He aced the test and manifested a *coup de théatre* to the surprise of those who considered him dense."

courtier [KORteeur] a person who seeks benefit through flattery. "Each new presidential administration is besieged with *courtiers* seeking office." "*Courtiers* surrounded the king." "The *courtiers* expected lucrative positions and grants." "Having failed as a *courtier*, the man retired to his house." This word is related to "court," as in "royal court."

couvade [kooVAD] a practice among certain tribes in which the husband of a woman giving birth takes to bed and feigns labor pains. "*Couvade* is a means by which a man declares his paternity." "When he saw his pregnant wife in labor, the man repaired to his room and began *couvade*." "The anthropologist traveled to Africa to study *couvade*." "*Couvade* was unknown to that particular tribe."

Coventry [KUVuntree] the state of ostracism. "He was sent to *Coventry* for not paying a union fee like his colleagues had." "She was in *Coventry* for having tattled." "She was sent to *Coventry* because of her racist belief." "He was in *Coventry* for having cheated on the test."

coxcomb [KOKSkohm] a fop or silly person. "The *coxcomb* was viewed contemptuously, as is almost anyone who plays the fool." "He was as surely a *coxcomb* as Beau Brummel." "The *coxcomb* dressed fastidiously." "The *coxcomb* was also a boulevardier." "The *coxcomb* had a sponsor who supported his life in the fashionable world." The term stems from the fool's cap worn by professional jesters. Syn.: dandy, gay blade.

covey [KUvee] a small group of persons. "The *covey* moved out onto the patio after dinner." "The *covey* dined al fresco in a golden sunset." "Three was an awkward number for the *covey*." "The *covey* of two couples took a short nature walk up the hill." "He excused himself from the *covey* because he had a headache."

cozen [KUzun] to cheat. "The buyer of the old clock felt *cozened*." "The youth was *cozened* out of $50." "The worker was *cozened* by an employment scam." "She felt *cozened* by her boyfriend." Syn.: bilk, cheat, defraud, dupe, fleece, hoodwink.

crapehanger [KRAYPhangur] a gloomy or pessimistic person. "The *crapehanger* gave up on his baseball team in the third inning." "The *crapehanger* contemplated death." "The *crapehanger* did not see through rose-colored glasses." "The *crapehanger* dwelled on sad events." Syn.: defeatist, negativist.

crapulous [KRAPyoolus] given to gross excess in drinking or eating; suffering from such excess. "The man was *crapulous* from eating too much candy." "She became *crapulous* on the holiday." "She broke her diet and became *crapulous*." "*Crapulous* people are certain to gain weight."

crass [KRAS] unrefined or coarse. "*Crass* materialism is to be criticized." "The paintings at the art fair were rather *crass*." "The wealthy family wallowed in *crassness*." "After receiving a monetary windfall they went on a *crass* shopping spree." Syn.: uncultivated, uncultured.

credo [KREEdoh] a creed. "Their *credo* was 'more money!'" "A *credo* is what a person lives by." "Examination of their *credo* shows that a whole culture can be wrong." "There was a conflict between their *credo* and the actual status quo." *Credo* literally means "I believe."

crestfallen [KRESTfolun] dispirited; depressed. "She was *crestfallen* when her husband died." "He appeared pale and *crestfallen* after losing his job." "The girl was *crestfallen* when the boy did not return her affection." "Unrequited love made him *crestfallen*." Syn.: dejected, low, sad. Ant.: cheerful.

crock of shit [KROK...] a pack of lies. "The teacher devised a *crock of shit* to cover her paranoid fear." (Spears.)

crocodile tears [KROKudihl TEERZ] false or insincere crying. "The heirs shed *crocodile tears* at the funeral of their grandfather." "She cried *crocodile tears* upon the death of her stepmother." "The first-grader's crying for his dead turtle was not *crocodile tears*." "It is the wisdom of the crocodiles, that shed tears when they would devour" (Francis Bacon). "Her *crocodile tears* on the witness stand did not fool the jury."

Croesus [KREEsus] a very rich man. "The *Croesus* gave much to philanthropy but nothing to charity." "Since his father was a *Croesus*, the young man was not compelled to go out and make a living." "The *Croesus*, who had inherited his money, provided trust funds for his children so that they could live off the labor of others." "The money inherited from the *Croesus* was lightly taxed."

crotchety [KROCHitee] characterized by whimsy or stubborness. "The *crotchety* old homesteader had few friends." "The old man was *crotchety*." "The media misrepresented the dissenting music group as lunatic and *crotchety*." "A mistaken rumor cast her as *crotchety*." Syn.: capricious, contrary, fickle, inconstant, perverse. Ant.: amiable.

crux [KRUKS] the most important point. "The *crux* of his argument is that—contrary to the reasoning of an idiot—noone wants to be poor." "The *crux* of socialism is equality." "The *crux* of conservatism is tradition." "The *crux* of Francis Bacon's magnificent essay 'Of Friendship' is that a friendless person eats his own heart out." *Crux* is Latin for "cross" and "trouble."

cuckold [KUKuld] a man whose wife has been unfaithful. "Any *cuckold* is likely to feel anger or rage." "The *cuckold* felt humiliated." "This is a great year for cuckolds" (François Rabelais, *Pantagruel*). "His wife *cuckolded* him for a second time."

cui bono [KWEE BOHnoh] (Latin) for whose benefit? "In analyzing American politics it is more useful to look for a *cui bono* rather than a general good." "The sociologist asked *cui bono* with respect to the lack of laws on wealth inheritance." "The man given a traffic fine he could ill-afford asked, *cui bono?*" "The radical looked at the condition and pay of the workers of the ritzy restaurant and wondered *cui bono*."

cull [KUL] to choose or gather. "She *culled* many years of learning and wrote an informative book of essays." "He *culled* many columns he had written and published them as a book." "She *culled* her years of experience to tell amusing anecdotes." "They carefully *culled* the food and equipment needed for the backpack trip up the Appalachian Mountains." Syn.: collect, pick.

cunctation [kungTAYshun] delay; tardiness. "Her *cunctation* was costly." "The train's *cunctation* wreaked havoc all along the line." "There was a *cunctation* as the bus was unloaded." "The teacher warned against *cunctation* in handing in the paper."

cunt [KUNT] the female genitals. Syn.: altar of hymen, cockshire, coosie, gash, Netherlands, prick purse, squanch, whelk. (Spears.)

cupidity [kyooPIDitee] greed. "The *cupidity* of endorsement opportunists was bountiful." "The arch *cupidity*, with which all petty cupidity has intelligence, is inheritance." "His *cupidity* showed in a boat, Mercedes, multiple houses and servants." "The family's *cupidity* ran to a huge haul of cybercash." Syn.: avarice, greediness, rapacity. Ant.: generosity.

cur [KUR] a mixed-breed dog; a despised person. "He called her a '*cur*' for eating his candy bar." "The dog was technically a *cur*, but the family loved it." "The *cur* was named Molly." "The *cur* was happy in his small yet cozy room."

curé [kyooRAY] a parish priest. "The *curé* gave his blessing to the marriage." "The *curé* was out when she called." "The *curé* hired a worker to mow the church lawn." "The *curé* insisted that everyone attend mass." "The *curé* embezzled money from the church account."

curmudgeon [kurMUJun] a cantankerous person given to criticism. "Although the so-called critic-at-large may have nothing to criticize, the newspaper critic of previous eras was a useful *curmudgeon*." "The sportscaster was a *curmudgeon* with a huge ego." "The political *curmudgeon* was denied access to television." "His *curmudgeon* ways brought him into conflict with some persons." The origin of *curmudgeon* is unknown.

cynosure [SIHnushoor] any person or thing that attracts interest. "The girl's beauty and vivaciousness made her a *cynosure*, the 'most popular girl in school.'" "The *cynosure* strode into the room with all eyes on her." "His six-five height made him a *cynosure*." "The *cynosure* did not always want attention."

D

dalliance [DALeeuns] dawdling, flirtation. "His *dalliance* with the rich girl got him nowhere." "The *dalliance* of the young couple went against the customs of the town." "He felt insecure during his *dalliance* with the police." "His *dalliance* with the woman was unplanned."

Darby and Joan [DARbee...] an elderly married couple who live happily together. "They were regarded as *Darby and Joan*." "Her parents were a real *Darby and Joan* and were inseparable." "A *Darby and Joan* was rare in that region." "The *Darby and Joan* had no grandchildren."

dawdle [DODul] to linger or loiter. "A sign on the parking lot of the fast-food restaurant prohibited *dawdling*." "He *dawdled* away the morning listening to music in bed." "He *dawdled* outside her home hoping she would show up." "He liked to *dawdle* in his car." Syn.: dally, linger, loiter, tarry.

deadpan [DEDpan] characterized by emphatic seriousness or emotional detachment; (verb) to make such an expression. "The comedian's *deadpan* humor was hilarious." "The sportscaster *deadpanned* as he narrated the humorous clips." "The stand-up comedian did a *deadpan* after telling the joke." "The *deadpanned* self-deprecating routine was very funny."

debauch [diBOCH] to degrade or lower morally; to corrupt with an excess of something, such as alcohol or drugs. "The older woman seduced and *debauched* the young man." "The woman was gripped with a desperate *debauchery*—she drank too much." "Thomas De Quincy (1785-1859), the English writer, was *debauched* by opium." "He was bothered by a *debauchery* of tobacco addiction." Syn.: debase, degrade. Ant.: uplift.

debonaire [debuNAR] pleasant, gracious and charming; carefree. "Cary Grant had a *debonaire* attitude." "His *debonaire* ways ingratiated him to women." "The man-about-town was *debonaire*." "He once directly claimed to be *debonaire* but later felt foolish about it." Syn.: amiable, courteous, genial.

debunk [deeBUNGK] to expose as untrue or pompous. "American society is the happy-hunting ground for the H.L. Mencken-type *debunker*." "The social critic *debunked* the myth of a liberal media." "She *debunked* the idea that he was a comedic genius." "The comedian made people laugh with his *debunking* humor."

deciduous [diSIJoous] shedding the leaves annually; transitory, impermanent. "The oak is usually a *deciduous* tree." "The opposite of a *deciduous* tree is an evergreen." "Children have *deciduous* teeth." "Her tatoo was *deciduous*."

declaim [diKLAYM] to inveigh against. "She *declaimed* against him for eating all the cake." "The angry woman *declaimed* against her children in a shrill voice for making a mess of the room." "He *declaimed* against Democrats for allegedly being soft on crime." "The senator *declaimed* against China for supposed human rights violations." Syn.: vilify, vituperate.

déclassé [daykluSAY] (French) reduced to a lower status. "The family was *déclassé*." "A *déclassé* professional man regards his loss of status as a tragedy." "History is full of *déclassé* aristocrats trying to restore their fortune." "The *déclassé* man wanted to marry an heiress."

décolleté [daykolTAY] (French) cut so as to expose the chest and much of the breasts; that is, having a low neckline. "Her *décolleté* dress brought her some impudent stares from men." "She looked sexy in her *décolleté* dress." "She wore a *décolleté* gown to the party." "The middle-aged woman's blouse was *décolleté*."

deep-six [DEEP SIKS] to get rid of or reject; to kill someone; (noun) a rejection. "His plans for finding buried treasure were *deep-sixed* by his friends." "The teacher's date proposal was *deep-sixed* by the young woman." "His job application was *deep-sixed* by one employer after another." "The conservative *deep-sixed* the book on lesbian love in his review."

de facto [dee FAKto] (Latin) actually existing (in contrast to *de jure*). "The *de facto* revolutionary government confiscated the property of the corrupt." "The *de facto* chairman would not be defied." "They constituted his *de facto* audience." "The *de facto* headquarters was destroyed."

defenestration [deefenuSTRAYshun] the act of throwing someone or something out a window. "The *defenestration* of the villain in the play was a violent spectacle." "The men attempted a *defenestration* of the fellow they held in contempt." "One can see cognates of *defenestration* in French *fenetre* and German *Fenster* (the words for window)." "The *defenestration* was dangerous because they were on the fourth floor."

defile [diFIHL] to pollute or corrupt. "'Masturbate' in its Latin root literally means to 'defile by hand.'" "He *defiled* the grave of his former enemy." "The actor was not going to *defile* himself by selling out for an endorsement." "He seemed to admit to *defiling* by hand." Syn.: befoul, debauch, dishonor, sully, tarnish.

dégagé [daygaZHAY] (French) easy-going; emotionally detached. "Schizophrenia and depression are marked by a *dégagé* affect." "The actor—far from being *dégagé*—was tense and uptight." "It can be psychologically disastrous to become *dégagé* with people." "The man knew he had to fight the *dégagé* habit, and as the smart psychiatrist told him, 'can't means won't.'" In French this word literally means "disengaged."

deign [DAYN] to think it not unworthy of oneself. "She *deigned* to rent out rooms in her house for extra money." "He *deigned* to ask out the plain but charming girl." "She *deigned* to shop at the discount department store." "He would not *deign* to wear the skull cap."

deism [DEEizum] the belief that God created the world but takes no interest in it. "*Deism* predominated in the 18th century." "He was a *deist* and not very interested in God." "The *deist* did not attend church." "Although a philosopher, he was also a *deist*."

de jure [dee JOORee] (Latin) by right; according to law (opposed to *de facto*). "The *de jure* difference between the rich man and poor man is nothing according to liberalism." "It was her money *de jure*." "The infant was *de jure* their son." "The circumstance was not supposed to be, was not *de jure*."

deleterious [deliTIReeus] causing harm. "The chemicals dumped by the company into the river were *deleterious*." "Strontium is very *deleterious*." "Aluminum is *deleterious*, not a nutritional element, and can cause Alzheimer's disease." "Excessive sleep is *deleterious* to someone suffering from depression." Syn.: baneful, detrimental, malignant.

delimit [diLIMit] to set the limits of. "He carefully *delimited* his daughter's behavior." "According to the book *Dare to Discipline*, proper behavior for children should be specified and *delimited*." "He did not want his income *delimited* at a low level." "He *delimited* the spending of his wife."

démarche [dayMARSH] (French) a maneuver. "The Munich Pact was Chamberlain's *démarche* at appeasing Hitler." "The peasants' retreat and then surrender to the treacherous prince's army turned out to be a disastrous *démarche*."

"The *démarche* settled the question of who was to lead the squad." "He dare not try the same *démarche* again."

demesne [diMAYN] an estate or realm. "Common law forbids interference with a man's *demesne*." "*Demesne* sometimes means private property." "His *demesne* went to his worthies on his death." "He had no *demesne* to speak of."

demimonde [DEMeemond] (French) a class of women whose reputation has been stained by sexual promiscuity or prostitution; a disreputable fringe group. "The literary *demimonde* that formerly met at that café achieved commercial success." "The *demimonde* of writers showed a creativity lacking in the best-selling novels." "The former prostitute was recognized as belonging to the *demimonde*." "The woman was part of the *demimonde*, since she violated sexual conventions." This word literally means "half-world" in French.

demoded [deeMOHdid] outmoded; out of date or fashion. "The dress she wore to the reception was *demoded*." "The *demoded* typewriter simply would not do." "He hated being forced to drive a *demoded* economy car." "Fashion makes *demoded* clothes that will otherwise do."

demure [diMYOOR] behaving modestly; coy. "*Demure* is probably not related to the word *demur*, which in its Latin root means to 'delay.'" "Grace Kelly is remembered for her aristocratic *demure*." "She completely lacked *demure* and used obscenities like a man." "She lost both her beauty and her *demure*."

denigrate [DENugrayt] to speak ill of someone; to sully. "The minister *denigrated* the mayor and his cronies." "The evangelist *denigrated* homosexuals as godless." "The British author *denigrated* American society." "The media critic *denigrated* the treacle of the television show." Syn.: badmouth, defame, soil.

denizen [DENizun] an inhabitant or dweller. "The *denizens* of East Los Angeles would rather live in Pacific Palisades." "The *denizens* of the trailer park would rather live in Palm Beach." "He was a *denizen* of the Hamptons, Long Island." "He was a *denizen* of a country cottage."

denouement [daynooMEN] (French) the resolution of a drama. "The *denouement* of *Moby Dick* is a disastrous fight with a great white whale." "The *denouement* of her battle with depression was successful drug therapy." "The *denouement* of the novel is the death of the hero." "The *denouement* of *The Merchant of Venice* is the foiling of the contract with the moneylender." "The *denouement* of the film is the rescue of the woman by the hero." Syn.: outcome.

deportment [diPOHRTmunt] behavior. "The foolish *deportment* of the missionaries in the tribal culture carried scandal with it, as it did not respect the tribe's social autonomy." "His *deportment* was foolish for too long." "Their *deportment* was characterized by constricted responsiveness." "The dancers' *deportment* seemed to take account of the fact that others were watching them." "Their *deportment* appeared to be based on calculation of how others would react to it."

deprecate [DEPrikayt] to belittle. "Critics *deprecated* the Technicolor of *The Wizard of Oz* as garish." "He *deprecated* his nephew's poem." "The artist *deprecated* the paintings of his rivals." "The social critic *deprecated* 'momism.'" Syn.: depreciate, disparage.

de profundis [DAY prohFOONdis] (Latin) from the depths of, for example, despair. "He wrote a letter to the girl expressing love *de profundis*." "He made the journey in hopes born *de profundis*." "He wrote the poem *de profundis*." "The novelist showed a *de profundis* desire to eliminate the ills of society." "She cried out for justice *de profundis*." "The old man tried to rebuild his life *de profundis*."

depurate [DEPyurayt] to cleanse; to ritually purify. "Ceremonial *depuration* is found in many religions, such as the Christian baptism." "The *depuration* was also a bath or shower." "The *depuration* took place at 8 a.m." "*Depuration* may have some sort of practical value, such as removing dirt."

de rigueur [du reeGEUR] socially obligatory. "Sideburns were *de rigueur* for men in 1971." "For the American middle class a yearly vacation to Hawaii or the Carribean is *de rigueur*." "For some money for treats for the children is *de rigueur*." "A guest bedroom in their house was *de rigueur*." There are many ways of saying something is in fashion, such as *a la mode, comme il faut, fashionable,* "in vogue," "all the rage."

derogate [DERugayt] to disparage, deride. "He *derogated* the police by joking 'they claim no need of an intellect.'" "The sociologist *derogated* the mothers' extraordinary lack of affect." "He *derogated* the artificial Christmas tree." "The teenagers *derogated* the music he liked." Syn.: bad-mouth, calumniate, deprecate. Ant.: laud, praise.

descant [DESkant] a song or melody; (verb) [desKANT] to discourse at great length. "Chopin's piano *descant* is beautiful." "She played a *descant* on guitar." "The scholar *descanted* on English history." "She *descanted* on chaos theory."

desideratum [disiduRAYtum] something desired. "The *desideratum* of liberalism has dried up into mere survival." "His *desideratum* was beyond attainment." "The *desideratum* always seems to be money." "A man's *desideratum* may sometimes coincide with a woman's."

despot [DESput] a tyrant. "The *despot* held power using a secret political police and propaganda." "France was long a despotism tempered by epigrams" (Thomas Carlyle). "The *despot* was a cruel ruler." "The *despotism* had no parliament or diet." "President Lincoln (1809-65) was occasionally somewhat of a *despot*." Syn.: autocrat, Caeser, dictator, Draco.

desultory [DEZultoree] digressive or disconnected. "The 'you know's' and 'uh's' in his *desultory* speech distracted the audience's attention." "The dissertation was rather *desultory*." "The drunken man's speech was *desultory*." "She could not think clearly and her speech was *desultory*." Syn.: erratic, fitful, rambling.

de trop [du TROH] (French) superfluous. "It is a bad habit to eat and gain *de trop* calories merely because you have nothing else to do." "He had *de trop* time on his hands." "Noone thinks he has *de trop* money." "Some laws on the books are *de trop*." Syn.: excessive, needless, unnecessary.

devoir [duvWAHR] civility; duty. "*Devoir* means 'duty' in French: *Il a fait son* *devoir* ('he did his duty')." "*Faites votre devoir, et laissez faire aux dieux*" (Horace): "Do your duty and leave the rest to the gods." "We must uphold *devoir*, even in war, said the woman." "Formerly tribal peoples were called barbarians or savages, as if they did not respect *devoir*." "The German people have a strong commitment to *devoir*."

devolution [devuLOOshun] a passing down, as of power or property. "The *devolution* of power in the Weimar Republic ended with Hitler's dictatorship." "The *devolution* of presidential power in America, with the exception of the Civil War, has been peaceful." "The *devolution* in Mexico was contentious." "The *devolution* of the man's estate was challenged in court."

diacritic [dihuKRITik] distinguishing. "The medical term for *diacritic* is 'pathognomonic.'" "German and Swedish have *diacritical* marks not found in English." "The *diacritical* sign of his disease, a bleeding ulcer, was sharp pain in the abdomen." "The *diacritical* feature of manic-depression is racing thoughts."

dialectic [dihuLEKtik] the Hegelian philosophy of a thesis, antithesis and synthesis; the Marxist philosophy of change and conflict; logic used to challenge an opposing argument by making light of its contradictions. "His approach to criticizing the bimbo reasoning was *dialectic*." "The philosophy student researched Hegel's *dialectic*." "The professor gave an example of the *dialectic* of Marx." "The sociologist's critical approach relied on the *dialectic*."

diatribe [DIHutrihb] a caustic denunciation. "The president's press conferences were criticized by the foreign press as *diatribes*." "'Don't go into a *diatribe*,' said the son to his father." "Without thinking too much about it, the student went into a *diatribe* in a college paper, to the despair of the instructor." "The dictator gave a *diatribe* about 'imperialism.'" Syn.: declamation, harangue, tirade.

dichotomy [dihKOTumee] division into two unequal or contrasting parts. "American politics is set in the *dichotomy* of Republican and Democrat." "The *dichotomy* good-evil, though a little trite, according to the sociologist still explains much about the world." "Some, but not all, societies are characterized by a conflicting rich-poor *dichotomy*." "The human gaze features a *dichotomy* of happy and trusting as against sad or indifferent and mistrusting."

dicker [DIKur] to trade or haggle, especially in a petty way. "Much *dickering* was going on at the market." "The two friends *dickered* over whose ten dollars it was." "The agent *dickered* over a contract with the team's representative." "Several people were *dickering* in the bar."

dictum [DIKtum] a maxim. "The *dictum* 'beauty is in the eye of the beholder' is from Shakespeare." "The professor consciously heeded some *dictums*." "When he saw the married pair arguing he thought of the *dictum* 'the quarrels of lovers are the renewal of love.'" "Horace (65-8 B.C.) is a good source of wise *dictums*." Syn.: adage, axiom, precept, proverb, saw, saying.

didactic [dihDAKtik] intended to instruct; preachy. "*Didactic* 'methods' courses for teachers are mind-emptying." "The film maker was accused of being *didactic*." "He avoided the *didactic* books in the library stacks." "The social critic *didactically* claimed 'they're all the same.'"

diffident [DIFidunt] timid. "American teachers are *diffident* when it comes time to assign students a grade." "*Diffidence* may vary by class and sex." "The woman was hardly *diffident*." "The *diffident* applicant did not get the job." Syn.: irresolute, timorous.

digress [diGRES] to wander away from the main subject in a speech or writing. "A good public speaker does not *digress* at length into parenthetical details." "He *digressed* so often that few wanted to talk to him." "The nonexistent 'Oedipal complex' is a desultory *digression* in psychology." "The writer needed a *digression* from his usual routine." Syn.: deviate, diverge, ramble.

diktat [dikTAHT] (German) a dictated agreement. "Driving a hard bargain— gaining a *diktat*—is par for the course in competitive business." "The *diktat* ceded valuable land to Germany." "Hitler imposed a *diktat* on Austria." "The defendant was stung with a judge's order that was essentially a *diktat*." Syn.: decree.

dilapidated [diLAPidaytid] fallen to ruins due to neglect. "Slums are characterized by *dilapidated* housing." "A *dilapidated* residence is a sign of unsuccessfulness." "The working-class neighborhood was full of depressing *dilapidated* homes." "The building was *dilapidated* beyond repair." Syn.: decrepit, derelict, ramshackle, rundown, tumbledown.

dilatory [DILutoree] referring to delay. "The much-castigated government welfare programs always seem, instead, *dilatory*, too little too late." "Help was *dilatory*, not punctual, so the injured man nearly perished." "Justice can be quite *dilatory*." "Her reply to his proposal was *dilatory*." Syn.: remiss, tardy.

dilettante [DILitahnt] an amateur at an art or subject of knowledge. "*Dilettante* actors are not hard to find at high school plays." "The *dilettante* was incapable of learning golf." "The *dilettante* college student was motivated and eager to learn." "The *dilettante* was a slow learner."

diminutive [diMINyootiv] very small; a word or name with a suffix indicating smallness, youth, familiarity or affection.. "The *diminutive* is used in languages like German and Spanish to indicate a female." "She referred to *diminutive* men wearing lifts as having a 'little-man complex.'" "*Ling* is a *diminutive* suffix, as in *darling*." "The word *Mrs.* comes from *mistress*, which in turn is derived from an old word for 'master,' it using the *diminutive* suffix -*ess*." Syn.: minute, small. Ant.: huge.

diminution [dimuNOOshun] a decreasing or decrease. "The *diminution* of foreign language teaching in America was an educational disaster." "The *diminution* of well-paying jobs hit the poor hard." "The *diminution* of business activity did not affect everyone equally." "The *diminution* of the price of oil stimulated more automobile vacations."

din [DIN] unpleasant noise. "The *din* in the classroom portended poorly for the teacher's effectiveness." "The *din* of kitchen workers is buffered from a restaurant's dining area by sound-absorbing baffles." "The activity of the men wrangling for financial gain emitted a *din*." "The *din* prevented his falling asleep." Syn.: cacophony, discord, racket.

Dionysian [dihuNISHun] wild and sensuous, especially sexually. "*Dionysian* 'swinging' is not exactly condoned by American society." "The Latins are purported to be *Dionysian*." "She was a *Dionysian* aesthete." "The Zeitgeist was not ripe for *Dionysian* festivities." Dionysus was the Greek god of wine, fertility and sexual license.

diptych [DIPtik] a pair of paintings or sculptures on panels that are hinged together. "The Cathedral contained a beautiful *diptych*." "The *diptych* portrayed a scene from the Bible." "The artist put gold leaves on the *diptych*." "The *diptych* was in very good condition, considering its age."

dirge [DURJ] a funeral song. "The congregation sang a *dirge* in memory of the late matriarch." "The priest wrote a famous *dirge*." "A dirge for her, the doubly dead, in that she died so young" (Edgar Allen Poe). "The *dirge* was simple and dignified." Syn.: threnody.

disabuse [disuBYOOZ] to set right. "He sorely wanted to *disabuse* his aunt of her habit of calling him 'sweetie.'" "After confiding that he needed a little help, the people were all over him and he needed to *disabuse* them of their insolence." "He *disabused* his acquaintance of the idea that the poor do not want more money." "The writer *disabused* her of the idea that a fifty-year-old woman could be beautiful." Syn.: rectify, straighten.

discomfit [disKUMfit] to frustrate or make uneasy. "The working-class couple seemed *discomfited* at the ball." "He was *discomfited* in his search for a job." "The lies *discomfited* him." "The turbulence *discomfited* the woman's plane trip." Syn.: disconcert. Ant.: ease.

discommode [diskuMOHD] to inconvenience. "He *discommoded* his parents by moving back home upon being discharged from the army." "The student in the cultural exchange was afraid that he was *discommoding* his host family." "The hurricane left many people homeless and *discommoded*." "There are many modern things to prevent a person's being *discommoded*, such as motels and fast-food restaurants."

discursive [diSKURsiv] digressive. "The lecture proved *discursively* lengthy when the visiting speaker began 'Modern Italian History' in the Middle Ages." "The novel *Debt of Honor* is *discursive*." "The instructor's unpublished tome was *discursive*." "The article was all over the place and *discursive*." Grammarians criticize as a discursive nuisance a sentence enclosed in dashes and placed between the subject and the predicate, as in this sentence: "Although out of money—he had lost his last spare cash to a fine for speeding—he was determined to complete the college semester." The sentence should be reformulated so that the insertion between dashes is by itself either in front of or behind the second sentence: "He had lost his last spare cash to a fine for speeding, and although thus out of money, he was determined to complete the college semester." Consider another example: "The controversial Surgeon General—she had advocated teaching 'self-abuse' in the school—was forced to resign." A better formulation: "Having advocated teaching 'self-abuse' in the school, the controversial Surgeon General was forced to resign."

disfranchise [disFRANchihz] (also *disenfranchise*) to deprive a person of the right to vote; to deprive of a right or privilege. "Their status as aliens effectively *disfranchised* them." "Being at work effectively *disfranchised* the employees." "The slaves were *disfranchised*." "Corporate censorship of the media *disfranchised* the people."

disingenuous [disinJENyoous] not straightforward. "The Congressman's *disingenuous* help in filling sandbags for an hour was merely a publicity gimmick." "Any impecunious worker who *disingenuously* hoots 'money doesn't make you happy' ought to be asked, 'So you would rather be poor than rich?'" "The lawyer was *disingenuous* and focused on something other than his clients' problems." "The chiropractor acted *disingenuously*."

disquietude [disKWIHitood] uneasiness. "Her *disquietude* at being charged with grand larceny was compounded by having to mortgage the house to pay a lawyer's retainer." "Being arrested and booked by the police involves considerable *disquietude*, considerable Angst, or sometimes guilt." "There was *disquietude* between the man and his sister's boyfriend." "The man felt *disquietude* after eating the whole cake, and not leaving some for others." Syn.: agitation, commotion. Ant.: peace of mind.

disquisition [diskwiZISHun] a treatise. "The professor's *disquisition* on Pope's *The Rape of the Locke* became a popular and standard work on the subject." "The graduate student was outraged that the assistant professor—whom he ill-advisedly called a 'demented degenerate'—stung his well-prepared *disquisition* with a D out of emotional dislike, it being true that some instructors grade according to their emotion." "The *disquisition* was an attack on all the 'pricks' he had come across in life." "She wrote a *disquisition* on penile circumcision." Syn.: dissertation, essay, monograph.

dissemble [diSEMbul] to conceal the true nature of; to affect some posture or appearance. "The politician *dissembled* the idea of being plain folks just like everybody else." "The radical asserted that all *dissemblance* in society should be questioned." "Why should the senator *dissemble*?" "He *dissembled* interest in the health of his friend's hospitalized mother." Syn.: counterfeit, fake, manipulate.

dissimilitude [dissiMILitood] dissimilarity. "The *dissimilitude* of the twins was striking." "There was a *dissimilitude* between the rich man and his poor brother." "The *dissimilitude* of their passions drove a wedge in their friendship." "There was considerable *dissimilitude* in the books written by the social critic, the second one having lacked conviction."

dissimulate [diSIMyulayt] to feign. "As the Bible says, 'Let love be without dissimulation.'" "Someone once said, 'He who knows not how to dissimulate knows not how to live'; that is, you should not always show your true opinions and emotions in social situations." "They often *dissimulate* in order to fulfill the expectations of others." "*Dissimulation* may not be a positive experience." Syn.: cloak, conceal, disguise, dissemble. Ant.: reveal.

dissolute [DISuloot] lacking moral integrity. "Edgar Allen Poe's *dissolute* drinking inevitably caught up with him, and he was found dead in an alcoholic stupor." "She was wild and *dissolute*." "The bachelor had a reputation for being *dissolute*." "The children of the strait-laced couple were not allowed to be *dissolute*." Syn.: debauched, degenerate, dissipated. Ant.: upright.

distrait [diSTRAY] (French) inattentive or absent-minded. "He had a history of being *distrait*, and losing concentration in school." "He was *distrait* when he had the automobile accident." "The people were seldom care-free enough to be *distrait*." "He tried to overcome his *distrait* habit." Syn.: preoccupied. Ant.: alert.

dither [DITHur] to act irresolutely. "He *dithered* when he should have acted firmly." "The army *dithered* in the face of the enemy." "'You *dithering* idiot,' declared the lieutenant to the private who 'screwed up.'" "The shift supervisor *dithered* and vacillated when he should have reprimanded the worker." Syn.: shilly-shally, vacillate, waver.

dithyrambic [dithuRAMbik] having a very irregular form; wildly enthusiastic; pertaining to a dithyramb (a poem or composition of irregular form). "The party was noisy and *dithyrambic*." "The partisan crowd at the tennis match was *dithyrambic* and cheering wildly." "His speech was *dithyrambic*." "The priest's sermon was rather *dithyrambic*."

doctrinaire [doktruNAYR] unreasoning in the face of evidence or experience; dogmatic. "Liberal cliché says that Marxists are *doctrinaire* and even 'totalitarian.'" "The radical asserted that broadcasters are *doctrinaire* in not allowing radicals on television." "The economics book *Free to Choose* is *doctrinaire*." "It is *doctrinaire* to hold that progressive and socialist presidential candidates are kooks." "The conservative dismissed the charge of being *doctrinaire* by referring to extremism." Syn.: inflexible, rigid. Ant.: liberal.

doddering [DODuring] shaky or trembling, as from old age. "The *doddering* old man slowly made his way with a cane along the sidewalk." "The unfortunate woman's hands were *doddering* as she held the newspaper." "'You *doddering* old fool,' said the old woman to her husband." "The fall breeze caused *doddering* in the tree leaves." Syn.: teetering, tottering, wobbling.

doggerel [DOgurul] crude slang verse, as graffiti. "Obscene *doggerel* was scribbled all over the toilet stalls." "A bit of feminist *doggerel* declared 'when God created man, She was only joking; I always thought that men were just a phallasy.'" "The *doggerel* in the men's room of the courthouse attacked the judge as a tyrant." "Sixties radicals chanted *doggerel* like 'hey, hey LBJ, how many kids did you kill today?'" Syn.: ditty.

dolce far niente [DOLche FAR NYENte] (Italian) "sweet idleness." "The leisure class, or idle rich, enjoys *dolce far niente*." "He retired early because he wished for more *dolce far niente*." "Whether the people can enjoy *dolce far niente* without social compulsion is very important." "She spent *dolce far niente* listening to music." Expressions associated with easy living include "the life of Riley," "the good life," "Shangri-La," and "Canaan."

dolor [DOHlur] sorrow; anguish. "The hero of Poe's poem 'The Raven' feels *dolor* for a lost girl named 'Lenore,' who is to be seen 'nevermore.'" "The single old woman was full of *dolor* after her pet poodle died." "It is *dolorous* to remember happy times when in misery." "*Dolor* reminds one that pain is experienced much like sorrow." *Dolor* is a cognate of the word for "pain" in the Romance languages. Syn.: grief, woe.

dolt [DOHLT] a dullard or stupid person. "Basically only *dolts* were hired to move the stacks of newspapers, which was very hard work." "The *dolt* did not know the answer to the teacher's question." "The *dolt*, astonishingly enough, was Vice-Chancellor for Student Affairs." "The *dolt* who tried to dabble in German confused *Fräulein* with *Frau*."

donnybrook [DONeebrook] a brawl; a free-for-all. "A *donnybrook* broke out at the high-school gymnasium." "The two gangs met at a predetermined site for a *donnybrook*." "He was injured in a *donnybrook*." "The *donnybrook* was started by an argument over a girl." After Donnybrook Fair, formerly held in Dublin and known for uproars.

Doppelgänger [DOPulgengur] (German) a ghostly double. "The whole town was astonished by the appearance of a cousin of a townsman, who resembled him like a *Doppelgänger*." "Both Hawthorne and Poe wrote a short story involving a *Doppelgänger*." "It was not as if the two friends were a *Doppelgänger*." "It seemed unlikely that she had a *Doppelgänger*." Syn.: double, look-alike.

double-entendre [doobluanTANdru] a word or phrase having two meanings, one of which is risqué: *joy stick*. "One of her favorite *double-entendres* went 'he who farts in church must sit in his own pew.'" "He told an amusing *double-entendre* in class." "The joke used the *double-entendre* 'beating around the bush.'" "There are many *double-entendres* in Shakespeare." Syn.: pun, wordplay.

dowdy [DOUdee] shabby; frowzy in appearance. "Compared to the others at the wedding, the best man looked *dowdy*." "Hobos, bums, the homeless and down-and-out alcoholics often have *dowdy* dress." "The farm family looked *dowdy* next to the family from the city." "He had a *dowdy* appearance not fit for formal occasions." Syn.: down-at-heels, frumpy, inelegant, seedy, threadbare. Ant.: classy, dapper, stylish.

down-at-heels [DOUN AT HEEL] shabbily dressed; run-down. "The train station was *down-at-heels*." "The rickety old *down-at-heels* house would soon be demolished." "The homeless man was *down-at-heels*." "The police station and its jails were *down-at-heels* and desperately in need of painting and remodeling." Syn.: bedraggled, disheveled, frowzy, ragged, scruffy, tousled, unkempt. Ant.: neat, well-groomed.

doyen [doiEN] the senior member, especially in age or rank, often a middle-aged male. "The *doyen* of the church was the reverend." "The conservative asserted that there will always be a *doyen* who leads a group, as opposed to inclusive democratic leadership." "The *doyen* of the criminal gang led it into a territory war with rivals." "Seldom is a *doyen* a woman." Syn.: leader, notable.

dregs [DREGZ] the least desirable part; trash. "The Lumpenproletariat is looked down on as inferior and shiftless, the *dregs* of society." "The *dregs* of the nation were considered to be the unemployed, the poor, the drunken and the criminal." "Working-class *dregs* hung out at the carnival." "The *dregs* of the society frequented taverns, pool halls and bordellos."

droit [druWAH] a legal right. "The *droit* of private property is a bulwark of the competitive profit economy." "His *droit* of seeing a lawyer was violated."

"There is no *droit* about being deprived of your right." "A *droit* without a remedy is no droit at all."

droit-de-seigneur [druWAHdusayNEUR] the institutionalized rape of lower class women by aristocratic men in historical Europe, by which a peasant's or worker's bride had to have sex with the "lord" on her wedding night; the Latin name of this practice is *jus prima noctis* ("the right of the first night"). "*Droit-de-seigneur* was last known about 1800, it having been the product of feudalism." "A few historians actually deny that there was such a custom as *droit-de-seigneur*." "*Droit-de-seigneur* was an oppressive custom." "*Droit-de-seigneur* must have been humiliating or infuriating to the groom."

droll [DROL] oddly amusing. "The *droll* comedy of the movie made it a cult success." "The man's *droll* humor cracked up his friend." "His *droll* humor was inappropriate at the school." "He was a *droll* and interesting old man." Syn.: buffoonish, farcical, jesting.

druid [DROOid] a member of a preChristian religion among the ancient Celts of Britain and Ireland. "The *druids* observed a religious rite marking the summer solstice." "He studied the *druids* to learn more about alternative religions." "The *druids* did not survive Christian competition." "The *druid* was content to pass his life as an anchorite in a monastery."

drunk [DRUNGK] alcohol-intoxicated. Syn.: barmy, basted, bibulous, flummuxed, hooched, polluted, shit-faced, taverned, zulued. (Spears.)

dry-as-dust [DRIH...] dull and boring. "Some people find baseball *dry-as-dust*." "The play was *dry-as-dust* and only attracted a half-full house." "The comedian asserted that *Beowulf* is *dry-as-dust*." "The life of the people at the village seemed *dry-as-dust*."

duenna [dooENu] an older woman serving as chaperon to a young woman. "Her *duenna* accompanied the woman to the soirée." "The woman was hired as the society girl's *duenna*." "The *duenna* went almost everywhere with the girl." "The *duenna* watched her charge."

duplicity [dooPLISitee] purposeful deceptiveness. "The *duplicity* of used-car salesmen is notorious." "The modern supermarket is full of *duplicity* intended to increase sales, everything from misleading prices ending in 9's to arrangement of the merchandise to expose the consumer to the most possible goods." "The teacher's *duplicity* was notable." "The pimp was *duplicitous*." Syn.: cheat, cozenage, fraud.

durance [DYOORuns] forced confinement; imprisonment. "He looked upon the *durance* of his new job in the mail room as a rip-off and brutal means of subsistence." "Some children view school as *durance*." "His *durance* he talked of as totalitarian meanness." "He was given *durance* of 20 years for possession of two ounces of cocaine."

duress [dooRES] coercion. "The police have numerous means of physical and psychological *duress* which the law does not recognize as violations of civil rights." "*Duress* was used to get him to confess." "He used *duress* to have sex with his girlfriend." "The *duress* consisted of showing the woman a gun." Syn.: compulsion, constraint.

Dutch uncle [DUCH UNkul] a person who gives candid advice or criticism. "He was like a *Dutch uncle* to the young artist." "The *Dutch uncle* told him precisely what to do." "The *Dutch uncle* did not mince his words." "The *Dutch uncle* threw cold water on the woman's plans." "The *Dutch uncle* advised his nephew to take up atheism rather than go into the ministry."

E

easy mark [EEzee MARK] a fool who is easily swindled. "The *easy mark* lost $200 to a woman who wrongfully promised to build a web site." "They were *easy marks* easily duped, but it is malicious to steal from poor people." "The *easy mark* paid $50 to a business which merely gave him public information otherwise available in the newspaper." "They were *easy marks* to the Bible salesman."

ebullient [iBOOLyunt] enthusiastic or perky. "Several journalists noted her *ebullient* national television presence but none suggested that perkiness might be a sign of demoralization." "The *ebullient* girl seemed to have everything." "She was a charming *ebullient* French girl." "He was *ebullient* about the possibility of entering college." Syn.: jovial. Ant.: lugubrious.

ebullition [ebuLISHun] an emotional outburst. "Grandpa surprised everyone with a joyous *ebullition* in response to the roller-coaster ride he had hesitated to take." "His *ebullition* was spontaneous though strident." "The birthday boy responded with *ebullition*." "Her *ebullition* revealed her true feelings."

éclat [ayKLAH] (French) brilliance; a brilliant performance. "He won the tennis tournament with true *éclat* rather than flashy play." "Jorge Luis Borges (1899-1986) is known for literary *éclat* for his redoubtable writing." "What *éclat* the acrobat had!" "Do you know someone with intellectual *éclat*?"

eclectic [iKLEKtik] selecting from the best. "His taste in classical music was *eclectic*, running from Puccini and Italian opera to Austrian waltzes and Russian symphonies and ballets." "Some critics slighted the Durants' *eclectic* summary of philosophy as oversimplified." "The book was an *eclectic* collection of quotations." "His library was very *eclectic*, though still cultivated." Syn.: catholic, diverse. Ant.: narrow.

economic determinism [eekuNOMik...] the theory that society is shaped by the total process of economic production. "The professor who taught *economic determinism* lost his position at the university." "The radical's view of society involved *economic determinism*." "The scholars debated whether Marx's *economic determinism* was scientific." "While part of it is complex, *economic determinism* can otherwise be direct and simple."

ecumenical [ekyooMENikul] general or universal. "An *ecumenical* pacifist movement seeks to make war a thing of the past." "The writer agreed that all religion ought to be *ecumenical* in organization." "The local pacifist organization had a provincial rather than an *ecumenical* outlook." "The *ecumenical* movement is opposed by local autonomy and struggles for independence." Syn.: interdenominational, interfaith.

edacious [iDAYshus] devouring; voracious. "After two weeks on a diet he had an *edacious* appetite." "The celebrity's hunger for money was *edacious*." "He *edaciously* consumed food at the wedding reception." "Her desire for an education was *edacious*."

edict [EEdikt] a decree. "Some *edicts* are notorious, like the Edict of Nantes." "The *edict* declared the king's assumption of power." "The emperor's *edict* was self-serving." "The *edict* punished the minority religion." Syn.: diktat, proclamation, pronouncement.

edification [edufuKAYshun] improvement in intellectual or moral character. "Monuments like the Lincoln Memorial seem to embody some kind of solemn lesson, some kind of *edification*." "The writer recalled the phrase 'for your *edification*.'" "The people needed *edification* as to the existence of a leisure class." "The humbug Baptist college did not *edify* its students." Syn.: enlightenment. Ant.: obfuscation.

edifice [EDufis] a building or imposing structure. "The Columbia Exposition in Chicago in 1892 inspired the building of many Greek and Roman style *edifices* across the country (court houses, museums, libraries, and so forth)." "The bank had an impressive *edifice*." "The *edifice* resembled a Greek temple." "There were many tall *edifices* downtown."

educe [iDOOS] to draw out an idea; to elicit. "The high school teacher *educed* the opinions of his students." "He daily *educed* his thoughts in a diary." "The speaker *educed* his knowledge of the subject." "Can you *educe* the history of your home city or town sufficiently for a lecture?"

effete [iFEET] exhausted; over-refined; effeminate. "President Carter's *effete* gambit to make Puerto Rican statehood an issue went nowhere." "The depressed man was *effete*, as opposed to courageous." "The radical argued that liberalism is *effete*." "The *effete* government was toppled in 1989." "The Roman Empire is said to have been *effete* in its last stages." Syn.: barren, debilitated, decadent, enervated, fruitless, sterile. Ant.: vigorous.

efficacious [efiKAYshus] effective. "The contrived movie was *efficacious* in turning a profit, but it was an artistic failure." "The antidepressant was not *efficacious*." "Zinc and selenium are *efficacious* for dandruff." "Vitamin A is *efficacious* for acne." Syn.: effectual, efficient, useful. Ant.: ineffective.

effigy [EFujee] a crude figure of a hated person. "The company's CEO was burned in *effigy* by a group of employees for arbitrarily transferring 5,000 jobs to another state." "The *effigy* of their boss much resembled him." "The traitor was burned in *effigy* as a patriotic celebration." "The teacher was burned in *effigy* as a joke at the picnic."

effrontery [iFRUNturee] audacity; shameless nerve. "The policeman resented the *effrontery* of the boy he arrested." "The teenager had the *effrontery* to step ahead of him in line." "The receptionist's cheeky *effrontery* insulted him." "He who thought highly of himself manifested *effrontery*." Syn.: cheekiness, discourtesy, impudence, insolence.

effusive [iFYOOsiv] emotionally unrestrained. "The *effusive* behavior of the game-show contestants does not seem spontaneous." "The *effusive* laughter on some television shows may not seem spontaneous or genuine." "His behavior on the trip was *effusive*." "*Effusiveness* was uncalled for in that situation." Syn.: demonstrative, ebullient, fulsome, profuse. Ant.: reserved.

egalitarian [igaliTAYReeun] pertaining to or believing in equality. "A class society is the opposite of an *egalitarian* society." "French society is basically *egalitarian*." "The radical claimed that all politics should be assessed in terms of *egalitarianism*." "European societies are more *egalitarian* than the U.S." Syn.: democratic, populist. Ant.: unequal.

ego trip [EEgoh TRIP] an act or course of action intended to magniloquently bolster one's self-image. "The rumors swirling around her fueled her *ego trip*." "The woman's lobbying seemed to some an *ego trip*." "The historian claimed that some of the student revolutionaries of the 60s were on an *ego trip*." "He was clearly on an *ego trip* when he denounced abortion—but otherwise allowed killing in war—and went on television as a God-fearing man."

egress [EEgres] emergence; exit. "His *egress* from his marriage was the beginning of his ruin." "His *egress* was difficult." "The magician accomplished an *egress* from the locked chest." "His *egress* from the navy was honorable."

egregious [iGREEjus] flagrant. "His military deferment was an *egregious* case of draft-dodging." "The player *egregiously* fouled the shooter." "Her hatred of her mother was *egregious*." "The referee made an *egregiously* bad call."

eighty-six [AYteesiks] to refuse to serve a customer in a restaurant or bar. "He felt humiliated in the restaurant as they *eighty-sixed* him." "He was ostracized and *eighty-sixed* at the sports bar." "They *eighty-sixed* the poor man who never left a tip." "The teacher bedeviled by rumors desired an end of the *eighty-sixing*."

élan [ayLAN] enthusiastic vigor and liveliness; style, flair. "She played golf with *élan*." "He wrote novels with *élan*." "The hotshot kid did everything with *élan*." "The employee sometimes used *élan* to liven up the work." Syn.: dash, panache, verve. Ant.: mediocrity.

eldritch [ELdrich] weird; eerie. "The October night was *eldritch*." "The big old house was *eldritch*." "The crime scene was *eldritch*." "That morning in the forest was *eldritch*." Syn.: disconcerting, uncanny, unnerving. Ant.: normal.

eleemosynary [eluMOSuneree] pertaining to gifts or charity. "The church was built with *eleemosynary* funds." "His *eleemosynary* donation was not substantial." "The impoverished man lived on *eleemosynary* generosity." "He made an *eleemosynary* bequest to the school."

elegy [ELijee] a melancholy poem. "One famous poem by Thomas Gray (1716-71), of the 'graveyard' literary school, is entitled 'Elegy Written in a Country Churchyard.'" "The student's *elegy* was contrived and dull." "The *elegy* dealt with the shortness of life." "The *elegy* was turned into a hit song." Syn.: dirge, requiem.

elision [iLIZHun] omission of a syllable; omission of something. "English and

French are full of *elision* in pronunciation." "The *elision* was of the third syllable." "The letter bore *elision* of a signature." "The *elision* was a drastic one." Syn.: abridgment, contraction, truncation.

elixir [iLIKsur] the quintessence of something; a panacea. "The *elixir* was sold as a general 'tonic.'" "The *elixir* of the movement was religion." "The *elixir* was supposed to be a remedy for everything from kidney stones to impotence." "The *elixir* of the business was conscientious employees."

elocution [eluKYOOshun] a style of public speaking. "Hitler had an aggressive, maniacal *elocution*." "Fussy insistence on using hand gestures in *elocution* should be ignored." "The *elocution* instructor tried to sting the student with a D, but he won a grade appeal to the chairman." "The teacher had an eloquent *elocution*."

Elysium [iLIZHeeum] (also Elysian Fields) paradise. "Probably each person has his own conception of *Elysium*." "The Champs Elysées (French for *Elysian Fields*) is a centrally-located boulevard in Paris." "The *Elysium* she was referring to does not exist." "It may be a bad idea to travel in search of an *Elysium*." Syn.: cloud nine, El Dorado, nirvana, seventh heaven, Shangri-la. Ant.: hell.

emblazon [emBLAYzun] to decorate; to celebrate. "Some people think that *emblazoning* the body with pierced jewelry is bad taste." "*Emblazoned* on the general's helmet were four stars." "They *emblazoned* Thanksgiving in fine style." "Everywhere you went people were *emblazoning* and making merry on the occasion of the New Year." Syn.: extol.

embonpoint [anbonPWAN] (French) stoutness; plumpness. "The *embonpoint* of the girl was not in fashion." "The boy's *embonpoint* indicated the need to diet." "Despite her *embonpoint*, she was pretty." "His *embonpoint* interfered with running." Syn.: obesity.

emboss [emBOS] to decorate in relief. "The Purple Heart has an *embossed* profile of George Washington." "The time piece had a small figure *embossed* on its case." "The triptych had an *embossed* portrayal of the angel Gabriel." "The *embossed* seal indicated the document was legitimate."

emend [iMEND] to edit or proofread a text; to correct. "The text was *emended* prior to publication." "The student *emended* his essay prior to submission to the teacher." "The editor worked with the novelist to *emend* the book." "Every paper or manuscript must be *emended* atleast once."

émigré [EMugray] an emigrant. "Hemingway was among the *émigré* American intellectuals in Paris during the 1920s." "The *émigrés* met at a cafe in the bohemian quarter." "The *émigré* writer settled in Mexico." "The *émigré* fled societal indifference to art."

éminence grise [aymeenans GREEZ] (French) a person who wields power behind the scenes. "Rasputin was an *éminence grise* in Czarist Russia." "He was an *éminence grise* in Bourbon France." "The railroad Titan was an *éminence grise*." "The *éminence grise* nixed the idea." In French this phrase means "gray eminence."

empathize [EMputhihz] to identify with another emotionally or intellectually. "The policeman said he *empathized* with the shoplifter but had to take her into custody anyway." "The man was incapable of *empathizing* with his children." "The politician had no *empathy* for the poor." "The upper-class women had no *empathy* for women of lower classes." *Empathize* in German is *Einfühlung,* literally meaning an "in-feeling." Whereas *sympathize* relates to emotion, *empathize* can refer to identification with another on the cognitive level.

empirical [emPIRikul] based on observation or experiment. "Psychoanalysis is nonsense because it is not *empirical.*" "*Empirical* means scientific." "The theory did not stand up to *empirical* testing." "Arm-chair theorizing is one thing, but *empiricism* is another." Syn.: experiential, pragmatic. Ant.: theoretical.

empyreal [emPIReeul] sublime. "The view from Yosemite Valley was *empyreal.*" "John Keats (1795-1821) wrote *empyreal* verse." "The paintings of Fragonard (1732-1806) are marked by rich, *empyreal* color." "The Grand Canyon affords an *empyreal* vista." Syn.: elevated, exalted, lofty.

encomium [enKOHmeeum] a formal expression of high praise. "Like most *encomiums* the eulogy at his funeral did not mention the man's shortcomings." "An *encomium* was read for the late politician." "The magazine featured an *encomium* about him." "The Catholic Church recited an *encomium* for the new saint." Syn.: eulogy, tribute. Ant.: condemnation.

encyclical [enSIKlikul] meant for general circulation; (noun) a papal bulletin. "The company memorandum was not meant to be *encyclical.*" "The prayer book was *encyclical.*" "The paperback was popular, *encyclical* and advertised as having millions in print." "The *encyclical* was designed to increase the Pope's power."

endemic [enDEMik] native; found in a particular region or country. "Polar bears are *endemic* to the Arctic." "Grizzly bears were originally *endemic* to much of North America." "The plant is *endemic* to the Great Plains." "Nutritional diseases were once *endemic* to Europe."

endue [enDOO] to provide with some quality. "Constant practice in keeping a diary—as Francis Bacon advised—*endued* her with a talent for writing." "Adversity *endues* virtue." "Exercise *endued* him with leanness and gymnastic ability." "Reading *endued* her with wisdom."

enervate [ENurvayt] to weaken. "Widespread self-absorption may mark an *enervated* society." "His will to continue was *enervated.*" "The conservative argued that allowing women in the military would result in *enervation.*" "The writer argued, though not without opposition, that the 'West' has become *enervated.*" Syn.: enfeeble, unnerve. Ant.: animate, invigorate.

en famille [EN faMIyu] (French) with the family. "The Germans have the habit of taking a Sunday walk *en famille.*" "The photographer got several photos of the celebrity *en famille.*" "They posed for a photo *en famille.*" "They took a vacation *en famille.*"

enfant terrible [ahnfahn teREEblu] (French) an incorrigible child; a person whose behavior is embarrassing and unruly. "Their daughter was a real *enfant terrible*, constantly throwing tantrums and saying 'no' to her impotent parents." "The *enfant terrible* finally met his match in an aunt who disciplined him." "Dare to discipline the *enfant terrible!*" "The *enfant terrible* made for an appalling spectacle."

engagé [angaZHAY] (French) socially committed, as opposed to remaining aloof or a loner. "He enjoyed life more when he was *engagé* and with friends." "The plain girl was *engagé* but longed for a husband." "Girls are *engagé* with one or two friends, whereas boys 'hang out' in larger groups." "The popular girl was very *engagé* and belonged to the student council, cheerleading and other groups."

enjoin [enJOIN] to order; to forbid. "Courts may *enjoin* a union from striking, but no court ever *enjoins* a corporation from laying off workers." "He *enjoined* his wife to stop spending money." "He felt *enjoined* into falling in love with her." "The high school principal *enjoined* him from teaching about control of Congress by the corporate lobby." Syn.: command, instruct.

en masse [an MAS] all together; in a group. "The angry police streamed out into the street *en masse* and confronted the protestors." "The crowd *en masse* started cheering." "The family took a joy ride *en masse*." "The fans left the stadium *en masse*." Syn.: collectively, en bloc. Ant.: singly.

ennui [onWEE] boredom. "After a mere half-hour at the park the children were already complaining of *ennui*." "He experienced much *ennui* as a child." "They drove around to kill *ennui*." "After an hour of viewing the movie *ennui* set in." Syn.: languor, tedium, weariness. Ant.: excitement.

en rapport [an raPOR] (French) in accord; congenial. "England's diplomacy was *en rapport* with economic prosperity." "The waitress was very *en rapport*." "His behavior was not *en rapport* with the rest of the group." "The marriage was not *en rapport*." Syn.: affable, amiable, good-natured, hospitable. Ant.: hostile.

ensconce [enSKONS] to hide; to settle snugly. "American professors often *ensconce* themselves away from students rather than being in the classroom or office more." "The couple *ensconced* themselves in the hotel suite to celebrate nuptual love." "He was *ensconced* in an armchair—and snug as a bug in a rug." "The couple was *ensconced* in their small though cozy home." Syn.: conceal, entrench. Ant.: expose.

eolian [eeOHleeun] pertaining to or formed by the wind. "In desert areas *eolian* swirls of sand can carve unique geologic structures." "Alternative *eolian* energy is just beginning to be harnessed." "*Eolian* energy swelled the waves of the sea." "*Eolian* turbulence can make a plane trip nerve-wracking."

ephemeral [iFEMurul] short-lived; having a life of just one day. "Several insects are *ephemeral,* completing their adult phase in merely a day, mating (if successful) and then dying." "The play featuring nude actors was *ephemeral*." "The fame of the movie star was *ephemeral*." "The obese woman's will to diet and lose much weight was *ephemeral*." Syn.: brief, evanescent, fleeting, momentary, short-lived, transient, transitory. Ant.: lasting.

epicene [EPuseen] common to both sexes; effeminate. "The transvestite exhibited *epicene* traits." "The unfortunate baby was born with *epicene* traits." "The homosexual man was *epicene*." "The rugged athletic man was the opposite of *epicene*." Syn.: androgynous.

epicure [EPikyoor] an adherent of Epicureanism, believing that tempered pleasure is the greatest good. "The radical asserted that not welfare recipients, but the idle rich are the true feeders at the sty of *Epicure*." "Think to yourself that every day is your last; the hour to which you do not look forward will come as a welcome surprise. As for me, when you want a good laugh, you will find me, in a fine state, fat and sleek, a true hog of Epicurus' sty" (Horace). "The *epicure* enjoyed wine and feasting." "It would be hard to be an *epicure* if deprived of leisure time." Syn.: gourmand, gourmet, sensualist, sybarite, voluptuary. Ant.: ascetic.

epigone [EPugohn] an inferior imitator of a distinguished writer or artist. "The *epigone* wrote a novel reminiscent of *The Da Vinci Code*." "The poet was an *epigone*." "The *epigone* imitated the artist in a bid for commercial success." "The work of the *epigone* was truckling." Syn.: dilettante. Ant.: expert.

epigram [EPigram] a witty and concise saying. "A Shakespearean *epigram* says that 'brevity is the soul of wit.'" "The artist kept the following *epigram* in mind: 'Hate as though you might love, and love as though you might hate.'" "It is a simple though smart *epigram*: Haste makes waste." "The *epigram* advises 'cross that bridge when you come to it.'" Syn.: aphorism, apothegm, axiom, witticism.

epiphany [iPIFunee] a revelation, especially a divine or intuitive one. "All at once the excited forty-niner dropped his tools and ran down toward the valley, leaving his partner to explain that he had an *epiphany* of where the gold lay." "The girl claimed to have been touched by an *epiphany* from God." "In the man's *epiphany*, the way was revealed to wealth by claiming to talk with God." "She suddenly had an *epiphany* of the chemical structure of the substance."

epistemic [epiSTEEmik] relating to knowledge. "For Thomas Carlyle (1795-1881), a library had great *epistemic* value: 'The true University these days is a collection of books.'" (In *Heroes and Hero-Worship*.) "His *epistemic* ability was very limited." "*Epistemically* she was bankrupt." "The university biologist made significant *epistemic* contributions." An epistemic note: In my opinion, teachers and classrooms are obsolete in this age of libraries and the mass production of books, and the growth of home study or schooling and "distance" or Internet college courses is a healthy trend. The demoralized, "do-nothing" teacher, together with the not-uncommon teacher who grades according to emotion, redoubles the value of self-teaching. In addition, modern media like the computer and television make home study even more appealing. There is still a place for childhood teachers and for research, and for miscellaneous laboratories and exhibits for hands-on learning, but classroom education—wherein one may communicate BO, flatulence, halitosis, dandruff and certain communicable diseases like the flu—is inefficient, clumsy, and antiquated. Ideally one ought to be able to earn a Ph.D. with courses that are almost all teacher-less.

epistle [iPISul] a letter. "The Catholic Church has for centuries been issuing *epistles* to regulate or edify its priests." "The novel is in the *epistolary* form." "Initially their friendship was entirely *epistolary*." "The *epistle* was lost in the mail." The German word for "letter," *Brief*, a cognate of the English word of the same spelling, suggests something short about a letter, or something which by contrast seems abbreviated. A letter is "brief" in some sense.

epithet [EPuthet] a word or phrase, often derisive, used to express contempt or hostility. "President Johnson had an obscene *epithet* for Robert Kennedy—'that little shit.'" "Rather than use his name, the man referred to him with an *epithet*." "His coworkers called him by an *epithet* rather than his name." "The two men angrily exchanged *epithets*." Syn.: appellation, moniker, sobriquet.

epitome [iPITumee] a person or thing with the highest qualities of: *the epitome of courage*. "Bounty hunting, and placing a dollar price on a human life—no matter what crime was commited—is the *epitome* of an evil style of 'justice.'" "A man so various that he seemed to be, Not one, but all mankind's epitome" (William Drummond). "The radical asserted that social hierarchy is the *epitome* of evil." "She was the *epitome* of charm." Syn.: embodiment, quintessence. Ant.: antithesis.

eponym [EPunim] a person whose name was given to a place, country or era. "King Edward Vll (1841-1910) is the *eponym* of the 'Edwardian period' of Britain (1900-1910)." "Queen Victoria (1837-1901) is the *eponym* of the Victorian Age." "The president is the *eponym* of the university." "Her name is an *eponym* for the institute."

equable [EKwubul] not easily annoyed or disturbed. "The aim of a Stoic philosopher is an *equable* life free of vices and obsessions." "He was an *equable* man who commanded the attention of townspeople seeking advice." "The duchess was an *equable* woman." "He was not *equable* in his 20s." Syn.: affable, good-humored, imperturbable, stolid, unflappable. Ant.: churlish, irascible, irritable, nervous, peevish, querulous.

equanimity [eekwuNIMitee] composure; the quality of never getting "worked-up." "His *equanimity* in adversity was his great virtue." "She lost her *equanimity* and lashed out at the clerk." "The easy-going man possessed remarkable *equanimity*." "His *equanimity* was not lost during the uproar." Syn.: imperturbability, nonchalance, sang-froid, serenity.

equipoise [EEkwupoiz] equilibrium; a socially or emotionally balanced state. "The *equipoise* of the *Sitzkrieg* in Western Europe was shattered when Nazi armored divisions attacked." "*Equipoise* is requisite in troubled times." "The woman possessed *equipoise* like an actress in front of a camera." "He had no *equipoise*, yet the job required it." Syn.: equanimity, equilibrium, imperturbability.

eremite [ERumiht] a recluse, especially a religious one. "The *eremite* mainly studied and prayed." "The *eremite* taught theology." "The *eremite* wanted to be alone." "The word *eremite* is related to *hermit*." "And watching, with eternal lids apart, Like Nature's patient, sleepless Eremite" (John Keats, "Bright Star").

eristic [iRIStik] relating to argument or debate. "The *eristic* skill of William Jennings Bryan (1860-1925) brought him prominence at a rather early age." "*Eristic* education in the form of rhetoric was formerly a separate school subject." "*Eristic* ability necessitates a good education." "Her *eristic* skill lay in able public speaking."

ersatz [erZATS] (German) artificial; (noun) an inferior substitute. "Radcliffe to women was an *ersatz* for Harvard." "TV dinners are a dull *ersatz* for a good meal." "The soft drink's sweetener was *ersatz*." "The used car was bought as an *ersatz* for a decent new one." Syn.: false, faux, mock. Ant.: genuine.

erudite [ERyudiht] learned. "The *erudite* author was a graduate of Eaton and Oxford University." "Bacon advised one not to wear *erudition* as ornament." "The scholar was very *erudite*." "She was *erudite* on the subject of Chinese history." Syn.: cultured, knowledgeable, learned, well-educated, well-read. Ant.: mindless, uneducated.

eschatology [eskuTOLujee] a doctrine or doctrines concerning final things, as death. "Christian *eschatology* says believing in God brings everlasting life in the next world." "The theology student studied *eschatology*." "Whether or not there is a heaven is an *eschatological* question." "The intellectual did not believe in Christian *eschatology*."

escheat [esCHEET] the reversion of property to the state in the absence of a rightful heir. "Through *escheat* the house became government property." "The last family member died and his property was *escheated*." "She stipulated that her property was to be *escheated* on her death." "Noone having claimed the house, it went to the state through *escheat*."

eschew [esCHOO] to shun. "The rich family *eschewed* contact with its poor neighbors." "Their daughter *eschewed* dolls for baseball and hunting." "The professor *eschewed* Christianity." "The radical was an atheist and *eschewed* all religion." Syn.: avoid, disdain, shun.

esoteric [esuTERik] restricted to a few people with specific knowledge; secret. "Professionals tend to attempt to keep their trade *esoteric*." "The sociologist stated that *esoteric* knowledge is a matter of control and power." "Knowledge of her seduction was *esoteric*." "Appreciation of her art was *esoteric*, since others did not view or understand it." "The idea that they're all the same was not actually *esoteric*." Syn.: abstruse, arcane, cryptic, mysterious, occult. Ant.: exoteric, straightforward.

espial [iSPIHul] the act of noticing. "He was aroused by the *espial* of a girl sunbathing in the adjoining backyard." "She was embarrassed by the *espial* of a neighbor peeking out the window at her." "The *espial* by the public of you doing what would be the most embarrassing?" "He caught an *espial* of his nude girlfriend coming from the shower."

estimable worthy of esteem; admirable. "His publications on zoology are *estimable*." "Her study of the Italian Renaissance was *estimable*." "Her skating ability is *estimable*." "The battle to dam the river for power, irrigation and flood control was *estimable*." Syn.: deserving, laudable, praiseworthy, reputable, venerable. Ant.: unimpressive.

estivate [EStuvayt] to spend the summer; to hibernate in the summer. "The mammal *estivated* in a burrow." "He *estivated* at a beach house on Long Island." "The couple *estivated* in the South of France." "The two boys and their parents *estivated* on Vancouver Island."

esurient [iSOOReeunt] hungry; greedy. "The *esurient* athlete signed endorsement deals with ten corporations." "The *esurient* laborers devoured their dinner." "The *esurient* actor hauled in $10 million merely for making a film." "The writer was not *esurient* but he did need to make a living."

ethereal [iTHEEReeul] light or airy; highly refined. "She was an *ethereal* beauty." "His 'genius' was vapid, *ethereal* or nonexistent." "The aura in the fancy hotel was *ethereal*." "The rich man's taste in household furnishings was *ethereal*." Syn.: developed, polished, sophisticated. Ant.: coarse.

ethos [EEthos] the morality or character of a person, group or community. "He realized that the *ethos* forbade him from socializing with the girls at the school where he taught." "The most sacred and praised *ethos* in one culture may be criminal in another." "The *ethos* of socialism holds that wealth is exploitation." "The *ethos* of capitalism holds that wealth is the just benefit of economic success." Syn.: code, norms, philosophy, principles, spirit, tenet.

euchre [YOOkur] to get the better of, as by scheming; to cheat. "He *euchred* the other players to win the prize." "The salesman *euchred* his competitors to get the promotion." "The conman *euchred* her out of her savings." "The cancer patient *euchred* death."

eudaemonia [yoodiMOHneeu] happiness. "*Eudaemonia* eluded the woman." "*Eudaemonia* is difficult if you are excessively self-conscious." "*Eudaemonia* was the people's professed goal." "*Eudaemonia* was hard to come by at that time and place."

eunuch [YOOnuk] a castrated man. "*Eunuchs* and homosexuals are trusted with one's wife." "*Eunuchs* were formerly used to watch a harem or sing in a choir." "The *eunuch* became a woman." "He became a *eunuch* only involuntarily, as punishment."

euphemism [YOOfumizum] a misleading or polite rephrasing. "'Pre-owned car' is a *euphemism* for 'used car.'" "The expression 'gee' developed as a *euphemism* for Jesus." "The word 'elderly'—as opposed to 'the aged'—sounds a little *euphemistic*." "A recent marketing *euphemism* for 'impotence' is 'E.D.'" Syn.: understatement, weasel word.

euphonious [yooFOHneeus] pleasant-sounding. "His singing was not *euphonious*." "The diva had a beautiful *euphonious* voice." "The rain was *euphonious* to the man in a sweet mood." "The noise of the birds was *euphonious*." Syn.: harmonic, lyrical, melodic. Ant.: harsh.

euphuism [YOOfyooizum] language overloaded with affected words. "The poet's reading, though full of interesting allusions, was marred by a bit of *euphuism*." "The book on medical consumerism was *euphuistic*." "His class paper was *euphuistic* and excessively rhetorical." "The otherwise solid report was marred by *euphuism*."

evanesce [evuNES] to fade away. "The school reform movement *evanesced*, dried up." "His struggle to lose weight *evanesced*." "The woman's beauty *evanesced*." "Watching his lover walk away and *evanesce* on the horizon made him sad."

ex cathedra [EKS kuTHEEdru] (Latin) with authority. "The Pope called *ex cathedra* for the release of the prisoner." "The cop acted *ex cathedra* in arresting the man." "The ukase was issued *ex cathedra*." "The foreign minister spoke *ex cathedra*."

excogitate [iksKOJitayt] to devise beforehand. "The famed remark of the Apollo astronaut upon touching the moon—something about a step and a leap—was undoubtedly *excogitated*." "On television reality shows it is hard to tell what is *excogitated* and what is spontaneous." "Her witticism was *excogitated*, rehearsed." "The beauty contestants gave *excogitated* examples of skill."

excoriate [iksKOReeayt] to harshly berate. "He was roundly *excoriated* in the press for his public ethnic slur, though everyone is free to say it in private." "Mrs. Frances Trollope (1780-1863) wrote a travel book that *excoriated* early 19th century American culture." "The conservative *excoriated* the work on moral relativism." "He *excoriated* his son for crying uncontrollably." Syn.: censure, condemn, denounce, reprove. Ant.: approve, laud, praise.

excrescence [iksKRESuns] an abnormal growth; an extension to, for example, a building. "The dog had an *excrescence* hanging from its muzzle which needed veterinary attention." "The *excrescence* to the garage was an eye sore." "An *excrescence*, a sun room, was added to their back yard." "The *excrescence* to the museum doubled its space."

exculpate [EKskulpayt] to clear of blame or guilt. "The Justice Department's investigation ended in limbo, and for some reason did not *exculpate* the anarchists." "The governor had the power to *exculpate* the man on death row." "The criminal was extremely grateful and relieved to be *exculpated* and get out of prison." "The emperor magnanimously *exculpated* the prisoner." Syn.: acquit, exonerate, free.

excursive [iksKURsiv] digressive, desultory. "Mehlville's *Moby Dick* begins with a rather *excursive* treatise on whaling." "The emotionally-ill man's speech was *excursive*." "The dramatic movie had a romantic *excursive* scene." "Every serious occasion should have a little light-hearted *excursiveness*." Syn.: discursive. Ant.: succinct.

execrable [EKsikrubul] very bad, abhorrent. "The quality of education at the high school was *execrable*." "She said most modern poetry is *execrable*." "The *execrable* book was full of filler." "The movie *California Suite* was so *execrable* that some people walked out in the middle or demanded their money back." Syn.: odious, offensive, repulsive. Ant.: excellent.

execrate [EKsikrayt] to abhor. "Some Americans seem to congratulate themselves with talk of 'soak the rich,' *execrating* what seems unfair, but in reality the effective rate of taxation of inherited wealth is a mere one percent." "The minimum-wage worker *execrated* the tax levied on his meager earnings and the fact that money was removed from his paycheck even before he saw it." "The radical tried to get people to justly *execrate* the highly-concentrated maldistribution of the wealth." "The conservative *execrated* the urban rioters for destroying property and overturning orderliness." Syn.: detest. Ant.: praise.

executant [igZEKyutunt] one who performs or executes: *the executant of the will*. "The ad hoc *executant* at the piano played Rachmaninoff beautifully." "He was a poor *executant* of the deceased man's estate." "The *executant* of the will withheld money from the minor for her own interest." "He was appointed *executant* of the philanthropic organization."

exegesis [eksuJEEsis] a critical interpretation, as of the Bible. "Tocqueville's *exegesis* of American society, *Democracy in America,* is recognized as a classic." "The scholar's *exegesis* on the history of medicine was voluminous and first-rate." "The woman wrote an *exegesis* on the problem of the origin of emotion and thought, of the James-Lange versus the Cannon-Bard theory." "The conservative's *exegesis* attempted to refute the theory of surplus value."

exegete [EKsugeet] a person with a talent for exegesis. "The most famous foreign *exegetes* of American civilization are St. John de Creve Coeur, Mrs. Trollope, Tocqueville, Lord Bryce and Werner Sombart." "The *exegete* concluded his study of the Bible by noting that the devil can quote scripture for his purpose." "The *exegete* was a noted scholar." "The *exegete* was employed by a university." Syn.: academician, scholar.

exemplum [igZEMplum] an example; a moral, as of a fable. "The *exemplum* of Aesop's fable 'The Dog and the Shadow' is 'beware that you do not lose the substance by grasping at the shadow.'" "'Look before you leap' is a simple though serviceable *exemplum.*'" "He was an *exemplum* of moral imbecility." "An *exemplum* applicable to his life is cultivate more thought."

exhume [igZOOM] to disinter a body; to revive or clarify. "The gold treasures *exhumed* by the Schliemanns was an extraordinary discovery." "The body was *exhumed* in order to test for a poison." "The hearing *exhumed* the fact that the teacher was paranoid." "Grave robbers *exhumed* the gold coffin of the pharaoh." Syn.: disinter, unearth.

exigency [EKsujunsee] an emergency; a drastic situation. "The *exigency* created by the hurricane was greater than the area's emergency crews could handle." "The *exigent* events in Francis Bacon's later life, especially the chastisement for taking a bribe, tempered the third edition of his powerful *Essays* (1625)." "The phone call at 4 a.m. seemed to hint of *exigency.*" "The man stung with a traffic ticket pleaded *exigent* circumstances." Syn.: necessity.

exiguous [igZIGyoous] meager. "The *exiguous* subsistence of its working class makes it hard to say that America is a rich country." "His *exiguous* tips, gratuities and donation to charity earned the well-heeled man the moniker 'tight wad.'" "The average world-wide income is extremely *exiguous.*" "According to the political scientist, the wealthy give *exiguous* tips." Syn.: scanty, sparse. Ant.: plentiful.

existential [egziSTENshul] relating to existence; pertaining to the philosophy of existentialism. "In *Being and Nothingness,* Jean-Paul Sartre (1905-80) made the *existential* claim that being exerts negativity, though that is not an easy concept to grasp." "The philosophy major studied *existential* philosophy." "The culture made, in effect, an *existential* claim to 'winning images.'" "The social critic asserted that in their *existential* agony, the people could not act without calculating how others would react to them."

ex officio [EKS uFISHeeoh] (Latin) by virtue of official position. "Should the president die in office, the vice-president, *ex officio,* becomes president."

"The governor, *ex officio*, pardoned the convict." "The prime minister governed *ex officio*." "She was uncertain of her duties *ex officio*." "The panjandrum claimed the *ex officio* right to dismiss the employee."

exorbitant [igZORbitunt] unduly expensive. "The landlord's rent was *exorbitant*." "The minimum or subminimum wage worker finds the price of almost everything *exorbitant*." "The rent charged the migrant farm workers for a tarpaper shack was *exorbitant*." "The poor are stung with *exorbitant* taxes." Syn.: overpriced. Ant.: inexpensive.

exoteric [eksuTERik] intended for a general audience. "Popular *exoteric* reference books are kept in a separate section of the library and may not be checked out." "How to drive a car is *exoteric* knowledge." "The manual used *exoteric* language." "The movie, although shown in art theatres, was *exoteric*." Syn.: communal, public. Ant.: esoteric, occult, specialized.

expatiate [ikSPAYsheeayt] to speak or write at length. "His impressive knowledge of Incan civilization was shown by his *expatiation*." "The sociologist *expatiated* on the fact that associations for the welfare of animals like dogs were founded before associations for the welfare of people." "The station's general manager *expatiated* on the reason that noone with a 'partisan political agenda' may go on his company's television channel." "The conservative *expatiated* on the idea that tradition is the best source on how to live."

expatriate [ekSPAYtreeayt] to banish a person from his country; exiled; (noun) an exiled person. "The *expatriates* lived in Paris in near poverty but were still content." Thomas Appleton (1812-84) declared, "Good Americans, when they die, go to Paris." "The *expatriates* lived in a commune in Oregon." "The *expatriate* criticized his former nation." "The *expatriate* intellectuals and bohemians made Vienna their new home."

expeditious [ekspuDISHus] marked by promptness. "The destruction of the Spanish fleet in Manila Bay in 1898 by an American naval squadron was accomplished quite *expeditiously*." "The professor replied to the email *expeditiously*." "The sheriff *expeditiously* ordered the drifter out of town." "The people were *expeditious* in their informal disapproval of deviance." Syn.: prompt, quick, swift. Ant.: slow.

expiate [EKspeeayt] to atone for. "Feeling guilty, he *expiated* for his rude treatment of his mother by helping her with chores." "He knew he would have to *expiate* for his gluttony on the holiday with dieting." "The old man tried to *expiate* for his greed by giving to philanthropy." "The man '*expiated*' for his crime through lethal injection." Syn.: propitiate.

expletive [EKsplitiv] a word or words used merely for emphasis or to fill in space; an obscene word. "A good writer or speaker avoids *expletives*." "One may not use *expletives* in court or church." "The fight was preceded by the belligerents' use of *expletives*." "The celebrity's *expletive* was reported in the press as 'shut the f*** up.'" Syn.: obscenity, profanity.

explicative [EKsplikaytiv] explanatory. "The chemistry text chosen site unseen, so to speak, by the instructor was as clear as mud, was not clearly *explicative*." "The psychiatric diagnosis was *explicative*." "The brochure on sexually-transmitted diseases was *explicative*." "The manual was obscure, not *ex-*

plicative."

ex post facto [EKS POST FAKto] (Latin) arising after some event. "The Battle of New Orleans took place *ex post facto* with regard to a peace treaty." "He married her *ex post facto.*" "She became a grandmother *ex post facto.*" "The dispute was solved *ex post facto* with regard to the court ruling." "The law was passed *ex post facto* and thus is irrelevant to the case." Syn.: retrospective.

expostulate [ikSPOSchulayt] to remonstrate. "The plaintiff realized that the judges were all the same and that it was futile to *expostulate* further." "She *expostulated* to no avail that she was innocent." "He *expostulated* that college tuition was steep." "He *expostulated* that the police could be niggling in issuing citations for trespassing and so forth." Syn.: protest, reprove.

expound [ikSPOUND] to state at length. "A radical speaker at the anti-war demonstration *expounded* sarcastically upon the advantages of fiery napalm." "She *expounded* on the role of B-vitamins in seizure prevention." "The attorney *expounded* on the progressive role of the Attorney General." "The teacher *expounded* on the beers served in Germany." Syn.: explain, explicate.

expropriate [ekSPROHpreeayt] to take something from another for oneself. "The economists found that nothing is ever *expropriated*, according to their economic analysis." "Employers *expropriate* the value created by workers." "The maid *expropriated* the car of her late employer." "*Expropriate* sometimes amounts to stealing." Syn.: steal.

expurgate [EKspurgayt] to remove objectionable material from a book, speech, etc. "The galleys were *expurgated* to avoid libel." "An aide *expurgated* the president's speech to avoid offending an interest group." "The 'standards and practices department' of the television network *expurgates* offending material from its programs." "The student *expurgated* his report to suit the taste of the instructor." Syn.: amend, censor.

extant [EKstunt] still existing. "Very few of the original folios of Shakespeare's works are *extant*." "Unfortunately for its fans, the *Speed Racer* show is no longer *extant* in broadcasting." "The *extant* paintings of the artist are in museums." "The collector could find but few *extant* stamps from the period." Syn.: surviving. Ant.: lost.

extemporaneous [ikstempuRAYneeus] spontaneous. "He did not doubt her appreciation of his joke, since her hearty laughter was *extemporaneous*." "*Extemporaneousness* is important to having fun." "The girl was care-free and *extemporaneous*." "His reaction to being fired was *extemporaneous* shock." "The politican's speech at the press conference was not *extemporaneous*." Syn.: impromptu, unrehearsed. Ant.: contrived, excogitated.

extemporize [ikSTEMpurihz] to improvise. "The cheer 'for he's the jolly good fellow' for the brave fighter pilot was *extemporized* by the men at the air base." "The mechanic used *extemporized* parts to rebuild the car." "The emcee *extemporized* when a nude man walked across the stage during the ceremony." "It was impossible to *extemporize* when the star of the play got sick and there was no understudy."

extenuate [ikSTENyooayt] to make or seem to make less serious. "In jurisprudence an *extenuating* factor mitigates a defendant's guilt." "When you shall these unlucky deeds relate, Speak of me as I am; nothing extenuate..." Shakespeare (*Othello*). "He did make an illegal right on a red light but there were *extenuating* circumstances." "He tried politeness to *extenuate* her fear of him." Syn.: justifying, mitigating, moderating, palliative. Ant.: magnifying.

extirpate [EKsturpayt] to thoroughly uproot. "The battle of Waterloo finally *extirpated* Napoleon's military strength." "She *extirpated* the weeds from the lawn." "He *extirpated* the bugs that had entered his house." "The army was *extirpated* by the enemy armored army." Syn.: annihilate, deracinate, eradicate, exterminate, root out.

extrapolate [ikSTRAPulayt] to conjecture. "His *extrapolation* did not seem to fit the evidence." "In logic or reasoning *extrapolation* is like an inductive leap." "He *extrapolated* that the man was murdered two days before." "The *extrapolation* proved incorrect." Syn.: conclude, induce, infer, reason.

extreme unction [ikSTREEM UNGKshun] last rites; a sacrament given to a person in danger of dying. "So many men were dying that the priest could not administer *extreme unction* to all of them." "The injured man requested *extreme unction*." "*Extreme unction* was given to the dying sinner." "The priest administered *extreme unction* to the wounded soldier."

extricate [EKstrikayt] to remove from difficulty. "He *extricated* himself from a potentially embarrassing situation by saying 'of course, next to the loveliness of our hostess, that is.'" "He *extricated* himself from legal trouble." "He was *extricated* by an alibi witness." "She could not *extricate* her toe from the bathtub faucet by herself." Syn.: detach, disconnect, disengage, extract, remove. Ant.: engage.

exurb [EKsurb] the outskirts of a city. "Since the late 19th century, elite American neighborhoods have moved from the urban core to the *exurb*." "The *exurb* contained 200,000 people." "The *exurb* was served by a commuter train." "The *exurb* was 25 miles from downtown."

exuviate [igZOOveeayt] to shed. "The *exuviated* exoskeleton of a spider may be mistaken for the spider itself." "The snake *exuviated* its skin." "The maple tree *exuviated* its leaves." "She *exuviated* 20 pounds in two weeks." "The dog *exuviated* some hair in summer." "The gambler *exuviated* $4,000 in Las Vegas."

F

facile [FASul] done easily; affable. "His *facile* comment to reporters was not exactly ingenious: 'I will not dignify that question by answering it.'" "The bike was *facile* to repair." "The man proved *facile* to intimidate." "The auto mechanic was a *facile* mild-mannered man." Syn.: casual, flippant, glib. Ant.: profound.

factious [FAKshus] divisive. "Radicalism has historically been weakened somewhat by *factious* competition with anarchism." "To die for faction is a common evil, But to be hanged for nonsense is the Devil" (John Dryden). "The political party was *factious*." "The celebration turned into a *factious* brawl." Syn.: contentious, discordant, divisive, schismatic, sectarian.

factotum [fakTOHtum] a major domo, chief servant. "The wealthy American family employed two *factotums*, neither of whom, it goes without saying, showed any resentment about their situation." "The *factotum* served the earl." "The *factotum* oversaw the servants of the manor." "Does your family employ a *factotum*?"

fainéant [faynayAHN] indolent; (noun) an idler. "Thorstein Veblen described the class of *fainéants* as though he were an anthropologist who had discovered an unknown tribe." "The *fainéants* formed a distinct class." "The *fainéants* inherited their wealth." "The *fainéants* by definition never worked, but other people did." Syn.: loafer, malingerer, slacker. Ant.: workaholic.

fakir [fuKIR] a Muslim or Hindu ascetic who is presumed to have special powers. A fakir is basically synonymous with "dervish," as in "whirling dervish" (a reference to the ritual dancing of the ascetic men). Fakir means "poor" in Arabic. "There was a *fakir* in the town square of the city they visited." "The family of the missing woman consulted a *fakir*." "The *fakir* was hired to pray for good weather for the festival." "The man was apprenticed to a *fakir*."

fait accompli [faytahkomPLEE] (French) something already done and beyond reversal; an accomplished fact. "The young couple eloped and presented their parents with a *fait accompli*." "Her resignation was a *fait accompli*." "The revolution was a *fait accompli* by the time the government reacted to it." "In the *fait accompli* the general was removed from power." "He lost his job in a *fait accompli*."

falderal [FALdural] foolish talk or ideas. "The boys' dream adventures led to *falderal* and things they would never actually do." "*Falderal* about buried treasure excited the youths." "The conservative labeled as *falderal* the idea of expropriating the expropriators." "Much of what went on in the head of the obsessed woman was *falderal*." From trivial refrains of old songs. Syn.: balderdash, bosh, humbug, twaddle.

fanfaronade [fanfuruNAYD] bragging; bluster. "Everyone around him was tired of his *fanfaronade*." "The politician spewed *fanfaronade* about the charges of corruption just before going to prison." "The fat old man was full of *fanfaronade*." "The actress strutted *fanfaronade* on the stage." Syn.: bravado. Ant.: humility, modesty, unpretentiousness.

farrago [fuRAgoh] a confused mixture. "The novel was a *farrago* of violence, a slow-moving plot and confusing scenes." "The restaurant offered a *farrago* of food." "The flea market sold a *farrago* of items." "His paper was all over the place, was an incoherent *farrago*." Syn.: hodgepodge, medley.

fashion plate [FASHun PLAYT] a person who dons the latest fashion. "She tended to be a *fashion plate* but could not afford serious fashionable clothes." "The *fashion plate* is usually a woman." "The *fashion plate* was sentimental." "The celebrity magazine covered all the *fashion plate* antics." "The woman was a *fashion plate*, just like all her friends from the upper-class, who could afford to continually buy the never-ending production of new fashion."

fatalism [FAYtulizum] the doctrine that all events are predetermined by fate and cannot be changed. "*Fatalism* may be a rather desperate philosophy." "The priest espoused a religious *fatalism*." "Their failure was countenanced by adoption of *fatalism*." "It is *fatalistic* to keep eating and say that obesity is in metabolism and cannot be overcome." Syn.: defeatism, resignation.

fatuity [fuTOOitee] foolishness or an act of foolishness. "It is actually a *fatuity* to get all worked up with excitement on a televised game show over the prospect of a new refrigerator or a weekend at a resort." "His *fatuity* was to shy away from friends." "The woman was involved in a *fatuity* of sleeping until noon." "Smoking, due to the health danger, may be a *fatuity*." Syn.: foolhardiness, inanity.

fatuous [FACHoous] foolish and stupid. "Trying to carry a can of kerosene on an airplane, and being rebuked by security, had the couple feeling *fatuous*." "Getting angered by trifles is *fatuous*." "He showed everyone he knew his *fatuous* poem." "Tolerance of inequality has some *fatuous* results." Syn.: asinine, ill-advised, inept, nonsensical.

faugh [FAU] an interjection expressing disgust; sickening. "*Faugh*, I lost my wallet!" "*Faugh*, this wine is disgusting!" "He said *faugh* but he was all alone." "*Faugh,* I just missed hitting the ball."

faute de mieux [fohtduMYEU] (French) for lack of something better. "They served sirloin steak *faute de mieux* at their dinner party." "Masturbation is done *faute de mieux*." "On the tawdry walls were cheap copies of famous paintings, *faute de mieux*." "The obsessed boy walked swiftly around the table, *faute de mieux*, again and again."

Fauve [FOHV] one of a group of French artists of the early 20th century. "The *Fauvist* painting was abstract." "The *Fauvists* used bright colors." "The *Fauvists* put their work on exhibition on the boulevard." "The art enthusiast did not like *Fauvist* painting."

faux pas [FOH PAH] (French) a social blunder. Literally "false step." "He committed a *faux pas* when he asked a married woman for a date." "The two women unintentionally committed a *faux pas* by wearing identical dresses to the gala." "Her *faux pas* consisted of calling her *Frau* instead of *Fräulein*." "She committed a *faux pas* by going to class without having showered." Syn.: contretemps, impropriety, solecism.

fawn [FAUN] to cringe in seeking the favor of. "His *fawning* countenance in the film gave him away as a hammy actor." "The right-wing columnist *fawned* when interviewing the arch conservative." Synonyms of fawning: fulsome, groveling, obsequious, servile, toady, unctuous. "To eat thy heart through comfortless despairs: To fawn, to crouch, to wait, to ride, to run, To spend, to give, to want, to be undone" (Edmund Spenser).

fealty [FEEultee] a vassal's contract with a lord; fidelity. "The commoner owed *fealty* to his grace the duke." "She maintained *fealty* to her husband." "The *fealty* of the Middle Ages could be oppressive." "The lords in turn owed *fealty* to a king."

feckless [FEKlis] ineffective; lazy. "If they did not have money, the idle rich would be considered as *feckless* as any 'welfare cheat.'" "His *feckless* lawsuit against the corporation was quashed, though noone can say who gave the judge the right to do that." "Her defense of her rights as a student was *feckless,* and she was suspended." "Only the *fecklessness* of the people allows the continuation of the injustice, asserted the radical." "The *feckless* young man quit his well-paying though strenuous job." "Her role in the play is *feckless,* since she does little but speak interjections." "The conservative claimed that the poor are *feckless.*" Syn.: indolent, slothful.

feculant [FEKyulunt] fecal; foul. "The *feculant* odor from the untreated sewage was unbearable." "A flatus is *feculant.*" "Humans can give off numerous *feculant* odors, including halitosis, body odor and the stench of death." "The odor in the septic tank was *feculant.*" Syn.: fetid, malodorous, mephitic, putrid, rank, rotten.

fecund [FEKund] fruitful; productive. "The *fecund* San Joaquin Valley of California does not yield its fruit without the groveling labor of migrant farm workers." "The psychology of gaze is a *fecund* area for scholarly research and publication." "The *fecund* woman bore five children." "The *fecund* historian wrote 40 books." Syn.: prolific. Ant.: infertile.

fecundate [FEEkundayt] to impregnate; to make fruitful. "The river's annual flooding *fecundated* the soil." "It seems impossible for a woman to be *fecundated* by two men at the same time." "Irrigation *fecundated* the desert." "With the help of certain insects the shrub's blossoms were *fecundated.*"

felicity [fiLISitee] an artful ability; bliss. "The *felicity* of their whirlwind relationship ended when the poor girl was introduced to the rich young man's family." "Still to ourselves in every place consigned, Our own felicity we make or find" (Oliver Goldsmith). "His *felicity* was based on good friends." "Her *felicity* was due to how she was raised." Syn.: contentment, happiness, joy.

ferule [FERyoolu] a stick of wood for punishing children. "The schoolmaster's use of a *ferule* has thankfully become a thing of the past." "Parents who cannot discipline their children could use a *ferule.*" "The father was reported to the police for using a *ferule* on his son." "The girl needed a rap on the knuckles with a *ferule*—or something."

festina lente [FEStinu LENti] (Latin) "hasten slowly." "*Festina lente* is excellent advice." "He had come across the proverb *festina lente* and followed the precept." "He ignored the idea *festina lente* and made trouble for himself by having an automobile accident." "*Festina lente* means act with dispatch but not so hurriedly."

fete [FET] a festive celebration; (verb) to honor someone with a fete. "Charles Lindbergh (1902-74) was *feted* almost immediately upon touching down at Le Bourget near Paris." "A few of the American *fetes* of the 1890s by the extremely wealthy, such as the notorious 'Monkey Ball,' evoked scandal."

"The general was lionized and *feted*." "Pizza was served at the *fete*." Syn.: commemoration, holiday.

fetid [FETid] foul-smelling. "The Turkish ingénue he met in Germany was very pretty but *fetid*, as though she had not bathed in months." "The room was *fetid*." "The dumpster was *fetid*." "The sweaty man was *fetid*." Syn.: malodorous, putrid, rotten, squalid.

fettle [FETul] a state or condition. "He was in fine *fettle*." "The *fettle* of the cattle was precarious." "The *fettle* of the car was excellent." "He needed to be in better physical *fettle* to beat his opponent in tennis."

fey [FAY] unreal; enchanted. "The theme park is full of sentimental *fey* characters." "They decorated their yard with porcelain *fey* figures." "The *fey* illustrations in the children's book were charming." "The boy drew a *fey* creature." "Children sometimes make up *fey* creatures as playmates." Syn.: fanciful, unworldly, whimsical.

fiat [FEEaht] an authoritative order or sanction. "The Federal Reserve, the 'Fed,' operates by *fiat*, and will even defy an order by Congress to produce documents." "The czar issued an oppressive *fiat*." "The corporation, by *fiat*, moved its headquarters and 20,000 jobs." "The *fiat* forbade political campaigning on military bases." Syn.: decree, ukase.

fiduciary [fiDOOsheeuree] someone entrusted to safeguard the property or power of someone else. "Upon turning 21, the heiress Barbara Hutton demanded the fortune held for her by a *fiduciary*." "The youth had an honest *fiduciary*." "The *fiduciary* decided how the estate would be divided." "The *fiduciary* had been selected by the deceased old woman."

filial [FILeeul] pertaining to a son or daughter. "Foreign visitors to America are shocked by *filial* disobedience." "English *filial* is reminiscent of French *fil* ('son')." "He did his *filial* duty and begat a child." "The French woman showed strong *filial* love."

finagle [fuNAYgul] to use deception; to wangle. "So far from losing everything, the very rich at the start of the Great Depression usually managed to save their position, *finagle* competing businesses and consolidate finances." "She *finagled* five dollars from her mother." "The corporate-board members *finagled* from their institution a few million dollars apiece." "He *finagled* a loan for $300 from his friend." Syn.: con, inveigle, machinate, wheedle.

firmament [FURmumunt] the heavenly vault. "Atheists are obviously not impressed that the *firmament* itself is an argument for God's existence." "The spacious firmament on high, And all the blue ethereal sky, And spangled heavens, a shining frame, Their great Original proclaim" (Joseph Addison). "The airplane disappeared into the blue *firmament*." "On that glorious spring day the *firmament* was blue and cloudless." Syn.: heavens, sky.

flagitious [fluJISHus] flagrantly wicked. "The teenager did not view shoplifting as *flagitious*." "The teenager thought his workplace supervisor was *flagitious*." "Marquis de Sade (1740-1814) was *flagitious*." "The misanthrope was mean and *flagitious*." Syn.: brazen, depraved, iniquitous, vicious, vile.

flâneur [flaNEUR] (French) an idler; a loafer. "The *flâneur* slept 12 hours a day." "The *flâneur* was involuntarily unemployed." "The forty-year-old *flâneur* was in the prime of his life but society failed to employ him." "The *flâneur* dawdled time away in little projects." Syn.: fainéant, malingerer, slacker. Ant.: workaholic.

flapdoodle [FLAPdoodul] nonsense. "What he said at the party while sauced was *flapdoodle*." "The radical claimed that the idea of national greatness is *flapdoodle*." "Stop writing that *flapdoodle* in your diary, said the woman to her son." "The college girl's letter to home was excited *flapdoodle*." Syn.: bosh, bunkum, drivel, falderal, rubbish.

flatfoot [FLATfoot] (pejorative) a policeman. "The *flatfoot* wrote a ticket for a trifling infraction of the law." "The *flatfoot* did riot-control." "The *flatfoot* walked the beat." "The *flatfoot* stopped for a doughnut." Syn.: constable, cop, officer.

fleer [FLEER] to smirk or laugh in contempt or derision; (noun) a contemptuous look. "After whistling loudly the boy shot a *fleer* of his fist shaken at his crotch—an unthinkable gesture of sexual derision." "She *fleered* at the teacher but he was shrewd enough to put down the jibe." "The *fleer* did nothing to mitigate the bully's teasing and taunting." "Who can refute a *fleer*?"

flimflam [FLIMFLAM] deceptiveness or trickery. "Save the *flimflam* for Halloween, said their father." "The con artist made a living from *flimflam*." "The *flimflam* earned for the youth some extra money." "The college student tried *flimflam* to change the arbitrary grade by the instructor." Syn.: deceit, dishonesty, disingenuousness, fraud.

flivver [FLIVur] an automobile of little worth. "His children complained of their father's car as a *flivver* until they grew older and realized the expense of upkeep of an automobile." "The *flivver* did not look like much, but you could tool around in it." "After coming into money, she exchanged her *flivver* for a Mercedes." "It was amazing that the family drove on vacation 500 miles and back in a *flivver*." The origin of *flivver* is unknown.

florid [FLORid] flowery; reddish. "In middle-age her formerly *florid* cheeks were now still so only due to make-up: She lost the rosy-cheeked complexion of youth." "The man had *florid* eczema all over his body." "He gave his mother a *florid* gift for her birthday." "A red *florid* bouquet is only appropriate for romantic love." Syn.: flowery, ornate, showy. Ant.: plain.

flummox [FLUMuks] to bewilder. "The crossword puzzle had him *flummoxed*." "Trigonometry *flummoxed* him." "Her beloved's behavior had her *flummoxed*." "He was *flummoxed* by the rules of the board game." The origin of *flummox* is uncertain. Syn.: baffle, confuse, disconcert, flabbergast.

flunkey [FLUNGKee] a servile lackey. "The judge was bitterly accused of being an establishment *flunkey*." "The magistrates are often the prosecutors' *flunkey*." "The gangster and his *flunkey* did the informant." "The leader had numerous *flunkeys* to assist him." Syn.: assistant, gofer.

foible [FOIbul] a minor flaw in character. "His wife habitually pointed out her husband's *foibles* before they became an embarrassment." "The man had *foibles* but he tried to prevent their becoming vices." "One of her *foibles* was combing her hair a dozen times daily." "The man insulted his wife by attributing a 'sackrat' *foible* to her." Syn.: eccentricity, fault, kink, shortcoming, weakness. Ant.: strength.

foil [FOIL] a person who makes someone else seem better by contrast, as in a comedic duo. "The comedian's sidekick was also his *foil*." "Harpo had Chico for a *foil*." "He refused to be his *foil*." "A wife is sometimes the *foil* of her husband." Syn.: accompaniment, counterpart, match.

folderol [FOLderol] (also *falderal*) foolish talk or ideas. "Their *folderol* about opening their own restaurant never came to anything." "It was all *folderol*, nothing came of it." "The two girls engaged in *folderol*." "Their *folderol* was about the Maine woods." Syn.: babble, balderdash, bosh, claptrap, drivel, gibberish, hot air, jabber, jabberwocky, poppycock.

font [FONT] a source of plenty. "Ancient philosophers held that the *font* of knowledge ought merely to promote virtue." "Television was a *font* for the actor." "Which do you believe is an economic *font* for the majority, capitalism or socialism?" "The practice of corporate law is a financial *font* for an attorney." Syn.: basis, fount, origin, supply, well, wellspring.

foofaraw [FOOfuro] much ado about nothing; excessive ornamentation. "He tried to say it was a *foofaraw* but the police had already shown up." "The party was a *foofaraw* but still fun." "She referred to her success as *foofaraw* but her father made much of it." "The argument was a *foofaraw* and concerned nothing important." The etymology of *foofaraw* is unknown. Syn.: donnybrook, hubbub, to-do.

fop [FOP] a dandy, or a male with an effeminate concern for his appearance and manner. "After watching the movie, he scornfully referred to its young star as a 'five-foot-five *fop*.'" "The *fop* was not employed and mooched money from others to support his fashionable life." "It is not hard to see the attraction being a *fop* has." "The *fop* attained success in music and movies." Syn.: Beau Brummel, popinjay.

force majeure [FORS mahZHUR] an unforeseen or uncontrollable event; in French literally "greater force." "The bold fellow's attempt to insert himself into national media events met with *force majeure*, and quickly folded into a heap of ignominy." "The party was cancelled because of purported *force majeure*." "The man was released from the contract because of *force majeure*." "*Force majeure* prevailed on the battlefield."

foreordain [fororDAYN] to predestine or predetermine. "The marriage was *foreordained* to failure." "The golf tournament seemed *foreordained* against him." "He told his beloved that it was *foreordained* that they should be together." "The flight was *foreordained* to disaster by mechanical failure."

forfend [forFEND] (also *forefend*) to defend or secure. "The battalion *forfended* the fort to the last man." "The army *forfended* the river bank." "Napoleon ordered his troops to *forfend* the church." "The Coast Guard *forfended* the shores against drug runners." Syn.: deter, obviate.

forlorn [furLORN] dreary or sad due to loss. "His scheme to make money left him broke and *forlorn* when it crashed." "Forlorn" is a cognate of German *verloren*, which means "lost." "Great God! I'd rather be, A pagan suckled in a creed outworn; So might I, standing on this pleasant lea, Have glimpses that would make me less forlorn." (William Wordsworth.) "He was *forlorn*

called attention to the 'art of social survival.'" "The *gadfly* eventually encountered strong criticism and had to sort of back off." Syn.: busybody, meddler, nuisance, pest.

gaffe [GAF] a social blunder. "She committed a *gaffe* on television that embarrassed her for weeks." "People generally wish to avoid a *gaffe* and making a scene." "Traveling as tourists in France, they committed a few *gaffes*, such as in the café: *ils mangeant comme une vache, it is said* ('they eat like a cow.')" "He made a *gaffe* in Germany by wearing a Bavarian hat in the wrong province." "Sneezing at the luncheon table was a *gaffe* he'd rather forget." "A *gaffe* at the interview cost him the job." Syn.: faux pas, howler, solecism.

Galahad [GALuhad] an honorable man of uncompromising principles and ideals. "The Congressman had a reputation of a *Galahad*." "The *Galahad* reached out and helped people in need." "The *Galahad* was generally charitable but it might be that, as an heir and Brahman, he was more charitable to his own children and lavished on them an untaxed trust fund." "All the reputed or supposed *Galahads*, it seems, are to be found in the upper-class." The term *Galahad* is derived from the Arthurian saga.

gall [GAL] rancor; effrontery. "He had the *gall* to send to him in the mail a summons for littering in the city." "He delivered the lecture with sullen *gall*." "The meeting became mired in *gall* and incriminations." "The nerve of him! The *gall* of him!' said the woman." Syn.: acerbity, bitterness, cholera, virulence.

galley slave [GALee SLAYV] an overworked person, in the manner of those who formerly propelled oars on a galley. "His brother complained of being a *galley slave*, of working in the 'salt mines,' such was his hatred of work at the warehouse." "Lower-class women, *ipso facto*, are *galley slaves*." "The trash collector, or 'sanitation worker,' was a *galley slave*." "Some nurses seem to have some slack time at work, while others are *galley slaves*." Syn.: drudge.

gallimaufry [galuMOfree] a hodgepodge. "He had a *gallimaufry* of souvenirs in his car." "He played a *gallimaufry* of games." "He had a *gallimaufry* record collection." "She read a *gallimaufry* of magazines." Syn.: assortment, jumble, medley, melange, miscellany, mishmash, potpourri, salmagundi.

gallivant [GALuvant] to wander about frivolously. "The youth *gallivanted* all summer long and never accomplished anything." "The young children *gallivanted* at the wedding reception." "The boys *gallivanted* in the park." "The family *gallivanted* in Yellowstone National Park." Syn.: ramble, saunter, wander.

gallows bird [GALohz BIRD] a person who deserves to be hanged. "The president of the country could think of many *gallows birds*." "They heaped ill-will and contempt on the *gallows birds*." "The men who thought of the convict as a *gallows bird* had a shallow intellect." "The men on death row were *gallows birds*, sometimes in a double sense."

gallows humor [GALohz HYOOmur] macabre humor. "The physicians engaged in *gallows humor* and spoke of having a lame horse shot." "The surgeon broke the tense silence and spoke with *gallows humor* in the O.R." "*Gallows* *humor* is sometimes necessary, since one should mingle bantering with seriousness." "They made jest running through the cemetery sporting *gallows humor*."

galoot [guLOOT] an awkward silly person. "The class *galoot* was respected by noone." "The *galoot* dared not try it." "The *galoot* threw 'like a girl.'" "The *galoot* was no athlete." Syn.: dolt, duffer, dunderhead, lackwit, schmuck.

gambol [GAMbul] to frolic. "The teenaged girl *gamboled* around the dance floor." "The collie *gamboled* in the grass." "The young couple *gamboled* in the meadow." "The grade-school students were supposed to be working at the school, not *gamboling*." Syn.: romp, skylark.

gamin [GAMin] a boy of the street left to his own devices. "In the eyes of society, *gamins* are headed for trouble or a life of crime." "Oliver Twist was a *gamin*." "The *gamin* had no parents." "The *gamin* eventually succeeded in life." Syn.: urchin, waif.

gamut [GAMut] the entire range. "The American media pass off 'conservative,' 'moderate,' and 'liberal' as the *gamut* of the political spectrum." "The manic-depressive man experienced the *gamut* of emotions." "The scholar possessed the *gamut* of knowledge." "There was a *gamut* of opinion on the subject of taxation." Syn.: array, breadth, extent, length, range, scale.

gamy [GAYmee] showing much spirit; plucky. "The *gamy* woman beat the man in chess." "The youthful but *gamy* soccer team won the championship." "The *gamy* woman went out and got her man." "The *gamy* old woman was not to be defied."

ganef [GAnuf] an unscrupulous opportunist in search of riches. "The *ganef* signed endorsement deals with several corporations." "The *ganef* rode around in Mercedes, flew in a jet and resided in an expensive villa." "The *ganef* collaborators were punished." "Many *ganefs* appear with a change in government." This is a Yiddish word that has a few alternative spellings.

garish [GARish] crudely elaborate or showy; excessively bright. "The movie's color is *garish*." "The peacock was almost *garish*." "His dream, in which he was back in kindergarten, seemed *garish*." "The school parade was a rather *garish* display." Syn.: gaudy. Ant.: tasteful.

garrote [guROHT] capital punishment through use of a strangulation device. "Compared to lethal injection, the *garrote*, hanging, electrocution and the gas chamber were inhumane means of capital punishment, although there are those who oppose lethal injection too." "A large crowd gathered to view the *garrote*." "The *garrote* is, of course, obsolete." "The man suffered while being killed through *garrote*."

garrulous [GARulus] excessively talkative. "Her *garrulous* behavior as hostess was one drawback to their party." "It is ironic that although women are generally *garrulous*, in the past, and even in some societies today, they are supposed to maintain silence among men, to be seen but not heard." "The *garrulous* man was just perfect for her." "The *garrulous* students had no capacity for silence." Syn.: loquacious, prolix, verbose. Ant.: reticent, taciturn.

gasconade [gaskuNAYD] boastfulness. "He was known for the *gasconade* of his football stories." "In reality, he has no basis for *gasconade*." "His *gasconade* was over the top, out-Heroding." "Her *gasconade* concerned an African safari." Syn.: bombast, braggadocio, bravado, rodomontade.

gauche [GOHSH] tactless. "To arrogantly refuse to adjust oneself to the norms of a foreign culture is *gauche*." The corresponding noun, *gaucherie*, means "social awkwardness," the opposite of which is *savoir-faire*. "The poor unfortunate lad was *gauche* with girls." "The *gauche* teacher wanted to give his students a grasp of English composition but they preferred to be amused." "He was *gauche* and nervous on the television interview." Syn.: awkward, callow, uncouth. Ant.: poised.

gaunt [GONT] drawn and worn-out. "President Woodrow Wilson's *gaunt* face in 1920 reflected the stress of intervening in World War l." "Her *gaunt* face told a tale of hardship." "His face was *gaunt* from belt-tightening." "The expremier was *gaunt* because of the stress of leadership." Syn.: haggard.

gauntlet [GAUNTlit] an ordeal, such as having to run through two lines of men armed with clubs. "The *gauntlet* is a senseless military brutality, like boot camp, K.P. duty and hazing." "The man died trying to run an actual *gauntlet*." "The marathon was an excruciating *gauntlet*." "The *gauntlet* seems to be on the decline, thankfully." Syn.: tribulation.

Gehenna [giHENu] any place of extreme suffering. "He viewed his former house as a *Gehenna*." "She associated the store with a kind of *Gehenna*, where everything went wrong." "The radical asked, 'the Vietnam War was a *Gehenna*, but for whom?'" "The concentration camp was a *Gehenna*." From the Old Testament.

Gemütlichkeit [guMUETlikhkiht] (German) good-natured fun, congeniality. "Bavaria and Austria are famous for their *Gemütlichkeit*." "The tourist sought out *Gemütlichkeit*." "There is nothing quite like enjoying *Gemütlichkeit* with *bons vivants*." "She soaked in the *Gemütlichkeit* at the Oktoberfest."

generation gap [jenuRAYshun GAP] a lack of communication and understanding between the young of one generation and the old of another generation. "The *generation gap* caused some chaos." "There was a *generation gap* between boys and fathers as to who were their baseball heroes." "The social critic called attention to the *generation gap* and the mortification of being aged." "Underlying the *generation gap* may be an ideology gone awry."

genius loci [JEEneeus LOHsih] the peculiarity of a place that impresses one. "The *genius loci* of the garden reminded him of Rome." "The *genius loci* of the hardware store was special to him." "The *genius loci* of the school reminded her of her childhood." "The *genius loci* of the slum made him uncomfortable."

genteel [jenTEEL] well-bred, belonging to polite society. "*Genteel* establishments exclude persons like hippies, hobos, flower-children, bums, ne'er-do-wells, and men without a necktie." "Only '*genteel*' people ate at the expensive restaurant." "Professionals are sometimes said to be *genteel*." "Polo is a *genteel* sport in a sense." Syn.: patrician. Ant.: coarse.

gentil [zhanTEE] (French) gentle or noble. "They were *gentil* people, not mean commoners." "He was *gentil*, aristocratic, upper-class." "The socialite was *gentil*, belonged to polite society." "The son and daughter attended a private, *gentil* school." "The *gentil* man was lost in the world of restaurant employees and unused to manual labor." *Gentil* is related to the word *gentle*, which formerly had the meaning "noble" or "chivalrous."

genuflect [JENyooflekt] to show a servile attitude. "The vice-president *genuflected* to the chairman of the board." "*Genuflection* shows hierarchy." "The student teachers *genuflected* to the teachers, who *genuflected* to the principals." "He was strangely eager to *genuflect* to the manager and so show his normalcy." "The politician *genuflected* to corporate interests."

germane [jurMAYN] pertinent. "The phrase would be more germane to the matter if we could carry cannon by our sides" (Shakespeare, *Hamlet*). "Whether an instructor has read a textbook he has assigned is quite *germane*." "Understandable language is *germane* to social science publications." "An intellect is *germane* to sensible living." Syn.: apposite. Ant.: irrelevant.

gerrymander [JEReemandur] to manipulate voting districts to one's own political advantage. "*Gerrmandering* is a corrupt political practice that continues to this day." "The political scientist studied *gerrymandering*." "The Congressman lost his seat when his district was *gerrymandered* by state legislators." "The progressive Democrat was unseated by *gerrymandering* on the part of both Democrats and Republicans." *Gerrymander* comes from the name of an early 19th century governor of Massachusetts combined with the word *salamander*, the latter referring to the lampoon in a cartoon of a county in the state which bore resemblance to this amphibian; that is, the name of the governor and the word *salamander* were combined to form this term. The circuitous, rambling boundaries on the map of some political districts, rather than neat geometric planning, is evidence of gerrymandering.

gilt-edged [GILTejd] of a high quality. "The furnishings in the Vanderbilt mansion were *gilt-edged*." "Her personal library was *gilt-edged*." "The Pulitzer-Prize-winning memoir was *gilt-edged*." "The university, which not many years before was a college, was not *gilt-edged*."

gist [JIST] the essential aspect of something. "The *gist* of his argument was that the right-wing avoids the crucial issue of wealth and poverty, of equality versus inequality." "The *gist* of his criticism was that the film lacked honest adversarial relationships, and so was a 'turkey.'" "The *gist* of his assertion is that the love of money was greater than the greed of even the Robber Barons." "The *gist* of the book is that every 'school of education' should be bulldozed." Syn.: essence, substance.

glabrous [GLAYbrus] bald, as of a plant or animal. "Some bald men are very sensitive about having a *glabrous* pate." "The man with a *glabrous* head bought a toupee." "The comedian made jokes about a *glabrous* head." "The man with a *glabrous* head combed his hair straight over to partly cover baldness."

glad hand [GLAD HAND] an effusive, often insincere welcome. "The CEO received the *glad hand* at the meeting of employees." "The mayor got a *glad hand*." "There were some boos in the *glad hand* given the singer." "The surgeon got the *glad hand* at the banquet."

glitch [GLICH] a minor problem. "Much trouble and expense is needed to blast off a communications or surveillance satellite without a *glitch*." "The new car had several *glitches*." "The *glitch* in the computer was that it lacked the desired software." "The *glitch* in communication was that they did not speak the same language." Syn.: anomaly, bug, fault, hitch, malfunction.

gliterati [gliteRATee] celebrities. "The television program said that the buxom actress belonged to the *gliterati*." "The *gliterati* are overpaid." "Everyone strives to join the *gliterati*, though the poor fall woefully short." "The *gliterati* reject people without financial means." *Gliterati*, a new coinage, is an alteration of "literati." Syn.: beau monde, high society.

glower [GLOUur] to stare sullenly. "His *glowering* face said everything she needed to know." "She *glowered* at her defiant daughter." "The *glowering* man was angry." "The boy was *glowering* out the window when she walked in." Syn.: frown, scowl. Ant.: smile.

gloze [GLOHZ] to gloss or underplay. "The press *glozed* his infidelity, perhaps because he was a famous politician." "The editor *glozed* the controversial story." "She *glozed* her son's shortcomings." "The media *glozed* the story that business does not pass on to consumers the savings due to technological progress."

gnomic [NOHmik] like an aphorism. "Some of Ben Franklin's *gnomic* advice, given in his rustic newspaper, is found in common sayings today." "In Shakespeare's *gnomic* phrase, 'brevity is the soul of wit.'" "Francis Bacon's powerful essays are *gnomic*.'" "The man gave his nephew *gnomic* advice." "The policeman's favorite *gnome* was 'the conscience is as good as a 1000 witnesses.'" Syn.: axiomatic, proverbial.

gnosis [NOHsis] mystical knowledge. "The guru had, or seemed to have, *gnosis*." "The traveling spiritualist advertised possession of *gnosis*." "Siddhartha had *gnosis*." "The skeptic declared that *gnosis* is not known to science."

gnothi seauton [GNOHthi seooTUN] Greek for "know thyself." "He commented that, in his opinion, *gnothi seauton* is so important because human character is fundamentally universal." "The mystic pondered *gnothi seauton*." "Men may need to heed *gnothi seauton* more than women." "In a crude sense, *gnothi seauton* might be called getting in touch with your feelings."

go-getter [GOHgetur] an aggressively enterprising person. "The classic *go-getter* is to be found in *Babbitt*, a novel by Sinclair Lewis (1885-1951)." "The head of the Chamber of Commerce was a *go-getter*." "The *go-getters* planned to bring a symphony orchestra to town." "The *go-getter* built segregated housing for the elderly." "The *go-getter* could only get self-esteem from others." Syn.: live wire.

golconda [golKONdu] a rich mine or other source of great wealth. "The *golcondas* found by the 49ers were, of course, quite few." "His invention turned out to be a *golconda*." "The *golconda* allowed the man's heirs to live in the leisure class, *in sudore vultus alieni*." "The society glorified the chance, however unlikely, to obtain a *golconda*." After Golconda, India.

goldbrick [GOLDbrik] a person, especially a soldier, who loafs on the job. "Some college employees work hard, while others are a *goldbrick*." "After a long period of slacking, the *goldbrick* was finally fired from his job as a waiter in the restaurant." "There were no *goldbricks* in that occupation." "The army *goldbrick* had no duties." Syn.: idler, layabout, loafer, malingerer, shirker, slacker.

golden rule [GOLdun ROOL] the Biblical injunction "Whatsoever ye would that men should do to you, do ye even so unto them." (From the book of Matthew.) "You know what they say about the *golden rule*: He who has the gold rules!" "In that country, at that time, the *golden rule* was ignored day-in and day-out, yet they were Christians." "The prevalent attitude toward the *golden rule* seems to be 'people aren't doing that to me, so why should I behave that way towards them?'" "It might be useless to invoke the *golden rule* when you are being mistreated."

golgotha [GOLguthu] a place of suffering. "The woman fled from the *golgotha*." "The *golgotha* was his old workplace." "The jail was a *golgotha*." "For him his old neighborhood was merely a *golgotha*." "Golgotha" is a Biblical term which in its Hebrew root means "skull."

gonfalon [GONfulun] a banner suspended from a crossbar. "A man with a *gonfalon* walked in front of the procession." "The *gonfalon* bore a symbol of the Italian republic." "The *gonfalon* was used in ecclesiastical ceremonies." "The *gonfalon* was red and white."

Gongorism [GONGurizum] an ornate, fussy literary style. "Inexperienced writers and poets should be wary of wandering into *Gongorism*, or what might be called the 'hothouse' style." "His attempt to infuse *Gongorism* into his novel miscarried." "The term *Gongorism* comes from the name of a Spanish poet." "The student's poem was not *Gongorism*, but noone knows just what it was."

good Samaritan [GOOD suMAYRitun] a person who unselfishly helps another. "The *good Samaritan* allowed the man with few goods to precede her in the checkout lane." "The *good Samaritan* helped the woman who fell get to her feet." "Those particular people felt no compassion and never played the *good Samaritan*." "Religion ought to bring out the *good Samaritan* in everyone." From the Bible, in Luke.

gook [GOOK] (derogatory) an Oriental. "Calling the enemy a *gook* made it easier to kill him." "The so-called *gooks* were no fools." "The *gook* was not actually Asian." "The so-called *gooks* braced for an attack."

gorgon [GORgun] a mean or repulsive woman. "His sister was a shrewish *gorgon*." "The movie called for the role of a *gorgon*." "The *gorgon* was a henpecker." "The play featured a *gorgon* who dominates her husband."

Gothic [GOTHik] pertaining to a style of architecture of the later Middle Ages marked by the use of the pointed arch and ribbed vault; barbarous or rude. "American Gothic is the name of a famous painting depicting an old farming couple." "The French town had a *Gothic* cathedral built in the 1300s." "The rustic accommodations were *Gothic*." "Cultural standards were *Gothic*." Syn.: coarse, crude, uncultivated.

gourmand [goorMAN] a person who loves to eat; a glutton. "The *gourmand* was fat." "He was often skinny, but also knew *gourmand* days." "The *gourmand* ate a five-course meal." "He knew that if he lived to eat like a *gourmand* he would gain weight." "The excesses of a *gourmand* never fail to show up in pounds of flesh." Syn.: gorger, overeater.

graft [GRAFT] booty; dishonest or illegal acquisition of money. "The *graft* of the Gilded Age—post-Civil War America—was extreme, and entire state legislatures were bought by big business." "The corporate officers cooked the books in order to gain *graft* from the value of their stock in the company." "*Graft* in the corporation is commonplace." "Opportunists in search of *graft* are never wanting." Syn.: boodle, bribery, corruption.

grail [GRAYL] the object of an arduous quest. "The *grail* of Narcissus in the Greek myth was never fulfilled." "The adventurous journalist went in search of the holy *grail*." "Finding the *grail* would be thrilling." "Would you ever join a treasure hunt for a *grail?*"

grandee [granDEE] a man of high social status. "His belle's father was a *grandee* who owned a plant employing many workers in the town." "The *grandee* had the money to bail out his son but refused." "The *grandee* was a Wall Street banker." "The *grandee* was a venture capitalist." Syn.: aristocrat, Brahman, blue blood, noble, nobleman, patrician, peer.

grandiloquence [granDILukwuns] pompous speech. "Hitler gave notorious *grandiloquent* speeches at the Nuremberg rallies." "His lecture was almost *grandiloquent*, as he spoke as if his words lent him greatness." "The speaker at the rally was in no way *grandiloquent*." "The book was a little flighty and *grandiloquent* in its expansive theme." The root of *grandiloquence* in Latin is "great" combined with "speaking." Syn.: bombast, pontification.

grand monde [GRAHN MOND] (French) high society, the elite. "The *grand monde* inhabits an exclusive world all its own." "The *grand monde* is exempt from doing the work that other people take for granted." "The middle-class man detested the *grand monde*." "The *grand monde* does no household work, but employs menials." *Grand monde* is French for "great world." Syn.: *beau monde*, fashionable society, *haut monde*, high society, polite society, upper crust. Ant.: riffraff.

gratis [GRATis] without charge. "The students were thankful that the university set up a textbook service to provide books *gratis* or at a nominal fee." "The pasta lunch was a perquisite provided *gratis*." "Carry out at the pizzeria was not *gratis*, since one had to give a tip." "According to economists, nothing in this world is *gratis*." *Gratis* comes from a Latin word meaning "grace." Syn.: complimentary, cost-free, costless, gratuitous.

gratuitous [gruTOOitus] gratis; done without provocation or reason. "Socialists viewed the hanging of a few men in the Haymarket affair as *gratuitous* and wrongful." "The teenaged boy *gratuitously* punched his coworker on the chin." "The school violence was *gratuitous*." "Inheritance of trust-fund fortunes is *gratuitous*." Syn.: needless, superfluous, uncalled-for, unjustified, unnecessary, unwarranted. Ant.: requisite.

gravy train [GRAYvee TRAYN] a position in which a person or group receives considerable profit for little or no effort. "They who inherit a fortune ride the *gravy train*." "There was much criticism of the 'welfare cheats' on the *gravy train*." "As a teenager he thought that working at the restaurant was like being on the *gravy train*." "The true *gravy train*, argued the radical, is being in the leisure class."

gray eminence [GRAY EMinuns] (also French *éminence grise*) a power behind the throne; a person who wields power through another person having formal power. "The king's wife was a *gray eminence*." "His advisor became a *gray eminence* when the premier suffered a stroke." "The *gray eminence* was the true ruler of the country." "The queen took steps to ensure that no *gray eminence* would usurp her power."

gremlin [GREMlin] an imaginary creature to whom mechanical problems in aircraft are sometimes attributed; a mischievous creature. "Bad luck seemed to follow the girl, who was deemed a *gremlin*." "The fact that the wheels would not come down on the plane was attributed to a *gremlin*, the real cause being unknown." "The boy was a *gremlin* who stole change from his mother and brother." "The breakdown of their car was attributed to a *gremlin*."

grift [GRIFT] money obtained by fraud or swindle. "The white-collar con men made *grift* from fees charged to job applicants." "The *grift* was deposited in the bank just as though it had been honestly earned." "The *grift* was divided among the three thieves." "The thief's *grift* was in turn stolen by another thief." Syn.: boodle, graft.

grimalkin [griMALkin] a splenetic old woman. "The *grimalkin* was not nice to be around." "The *grimalkin* was frail and lonesome." "The widowed *grimalkin* had no family." "The *grimalkin* did not get along with her neighbors in the apartment building." Syn.: beldam, hag, harridan.

grizzle [GRIZul] to grow gray. "His *grizzled* hair and beard belied his otherwise youthful appearance." "The *grizzly* bear is so-called because of some gray hairs." "She dyed her hair to cover *grizzling*." "The man dyed his *grizzled* beard brown."

grog [GROG] strong drink; liquor. "The *grog* he imbibed at the tavern made him sway to and fro in walking home." "He had drank too much *grog* to drive." "The teenager was not allowed to drink *grog*." "The *grog* affected his mind quickly." This word derives from the nickname, Old Grog, an 18th century British admiral.

grouse [GROUS] to complain. "Right-wingers often use the word *grouse* to describe the claims of liberals and radicals: *grousing about sexual discrimination; grousing about expensive health care*." "He *groused* about tasteless food." "She *groused* that her bedroom was too small." "He *groused* that everything was expensive." Syn.: grumble, lament, repine. Ant.: commend, praise.

grovel [GROVul] to humble oneself or act abjectly. "His show of *groveling* in front of his boss was a clear demonstration of office politics." "He *groveled* before his wife asking for forgiveness." "He was *groveling* in order to avoid a fight with the mean coworker." "He did not need to *grovel*, being over six feet tall." Syn.: bootlick, cower, cringe, kiss one's ass, kowtow, truckle.

guerdon [GURdn] a reward. "A *guerdon* of $10,000 went with the prize for best essay." "There was a *guerdon* on the outlaw's head." "The poster announcing the *guerdon* said the man was wanted dead or alive." "The *guerdon* was for $1500."

guile [GIHL] duplicity. "The *guile* of the Bible salesman was persistent and not a little unfriendly." "He acted with mean *guile*." "There was a good reason for her *guile*." "He had the *guile* of a used-car salesman." Syn.: astuteness, cleverness, craftiness, cunning, deceit, deviousness, duplicity, slyness, treachery, trickiness.

guru [GOOroo] a Hindu personal religious instructor; an intellectual or spiritual guide. "The *guru* helped the anguished 'see the light.'" "The well-to-do family engaged a *guru* to revive their spirits." "The *guru* practiced enlightenment with people in Los Angeles." "She saw a *guru* who tried to help her overcome depression." "The popular *guru* aided people needing psychic healing." Syn.: mentor, yogi.

guttersnipe [GUTursnihp] a person of the lowest class. "The *guttersnipe* was unemployed." "The *guttersnipe* was looked down upon." "She was a *guttersnipe,* although the only thing she really lacked was money." "The radical, in part, blamed the system for *guttersnipes,* whereas the conservative blamed the *guttersnipes* themselves." Syn.: bum, hobo, tramp, vagabond, vagrant.

H

hackles [HAKulz] anger. "Do not get your *hackles* up over that." "She got her *hackles* up over the traffic ticket." "It is not wise to get your *hackles* up over trivia." "After some bad experiences with rage, he decided to avoid whenever possible getting his *hackles* up." Syn.: ire, wrath.

Hades [HAYdeez] the underworld of departed souls; hell. "The raging evangelist threatened sinners with *Hades*." "The writer claimed agnosticism as to whether there is a *Hades*." "The meaning of the Biblical *Hades* was uncertain to him." "The priest earnestly believed in *Hades*." Syn.: inferno, perdition, purgatory.

hagridden [HAGridun] worried or tormented, as by unfounded fears. "She became *hagridden* after lapsing into depression." "All the bills generated by his wife and four children made the hard-working father *hagridden*." "The stagnant economy and slumping income caused many people *hagridden* days." "The decline of her physical health made the old woman *hagridden*." Syn.: harassed. Ant.: carefree.

halcyon [HALseeun] peaceful; very pleasant. "Adversity tends to make a man reflect on the *halcyon* days of yore." "Those years were not *halcyon* at all." "At last he had peace of mind and a *halcyon* life." "Her life was *halcyon* until age 21." *Halcyon* is derived from the name of a fabled bird. Syn.: placid, serene, soothing, tranquil. Ant.: troubled.

hamartia [hamarTEEu] (Greek) in ancient Greek tragedy, a tragic flaw, the means by which a person meets doom. "The *hamartia* of the novel's hero was bashfulness." "The author gave his protagonist a *hamartia*." "His *hamartia* was a mean temper." "He thought about *hamartia* and believed he had no tragic flaw."

handsel [HANDsul] a gift in commemoration of something; a foretaste. "She sent her parents a *handsel* on their wedding anniversary." "The *handsel* was for his birthday." "The *handsel* told him he ought to leave immediately." "She had a *handsel* of death."

harlequin [HARlukwin] a buffoon. "It is hard to get respect when dressed as a *harlequin*." "The *harlequin* dared to mock his own patron." "The circus *harlequin* amused the audience." "The ice cream vendor was dressed as a *harlequin*." Syn.: clown, jester, merry-andrew.

harpy [HARpee] a greedy, grasping person; a shrew. "The *harpy* raided the workers' pension fund." "He did anything to escape his wife, a *harpy*." "The *harpy* finally went to prison after a career of defrauding others." "The *harpy* always had on his mind a promotion and getting ahead."

harridan [HARidun] a shrewish woman. "The psychologist, in his lecture, said that although female misanthropes do not exist, an otherwise misanthropic woman is manifest in the *harridan*, the vicious hag." "He spitefully called her a 'horrid *harridan*.'" "The *harridan* changed her stripes when her husband got home from work." "The *harridans* were scattered across the middle class." Syn.: fishwife, scold, termagant.

hatchet job [HACHit JOB] a maliciously destructive act. "The magazine reviewer did a *hatchet job* on the book." "The henchmen of the secret police did a *hatchet job* on the suspect." "The *hatchet job* of gutting middle management was done by the new chairman brought in by the board." "The media did a *hatchet job* of reporting the facts in his arrest."

hatemonger [HAYTmongur] a person who excites hatred in others. "The *hatemonger* despised Jews, blacks and socialists." "He was labeled a *hatemonger*, though he really was calling for equality." "The *hatemonger* was imprisoned for conspiracy to commit murder." "The *hatemonger* was a libertarian."

haute couture [OHT kooTEUR] (French) high fashion; the fashion of stylish dressmakers. "The working girl could not afford *haute couture*." "Designers of *haute couture* were very rich." "The models strolled back and forth on the stage showing off *haute couture*." "The radical asserted that powerful women shun *haute couture* for tasteful, dignified clothing."

hauteur [hohTUR] haughtiness or arrogance. "The queen deigned not to lend her *hauteur* to the primary school which had declared a scholarship in her honor, it having been beneath her." "His desire for vengeance resulted in *hauteur*." "Her *hauteur* was reinforced by being rich." "He was gripped with *hauteur*." Syn.: arrogance, conceit, domineeringness, effrontery, overbearance. Ant.: modesty.

haut monde [OH MOND] (French) high society. "When a commoner comes into contact with the American *haut monde*, the society people politely say, 'he's not our kind.'" "Is there anyone who would not want to be in the *haut monde?*" "She was wealthy but not in the *haut monde.*" "The *haut monde* did not accept him." "The *haut monde* is very exclusive." Syn.: *beau monde, grand monde,* high society, polite society. Ant.: riffraff.

hayseed [HAYseed] a hick. "It does not take much to start a fight, least of all alcohol, among *hayseeds.*" "He was a country boy, a *hayseed,* and proud of his origins." "He was a *hayseed* from the boondocks." "The *hayseeds* drove along the road screaming yahoo." Syn.: bumpkin, hoosier, oakie, redneck, rube, yokel.

hebdomadal [hebDOMudul] weekly. "The gazette appeared *hebdomadally.*" "The concert was a *hebdomadal* event in summer." "The magazine was issued *semihebdomadally.*" "He walked to the store *hebdomadally.*"

hebetude [HEBitood] mental lethargy. "The elderly afflicted with *hebetude* in America suffer from added stigma." "The rioting crowd displayed moral *hebetude.*" "He acquired *hebetude* in middle age." "The unmotivated school children manifested *hebetude.*" Syn.: senility.

hector [HEKtur] a bully; (verb) to bully. "Being the victim of *hectoring* is sufficient grounds for unemployment compensation, according to the government." "*Hectoring* at the military academy still goes on." "The neighborhood *hector* finally met someone stronger and was taken down." "The *hector* put up a big bluff, apparently to hide his fear." Syn.: badger, harass.

hedonism [HEEDnizum] the pursuit of pleasure for its own sake. "Conservatives attack *hedonism,* but it is very questionable whether the work ethic is in decline." "The *hedonists* just could not attain what they sought." "The social critic discussed *hedonism* and 'the void within.'" "The opposite of pleasure is *anhedonia,* wherein *hedonism* is of little use." Syn.: intemperance, pleasure-seeking, profligacy, self-indulgence, self-satisfaction.

hegira [hiJIHru] a flight or journey to escape danger. "His *hegira* to escape arrest landed him in Algeria." "A *hegira* was impossible because the man was broke." "Their honeymoon was like a *hegira,* since they stayed put to avoid her father." "The man's *hegira* was an attempt at religious freedom." This word is from Arabic, and originally denoted the flight of the prophet Muhammed in A.D. 622.

heinous [HAYnus] odious. "They denounced the bombing of Guernica, Spain, as a *heinous* crime." "The football player committed a *heinous* crime." "The leader was denounced for *heinous* immorality." "His actions were *heinous.*" Syn.: atrocious, dreadful, evil, monstrous, scandalous, shocking.

Helen of Troy [HELun UV TROI] in Homeric myth, the most beautiful woman in the world. "The magazine declared the actress a *Helen of Troy.*" "The blonde-hair, blue-eyed woman was a genuine *Helen of Troy.*" "The man said that if he waited for a *Helen of Troy* to marry he would be single his whole life." "The *Helen of Troy* married at age 28."

hellcat [HELkat] a witch or shrewish woman. "The *hellcat* dominated her husband, in much contrast to the expectations of others." "The *hellcat* hollered at her children." "The *hellcat* wore the pants in the family." "The *hellcat* was not fun to be around." Syn.: harridan, scold, termagant.

helot [HELut] a slave. "*Helots* are rarely passive or submissive, however much some societies have thus portrayed them." "The *helots* revolted." "The man acquired wealth as a *helot*." "A *helot* necessarily lives for another." A helot was originally a slave in ancient Sparta. Syn.: bondman, peon, serf.

henpeck [HENpek] to regularly scold or nag one's husband. "The *henpecked* husband wanted a divorce." "The *henpecked* husband preferred the company of his male friends over that of his vicious wife." "The wife of Socrates *henpecked* him." "Why he ever married a *henpecking* woman is a mystery." "His friends sympathized with the *henpecked* husband."

heresy [HERisee] a belief that defies orthodoxy, especially religious orthodoxy. "Anthropologists insist that modern society has its own forms of *heresy,* just as did Europe in the Dark Age." "It would be *heresy* to discuss inherited wealth in the media." "The historian wanted to unmask the *heresy*." "The *heresy* consisted in criticizing corporate hegemony." Syn.: deviation, dissent, heterodoxy, misbelief, profanation, sacrilege. Ant.: faithfulness.

Herrenvolk [HERenfolk] (German) a master race. "Nazi Germany trumpeted itself as a *Herrenvolk* destined to dominate other peoples." "The tribe attempted to dominate and rule other tribes as a *Herrenvolk*." "The group of plotters imagined themselves as leaders of a *Herrenvolk*." "The self-styled *Herrenvolk* was defeated while trying to spread its power."

heterodox [HETurudoks] holding unorthodox doctrines or opinions. "His friends were shocked by his *heterodoxy*." "She persisted in holding *heterodox* beliefs despite everything that happened around her." "The radical's *heterodoxy* went against the ways of his fellow citizens." "Everything about society's institutions discourages *heterodoxy*." Syn.: nonstandard, unconventional. Ant.: orthodox.

heuristic [hyooRISTik] using practical discovery to learn more; serving to point out; (noun) a teaching method of learning through practical experience or application. "Scientists speak of a *heuristic* working hypothesis to discover facts and principles." "The kindergarten employed the *heuristic*." "Psychoanalysis is neither scientific nor *heuristic*." "Students say that *heuristic* learning is best, but some scientific principles cannot be demonstrated so easily." "The sociologist proceeded with research using the *heuristic* idea that the collective means of making a living determines culture." "The historian discovers the past by the judicious use of such a heuristic device as the 'ideal type'" (Karl J. Weintraub).

heyday [HAYday] the period of greatest success, influence, etc.; prime. "The *heyday* of her career was in the 1930s." "The *heyday* of social Darwinism was late in the 19th century." "Looking back on it the man realized that he experienced his *heyday,* maybe not his last one, in 1960." "The *heyday* of the drive-in theatre was the 1950s." Syn.: halcyon days, peak, prime, zenith. Ant.: nadir.

hiatus [hiyAYtus] an interruption or gap. "There was a rather long *hiatus* between his asking her to marry him and their wedding." "The boys enjoyed the summer *hiatus* when school was out." "American professors have a long *hiatus* off work, from early May to late August." "The *hiatus* was not long, since a shot was fired in anger after the threat." Syn.: break, gap, interruption, interval, lull, pause.

hibernal [hiyBURnul] pertaining to winter. "The *hibernal* woods of the Midwest are dreary." "Noone likes the *hibernal* season." "A *hibernal* landscape can have its own bleak beauty." "The word *hibernal* is reminiscent of 'hibernate.'" Syn.: brumal.

hidalgo [hiDALgoh] a minor noble in Spanish-speaking countries. "An *hidalgo* might be likened to a count (or a *Graf* in German, *compte* in French, and *conte* in Italian)." "The *hidalgo* spent his time doing scientific research." "The *hidalgo* was pressed for money." "The *hidalgo* resided in a small manor house."

hidebound [HIHDbound] having a narrow, rigid opinion. "The methods teacher, a 'teacher teacher,' had her *hidebound* ways." "Government and corporate bureaucracy are *hidebound*." "He had to admit that in his own way he was what he sometimes criticized in others—*hidebound*." "The seventy-year-old man was *hidebound*, and not about to change his ways at his age." Syn.: bigoted, illiberal, inflexible, narrow-minded. Ant.: cosmopolitan.

high jinks [HIHjinks] boisterous celebration or fun. "A group from the party engaged in *high jinks* in the back yard." "He sorely missed the spontaneous *high jinks* with friends." "She was sometimes a part of the *high jinks* with her brother and his friends." "Many of the best *high jinks* of his life came at elementary school."

hippie [HIPee] a person, especially of the 1960s, who rejects certain social institutions and seeks more fulfilling roles and relationships and, in some cases, uses illicit drugs. "The *hippies* and flower children opposed the war in Vietnam." "What seemed to have given rise to the *hippies* and the counterculture was the expanding economy and easy availability of jobs." "The *hippies* sought to get closer to nature and enjoy primal beauty." "The clothing of *hippies* consisted of jeans, beads and flower patterns." *Hippie* is from the word *hip*, meaning in touch with fashion and social trends; the latter word, however, has an unknown origin. Syn.: bohemian, free-thinker, nonconformist.

hipster [HIPstur] a person who is hip, or in sync with the latest fashion and social trends. "The *hipster* had the money to follow the latest fashion." "The *hipster* knew the dance craze and new lingo of the day." "The *hipster* was in demand in social circles." "She outgrew her *hipster* days and became a wife and mother." Syn.: hippie. Ant.: nerd, square.

historied [HIStureed] containing history; historical. "The building housing the art museum was *historied*." "The gated neighborhood with big old homes was *historied*." "The grandfather clock was a *historied* antique." "The silver Roman coin was a *historied* collectible."

histrionic [histreeONik] affected, feigned for the purpose of creating a dramatic appearance or calling attention to oneself. "His numerous press conferences were marked by *histrionics*." "The youth was *histrionic* from an early age." "The social critic scathingly maintained that people now *histrionically* must perform a role and be a connoisseur of their own performance." "The woman was *histrionic* because she knew she was on television." Syn.: pretentious. Ant.: ingenuous, unaffected.

Hobbism [HOBizum] the doctrine of a strong central government that suppresses the anarchy of competing individual interests. "*Hobbism* sounds close to totalitarianism." "*Hobbism* as a practical *modus vivendi* is a common solution to the problems of mass society." "The *Hobbism* was overthrown by a socialist government." "*Hobbism* affected everyone in the society." After the English political philosopher Thomas Hobbes (1588-1679), who formulated the doctrine in *Leviathan*.

hobbledehoy [HOBuldeehoi] an awkward, clumsy youth. "The *hobbledehoy* could not learn to play tennis." "The *hobbledehoy* desperately wanted to participate in athletics." "The *hobbledehoy* was the last boy to be picked for the basketball teams." "The *hobbledehoy* was merely a benchwarmer on the football team." Syn.: galoot.

hobgoblin [HOBgoblin] a bogy; a bugbear; something one obsessively dreads. "The *hobgoblin* of economists is inflation." "A foolish consistency is the hobgoblin of little minds...." (Ralph Waldo Emerson, *Essays,* "Self-Reliance.") "The boy's *hobgoblin* was being found out or discovered." "The woman's *hobgoblin* turned out to be baseless."

hobnob [HOBnob] to associate with on friendly terms. "The nouveau-riche family liked to *hobnob* with nobility." "The two boys became good friends and liked to *hobnob* at the shopping center." "The two women *hobnobbed* at the café." "*Hobnobbing* was the teen's favorite activity." "After discovering *hobnobbing* with socialites, the priest abandoned his faith and preached atheism."

hog-wild [HOGWIHLD] extremely enthusiastic or excited. "The eight-year-old boy was *hog-wild* on his birthday." "The *hog-wild* crowd erupted from the stands after the game." "He was *hog-wild* after picking up the check for $1.2 million." "He was *hog-wild* for the hometown hockey team." Syn.: eager, energetic, exuberant, lively, spirited. Ant.: phlegmatic.

hoity-toity [HOItee TOItee] putting on airs; haughty. "The upper-class woman was *hoity-toity* to the servants." "He claimed that he could not be *hoity-toity* because he was not rich." "The girl was 'stuck-up,' or *hoity-toity*, because her mother was a *grande dame*." "The *hoity-toity* woman was from an aristocratic family." "The young doctor was *hoity-toity*." "The fifth-grade boys gleefully put on *hoity-toity* and pretended to be superior." Syn.: arrogant, high-falutin, stuck-up, uppish. Ant.: modest.

hokey [HOHkee] faked; contrived. "The flaw of the novel *Catch-22* is that it is *hokey*." "The ID saying she was over 21 was *hokey*." "He had the habit of often saying 'bogus' and '*hokey*.'" "The host's laughter on the television program was *hokey*, forced." Syn.: counterfeit, ersatz, imitation, mock, sham. Ant.: genuine.

Homeric [hohMERik] heroic or imposing. "The Hoover Dam is a *Homeric* structure." "Redwood trees are *Homeric*." "The battle of Iwo Jima was a *Homeric* struggle." "The size of the Sahara Desert is *Homeric*." The term comes from the Greek epic poet Homer.

homily [HOMulee] a sermon, either religious or lay; a tedious moralizing discourse. "The *homily* included the observation that 'from this evil some good may come.'" "The minister gave a *homily* asking for money." "The reviewer said the book was preachy, a *homily*, and so he preached against preaching." "He criticized the film as preachy, as a kind of *homily* for the general public." Syn.: moral, preachment.

honky-tonk [HONGkeetongk] a cheap nightclub. "They had a good time at the *honky-tonk*." "The worker took his girlfriend to a *honky-tonk* in the city." "The *honky-tonk* was a noisy, boisterous place." "The married man and wife met at a *honky-tonk*."

hoosegow [HOOSgou] a jail. "He was thrown into the *hoosegow* for shoplifting." "The *hoosegow* held a number of unsavory men." "The *hoosegow* was located in the county seat." "The burglar broke out of the *hoosegow*." Syn.: clink, cooler, pokey, slammer, stir.

horn-mad [HORNMAD] intensely angry. "He was *horn-mad* after discovering that someone had stolen his ten-dollar bill." "She was *horn-mad* that the children had dragged mud into the house." "The scold was often *horn-mad* about something." "The actor was *horn-mad* that his credit line was not first in the movie." Some phrases meaning horn-mad are "beside oneself with rage," "fighting mad," "fit to be tied," "het up," "hot under the collar," "hot and bothered," "in a lather," "livid with rage," "out of sorts," "teed off," "ticked off." Syn.: incensed, indignant, irate, livid, mad, pissed-off.

hornswoggle [HORNswogul] to swindle or deceive. "The dishonest man *hornswoggled* the couple out of $12,000." "The gold digging woman was looking for a rich husband to *hornswoggle*." "The pair *hornswoggled* businesses with a stolen credit card." "The man *hornswoggled* his girlfriend into believing he was five years younger than his true age." "The conservative radio ideologue *hornswoggled* his way out of serving in the Vietnam War." Syn.: bamboozle, dupe, gull.

hors de combat [ordekonBA] (French) no longer able to fight; disabled. "The fighter pilot was *hors de combat*." "The car he normally cruised in was *hors de combat*." "The soldier was *hors de combat* with a bullet wound." "The captain was *hors de combat* from the effect of a poison gas attack."

horselaugh [HORSlaf] a loud derisive laugh. "Though trying to be polite, she emitted a *horselaugh* on the television show." "A *horselaugh* greeted his entry into the room." "The *'duh'* *horselaugh* was for him." "The comic routine got more *horselaughs* than laughs." "*Horselaughs* and cheering came from the raucous pub." Syn.: guffaw.

horse trade [HORS TRAYD] a transaction marked by shrewd and intense bargaining. "The Congressman engaged in *horse trade* to get the bill passed." "The *horse trade* resulted in a $90,000 profit for the man." "The president agreed to a *horse trade* to get approval for his foreign policy." "He gained much knowledge of politics through *horse trade* at the state capital."

hortatory [HORtutoree] relating to exhortation; encouraging. "The tone of voice of a television newsreader very well might be biased and *hortatory*." "The politician's *hortatory* speech favored universal military service." "The *horta-*

tory billboard opposed abortion rights." "The *hortatory* television commercial said 'receive Jesus.'" "The *hortatory* sermon urged adoption of the Golden Rule." "The fans' *hortatory* cheers were not enough for their team to come from behind and win the game."

hospice [HOSpis] a shelter for travelers, especially a religious one; a hospital for terminally ill patients. "Her altruistic volunteer work at the *hospice* was pure selflessness." "A psychologist was employed by the *hospice* to counsel the dying." "The *hospice* had many cancer patients." "The old man refused to go to a *hospice*." Syn.: clinic, sanatorium.

houri [HOORee] in Islam, a beautiful virgin of paradise. "Besides being an Indian-British physician, she could easily have qualified as a *houri*." "The fallen Islamic man is said to be surrounded by *houris* in paradise." "The Islamic martyr is promised many *houris*." "The man was not content to have a *houri* only in an afterlife."

house of cards [HOUS…] a plan or structure vulnerable to collapse. "The Washington journalist's articles were flighty, were like a *house of cards* and needed rewriting." "His claim to happiness was like a *house of cards*—that is, he was lacking emotional support." "The text on the history of ancient Rome was an obscure *house of cards*, the writing was so bad." "He who builds on a bad site commits himself to prison, builds, in effect, a *house of cards*, said Francis Bacon."

hovel [HUVul] a mean and cramped dwelling. "The poor live in *hovels*, the rich in villas and mansions, and the one would go to the furthest extremes to trade places with the other." "Under the highway overpass was a homeless man in a makeshift *hovel* of cardboard trying to stay warm." "Privileged people do not live in *hovels*." "The conservative commented that although *hovels* are a mean place to live in, the poor must bear down and work for something better." Syn.: dump, rat hole, tumbledown shack.

hoyden [HOIdun] a boisterous girl. "The *hoyden* was the beloved of her mother." "The *hoyden* was charming." "The *hoyden* was afraid to love." "The *hoyden* made up for her plumpness with her talent." "The girl was a *hoyden* who liked to play with the boys."

hubbub [HUBub] a tumult; a confused din. "Approaching the door to the school cafeteria, the youth heard a *hubbub*." "The *hubbub* at the sorority did not cease until midnight." "There was *hubbub* at the fast-food restaurant at lunch on Saturday." "Women competing to purchase a doll that just went on sale caused a *hubbub* at the department store." Syn.: commotion, fracas, racket, uproar.

hubris [HYOObris] overbearing pride, often the fatal flaw of protagonists, and a theme in ancient Greek and subsequent literature. "He had to admit to himself later that his vindictive attitude after being denied tenure was due to *hubris*." "His *hubris* led him to revenge." "Only *hubris* led her to continue the law suit." "His *hubris* got him into trouble with the law." *Hubris* is variously literally translated as "insolence" or "violence." Syn.: vanity. Ant.: humility.

hue and cry [HYOO…] a public protest or alarm. "The woman raised a *hue and cry* about a thief." "The police action caused the young protestors to utter a *hue and cry.*" "A *hue and cry* was raised that the bank had been robbed." "The poor man would have raised a *hue and cry* about his poverty if that would have done any good."

hugger-mugger [HUGur MUGur] secrecy; disorder or confusion. "The *hugger-mugger* behind their actions was intended to conceal their fraud." "*Hugger-mugger* prevailed in the army after the enemy's cavalry charge." "The *hugger-mugger* in the high schools was not conducive to learning." "The society of anomie was full of *hugger-mugger.*" "As the proverb says, the *hugger-mugger* of one crime must be concealed with another crime." Syn.: chaos.

humbug [HUMbug] a hoax; deception; nonsense. "Schools of Education are *humbug.*" "The worker's life was *humbug.*" "The police said *humbug* to the man's complaint of harassment." "The conservative pronounced the anti-war demonstrations to be *humbug.*" Syn.: bunkum, claptrap, hokum.

hurly-burly [HURlee BURlee] commotion; uproar. "The *hurly-burly* on the street was about a motor vehicle accident." "He walked in the bar into a scene of *hurly-burly.*" "The touchdown sent the fans into a *hurly-burly.*" "The large security guard put an end to the *hurly-burly.*" Syn.: bustle, chaos, commotion, turmoil. Ant.: peace.

hussy [HUSee] a bold or immoral woman. "She was stigmatized as a *hussy.*" "The *hussy* chased after the man." "The *hussy* stood accused of breaking up a marriage." "The *hussy* had two lovers at the same time." *Hussy* is an alteration of "housewife." Syn.: bitch, Jezebel, slut, strumpet, trollop.

hustings [HUStingz] the site of political speeches; political campaigning. "The American *hustings* of today is the airwaves, television and radio." "His *hustings* was characterized as 'negative.'" "The *hustings* of the third-party candidate was stigmatized as lunatic." "*Hustings* is also called 'running' for office." *Hustings* has its origin in campaigning for the British parliament.

hydra [HIYdru] a thorny and almost irrepressible problem. "Social problems, a discipline in sociology, may impress one as a sort of *hydra.*" "Nuclear weapons are a *hydra* hanging over the head of modern civilization." "Global warming may become another *hydra.*" "Storing nuclear waste is a *hydra.*" In Greek mythology, a "hydra" is a many-headed water serpent slain by Hercules.

hypocorism [hiyPOKurizum] a pet name or its use. "*Ma belle* is a *hypocorism* in French, equivalent to *mein Liebchen, amore,* and *querida* in, respectively, German, Italian and Spanish." "She went by the *hypocorism* 'honey.'" "The boy's *hypocorism* was Mickey." "Edgar Allen Poe (1809-49) used female *hypocorisms* plentifully in his writings." Syn.: nickname.

hypostatize [hiPOStutihz] to reify; to treat an idea, concept, etc., as a distinct or material entity. "To say that society was shocked by his death is to *hypostatize.*" "The sociologist *hypostatized* social structure." "The writer *hypostatized* certain ideas to make a point." "She claimed her opponent in debate *hypostatized* class conflict."

I

iconoclast [ihKONuklast] a person who criticizes cherished beliefs and values. "H.L. Mencken (1880-1956) was an *iconoclast.*" "Because of her *iconoclastic* views she was somewhat of a social leper." "The sociologist was also an *iconoclast.*" "American teachers are not allowed any *iconoclasm.*" Syn.: idoloclast, irreligionist.

ideation [ihdeeAYshun] the process of conceiving. "Schizophrenic *ideation* takes the form of auditory hallucinations." "His *ideation* was oppressive." "Her *ideation* was excessively self-conscious." "The psychology student studied *ideation.*"

idée fixe [eeday FEEKS] (French) an obsessive idea. "After his father was ruined by a Jewish banker, he developed an *idée fixe* about Jews." "His *idée fixe* was so severe that he needed medication." "She had a phobic *idée fixe* about snakes." "His pet dog was part of his *idée fixe.*" "Her *idée fixe* was to win the pageant."

ignis fatuus [IGnis FACHoous] (Latin) a will-o'-the-wisp; something that deceives. "His attempt to find idyllic happiness degenerated into an *ignis fatuus.*" "The extremist idea that anyone can attain great wealth is an *ignis fatuus.*" "In the 1960s his *ignis fatuus* was to be constantly prepared for anything." "It is an *ignis fatuus* to grasp at shadows instead of embracing substance." *Ignis fatuus* means "foolish fire" in New Latin.

ignoble [igNOHbul] mean; base; born as a commoner rather than an aristocrat. "The coal miner was from an *ignoble* family." "His intentions in flirting with the girl were *ignoble.*" "She met an *ignoble* end in an auto accident." "He was *ignoble* and did not belong in high society." Syn.: proletarian. Ant.: noble.

ignominy [IGnuminee] disgrace. "Quisling became an *ignominious* traitor when the Allies retook Norway." "He felt *ignominy* over what he said to his mother." "Her failure to handle college was *ignominious.*" "The journalist's comments were *ignominious.*" Syn.: discomfiture, dishonor, humiliation, infamy, shame. Ant.: honor.

illative [ILutiv] inferential; pertaining to inference. "Sherlock Holmes was engaged in *illative* reasoning." "The witness was not allowed to make an *illative* statement." "His speech was *illative.*" "His reason for taking the herbal medicine was *illative.*" Syn.: empirical, logical, rational, reasonable. Ant.: illogical.

illiberal [iLIBurul] bigoted. "His political outlook was very *illiberal.*" "He had 'old fashioned,' that is, *illiberal,* views on the role of women." "The radical criticized the media as *illiberal,* as having a right-wing bias rather than a liberal bias." "The television station emitted *illiberal* news and propaganda." Syn.: intolerant, narrow-minded, parochial, reactionary. Ant.: liberal.

illimitable [iLIMitubul] limitless. "The power of the American president, according to some observers, is becoming dangerously *illimitable*." "The Croesus had *illimitable* purchasing power." "The country had almost *illimitable* coal." "The man sold his soul to the devil for *illimitable* knowledge."

illusory [iLOOsuree] deceptive. "Although he was loathe to admit it, his progress was *illusory*." "The height of the mountain was *illusory*." "The treacherousness of the river was hidden and *illusory*." "His wealth was *illusory* and tied up in real estate investments." Syn.: beguiling, misleading. Ant.: realistic.

imbroglio [imBROHLyoh] a confused or complicated situation. "His attraction to his girlfriend's friend made an *imbroglio* of the group of friends." "As the proverb says, what an *imbroglio* results when one first tries to deceive." "The woman was able to untangle her daughter's *imbroglio*." "Conspiracy or the charge of conspiracy opens up an *imbroglio*." Syn.: complication, entanglement, mess.

immanent [IMunent] inherent. "There is an *immanent* danger in taking to the road in a car." "She suffered from an *immanent* or inherited disease." "Violence is *immanent* in football." "Fatuous waste of time is *immanent* in overemphasis on educational method." Syn.: implicit, intrinsic. Ant.: foreign.

immiscible [iMISubul] incapable of being mixed. "The two sides of one's family, the mother's kin and the father's kin, are basically *immiscible*." "Oil and water are *immiscible*." "The conservative maintained that equality and prosperity are *immiscible*." "Misanthropy and love are *immiscible*."

immitigable [iMITigubul] incapable of being mitigated. "The cause of emotional depression may be a vicious cycle, but it is not *immitigable*." "The manner that social control affects an individual is *immitigable*, cannot be changed but can be altered as to how it is experienced." "His poverty proved *immitigable*." "Their marital difficulty was *immitigable*."

immolate [IMulayt] to kill as a sacrifice. "Hopefully, human *immolation* will become a thing of the past." "The Bible speaks much of *immolation*." "The Aztecs practiced human *immolation*." "The Romans *immolated* men in the arena."

immure [iMYOOR] to shut in; confine. "Some consider being *immured* in 'solitary confinement' to be cruel and unusual punishment." "The scholar was *immured* with her books." "The German shepherd was *immured* with his master." "The word *immure* is reminiscent of 'intramural,' meaning 'within the walls.'" "The body of the slain president was *immured* in the cemetery."

impalpable [imPALpubul] intangible. "Economics cannot quantify or put a dollar value on many *impalpable* phenomena, such as freedom from air pollution and the recreational value of land." "The philosopher's ideas were *impalpable*." "Evidence for UFOs is thus far *impalpable*." "The human spirit is *impalpable*." Syn.: shadowy, vague. Ant.: palpable, tangible.

impassive [imPASiv] apathetic; phlegmatic. "The masses seem politically *impassive* to some." "The father in that society was *impassive* about family life." "Apparently only men can be *impassive*, if women are considered to be inherently emotional." "His rule depended on the people being *impassive* about some things and excited about others." Syn.: aloof, blank, cool, deadpan, emotionless, expressionless, inexpressive, poker-faced, unemotional, unrevealing. Ant.: expressive.

impecunious [impeKYOOneeus] having no money. "She was *impecunious* and brought her lunch in a brown bag." "The *impecunious* man could not afford a good lawyer or an expert witness to defend his rights in court." "The *impecunious* workers are the losers, and the rich the winners, in the war of everyone against everyone." "Because he was *impecunious* he asked for aid from the senator's office." "He was *impecunious* and hard-up for money throughout his college years." Syn.: indigent, penniless, poor. Ant.: rich.

imperious [imPEEReeus] domineering. "The *imperious* system of justice crushes the poor." "The brute *imperiously* used his girlfriend for sex." "He was *imperious* at work but turned a different face to the public." "It is foolish to try to be *imperious* when you have no power." Syn.: authoritarian, dictatorial, highhanded, overbearing. Ant.: permissive.

imperturbable [impurTURbubul] not easily excited. "The British, atleast compared to Americans, are *imperturbable*." "She was an *imperturbable* woman." "The polo team was *imperturbable*." "The poker-faced man was *imperturbable*." Syn.: calm, collected, composed, cool, level-headed, steady, unflappable, unflustered. Ant.: excitable.

impiety [imPIHitee] ungodliness; an impious act. "*Impiety* in church is considered to be such things as falling asleep and carrying on a conversation." "He was *impious* in church, and could not stop staring at a woman." "The atheist did not believe in *impiety*." "The reprobate was guilty of *impiety*." Syn.: blasphemy, desecration, profanity, sacrilege.

implacable [imPLAKubul] impossible to appease. "Her nymphomania, far from being pleasurable, was of the hysterical, *implacable* type, which hungered as it fed." "The actor's rapacity was *implacable*." "The rube's meanness was *implacable*." "The teenager's need for acceptance was *implacable*." Syn.: unappeasable. Ant.: placable.

impolitic [imPOLitik] inexpedient; unwise. "It was *impolitic* to ask to marry her so soon." "It is *impolitic* to say the first thing that comes to mind." "Bombing in place of diplomacy is extremely *impolitic*." "You could see the *impolitic* frustration on his face." Syn.: inconsiderate, injudicious, undiplomatic. Ant.: astute, politic.

importunate [imPORchunit] persistent in asking for. "The girl *importuned* her mother for candy." "He *importuned* the doctor for an answer to his letter." "He was *importunate* in asking her to marry him." "The man *importuned* his wife about the man who phoned." Syn.: annoying, demanding, persistent, pertinacious, unrelenting. Ant.: satisifed.

imprecate [IMprikayt] to invoke evil upon. "His *imprecations* and thoughts of vengeance did him no good." "Psychology has concluded that *imprecations* and fantasies of violence are ineffective in releasing frustration." "The witch doctor chanted *imprecations*." "It seemed as though the cheerleaders were shouting *imprecations* at the opposing team." Syn.: damn, execrate. Ant.: bless.

impresario [impriSAReeoh] a manager or organizer of public entertainment. "The circus *impresario* stuck his head in the mouth of the pliant tiger to amuse the audience." "The *impresario* attended plays and fairs to look for recruits." "The *impresario* set the salaries of the performers." "The *impresario* hired a woman to jump into a pool from up-high." Syn.: promoter.

imprimatur [impruMAtur] sanction or approval. "The book was denied *imprimatur* and officially censored." "The film received *imprimatur* from the prime minister." "He had no *imprimatur* to arrest the man." "The television series had the *imprimatur* of the critics." Syn.: approbation.

impropriety [impruPRIHitee] the condition of being improper. "The *impropriety* of living off the labor of others did not seem to be recognized by the society." "Talking back to your mother is an *impropriety*." "Using obscenities is an *impropriety*." "Certain things are considered an *impropriety* in reference to minorities." Syn.: immodesty, inaptness, indecency, indecorum, offensiveness, unseemliness, unsuitability. Ant.: appropriateness, propriety.

impudicity [impyooDISitee] immodesty. "He thought the teenager guilty of cheeky *impudicity*." "The *impudicity* towards the elderly was a disgrace, claimed the anthropologist." "The stripper showed *impudicity*." "The judge held him in contempt for *impudicity*." Syn.: boldness, disrespect, impertinence, impoliteness, insolence, presumptuousness.

impugn [imPYOON] to oppose as false; to criticize. "The writer *impugned* 'impression management' as oppressive." "He *impugned* her integrity." "She *impugned* her husband's honesty." "The actions of the priest were *impugned*." "The conservative *impugned* government spending as destructive of useful private spending by business and consumers." Syn.: assail, challenge, dispute, doubt, question.

impute [imPYOOT] to attribute a negative trait to a person. "She was *imputed* as, to put it politely, a lady of the night." "He was *imputed* to be a crime boss." "He did not like being *imputed* to be a sort of monster." "They *imputed* to him a nastiness he did not actually have." "The tactful manner of referring to a brothel for Mrs. Frances Trollope was the *imputation* 'a house of more than doubtful repute.'" Syn.: accuse, allege, charge, implicate.

in absentia [IN abSENshu] in absence. "He was convicted of desertion of the army *in absentia*." "The former dictator was convicted of crimes *in absentia*." "His wife was guilty of adultery *in absentia*." "They celebrated Christmas while the father was *in absentia*."

inamorata [inamuRAHtu] a female lover. "Unknown to his family, the traveling journalist kept an *inamorata* in North Dakota." "At age 17 she was his *inamorata*." "The *inamorata* was a beautiful brunette." "His *inamorata* was named Odill."

inane [inAYN] lacking substance. "The report of the commission was timid and *inane*." "His speech was *inane*, full of 'you know's' and 'like's.'" "The manuscript was *inane* and unpublishable." "The study of 'communications' is *inane*." Syn.: crass, mindless.

inapposite [inAPuzit] unsuitable. "Wearing a tuxedo to a funeral is *inapposite*." "Her remark in class was inappropriate and *inapposite*." "What is *inapposite* in one class is appropriate in another." "The teacher's knowledge was *inapposite* for the course." Syn.: inappropriate, inapt, misguided.

incense [inSENS] to enrage. "The policeman was *incensed* that the man did not obey his order to get on the ground." "In its Latin root, *incense* is related to the word for 'to kindle.'" "He was *incensed* that his wife had been unfaithful." "The man guilty of road rage had been *incensed* that another car pulled in front of him." Syn.: pique, provoke, rankle.

inceptive [inSEPtiv] beginning. "Like an alpine flower, no sooner was her beauty *inceptive* than it began to fade away." "The girl was an *inceptive* woman at age 11." "The restoration work was merely *inceptive*." "The couple made an *inceptive* bequest of money to the library." Syn.: incipient.

inchoate [inKOHit] incomplete. "The study was *inchoate* without an examination of the role of biology." "She felt *inchoate* when her husband left town." "The article was *inchoate*, since it did not discuss class factors." "The man's life was *inchoate* without employment." Syn.: developing, emergent, incipient, undeveloped. Ant.: mature.

incognizant [inKOGnizunt] unaware. "She was *incognizant* of her son's actions when he was awarded a medal." "Her boyfriend was *incognizant* of her pregnancy." "Snug in a cabin, they were *incognizant* of the snowstorm outside." "He was *incognizant* that she was attracted to him."

incommensurable [inkuMENsurubul] having no common measure. "The two works of art were *incommensurable*." "It was *incommensurable*, like comparing a fruit and a vegetable." "The two modes of transportation, a plane or a train, were *incommensurable*." "The two national parks they visited were *incommensurable*." Syn.: incommensurate. Ant.: comparable.

incommode [inkuMOHD] to discommode, inconvenience. "A guest who stays too long *incommodes* his host: As Ben Franklin put it, 'fish and visitors stink in three days.'" "He did not want to *incommode* his friend, but he had nowhere to stay." "The man felt that he was *incommoding* his aunt and uncle." "She was loathe to *incommode* her grandmother." Syn.: bother, disturb, put out.

incongruous [inKONgroous] inconsistent; unbecoming. "His green shirt was *incongruous* with the blue shorts he had on." "The pigtails she wore were *incongruous* with her beauty." "Her embonpoint was *incongruous* with the fashion." "Schizophrenic grimacing is *incongruous*." Syn.: inappropriate, incompatible, inharmonious, odd, unsuitable. Ant.: consistent.

incontinent [inKONtununt] uncontrolled; unable to contain, as sexual desire. "The shy teenager was *incontinent* of talk in one class yet reticent in another." "She developed urinary *incontinence* in old age." "The middle-aged woman's desire for sex was *incontinent*." "The old woman was *incontinent* regarding her own paranoia." Syn.: unrestrained.

incorrigible [inKORijubul] not capable of being reformed. "He was an *incorrigible* womanizer." "The parents acted as though they were impotent and their unruly children *incorrigible*." "The parent of the *incorrigible* four-year-old complained of 'the world's toughest job.'" "His bad psychological habit seemed *incorrigible*." Syn.: dyed-in-the-wool, incurable, intractable, inveterate, irreclaimable, irredeemable. Ant.: tractable.

incubus [INkyubus] something that causes worry or anxiety; something oppressive like a nightmare; a demon said to descend upon and have sexual intercourse with sleeping women. "Her delusion developed into an *incubus*." "His arrest for drunken driving disturbed his sleep like an *incubus*." "She suffered an *incubus* for three weeks after the assault." "Her pregnancy was attributed to an *incubus*, but others in the tribe knew better."

inculcate [inKULkayt] to instill. "The highly regarded teacher *inculcated* her students with a love of geometry." "The uncle *inculcated* his nephew with a love of football." "Sloth and laziness *inculcate* bad habits." "Libraries *inculcate* knowledge and understanding." Syn.: indoctrinate, instruct.

inculpate [inKULpayt] to accuse; to incriminate. "During his testimony he was aware that not many people are formally *inculpated* for perjury." "The minister was *inculpated* for murder." "The youth was *inculpated* as the thief." "They did not know whom to *inculpate* for the arson." Syn.: implicate. Ant.: exonerate.

incumbent [inKUMbunt] already in a given position or office; obligatory. "*Incumbent* members of Congress have many advantages when seeking re-election." "It is felt by certain theorists that it is *incumbent* on the people to be good consumers, to buy and buy again, to keep the nation prosperous." "It is *incumbent* on the poor to go out and be gainfully employed." "The *incumbent* governor won re-election."

incurious [inKYOOReeus] not curious or inquisitive. "One problem with the high school was that the teachers did nothing to stimulate the intellect of their *incurious* students." "The man was *incurious* about the affairs of his neighbors." "The university students were *incurious*." "The chemistry major was not *incurious*." Syn.: apathetic, detached, indifferent, uninterested.

indelicate [inDELikit] rough; socially offensive. "His manners at the reception were *indelicate*." "His wife was temperamental and *indelicate* at the reunion." "He was rude and *indelicate* at the softball game." "The cad was *indelicate* with his date." Syn.: coarse, crude, impolite, indecent, offensive, tactless. Ant.: polite.

Indian summer [INdeeun SUMur] a period of mild weather in the U.S. and Canada in November or December. "He experienced a beautiful *Indian summer*." "The *Indian summer* lasted from December 14 to 18." "During that *Indian summer* the young couple visited the zoo and botanical garden." "On that *Indian summer* day the temperature reached 68 degrees F." "November turned out to be an *Indian summer*."

indigent [INdijunt] impoverished. "He was homeless and *indigent* three years after losing his job." "The *indigent* man relied on state alms." "The *indigent* people of the city viewed their failure as their own fault." "The conservative believed that the *indigent* should receive work, any kind of work, rather than hand-outs." Syn.: destitute, impecunious, penurious. Ant.: rich.

indirection [indiREKshun] aimlessness; deceitfulness. "Sociologists have enumerated the *indirection* of certain codes and laws, such as a law that, rather than exisiting to be obeyed, is meant to be evaded." "The advertising for the mop used *indirection* to try to make it look glamorous." "He used *indirection* to shoplift a watch." "She was not good at *indirection*."

indite [inDIHT] to compose or write. "He *indited* an essay on prehistory." "John Philip Sousa (1854-1932) *indited* 'Stars and Stripes Forever.'" "She *indited* an economics text." "They *indited* a treatise on government regulation of the poor." Syn.: create.

induction [inDUKshun] reasoning or argumentation that is not necessarily true according to its premises. "The scientist's reasoning was *inductive*." "*Induction* is the method of science." "*Induction* sometimes involves making a generalization about a class based on some of its members." "The student's conclusion used *inductive* reasoning."

indurate [INdurayt] callous; (verb) to make hard. "Modern impersonal institutions of mass society have made people *indurate* and selfish, compassionless and indifferent." "He was *indurate* after overexposure to doing good." "The *indurate* man was guilty but felt no remorse." "Why she was *indurate* was unknown." Syn.: cold, cold-hearted, hardhearted, heartless, insensitive, pitiless, uncaring, unfeeling, unsympathetic. Ant.: warmhearted.

inebriated [inEEbreeayted] intoxicated. "It did not take much drink to get her *inebriated*." "Only time can detoxify an *inebriated* person; coffee, a shower and other measures cannot hasten detoxification." "The *inebriated* driver wrapped the car around a tree." "The *inebriated* man fell down the stairs and broke his hip." Syn.: aced, awry-eyed, bamboozled, barmy, basted, bibulous, bladdered, blithered, blitzed, boffed, bosco absoluto, buoyed, catsood, dizzy as a goose, drunk as muck, drunkulent, feeling right royal, fishy about the gills, flummoxed, frazzled, gone Borneo, got a glow on, grogged, half up the pole, higher than Gilroy's kite, hooched, impixlocated, in fine fettle, lit up like Main Street, loaded to the Plimsoll mark, lockjawed, logged, mashed, mawdlin, mizzled, muy tostado, nazy, on the kip, on the shikker, owled, pasted, petrificated, piper drunk, pixilated, pizzicato, polluted, schlockkered, schnoggered, shellacked, shit-faced, spoony, stewed to the gills, swacked, taverned, topsy-boozy, waazooed, wiggy, woofy, zulued. (Spears; see bibliography.)

ineffable [inEFubul] unspeakable; inexpressible. "His face beamed with *ineffable* joy that Christmas morning." "She felt *ineffable* frustration at not being invited to the party." "He showed *ineffable* Schadenfreude after hearing the news." "His anguish was *ineffable*." Syn.: indescribable, inexpressible, unutterable.

ineffaceable [iniFAYsubul] indelible; not capable of being erased. "The embarrassment of having been caught working as a prostitute proved *ineffaceable*, and she moved to another state." "Her sin of stinging a student with an F was *ineffaceable*." "The chairman of the board got away with greed, his actions were not *ineffaceable*." "If you have no friend with whom to commiserate, past embarrassments can prove *ineffaceable*." Syn.: deep-seated, enduring, unforgettable.

ineluctable [iniLUKtubul] inevitable. "Laughter has an *ineluctable* limit." "The clash of the two headstrong brothers was *ineluctable*." "The war became *ineluctable*." "The conservative asserted that some form of failure in life is *ineluctable* and that progress consists of overcoming it." Syn.: inescapable, inexorable, unavoidable, unpreventable. Ant.: avoidable.

inexorable [inEKsurubul] unyielding. "The mother *inexorably* defied the social worker's intrusion into her life." "The Marquis de Sade's meanness was *inexorable*." "She was stubborn and *inexorable*." "The army put up an *inexorable* stand." Syn.: adamant, firm, inescapable, obdurate, relentless, unstoppable. Ant.: flexible.

inexpugnable [inikSPUGnubul] impregnable; incapable of being obliterated. "The old castle, or *Schloss*, on the Rhine had proven *inexpugnable* to invaders, but the wear of centuries finally made it a ruin." "The football team's front line was almost *inexpugnable*." "The Greek monastery set high on a cliff was like an *inexpugnable* fort." "The rural people turned out to be *inexpugnable*, even to carpet bombing." Syn.: invulnerable, unassailable.

inextirpable [inikSTURpubul] ineradicable. "Despite the therapy, her checking compulsion was *inextirpable*." "The termites were *inextirpable*." "Not even modern medicine could alleviate the *inextirpable* illness." "The weeds were *inextirpable*."

in extremis [IN eksTREmees] (Latin) near death. "He knew he was *in extremis* and asked for a priest." "The doctors did everything to try to save the ninety-year-old man *in extremis*." "The unlucky man was *in extremis* with a gunshot wound to the chest." "The victim lay *in extremis* with no hope of recovery." "While *in extremis*, he tried to dictate a will." Syn.: critical, dire, dying, moribund, near-death.

infelicitous [infiLISitus] sad; unfortunate. "The arrival of the police at the Saturday night party was *infelicitous* for the teenage revelers." "Desperate by too quick a sense of constant infelicity" (Bishop Jeremy Taylor). "The bus driver was lonely and *infelicitous*." "The actress was *infelicitous* because her cat was killed." Syn.: dejected, depressed, despondent, forlorn, gloomy, melancholic. Ant.: happy.

infrangible [inFRANjubul] inviolable. "The ex-ruler's political asylum was *infrangible*." "Their marriage was ideal and *infrangible*." "Her sexuality was *infrangible*." "The hallowed ground was *infrangible*." Syn.: firm, inviolate, sacrosanct, unbreakable.

ingénue [ANzhunoo] an artless girl. "He could not help falling in love with the pretty *ingénue* while on vacation in Italy." "The *ingénue* asked her mother how to handle boys." "The *ingénue* married at age 18." "The *ingénue* wore no makeup."

ingenuous [inJENyoous] artless; candid. "The writer's *ingenuous* lecture persuaded many of the validity of his argument." "The entreaty of the politician was not *ingenuous*." "They had an *ingenuous* conversation." "The judge's actions were not *ingenuous*." Syn.: artless, gullible, inexperienced, innocent, trusting, unworldly. Ant.: dishonest.

ingrate [INgrayt] an ungrateful person. "He was such an *ingrate* that he did not attend his mother's funeral." "The arch *ingrates*, with whom all petty *ingrates* have intelligence, are the idle rich." "The *ingrate* did not thank her uncle for the money." "Far from being an *ingrate*, he daily acknowledged his father as his meal ticket."

inimical [inIMikul] hostile. "From its beginning the American establishment was *inimical* to socialism." "Calculation is *inimical* to happiness." "The best is *inimical* to the good." "The resident was *inimical* to the stranger." Syn.: antagonistic, antipathetic. Ant.: amicable.

iniquity [iNIKwitee] wickedness; sin. "Much of the *iniquity* of modern society stems from social institutions, which mediate behavior impersonally rather than personally." "He saw *iniquity* in their careless behavior." "But the iniquity of oblivion blindly scatters its poppy, and deals with the memory of men without distinction to merit of perpetuity" (Thomas Browne). "Ye have plowed wickedness, ye have reaped iniquity" (the Bible, *Hosea*). Syn.: immorality, transgression, wickedness, wrongdoing. Ant.: innocence.

in loco parentis [in LOHkoh paRENtees] (Latin) in the place of a parent. "Professionals have gained control of children and their health and upbringing *in loco parentis.*" "A guardian was appointed for the child *in loco parentis.*" "The court acted *in loco parentis.*" "The law provided for situations *in loco parentis.*"

insalubrious [insuLOObreeus] unhealthful. "It is quite *insalubrious* to lie around all day without exercising." "The habits of the 'couch potato' were *insalubrious.*" "Age had taken its toll and he was so *insalubrious* that he could no longer climb a fence." "A diet of fast food is *insalubrious.*" Syn.: harmful, unhealthy, unwholesome. Ant.: healthy, salubrious.

insensate [inSENsayt] unconscious; foolish. "His *insensate* retribution cost him dearly, as he failed to heed the proverb 'look before you leap.'" "The fall knocked the man *insensate.*" "The *insensate* teachers gave them all a passing grade." "He had an *insensate* urge to lie with her." Syn.: fatuous, heedless, inattentive, thoughtless, unthinking, witless. Ant.: considerate, wise.

insipid [inSIPid] dull; lacking flavor. "The movie was *insipid*, with weak and stilted dialogue." "Lunch at the roadside stand was *insipid.*" "The reheated meat was *insipid.*" "The adventure novel was *insipid.*" Syn.: banal, bland, boring, colorless, dull, inane, tame, unexciting, uninteresting, wishy-washy. Ant.: exciting.

insouciant [inSOOseeunt] carefree. "His childhood was blissfully *insouciant* compared to his adult life." "*Insouciance* is tied up with spontaneity." "He and his friend knew happy *insouciant* times." "Their day in the park was *insouciant.*" Syn.: calm, cool, informal, laid-back, nonchalant, unconcerned. Ant.: terse.

intaglio [inTALyoh] a gem, piece of jewelry, etc., having an incised or sunken design. "The *intaglio* had a date of 1911 on it." "The *intaglio* was made of jade." "Someone stole her beautiful *intaglio.*" "He pawned an *intaglio* for some cash."

intelligentsia [inteliJENTseeu] the class of intellectuals. "The *intelligentsia* opposed the president." "The *intelligentsia* was divided into conservatives, liberals and radicals." "The *intelligentsia* favored abortion rights." "The *intelligentsia* leaned toward atheism." Syn.: cognoscenti.

internecine [inturNESin] mutually destructive; relating to conflict within a group or faction. "As far as basic policy is concerned, Republicans and Democrats do not engage in *internecine* strife." "The battle was an *internecine* slaughter." "The Christians were in an *internecine* struggle." "Their game ended in *internecine* bitterness." Syn.: civil, domestic, internal, pyrrhic. Ant.: nonpartisan.

interregnum [inturREGnum] a gap; a transition period between two rulers. "A few unholy papal *interregnums* saw rival pope's battling for the title *Pontifex maximus*." "Chaos prevailed in the *interregnum*." "In the *interregnum* two would-be emperors struggled for power." "In the *interregnum* Oliver Cromwell (1599-1658) held power." The Latin root of *interregnum* means "between reign." Syn.: hiatus, interruption, interval, lacuna, lag, lapse, pause.

in toto [IN TOHTOH] (Latin) in all; totally. "The estate of his parents was awarded to his brother *in toto*." "The emperor's army was defeated *in toto*." "The accident left him paralyzed *in toto*." "The writer expurgated the manuscript *in toto*."

intransigent [inTRANsujunt] uncompromising. "The noble leader of the counter-insurgent forces who put down the German Peasants' War (circa 1520) was *intransigent* and brutal." "The teacher's *intransigence* about the grade was overruled by the chairman." "The dog was *intransigent* and would not go for a walk." "The journalist was *intransigent* that the story he wrote should be unedited." Syn.: inflexible, intractable, obdurate, obstinate, unbending, unyielding. Ant.: flexible.

inure [inYOOR] to accustom to. "Good habits *inure* one to overcome adversity." "She was *inured* to sleeping late." "The salesman was *inured* to working hard." "They were *inured* to trying to survive socially." Syn.: acclimatize, habituate, harden, season. Ant.: desensitize.

invective [inVEKtiv] abusive denunciation. "American priests are not known for *invective*." "*Invective* is his strong suit." "After reading the notice that he had not gotten the job, the man wanted to go into *invective*." "Hitler went into *invective* at Nuremberg." Syn.: broadside, diatribe, objurgation, tirade, vilification, vituperation. Ant.: approbation, commendation.

inveigle [inVAYgul] to persuade using deceit or flattery. "The defendant's lawyer tried to *inveigle* the jury." "He tried to *inveigle* his boss." "He tried to *inveigle* his girlfriend." "*Inveigling* does not work with some people." Syn.: beguile, cajole, entice, wheedle.

investiture [inVEStichur] the act of investing, as an office or position. "The *investiture* of the queen was attended by much pomp." "The *investiture* took place on a Sunday in May." "Protests accompanied the *investiture* of the chancellor." "The *investiture* was a simple affair." Syn.: inauguration, installation.

invidious [inVIDeeus] offensive. "Comparing persons from different classes is *invidious*." "The magazine was *invidious* to people of color." "The wardrobe malfunction was *invidious* to puritanical right-wingers." "He found her words *invidious*." Syn.: insulting, odious, spiteful.

inviolable [inVIHulubul] incapable of being profaned. "The family of a deceased man is hurt if he is not laid to rest in an *inviolable* manner." "The truth is not always *inviolable*." "The former senator had an *inviolable* reputation." "Her

Ph.D. dissertation was *inviolable*." Syn.: unchallengeable, uninfringeable.
involute [INvuloot] complex or involved. "Every language is *involute* and has unique features, even the so-called primitive ones." "His story of how he became lost was *involute*." "The novel on submarine warfare is *involute*." "Learning Greek can be *involute*." Syn.: intricate. Ant.: simple.
iota [ihOHtu] a very small amount. "He angrily replied that he owed his ex-wife not one *iota* of money." "He exclaimed that there was not one *iota* of truth in what she said." "The conservative asserted that the rich are not one *iota* responsible for the state of the poor." "He got not one *iota* of sleep that night." Iota is the ninth letter of the Greek alphabet. Syn.: bit, scintilla, scrap, smidgen, speck.
ipse dixit [IPse DIKsit] (Latin) an unsupported assertion. "His *ipse dixit* was not well received by people who had heard of his extraordinary claims." "Her statement amounted to an *ipse dixit*." "The conservative stated that evolution theory is an *ipse dixit*." "The encyclopedia listed the teaching as an *ipse dixit*." "Ipse dixit" is Latin for "he himself said it."
ipso facto [IPsoh FAKtoh] (Latin) by that very fact itself. "Her lack of large breasts, *ipso facto*, almost disqualified her from the beauty pageant." "Class position, *ipso facto*, is a large factor in type of crime." "His love for the child *ipso facto* was suspicious." "His guilty feeling *ipso facto* made him uneasy." "By telling him that, *ipso facto*, the man suborned perjury."
irascible [iRASubul] easily angered. "*Irascible* men given to drink should be feared." "After seeing what a vice it was, he overcame his *irascibility*." "Hard work makes people *irascible*." "He was *irascible*, but not a fool." Syn.: bellicose, cantankerous, churlish, irritable, petulant, querulous, testy. Ant.: easy-going.
irrecusable [iriKYOOzubul] unobjectionable; not allowing for rejection. "His treatment of her was *irrecusable*." "His behavior in court was *irrecusable*." "She could not appeal the *irrecusable* decision made by the judge." "The social critic's observations were straightforward and *irrecusable*." Syn.: blameless. Ant.: blameworthy.
irredentist [iriDENTist] a person who advocates the acquisition of his country's lost or allegedly lost land. "Nazi *irredentist* propaganda preceded the annexation of Czechoslovakia in 1938." "*Irredentism* sometimes causes war." "The *irredentist* party sought to invade the country." "The *irredentists* called for a peaceful referendum."
irrefragable [iREFrugubul] undeniable. "That he was mistaken is *irrefragable*." "It is axiomatic or *irrefragable* that the cause of any event lies in history." "The police proved *irrefragably* that he had robbed the bank." "It is *irrefragable* that he won the bank."
irresolute [iREZuloot] indecisive. "People often become *irresolute* when faced with multiple paths to escape danger." "It was an *irresolute*, disastrous decision." "He was *irresolute* when he should have been decisive." "The writer believed that women are *irresolute* compared to men." Syn.: fickle, procrastinating, vacillating, wavering.
irreverence [iREVuruns] disrespect. "*Irreverence* in church or court is frowned

on." "She was *irreverent* with the man but she did not intend to be." "No *irreverence* was implied in his letter." "The men at the stag party were *irreverent*." Syn.: derisiveness.

irruption [iRUPshun] a violent incursion or invasion. "The army *irrupted* into enemy territory." "The burglar *irrupted* into the couple's house." "The guest practically *irrupted* into the host's home." "The *irruption* of the bullet into the victim's body killed him."

Ishmael [ISHmeeul] an outcast. "The *Ishmael* of the Bible was in Abraham's family." "He behaved like an *Ishmael* when his friends turned on him." "He had one true friend and was otherwise an *Ishmael*." "The *Ishmael* wandered the desert for six years." This word is from the Old Testament. Syn.: exile, pariah, recluse.

Ivy League [IHvee LEEG] a group of universities in the Northeast, including Harvard, Yale, Princeton, Columbia, Pennsylvania, Cornell, Dartmouth and Brown. "The lawyer had an *Ivy League* education." "He taught at a small college that was not exactly *Ivy League*." "For some the true value of an *Ivy League* education is the friends and colleagues one makes." "He learned to analyze chemicals at an *Ivy League* university."

J

jabber [JABur] to talk rapidly, unintelligibly or nonsensically. "They could not understand his *jabbering* as the police led him away." "She was still *jabbering* and gesturing as she walked out of sight." "The child was *jabbering* by himself to noone in particular." "The student *jabbered* during the entire class." Syn.: chatter, gabble, prate.

Jabberwocky [JABurwokee] nonsense or gibberish. "What she told the police was *Jabberwocky*." "His Ph.D. dissertation was *Jabberwocky*." "The boy's fibbing to his mother was *Jabberwocky*." "The college instructor's book on court-ordered busing was *Jabberwocky*." From the name of a poem in *Through the Looking Glass,* by Lewis Carroll (1832-98).

jackanapes [JAKunayps] an impudent young man; a whippersnapper. "The *jackanapes* interrupted the colonel's sleep." "He was a *jackanapes* unfit for her company." "The *jackanapes* halted the teacher to ask an impertinent question." "The job of dismissing the employee fell to the *jackanapes*."

jackbooted [JAKbooted] marked by violent cruelty. "The Marquis de Sade (1740-1814) is notorious for having written *jackbooted* novels." "He was mean, but never *jackbooted*." "It is not easy for a woman to be *jackbooted*." "The radical tarred the general as a '*jackbooted* misanthrope.'" Syn.: brutal, harsh, merciless, nasty, pitiless, ruthless, sadistic, savage, vicious. Ant.: benevolent, kind.

Jacobinism [JAKubinizum] extreme political radicalism. "He was involved in the *Jacobinism* of the day." "Their *Jacobinism* sought to abolish all government." "*Jacobinism* was opposed by liberalism." "He joined *Jacobinism* hoping to help bring about equality." After the name of the radicals in the French revolution.

jaded [JAYdid] weary or dull, as from overuse. "In an age of unbelief, the clergy is frequently seen as *jaded*." "We live in a *jaded* age, claimed the social critic." "After a while of binging on candy, her taste buds were so *jaded* that she could not taste it." "The *jaded* priest preferred watching television to preaching." Syn.: exhausted, satiated, surfeited.

jailbait [JAYLbayt] a girl with whom sexual intercourse is statutory rape because of her young age. "The '*jailbait*' got him into trouble." "*Jailbait,* joked the men as she walked by." "The zaftig girl was *jailbait*." "He had sex with the *jailbait* and had to endure the consequences."

jamboree [jambuREE] a noisy celebration. "The *jamboree* in the countryside lasted a week." "They had a *jamboree* in Oregon." "The summer rock *jamboree* became legendary." "Several famous bands played at the *jamboree*." Syn.: festival, gala.

Janus-faced [JAYnusfayst] hypocritical. "The government was *Janus-faced,* variously serving the public and big business." "The politician was *Janus-faced,* only pretending to serve the people's interest." "The multi-millionaire was *Janus-faced*." "The school's policy was *Janus-faced*." Syn.: disingenuous, insincere. Ant.: sincere.

jape [JAYP] to jest; to mock. "The bully *japed* the boy ceaselessly." "The friends sometimes fell to *japing* each other." "The entertainer loved to *jape*." "The group of old men could not get along without constant *japing*." "The *jape* was not made in a spirit of amiability." Syn.: gibe, jeer, scoff, sneer, taunt.

jaundiced [JAUNdist] biased due to resentment or prejudice. "The state's prosecutor was *jaundiced*." "The ad hoc jury was *jaundiced*." "The mayor was *jaundiced* with a class bias." "The view of the social critic was not *jaundiced*." From an Old French word meaning "yellow."

jejune [juJOON] dull, insipid; nutritionally deficient. "She found the weekday *jejune*." "The *jejune* movie had a cumbrous plot." "The mother's *jejune* diet while pregnant led to tragedy: A deficiency of the B-vitamin folic acid caused her child to be born with spina bifida." "That September day was *jejune* for him." "Many illnesses are marked by *jejune* states that may respond to vitamin therapy." Syn.: boring, uninteresting.

jeremiad [jeruMIHad] a lamentation. "He launched into a *jeremiad* of all that he had done for his son." "The social critic's book was called a *jeremiad* for our time." "The college student wrote to the chancellor a letter with a *jeremiad* of complaints and wrongs." "The convict's *jeremiad* was long." After Jeremiah, a Hebrew prophet of the Bible.

jerkwater [JURKwotur] remote and insignificant. "He is from a benighted *jerkwater* town called Valley Park." "He regarded the whole state as *jerkwater*." "Belize seemed *jerkwater* to her." "Their home was in a *jerkwater* area."

Syn.: out-of-the-way.

jerry-build [JERee BILD] to build cheaply and flimsily. "The table was *jerry-built*." "The house was a dangerous place because it was *jerry-built*." "The charity organization was *jerry-built* using two defunct religious groups." "The boys *jerry-built* a clubhouse."

jeunesse dorée [zhoeNES doRAY] (French) wealthy and sophisticated young people. "'Oh, to be part of *jeunesse dorée*,' declared the social critic." "The *jeunesse dorée* inherited their money." "The *jeunesse dorée* did no labor." "She was young, rich and beautiful, a true member of the *jeunesse dorée*."

jew-down [JOO DOUN] (offensive) to drive a hard bargain; to beat down a price. "They walked into the cosmetics store and tried to *jew-down* the prices." "'Your prices ought to be *jewed-down*,' said the customer to the coin dealer." "'You are not allowed to *jew-down* the prices,' said the antiques dealer to the customers." "Someone would always come into the store and try to *jew-down* prices." Syn.: barter, haggle, quibble.

Jezebel [JEZubel] a wicked woman. "A *jezebel* is a stock character in television 'soap' shows." "The *jezebel* was trying to get rich through marriage." "The *jezebel* pursued a married man." "The woman was slandered as a *jezebel* but had a heart of gold." Syn.: hussy, slut, trull.

Jim Crow [JIM KROH] the practice of segregating or discriminating against blacks. "Formal *Jim Crow* was finally overturned in the 1960s." "*Jim Crow* established separate restrooms for whites and blacks." "The crowd of demonstrators protested against *Jim Crow*." "*Jim Crow* barred blacks from eating at the lunch counter." From a song in a black minstrel show (about 1860).

jim-dandy [JIM DANdee] excellent; superior. "He bought himself a *jim-dandy* beach cottage." "He wore *jim-dandy* clothes to the wedding." "She remembered as *jim-dandy* the television commercial in which Santa Claus rode in on an electric razor." "The play about the orphan was *jim-dandy*."

jingoism [JINgohizum] nationalist chauvinism. "The *jingoism* of World War 1 was appalling." The term *jingoism* stems from a stanza by a G.W. Hunt: "We don't want to fight; but by Jingo, if we do, we've got the ships, we've got the men, we've got the money too." "*Jingoism* ran high as the European powers declared war on each other in 1914." "The *jingoists* in the party favored war." "The newspapers were actively *jingoistic*."

jocose [johKOHS] jesting or bantering. "His *jocose* sparring made her laugh." "One is not supposed to be *jocose* at a funeral." "He had a *jocose* winning way." "The servants were not allowed to be *jocose* with the duke." Syn.: facetious, flip, humorous, jovial, witty. Ant.: serious.

Judas [JOOdus] the disciple who betrayed Jesus; a traitor. "He was a *Judas* to his own country." "The *Judas* betrayed his own father to the police." "The *Judas* informed against the leader for 26 pieces of silver." "A *Judas* showed the enemy a route around the guarded pass." Syn.: defector, deserter, turncoat.

junket [JUNGkit] a pleasure trip; a trip by an official that is paid for by the public. "The senator's *junket* caused protest, but perquisites await almost all politicians." "The corporation *junket* caused no protest." "They made a *junket* on corporation expense." "Several politicians went on the *junket*." Syn.:

excursion, outing, spree.

Junoesque [joonohESK] pertaining to a beautiful or elegant woman. "Her *Junoesque* features drew attention wherever she went." "In her 20s she was *Junoesque*, but she aged rapidly in her thirties." "He went to the swimming pool to watch the *Junoesque* women." "She did not win the beauty contest, but Miss Mississippi was *Junoesque*." Syn.: beauteous. Ant.: haggard, ugly.

junta [HOONtu] (also *junto*) a small group of persons that has assumed power. "The *junta* was not a democratic form of government." "For a time one *junta* succeeded another in the unstable country." "The *junta* eventually yielded to democratic elections." "The *junta* set up a secret police."

junto [JUNtoh] a group or committee with political aims; a cabal. "The military *junto* ruled the country." "The dictator gave way to a *junto*." "The *junto* tried to defeat the opposition by shocking the economy." "The *junto* became the basis of a new government." This word is an alteration of *junta*.

juvenescent [joovuNESunt] becoming or making youthful. "Age can be hidden a little, but no actual *juvenescent* cosmetic exists." "The woman looked into *juvenescent* cosmetic surgery." "Because youth is in and age out, they wanted something *juvenescent*." "She would have paid much money for *juvenescence*."

K

kaffeeklatsch [kahFE KLATSH] (German) conversation over coffee. "War was the subject for most of the *kaffeeklatsch*." "The *kaffeeklatsch* of the two women was singularly trivial." "The French and Austrians really love the *kaffeeklatsch*." "He found it impossible to enjoy the *kaffeeklatsch*."

kaput [kaPOOT] broken; demolished; ruined; done for. "After 76,000 miles the car was *kaput* and scrapped at a junkyard." "The boxer was *kaput* after six rounds in the ring." "The last word of The Red Baron (Manfred von Richthofen, 1892-1918) was '*kaput*.'" "When the car's window went *kaput*, its angry owner had to pay $500 to have it fixed."

karma [KARmu] fate or destiny; a distinctive aura or atmosphere. "The *karma* of the new stadium seemed jinxed." "The room's *karma* was heavenly and peaceful." "Feeling bad *karma* in the building, they left quickly." "His *karma* was to live a condemned life in prison." "The *karma* of the couple was wedded bliss." *Karma* is from Sanskrit, in which it originally meant "deed." Syn.: kismet.

katabasis [kuTABusis] a military retreat. "The *katabasis* dragged on for 12 days." "The *katabasis* was a complete route." "The *katabasis* was continued over the sea." "The *katabasis* was accompanied by the slaying of many men."

Katzenjammer [KATsunjamur] (German) a hangover; a state of depression. "The long winter left him in a *Katzenjammer*." "He had a bad *Katzenjammer* on the Sunday after the big party." "She treated her *Katzenjammer* with St. John's Wort." "Unemployment left him in a *Katzenjammer*." In German this word is a compound meaning "cat's misery." Syn.: blues, melancholy. Ant.: joy.

keck [KEK] to retch; to show disgust. "He *kecked* when presented with the idea of spending the weekend with the woman." "He *kecked* on the steak while trying to eat and talk at the same time." "He *kecked* at the idea of reading the book by the monetary economist." "She *kecked* at the thought of kissing the man."

keelhaul [KEELhol] to rebuke severely. "After being caught stealing some candy bars the youth was *keelhauled* by the police." "The father *keelhauled* his son for being lazy." "The student was *keelhauled* for not being prepared for class." "They *keelhauled* and 'grounded' their son for hitting his sister." The original meaning of *keelhaul* is to drag a man attached to a rope in the water behind a ship as punishment.

ken [KEN] knowledge, understanding. "The sportscaster's *ken* did not surpass an eighth-grade parochial education." "His *ken* of geography was inadequate." "His *ken* of Spanish was excellent." "The journalist had great *ken* of a subject he researched for an article—satellite surveillance." This word is reminiscent of German *kennen*, "to know." Syn.: acquaintance, awareness, cognizance. Ant.: ignorance.

kibbutz [kiBOOTS] (Hebrew) an Israeli agricultural commune. "The *kibbutz* practiced socialist collectivism." "Everyone worked at the *kibbutz*." "There was no inequality at the *kibbutz*." "There was social harmony at the *kibbutz*."

kibitzer [KIBitsur] (Yiddish) a person who gives unwanted or unsolicited advice. "The *kibitzer* watched over their game of chess." "The *kibitzer* gave his opinion on her trouble with money." "The *kibitzer* gave his opinion to everyone." "The *kibitzer* was not welcome at the poker table."

kilter [KILtur] good condition; proper form or functioning. "The television was out of *kilter*." "On that Friday his golf game was in *kilter*." "The surgeon's nerves were out of *kilter*." "The softball team was out of *kilter*." The origin of *kilter* is unknown.

kinky [KINGkee] unusual or offbeat, especially sexually. "She dressed for the prom in a *kinky* manner." "The men thought her remark was *kinky*." "The actress in the movie did a *kinky* dance." "A *kinky* scene in the movie had a nude woman riding a motorbike." Syn.: capricious, unconventional, whimsical.

kino [KEEno] in Europe, a cinema. "They religiously went to the *kino* every Saturday." "The *kino* showed a good movie." "The *kino* sold popcorn and candy." "The drive-in *kino* has almost disappeared."

kismet [KIZmit] destiny. "The *kismet* of the protagonist of Franz Kafka's 'The Metamorphosis' as a sort of huge dung beetle is truly miserable." "Occasionally the *kismet* of a person in this world is to be condemned to live on." "His *kismet* was not in his own hands." "The *kismet* of the priest was ostensibly heaven." Syn.: fate, lot, portion.

kitchen police [KITshun PUlees] (abbreviated K.P.) soldiers assigned to work in the kitchen as punishment: *K.P. duty.* "The sergeant threatened the soldiers with *K.P.* duty." "The soldier hated *K.P.*" "*K.P.* is what the dishwasher did for a living." "*K.P.* consisted of peeling vegetables."

kith and kin [KITH AND KIN] acquaintances and relatives. "All *kith and kin* showed up at their barbeque." "*Kith and kin* attended her lavish wedding." "He contacted all his *kith and kin* looking for a job." "He saw no *kith or kin* at church."

kitsch [KITSH] bad taste, especially in art. "He disliked the *kitsch* in the form of birdbaths and tasteless ornaments in his neighbor's yard." "The movie *Love Story* was criticized as sentimental *kitsch.*" "*Kitsch* in the form of abstract art hung on the wall." "The multi-millionaire's art collection was no *kitsch.*" Syn.: frippery, showiness, vulgarity.

kowtow [KOUtou] to act obsequiously. "He was all *kowtow* to the boss." "The peasants *kowtowed* to the khan." "Do not *kowtow* to him, he's a tyrant! said the man to his friend." "Be assertive, not passive or aggressive, and do not *kowtow.*" Syn.: fawn, grovel.

kudos [KOOdos] praise; glory. "The film *Patton* won *kudos*, though one critic noted that the general crowded out all other characters, who were lifeless and monotone." "Her painting received *kudos.*" "The teacher won *kudos* from conservatives for imposing decent standards of grading." "The student received *kudos* from the teacher for knowing the answers." Syn.: acclaim, cachet, commendation, fame, glory, honor. Ant.: disapprobation.

L

lace-curtain [LAYSkurtin] (adj.) aspiring to the middle-class. "He was born to the working-class but had a *lace-curtain* outlook." "The couple was poor but still *lace-curtain.*" "The term *lace-curtain* is reminiscent of 'the American dream.'" "Immigrants to America sometimes quickly became *lace-curtain.*"

lachrymose [LAKrumohs] tearful. "It was a very *lachrymose* funeral." "*Hinc illae lacrimae*" (Terence): "Hence these tears." "She was joyfully *lachrymose* upon the announcement of her name as the prize winner." "The boy turned *lachrymose* on losing the birthday game." Syn.: melancholy, sad. Ant.: gay, joyful.

lackluster [LAKlustur] lacking brilliance; dull. "The figure skater put in a *lackluster* performance at the Olympics." "The two books the late historian wrote after his bestseller were *lackluster.*" "His critique of class society was *lackluster.*" "The administration of the liberal mayor was *lackluster.*" Syn.: faded, lusterless, washed-out. Ant.: brilliant.

laconic [luKONik] concise. "*Laconic* writing is best, but it takes practice." "Lincoln's Gettysburg Address is *laconic* and eloquent." "He wrote a *laconic* short story." "The tales of Edgar Allen Poe and Franz Kafka are *laconic*." Syn.: terse. Ant.: prolix, verbose.

laissez faire [lesay FAR] (French) the doctrine that government should intervene in the economy as little as possible. "*Laissez faire* advocates cannot explain why government war spending revives the economy." "The *laissez faire* economist was actually an ideologue." "The advocate of *laissez faire* favored a huge defense budget." "Some people got rich under *laissez faire* but more got rich under government spending."

lambaste [lamBAYST] to reprimand harshly; to censure. "The journalist was *lambasted* for writing a story on the stinginess of the rich." "The conservative *lambasted* liberal support of abortion." "The black, progressive politician was *lambasted* by Republicans." "The boy was *lambasted* by his mother for biting another boy in school." Syn.: attack, castigate, condemn, deride, excoriate, lay into, reprove, scold.

lambent [LAMbunt] gleaming; effortlessly brilliant. "Mark Twain (1835-1910) had a *lambent* wit, which turned caustic in old age." "She played the piano *lambent*-like." "The wide-receiver had a *lambent* stride." "The beautiful actress had *lambent* grace." Syn.: luminous. Ant.: tenebrous.

landsman [LANTSmun] a person from the same town, region, etc., as someone else. "He and his *landsman* from Germany were good friends." "As if to say it is a small world, the American met a *landsman* acquaintance in Europe." "He and a *landsman* took a charter-bus tour of Western Europe." "They were close friends and schoolmates, which meant they were also *landsmen*." Syn.: compatriot.

languid [LANGgwid] weak; indifferent. "The teacher had a *languid* stutter which challenged the attention span of students." "He was rendered *languid* by the flu." "The essay on prosperity was a *languid* bid for money." "His interest in her was *languid*." Syn.: apathetic, indolent, languorous, lethargic, listless. Ant.: lively.

languor [LANGgur] lassitude. "The unmitigated heat produced *languor* at the July celebration." "Some of Debussy's melodies are marked by dreamy *languor*." "The lotus-eaters were *languorous*." "He was tired and could not overcome *languor*." Syn.: lethargy, listlessness, torpor. Ant.: vivaciousness.

Laodicean [layodiSEEun] indifferent to religion. "The minister tried to counter his assemblage of *Laodicean* church-goers with moral appeals." "The people were *Laodicean* and materialistic." "In a purposeless world she could not help but feel *Laodicean*." "The novelist explored *Laodicean* anarchy." "The *Laodicean* minister killed his wife for insurance money."

lapsus linguae [LAPsus LINGwee] (Latin) a slip of the tongue. "She was the brief victim of a sexual *lapsus linguae*." "According to Confucius, better a slip of the foot than a *lapsus linguae*." "She betrayed her own thoughts in a *lapsus linguae*." "Psychoanalytic quacks make much of the *lapsus linguae*."

largesse [larJES] generous gift-giving; a gift of money. "The new couple thanked him for his *largesse*, but it was only $25." "Those with the most money are capable of the greatest *largesse*." "The upper-class family's *largesse* to its children was a multi-million-dollar trust fund, while nothing was given to charity." "The wealthy family's philanthropy was really no *largesse*, since it did not benefit the poor and merely added to its own fame and 'immortality.'" Syn.: bounty, generosity, liberality, munificence. Ant.: cheapness, parsimony.

lark [LARK] to frolic; (noun) a good-natured prank. "On a *lark* he asked her for a date." "They *larked* on the beach and had a picnic." "Instead of going to school, he played hooky and *larked* at a shopping mall." "She took the *lark* seriously and grew angry." The origin of *lark* is unknown. Syn.: caper, escapade, revel, shines, spree.

larrup [LARup] to wallop. "He was *larruped* by his father for eating the whole cake." "Their car was *larruped* by another car from behind." "The bully met his match in a boy who *larruped* him." "The policeman *larruped* the suspect with a baton." Syn.: clobber, whop.

lascivious [luSIVeeus] lustful. "His *lascivious* behavior in public was an embarrassment." "The *lascivious* man looked at the pornographic magazine." "She was as *lascivious* as a man." "He viewed *lasciviousness* as a useless distraction." Syn.: indecent, lewd, libidinous, salacious. Ant.: prudish.

latitudinarian [latitoodnAReeun] pertaining to liberal-mindedness. "He was *latitudinarian* and opposed a few Catholic practices." "The *latitudinarian* tolerated social differences." "The *latitudinarian* was a political activist." "The *latitudinarian* organization favored the abolition of nuclear weapons." Syn.: free-thinking. Ant.: bigoted, illiberal, narrow-minded.

lazaretto [lazuREToh] a hospital for persons with a contagious disease, as lepers. "The woman believed to be spreading typhoid was confined to a *lazaretto*." "On the South American island was a *lazaretto* for lepers." "The *lazaretto* was staffed by dedicated and self-less nurses." "The doctors at the *lazaretto* were careful to wear protective clothing."

legerdemain [lejurduMAYN] sleight of hand. "Through such *legerdemain* as 'cooking the books' and 'creative accounting,' corporate leaders can enrich themselves." "He had the *legerdemain* of a fast-buck operator, and he was the company's CEO!" "The chancellor's *legerdemain* in manipulating appearances exceeded the propaganda of many other universities." "He carefully watched the gamester's *legerdemain* and noticed that he had secretly palmed the pea." Syn.: trickery. Ant.: honesty, rectitude.

lemma [LEMu] an argument or theme. "The *lemma* of his paper was that the faculty of universities was overstaffed and underworked." "The *lemma* of her book is the laying waste to the environment." "His *lemma* or intent is vague." "The *lemma* in her book was not meant to be publicized." Syn.: subject, theorem, topic.

lenitive [LENitiv] soothing or ameliorating, as a medicine. "The poppy worked its magic, and was *lenitive* for the patient." "Rotting in jail for two months was not exactly *lenitive*, contrary to what the court said." "He found meditation *lenitive*." "She enjoyed a *lenitive* dip in the hot tub." Syn.: tranquil. Ant.: disturbing.

lese majesty [LEEZ MAjestee] a crime against a country's leader; an attack on a custom or belief. "The misanthrope Marquis de Sade committed *lese majesty* against Napoleon." "*Lese majesty* can be a foolish offence." "The writer deliberately engaged in *lese majesty* in examining culture." "*Lese majesty* takes different forms depending on the culture."

lethargic [luTHARjik] sluggish. "The scholar's *lethargic* habits made her physically unfit." "At age 40 he was *lethargic*." "The player-coach was *lethargic* compared to other players." "He was *lethargic* and could not play soccer well." Syn.: indolent, slothful, torpid. Ant.: active, robust.

levity [LEVitee] fickleness. "He was roundly criticized for the *levity* with which he announced the criminal charges." "His *levity* at the dinner table was rebuked by his father." "*Levity* in that situation was inappropriate." "Her *levity* was charming." Syn.: frivolity. Ant.: seriousness.

lex talionis [LEKS taleeOHnis] (also called *talion*) the legal principle of an eye for an eye in the punishment of an offender. "When there is a formal justice system in society, a person should not pursue *lex talionis*." "*Lex talionis* may make the law seem like institutionalized revenge." "*Lex talionis* is more common in tribal society." "The court bowed to *lex talionis* in setting punishment for the convict."

libertine [LIBurteen] a dissolute person. "The Marquis de Sade was one mean *libertine* who hated all mankind." "The *libertine* faced criminal charges." "The *libertine* preferred boys to women." "The *libertine* became notorious." Syn.: debauchee, profligate, roué, voluptuary. Ant.: stoic.

libidinous [liBIDnus] lustful. "She had a *libidinous* appetite for boys and then men." "The *libidinous* man suffered from satyriasis." "The teacher felt *libidinous* toward his female student." "He felt *libidinous* at the wrong times." Syn.: lascivious, lewd, salacious, wanton. Ant.: chaste, pure.

licentious [lihSENshus] lacking moral or sexual restraint. "The bully was *licentious*, a real punk." "He was mean and *licentious*." "The party grew *licentious*." "The fifth-grade class was *licentious*." Syn.: debauched, dissolute, immoral, wanton. Ant.: proper.

liege [LEEJ] a feudal lord or a feudal vassal. "The lord witnessed his *liege* vow loyalty." "The *lieges* were in thrall to the lords." "The *liege* was killed on his horse." "The *liege* system died out with the Dark Age." "The *liege* received in his chamber all the maidens in his province on their wedding night."

limbo [LIMboh] a place halfway between two extremes. "Her inability to pay the rent left her in *limbo*, expecting to be evicted." "They ran out of gas and were stuck in *limbo*." "He painted half the room and then left the customer in *limbo* for the other half." "He paid only part of the bill, leaving the store in *limbo* for the other part."

limpid [LIMpid] free from obscurity; completely calm, worry-free. "The manual was not *limpid* and was hard to understand." "The police found the man they questioned *limpid* and unafraid." "The soldiers performed their duty *limpidly*." "The child was *limpid* even far from home." Syn.: composed, cool, relaxed, serene, tranquil. Ant.: agitated.

lineaments [LINeeumunts] typical features. "The *lineaments* of American society are anomie and rapid social change." "Her *lineament* is a zaftig bust." "The *lineaments* of poverty are lack of choice and sacrifice." "The *lineament* of gluttony is obesity." Syn.: characteristics.

lingua franca [LINGgwu FRANGku] a language used as a means of communication among speakers of other languages. "German is often a *lingua franca* in Central Europe." "The traders used French as a *lingua franca*." "The Africans used Swahili as a *lingua franca*." "English is widespread as a *lingua franca*." In Italian, this term literally means "Frankish tongue."

lionize [LIHunihz] to treat a person as a celebrity. "The actor was *lionized* by his native city after starring in a blockbuster film." "Charles Lindbergh (1902-74) was *lionized* after his solo transatlantic flight." "The Roman general was *lionized* as a hero and the country's savior." "The president *lionized* the scientist who made the great discovery."

lissome [LISum] supple. "Her body seemed *lissome* as she swam in the pool." "The athlete had a *lissome* body." "The couch seemed *lissome*." "The woman who 'worked out' was *lissome*." Syn.: limber, lithe, pliant. Ant.: inflexible, stiff.

litany [LITnee] a recital or monotonous account. "His *litany* of complaints included not having enough money." "His *litany* for things to do sounded like he allowed no room for surprise or spontaneity." "Almost everyday she went through a *litany* of complaints with her husband." "The lecture sounded like a *litany*." Syn.: catalog, iteration, narrative, recitation.

literati [lituRAHtee] the class of literary intellectuals. "Thomas Jefferson (1743-1826) claimed that America first had to establish itself as a nation before it could produce *literati*." "The *literati*, by definition, question what others take for granted." "The *literati* opposed the new government." "America did not produce *literati* until about 1820." Syn.: clerisy, cognoscenti, intelligentsia.

lithe [LIHTH] pliant or limber. "At 180 pounds, she was not exactly a *lithe* athlete." "His build was not *lithe*, and, moreover, he had a bad back." "He was not *lithe* enough to be able to do sit ups." "He lost his *lithe* body to middleage." Syn.: agile, flexible, lissome, nimble, supple. Ant.: stiff.

litotes [LIHtuteez] an understatement using the negative of an assertion: *no athlete; not really ugly; not exactly rich.* "He used *litotes* to make his point." "It can be phrased more delicately if *litotes* is used." "His *litotes* was euphemistic." "*She is hardly rich* is an example of *litotes*." Litotes is a very common figure of speech. It is often used because it can be euphemistic and because it may be hard to phrase something as a positive assertion. *She is hardly an athlete,* an example of a sentence in litotes, thus means "she is cumbersome or fat."

live wire [LIHV...] a vivacious, energetic person. "Her babysitting charge was a *live wire* rather than a shy little girl." "The pupil, a *live wire*, refused to follow directions for the test." "The *live wire* had his own idea for furnishing his room." "The *live wire* made a dynamic quarterback." Syn.: go-getter, high-flier.

locution [lohKYOOshun] phraseology. "The *locution* of people careful with their words avoids 'aren't I?'" "In Spanish it is still good *locution* to use double and even triple negatives." "His *locution* was awkward." "The waitress had good *locution* despite her lack of education."

lodestar [LOHDstar] a star that shows the way; something that serves as a guide. "The caravan followed a *lodestar* on the journey." "The *lodestar* shown brightly in the northern sky." "An old map was their *lodestar*." "The navigator knew how to find the way using a *lodestar*."

Lothario [lohTHAReeoh] a seducer of women. "The actor laughed and admitted that he was no *Lothario*." "The *Lothario* tried to get his coworker into bed." "The *Lothario* finally got married." "The *Lothario* was also a masher." Syn.: Don Juan, womanizer.

lotus-eater [LOHtus EEtur] an indolent sybarite. "The *lotus-eaters* of this world are in the leisure class." "The *lotus-eater* never went hungry." "The *lotus-eater* never had a job." "The *lotus-eater* enjoyed luxury." From classical mythology.

lout [LOUT] an oaf. "She had a negative opinion of her son-in-law, whom she labeled a *lout*." "The bumptious *lout* was ill at ease with his friend's family." "He was a *lout* and a cad." "The *lout* lived in a menage-à-trois." *Loutish* is the adjectival form of "lout." Syn.: dullard, fool.

lubricity [looBRISitee] salaciousness; fleetingness. "His reputation for *lubricity* and sexual deviance shocked his middle-class neighbors." "His *lubricity* got a girl into trouble." "Women are not generally allowed *lubricity*." "He finally realized that he was guilty of *lubricity*." Syn.: lewdness, wantonness.

lucubrate [LOOkyubrayt] to study hard, especially at night. "All the time his censorious parents thought he was sleeping, he was actually *lucubrating*." "She crammed, *lucubrated* all night, before the big exam." "The scholar enjoyed *lucubrating*." "The high school student never *lucubrated*."

lugubrious [looGOObreeus] excessively gloomy or mournful. "Whether he 'cared' was doubtful, but it is certain that he affected *lugubrious* airs at the funeral." "The *lugubrious* old woman was a ludicrous spectacle in the town." "The teenaged boy felt *lugubrious*." "The man was *lugubrious* about prospects for happiness." Syn.: dejected, disconsolate, doleful, melancholy, sorrowful. Ant.: cheerful, optimistic.

luminary [LOOmuneree] an eminent person, especially a noted intellectual. "The *luminaries* at Brook Farm (West Roxbury, Massachusetts) included Nathaniel Hawthorne (1804-64) and Herman Melville (1819-91)." "The presidents of the 20th century were not really *luminaries*." "The *luminary* attracted a crowd wherever he went." "He was famous but not really a *luminary*." Syn.: celebrity, leading light.

lummox [LUMuks] a clumsy, stupid person. "He was maligned as a *lummox*." "The so-called *lummox* was no good at sports." "The *lummox* was illiterate." "The *lummox* had a low I.Q." The origin of *lummox* is unknown. Syn.: dolt, klutz.

lumpen [LUMpun] pertaining to the lowest class of society, to down-and-out people. "They were *lumpen*, for whose behavior, allegedly, there was no accounting." "The *lumpen* poor were desperately trying to improve their lot." "The *lumpen* people wore shabby clothes." "The *lumpen* people were very poor." This term comes from the word *Lumpenproletariat,* a German coinage, with the word *Lump* meaning "ragamuffin."

lunatic fringe [LOOnutik FRINJ] a derogated group holding or allegedly holding extreme views. "The conservative accused the socialist of being in the *lunatic fringe.*" "The *lunatic fringe* of the right-wing is probably libertarians or neo-Nazis." "The social critic branded prominent 60s radicals as the *lunatic fringe.*" "The *lunatic fringe* exploited the media."

lunker [LUNGkur] something very large of its kind; a very large fish, especially a bass. "The fisherman reeled in a *lunker.*" "The anglers were after a *lunker.*" "The hiker's eyes grew wide when he saw the *lunker* bear." "The *lunker* bass was a state record."

lush [LUSH] an alcoholic. "He was a *lush* without hope." "The *lush* went to the A.A. meeting." "The *lush* was treated with counseling, B vitamins and a minor tranquilizer." "The *lush* was put in the chemical dependency unit." Syn.: drunkard, tippler.

lustration [lusTRAYshun] a ceremonial purification. "After a week in jail she took a bath as though it were a *lustration.*" "The *lustration* felt good to the man." "The baptism was also a *lustration.*" "The *lustration* did not take very long."

M

macabre [muKAHbru] gruesome. "The burial catacomb of Paris was *macabre,* with thousands of skulls lining the path." "The *macabre* is at the center of many of Poe's stories." "The room held *macabre* secrets." "The walk down the chamber was *macabre.*" Syn.: ghastly, hideous, morbid.

macaronic [makuRONik] pertaining to a word with both Latin and vernacular parts; jumbled. "Some newly-coined scientific words are *macaronic.*" "Some grammarians object to modern *macaronic* coinages of Latin and Greek syllables." "The quilt they made was *macaronic.*" "The language of the report was *macaronic.*" Syn.: hodgepodge.

Machiavellian [makeeuVELeeun] marked by unscrupulous politics or ethics. "Francis Bacon has gone down in history as *Machiavellian,* as the 'wisest, brightest, meanest of mankind.'" "He was *Machiavellian* in his pursuit of business success." "The business and politics of the robber barons were *Machiavellian.*" "We are much beholden to Machiavel and others that write what men do, and not what they ought to do" (Francis Bacon). Niccolò Machiavelli (1469-1527) was an Italian statesman and author of *The Prince,* in which morality is displaced by political expedience. Syn.: expedient, manipulative, opportunistic, unprincipled. Ant.: principled.

machinate [MAKunayt] to contrive or plot with evil intent. "His political maneuvering was seen by the rival candidate as *machination*." "He thought up various *machinations* for vengeance, but rejected them all." "Hamlet *machinated* a play to draw out his suspicion of the king." "His *machination* led to prosecution for obstruction of justice." "All her *machinations* did not lead to greater social success, to her disappointment." Syn.: scheme. Ant.: entreat.

machismo [muCHIZmo] aggressive masculinity. "His *machismo* turned off sensible women." "His *machismo* was out of place at the restaurant." "The juvenile gang showed off its *machismo*." "The brothers' *machismo* led them to fight each other." Syn.: chauvinism, manliness, virility.

Machtpolitik [MAKHpolitik] (German) power politics, especially the use of force. "Tens of thousands of people marched in protest against the war and *Machtpolitik*." "The dictator wielded *Machtpolitik*." "The Allies defeated the *Machtpolitik* of the Nazis." "*Machtpolitik* crushed small countries."

maelstrom [MAYLstrum] a large, powerful whirlpool; a turbulent state of affairs. "Edgar Allen Poe wrote a short story called 'A Descent into the Maelstrom.'" "Their ten children made life in the house a *maelstrom*." "A *maelstrom* broke out when tickets were running out and the crowd was surging forward." "The ship steered a course that avoided the *maelstrom*." Syn.: bustle, fluster, tumult, turbulence, turmoil.

magnifico [magNIFukoh] a grandee; a Venetian grandee. "The *magnifico* was the arbiter of justice in the entire republic." "The *magnifico* was very rich, though not democratically elected." "He was widely recognized as the *magnifico* of the city." "The city-state had never had such a powerful *magnifico* as the one then in power." Syn.: blue-blood, Brahmin, nobleman, patrician.

magniloquent [magNILukwunt] spoken or done in a grandiose manner; pompous. "The politician gave a *magniloquent* speech." "His behavior after promotion to dean was rather *magniloquent*." "Her defense of patriotism was either eloquent or *magniloquent*." "Without intending it he behaved *magniloquently*." Syn.: bombastic, inflated, self-important, stuffy. Ant.: calm, cool, down-to-earth.

magnum opus [MAGnum OHpus] a great work, especially the best work of a writer or artist. "The baroque palace was the architect's *magnum opus*." "*The Grapes of Wrath* was the *magnum opus* of John Steinbeck (1902-68)." "The music of Tchaikovsky (1840-93) forms the *magnum opus* of ballet." "The anthropologist regarded his theory of the societal following as his *magnum opus*."

magpie [MAGpih] a chatterbox. "Women are said more often to be a *magpie* than men." "He wished the *magpie* would shut up for once." "He bitterly referred to his wife as a nagging *magpie*." "He was reticent, no *magpie*." Syn.: chatterer.

major-domo [MAYjurDOHmoh] the chief steward; a butler. "The *major-domo* answered the door at the mansion." "At the lord's estate he was *major-domo, in charge of 25 servants." "The *major-domo* was smarter than his master." "The *major-domo* had no expectance of better things."

malaise [maLAYZ] a sense of physical weakness; a vague feeling of uneasiness.

"The antidepressant fluoxetine relieved his *malaise.*" "He suffered from *malaise* for 48 hours, during which he got no sleep." "The athlete overcame his *malaise* by psyching himself up." "Due to *malaise* he could not go on playing tennis." Syn.: anxiety, disquietude, nervousness. Ant.: calm, cool, ease.

malapropism [MALupropizum] the misusage of words with a ridiculous effect. "His favorite *malapropism* came from a television program: 'There's a reason clichés survive—they're true.'" "Her words contained a notable *malapropism*: saying 'out-laws' instead of in-laws." "The nice old woman often spoke a *malapropism.*" "The otherwise intelligent student committed a *malapropism* by mispronouncing 'denouement.'" After Mrs. Malaprop, a character in *The Rivals* (1775), a comedy by Richard Sheridan (1751-1816). Syn.: solecism.

malapropos [malapruPOH] inappropriate. "Her archaic smile at the funeral was *malapropos.*" "To say the least it is *malapropos* to wear a swim suit to class." "His remark to the married woman was *malapropos.*" "He should not have done it, it was *malapropos.*" Syn.: improper. Ant.: fit, suited.

malediction [maliDIKshun] slander. "A legal joke says that a *malediction* against someone may bring a suit for 'definition of character' (instead of defamation of character)." "The politician's ad came close to personal *malediction.*" "The *malediction* was mean-spirited." "The *malediction* cost him plenty." Syn.: imprecation. Ant.: complement.

malefactor [MALufaktur] evil-doer. "The radical claimed that *malefactors* of inherited wealth have by no means disappeared." "The financial *malefactor* had his critics, but also a few apologists." "The president spoke of *malefactors* of great wealth." "The *malefactor*, to put it rudely, had his victim by the balls." Syn.: criminal, miscreant, wrongdoer. Ant.: benefactor.

maleficent [muLEFisunt] evil. "Much that is *maleficent* in criminal justice is owing to the impersonality of mechanisms that are supposed to dispense justice." "It's an evil, it's *maleficent*, he claimed, afterwards swearing once again that he would not let it bother him." "*Maleficence* is the product of treating as abstract that which is concrete." "The sociologist asserted that impersonal social institutions are *maleficent.*" Syn.: corrupt, malevolent, vicious. Ant.: salutary.

malfeasance [malFEEzens] an illegal act by a public official. "Accepting $200,000 from the utility company was not technically *malfeasance* for the Congressman." "Francis Bacon (1561-1626) took a bribe as a judge and was guilty of *malfeasance.*" "The *malfeasance* was reported in the newspaper." "He was sent to prison for *malfeasance.*" Syn.: breach, malefaction. Ant.: benefaction, welfare.

Malthusian [malTHOOzeeun] pertaining to the theory of Thomas Malthus (1766-1834) that population tends to increase faster than the resources to support it, and that the resulting overpopulation causes war, famine and disease. "*Malthusianism* was popular in the 19th century and is still a force today." "The scholar researched Marx's view of *Malthusianism.*" "*Malthusianism* may be part of the explanation of poverty in late-modernizing countries." "What *Malthusianism* cannot explain is the maldistribution of the wealth."

malversation [malvurSAYshun] misconduct in public office. "The media are very concerned with trivial *malversation* by members of Congress." "The *malversation* forced her to resign." "Viewed from one angle his *malversation* was harmless." "The governor's *malversation* set off a great scandal." Syn.: malfeasance.

mammon [MAMun] riches considered as an evil influence. "The radical claimed that those with *mammon* exploit common workers." "The minister decried the addiction to *mammon in sudore vultus alienii*—in the sweat of other men's brows." "*Mammon* is supported by mind-numbing work." "The conservative saw nothing wrong with having *mammon*." Syn.: lucre.

mana [MAna] a supernatural force in a person or object believed to give one power; authority. "The Maori people believed in *mana*." "He had no *mana* with which to detain the man." "The Polynesians ascribe much *mana* to their chiefs and gods." "The islander acted as though he had *mana*, and if he actually did not before his pretension, he perhaps actually did afterwards."

man about town [MAN...] an urbane, socially active man. "He was well-known as a sort of *man about town*." "The *man about town* was opposed to the unequal distribution of wealth." "The *man about town* was shot in an armed robbery." "The *man about town* supported himself through the charity of socialites." Syn.: boulevardier.

man Friday [MAN FRIHday] a male employee with general duties. "The *man Friday* supervised the other servants." "He had a *man Friday* who did such work." "He dismissed his *man Friday* for being drunk too often." "The industrialist had a *man Friday*." After a character in *Robinson Crusoe*, a novel by Daniel Defoe (1660-1731).

manful [MANful] full of manly vigor; resolute. "They say a man is not *manful* until he has sex with a woman and thereby 'proves' himself." "He made a *manful* decision to continue the struggle rather than give up." "He was *manful* at the difficult funeral, while women cried." "The shrewd teacher acted *manful* and kept discipline in the class." Syn.: mannish, masculine.

mangy [MAYNjee] mean; squalid. "The *mangy* burg had nothing to recommend itself except several fast-food restaurants." "It was a *mangy* trick to pull." "The house was *mangy* and small." "The poor *mangy* dog was underfed and in need of a bath." Syn.: shabby, sordid.

Manichean [manuKEEun] pertaining to a dualistic religious system dating from the third century A.D., composed of elements of various religions, and viewing the world as a contrast of good and evil. "The *Manicheans* were declared heretics by Rome." "The *Manicheans* practiced meditation and mysticism." "He learned to go in a trance from a *Manichean* mystic." "*Manicheanism* spread through Persia."

Manifest Destiny [MANufest DEStinee] the 19th century doctrine that it was the destiny of the U.S. to take possession of the North American continent. (See also Monroe Doctrine.) "*Manifest Destiny* was maligned as imperialism by radicals." "The conservative asserted that *Manifest Destiny* was natural and reasonable." "The rapid spread westward of the Americans was guided by their belief in *Manifest Destiny*." "The teacher failed to discuss *Manifest*

Destiny."

manna [MANu] divine or spiritual food; something of value received unexpectedly. "He regarded his benefit, his only source of income, as *manna* from heaven." "His grandmother willed to him *manna*, as he regarded the $50,000." "The Melanesian tribesman eagerly ate the *manna*." "He used the *manna*, the grant from the government, for support of his scholarship." This term comes from the Old Testament. Syn.: blessing, boon, godsend.

man on horseback [MAN...] a military man who, posing as the savior of the country, assumes dictatorial power during a crisis. "The *man on horseback* took power during the revolution." "He swore to the people that he was not an autocratic *man on horseback*." "The conservative asserted that there would always be a *man on horseback* in nondemocratic countries." "Napoleon is the classic *man on horseback*."

manqué [manKAY] (French) having failed; unfulfilled. "His desire for love was *manqué* until age 30." "The artist's life was *manqué*, since she wanted fame and fortune." "The widowed middle-aged woman felt *manqué*." "The obese *manqué* woman ate in order to cover the void in her life."

mansuetude [MANswitood] mildness or gentleness. "After so much hardship, he embraced the *mansuetude* of humanity." "The beautiful June night breathed *mansuetude*." "The *mansuetude* of her young skin was lovely." "The *mansuetude* of the summer morning contrasted with the storm the previous night."

mantra [MANtru] in Hinduism, a phrase or formula used in prayer and incantation and believed to possess divine magic. "The psychiatrist wondered whether a *mantra* might develop into auditory hallucination." "The swami invoked a *mantra*." "The *mantra* of the group was 'live and let live.'" "His *mantra* for pulling through difficulty was 'have courage and die only once.'" From a Sanskrit word.

manumit [manyuMIT] to liberate from slavery or servitude. "He was part of a group *manumitted* by an act of parliament." "*Manumission* did not come easily." "The slaves were *manumitted* by the president." "The South and the North fought over secession and *manumission*."

mare's nest [MARZnest] a fraud or hoax that at first deceives one; an extremely complicated situation. "The job hunter ran into an occupation too good to be true, a *mare's nest*." "What at first seemed a windfall was actually a *mare's nest*." "During moving the family ran into a *mare's nest* as to where to put all their belongings." "The *mare's nest* proved hard to put in order." "The discovery of gold turned out to be a *mare's nest*." Syn.: deception, fake, humbug, sham.

marquee [marKEE] a projection above a theater entrance with a sign indicating the name of the show and its star or stars. "The actors argued over who would be listed on the *marquee*." "The *marquee* names in the business brought in the audience." "The modern *marquee* had neon lights." "She was thrilled on seeing her name in big letters on the *marquee*."

martinet [martuNET] a rigid disciplinarian. "The army veteran never stopped denouncing the *martinets* he encountered in the service." "The radical criticized boot camp *martinets* as unnecessary bullies." "The marine recruit who refused to obey the *martinet* was discharged from the military." "Even the woman drill master for female recruits was a *martinet*." After a French general of the 17th century.

martyrize [MARturihz] to make a martyr of; to torment. "The mean misanthrope *martyrized* his rival." "The dominant class *martyrized* minorities." "The malign man *martyrized* his unfortunate German shepherd." "The *martyrized* saint was burnt at the stake." Syn.: crucify, persecute, torture.

Marxism [MARKsizum] the political doctrines of Karl Marx (1818-83) and Friedrich Engels (1820-95), featuring class conflict, surplus value and dialectical materialism. "*Marxism* swept the country." "Soviet-style *Marxism* was not what Marx had in mind." "*Marxism* is basically superficially rejected by Americans, but that rejection is not a deep-seated intellectual conviction." "The conservative claimed that *Marxism* was on the wane."

masher [MASHur] a man who propositions women, especially those whom he does not know. "The *masher*, though found everywhere, is said to be particularly common in Latin America." "After a first dance, he propositioned her, and then she slapped the *masher* in the face." "The *masher* was rejected by the woman." "The *masher* was not appreciated at the party." "He was more a *masher* than a Casanova."

Mason-Dixon line [MAYsun...] the boundary between Maryland and Pennsylvania, partly surveyed by men named Mason and Dixon, and popularly regarded as the dividing line between the North and the South (Dixie). "General Sherman crossed the *Mason-Dixon line* to attack the Confederates." "The carpetbagger crossed south over the *Mason-Dixon line* to seek his fortune." "Mason and Dixon made their survey of the *Mason-Dixon line* in the 1760s." "Yankees were not usually welcome over the *Mason-Dixon line*."

matriculate [muTRIKyulayt] to enroll, especially in a college or university. "She *matriculated* into Yale." "The young man *matriculated* into the college as a high school senior." "Because she was handicapped, *matriculation* was difficult." "Because he needed a degree quickly, he *matriculated* into an Internet 'university.'" Syn.: register.

matter-of-course [MATuruvKORS] expected or inevitable; accepting things as if they were inevitable. "They live *matter-of-course* but they do not have to conform with so little thought." "She was happy experiencing life *matter-of-course*." "*Matter-of-course* life was not for him." "He more and more wanted to experience things *matter-of-course*." Syn.: ineluctable, inescapable.

matutinal [muTOOTunul] pertaining to the morning. "A chief *matutinal* pleasure is to awaken peacefully after a night of troubles." "He who wishes to get much business done must get an early *matutinal* start." "The *matutinal* storm was violent." "The college student prepared for a *matutinal* exam."

maudlin [MODlin] tearfully sentimental. "The problem with a *maudlin* movie is that the self-consciousness it engenders hinders viewing satisfaction." "They seemed *maudlin* but not really mournful." "The *maudlin* musical play had an overflow crowd." "Goering and Hitler displayed an almost maudlin concern for the welfare of animals" (Aldous Huxley). Syn.: lacrimose, mawkish.

Ant.: cheerful, uplifting.

maunder [MONdur] to talk or wander aimlessly. "His speech went off on a tangent and *maundered* aimlessly." "She went off one afternoon in the car, *maundering* through the suburbs without care." "The drunk man's speech *maundered*." "They *maundered* through the park." Syn.: digress, ramble, straggle, stray.

maven [MAYvun] an expert on everyday matters. "She was a *maven* of cooking." "He was a *maven* in numismatics." "He was a sports *maven* and a walking encyclopedia of baseball." "As a child he was a *maven* of hockey, a strictly working-class sport." Syn.: aficionado, authority, specialist.

maw [MO] a cavernous opening that seems to gape voraciously. "Into the army's *maw* went the produce of the nation." "Her *maw* devoured her husband's savings." "The *maw* of the rich gulps down the lion's share of the GNP." "The *maw* of time annihilated his happiness at last."

mawkish [MAUkish] excessively sentimental. "The painter went through a *mawkish* period of reflection but returned to what is considered 'normalcy.'" "The *mawkish* romance novel had a readership consisting entirely of females." "The film is *mawkish* ('love means never having...')." "*Touched By an Angel* was *mawkish*." Syn.: lachrymose, maudlin. Ant.: realistic.

May Day [MAY DAY] the first day of May, the occasion of various celebrations, including the Maypole, and socialist demonstrations. "The *May Day* of Europe is not very similar to America's Labor Day." "*May Day* is sometimes confused with the distress call '*m'aidez*,' French for 'help me!'" "The *May Day* celebration included fertility rituals." "The *May Day* in France featured speeches and demonstrations by communists and socialists."

McCarthyism [muKARtheeizum] the attempt to limit dissent or political criticism by claiming it is communistic or unpatriotic. "*McCarthyism* has a vast chilling effect on freedom of speech." "The president used *McCarthyism* to chasten the media." "The attack on *McCarthyism* was branded unpatriotic." "The conservative claimed that *McCarthyism* was only half bad and had good intentions." After Senator Joseph McCarthy (1909-57), the notorious investigator of alleged communist infiltration of the government.

McCoy [muKOI] the genuine article or person: *the real McCoy*. "He bought the real *McCoy*, not an imitation." "The *McCoy* himself showed up at the store's grand opening." "The real *McCoy* sent him a letter." "She had the real *McCoy*, a genuine Monet, not a copy." After Kid McCoy, real name Norman Selby (1873-1940), American boxer.

mea culpa [MEEu KULpu] (Latin) my fault; an admission of error or fault. "He issued a *mea culpa* saying that they had put the wrong man in prison." "The judge, in a *mea culpa*, stated that he should have recused himself." "The media reported it as a sort of *mea culpa*." "He gave a *mea culpa* in court and allocuted to murder."

meal ticket [MEEL TIKit] someone on whom one is dependent for a livelihood. "The scholar knew better than to criticize his *meal ticket*." "His *meal ticket* was his late aunt's pension." "He made a *meal ticket* out of 'skewering radicalism.'" "The U.S. army was the poor man's *meal ticket*."

mealy-mouthed [MEElee MOUTHD] not using direct and forthright language. "The *mealy-mouthed* teacher could not explain why teaching the variable-case prepositions was a 'waste of time.'" "The writer at one time, in his inarticulate teens, used *mealy-mouthed* language." "She was never *mealy-mouthed* with her mother." "The suspect was *mealy-mouthed* with the police." Syn.: devious, diffident.

megalomania [megulohMAYneeu] an obsession of grandiosity. "The political candidate was afflicted with *megalomania*." "The woman with *megalomania* made up ideas for bringing fame and power to herself." "The depressed man suffered from *megalomania* and found it hard to enjoy life." "*Megalomania* is sometimes considered a psychiatric disease."

megrims [MEEgrimz] depression. "He developed *megrims* after losing contact with his friends." "A single stressful event in his life led to *megrims*." "She suffered post-partum *megrims*." Syn.: blues, dejection, melancholy. Ant.: optimism.

melancholia [melunKOHleeu] depression. "He took paroxetine, an SSRI antidepressant, for *melancholia*." "*Melancholia* involves the neurotransmitter serotonin, though other important neurotransmitters have a role in the illness." "The psychiatrist approached *melancholia* as a nutritional problem and told patients to take B vitamins, including a handful of folate." "He was diagnosed with *melancholia*, also technically known as 'major depressive disorder.'" Syn.: blues, melancholy.

meliorism [MELyurizum] an optimistic doctrine or belief that the world is growing better. "The liberal politician's *meliorism* came down in the end to resignation." "All is for the best in this the best of all possible worlds is a *melioristic* idea." "*Meliorism* is opposed to pessimism." "His philosophy of *meliorism* could not explain world events." Syn.: optimism. Ant.: pessimism.

mellifluous [muLIfloous] sweet-sounding. "The poetry of John Keats is *mellifluous*." "The noise from the street could actually be peaceful and *mellifluous*." "The woman's voice was *mellifluous*." "The drone of the bees was *mellifluous*." Syn.: dulcet, melodious. Ant.: discordant, jarring.

mellow [MELoh] genial or laid-back. "He was not *mellow*, but, on the contrary, sullen and tense." "He was *mellow* just lying there listening to music." "His *mellowness* was accompanied by thought when left to his own devices." "He loved the *mellow* yellow lights of the frozen custard store." Syn.: agreeable, relaxed. Ant.: uptight.

melting pot [MELTing POT] a country or condition in which many peoples of diverse background are assimilated to the host culture. "The '*melting pot*' somehow resulted in social homogeneity, as expressed in 'they're all the same!'" "There are many *melting pot* nations in the world, such as Canada, South Africa and Australia." "In some other *melting pot* cultures the Old World language and customs were largely kept by colonies of immigrants." "It was a *melting pot*, however, that demanded conformity."

memento mori [muMENto MOHRee] (Latin) "remember that you must die." "There are signs of *memento mori* all around us—cemeteries, the obituary pages, black clothes, hearses, cenotaphs, and so forth." "*Memento mori,* he shouted, 'and live every day as though it would be the last.'" "*Memento mori* means to an Epicure seize the day." "A sign saying *memento mori* hung on the philosopher's wall."

mendacious [menDAYshus] untruthful. "His *mendacious* resume listed an employment position he never had." "His *mendacious* habit had others mistrusting him." "Her *mendacity* finally got her into trouble." "His whole way of life was *mendacious*." Syn.: deceitful, prevaricative. Ant.: ingenuous, straightforward.

mendicant [MENdukunt] living on alms; a beggar. "The man was a *mendicant* because there were no good, available jobs in society." "The *mendicant* was begging for money on the street." "The *mendicants* ate in the soup kitchen." "The *mendicants* were polite and did not want to impose on anyone."

mens sana in corpore sano [MENS SAna...] (Latin) "a healthy mind in a healthy body." The idea that a fit body will assure emotional health. "He jogged one hour every morning, believing in *mens sana in corpore sano*." "He put his faith in vitamins and *mens sana in corpore sano*." "The principle of *mens sana in corpore sano* suggests that overindulgence causes emotional harm." "The medical researcher sought to disprove the concept of *mens sana in corpore sano*."

Mephistopheles [mefiSTOFuleez] the devil in the legend of Faust (a man who sells his soul to the devil in exchange for power and sensuous pleasure). "The best version of *Mephistopheles* and Faust is by Johann Wolfgang von Goethe (1749-1832)." "Faust eventually wins back his soul from *Mephistopheles*." "*Mephistopheles* is also called Mephisto." "Besides *Mephistopheles* legend has it that there are six other chief devils." Syn.: demon, satan.

mephitis [muFIHtis] a stench. "The *mephitis* from the bathroom was unbearable." "A terrible *mephitis* arose from the landfill." "The trash can emitted a *mephitis* that could not be washed away." "His sneakers gave off a *mephitis*."

mercurial [murKYOOReeul] changeable; flighty. "He had a *mercurial* temper that frightened those around him." "The weather at the airport was *mercurial* in winter." "She was fickle and *mercurial*." "He was *mercurial* that day." Syn.: capricious, erratic, volatile, wavering. Ant.: imperturbable, settled, steady, stolid.

meretricious [meriTRISHus] vulgarly attractive. "The neon signs in the neighborhood were a *meretricious* presence." "The abstract art on the walls was *meretricious*." "The girl's outfit was *meretricious*." "The student's room was *meretricious*." Syn.: flashy, gaudy, mangy, tawdry. Ant.: inconspicuous, plain.

mésalliance [mayZALeeuns] (French) a marriage with someone of lower status. "A *mésalliance* of an upper-class woman and a working-class man is the rarest type of marriage." "The *mésalliance* showed trouble from the beginning." "The celebrity's *mésalliance* with a working-class man was doomed to fail." "The *mésalliance* was between a maid and a millionaire." "The *mésalliance* between the waitress and the banker ended in divorce." Syn.: misalliance.

mestizo [meSTEEzoh] a person of mixed blood, especially in Spanish America. "The *mestizo* was born to peasants." "The country's *mestizos* were well-integrated into the governing class." "The *mestizo* had a white father and native American mother." "The *mestizos* were considered inferior to whites." Syn.: half-breed.

metaphysics [metuFIZiks] the branch of philosophy that treats of profound things like ultimate reality. "The *metaphysics* student studied the nature of experience." "*Metaphysics* can be abstruse." "His occupation was librarian, but he regarded himself as a *metaphysician*." "The *metaphysician* rejected Bishop Berkeley's assertion that there is no matter."

métier [mayTYAY] (French) an occupation or forte. "The *métier* of the protagonist of Kafka's short story 'The Metamorphosis' is a traveling salesman." "She was very happy with her *métier*—clinical psychologist." "The scholar's *métier* was etymologist." "She spent long hours working in her *métier*." Syn.: business, calling, profession, trade.

metonymy [miTONumee] the use of a word to indicate a greater meaning of which it is a part; for example, the "throne" to indicate a "kingdom." Metonymy can be a convenient way to show an abstraction. "The 'sword' is *metonymy* for the 'military.'" "The term 'bank account' was used as *metonymy* to indicate the greedy man's personal finances." "The word 'bed' can be *metonymy* for sex." "The word 'purse' can be *metonymy* for finances."

Mexican standoff [MEKsukun...] a standoff or impasse. "Trade talks between the two countries reached a *Mexican standoff*." "The criminal took a hostage and came to a *Mexican standoff* with police." "The *Mexican standoff* was a dangerous situation." "Peace talks in Paris reached a *Mexican standoff*."

miasma [mihAZmu] an atmosphere suggestive of danger. "The air was thick with apprehension, like a *miasma*." "The big old house at the end of the street—the 'haunted house'—was a *miasma* that scared children." "The army sergeant had a gift for sensing a *miasma*." "The strong wind and dark clouds made for a *miasma*." "The *miasma* of the place boded ill for the family's vacation." "The stream was turned into a *miasma* through the dumping of chemical waste by the plant." Syn.: brume, murk.

Midas [MIHdus] in classical mythology, a Phrygian king whose touch turned anything to gold; a man of great wealth. "The *Midas* was miserable despite his wealth." "The *Midas* bought himself five luxury vacation homes." "The *Midas* and his family never did any work." "The *Midas* expected to leave to his children a multi-million-dollar trust fund." Syn.: Croesus.

mien [MEEN] bearing or appearance. "His *mien* showed hostility." "She had a pleasant and dignified *mien*." "The French king had a dignified *mien*." "The dog had a sweet *mien*." Syn.: demeanor, deportment.

miff [MIF] to offend. "The big movie star *miffed* the little star." "She felt *miffed* when he hung up the phone early on her." "Do not *miff* someone powerful, advised the writer." "*Miffing* can be very contumelious." Syn.: annoy, exasperate, incense, irritate, pique, vex.

milksop [MILKsop] an effeminate man or boy. "He was a *milksop* but not homosexual." "The *milksop* had no athletic ability." "The *milksop* had constricted speech." "The girls but not the boys liked the *milksop*." "He was an open homosexual of the *milksop* type."

millstone [MILstohn] a heavy emotional or financial burden. "Schizophrenia is a true *millstone*." "Being poor is a *millstone* no matter how you view it." "The conservative asserted that the *millstone* of poverty must be overcome by hard work, not government handouts." "The radical asserted that the actual issue is who will live with a *millstone* and who will live off the labor of others." A millstone is a large round stone used in the past to grind wheat in a mill. Syn.: affliction, care, curse, load.

minatory [MINutoree] menacing. "The mere presence of a firearm is *minatory* and facilitates aggression." "The storm was a *minatory* foreshadowing." "His behavior was *minatory*." "The student affairs office was *minatory*." Syn.: foreboding, ominous.

minstrel [MINstrul] a musician, singer or poet; one of a troupe of comedians in blackface. "As a youth the governor participated in a *minstrel* show." "The *minstrel* told insensitive jokes about blacks." "The medieval *minstrel* played tunes at the court in Nuremberg." "The *minstrel* played the lute for the aristocratic audience."

mir [MEER] a Russian commune. "The *mir* is a model of equality." "Impersonal mass society is the converse of the *mir*." "The Israeli *mir* is called a kibbutz." "The *mir* was not agricultural."

misanthrope [MISunthrohp] one who hates mankind, known in German as *Menschenfeind*, and in Latin as *hostis humani generii*. "The Marquis de Sade (1740-1814) was the archtypical vile *misanthrope*." "He became known as a *misanthrope* because it was discovered that he planted a poisonous tree in his front yard." "The *misanthrope* irrespectively hated all mankind." "The *misanthrope*, unfortunately for humanity, was rich." Syn.: miscreant. Ant.: humanist, humanitarian.

miscegenation [misijuNAYshun] marriage between persons of different races. "*Miscegenation* is often a taboo." "*Miscegenation* became tolerated as the country emerged from colonial rule." "The *miscegenation* was scandalous." "*Miscegenation* in the United States seldom takes the form black-woman white-man."

miscreant [MISkreeunt] villain. "The *miscreant* in Shakespeare's *Hamlet* is both Hamlet's inner turmoil and his uncle." "At long last he realized that the *miscreant* in his life was the vice of hallucination." "The *miscreant* slew the hero." "The *miscreant* passed for normal." Syn.: misanthrope. Ant.: humanitarian.

mise en scene [mee zan SEN] (French) the stage setting of a play; environment. "The play's director took pains to create a memorable *mise en scène*." "The *mise en scène* of a psychiatric hospital is not conducive to recovery." "The *mise en scène* of the college classroom is absurd and obsolete: Students may communicate in class their B.O., eructations, etc., while the demoralized teacher exclaims 'What am I doing here? You can all get this from the book!'" "The *mise en scène* of the working-class breeds obscenity." Syn.: ambience, surroundings.

misericordia [miseriKOHRdeeah] (Latin) compassion. "According to Bacon, showing *misericordia* instead of taking retribution is the part of a prince, a person of noble character." "They lack *misericordia*, she claimed." "Nothing doth magnify *misericordia* like the Christian religion (Bacon)." "The radical asserted that *misericordia* is an essential part of one's humanity." Syn.: commiseration, empathy, ruth, sympathy. Ant.: misanthropy, Schadenfreude.

misnomer [misNOHmur] something mistakenly named. "A *misnomer* pointed out by Voltaire (1694-1778) runs, 'This agglomeration which was called and still calls itself the Holy Roman Empire was neither holy, nor Roman nor an empire in any way.'" "It is a *misnomer* to attribute the play to Shakespeare, declared the scholar." "The 'Department of Defense,' because it has engaged in wars, might be a *misnomer*." "Calling male masturbation 'solo sex' might be a *misnomer*."

misogamy [miSOGumee] hatred of marriage. "Since most people marry, *misogamy* would seem rare, though there are unhappy marriages, divorces, re-marriages and re-divorces." "The old bachelor's *misogamy* and denunciation of 'nagging wives' were notorious." "One might question the character of a *misogamist*." "He was not really a *misogamist*, since he planned to eventually marry."

misogyny [miSOJunee] hatred of women. "Many cultures have *misogynist* practices." "He is a *misogynist,* but his opinion hardly matters." "In German, *misogynist* is *Weiberfeind*, literally meaning 'women's enemy.'" "The *misogynist* hated people, not just women."

misology [miSOLujee] hatred of reasoning. "The students' *misology* was the despair of all the teachers at the school." "The boy's *misology* led him astray." "The conservative assailed the supposed *misology* of the working class." "Her *misology* had deep roots in working-class culture."

mithridatism [MITHridaytizum] the acquisition of tolerance to a poison by taking increasingly larger doses of it. "The king practiced *mithridatism* just in case." "*Mithridatism* cannot be used for poison ivy." "To implement *mithridatism* one apparently needs to know what poison an assassin would use." "The fearful queen took up *mithridatism*." After Mithridates VI (132?-63 B.C.), king of Pontus (in Asia Minor), who reputedly engaged in the practice.

mod [MOD] being up-to-date in fashion, especially in clothes. "The three boys called themselves the '*mod* squad.'" "She cultivated *mod* by shopping at expensive department stores." "He liked to appear not *mod* but classical, the kind of fashion that is always in style." "*Mod* varies from class to class." From the shortening of *modern*. Syn.: chic, cool, hip, modish, stylish, swank, trendy. Ant.: dowdy.

modus vivendi [MOHdus viVENdih] (Latin) a practical means of living or getting along. "The two nations reached a *modus vivendi* and concentrated on strife with bordering countries." "The husband and wife had a *modus vivendi* but stopped speaking to each other." "Their *modus vivendi* was disrupted by continual cheating." "They needed a better *modus vivendi* to end their dispute." "They lived in the same house as a *modus vivendi* pending the divorce." Syn.: arrangement, compromise, settlement.

moil [MOIL] to work hard; (noun) a drudge. "The radical asserted that *moil* ought to be equally distributed throughout society." "The tuck pointer *moiled* the day away but felt good afterward." "I hate *moil*, she declared, though she did do some manual work around the house and yard." "He preferred the scholar's *moil* in books to the *moil* of an accountant, nurse, typist, and so forth." "The *moil* of assembly-line work made him numb." "Being a mailman, in his opinion, was mindless *moil*." Syn.: grind, toil, travail.

moll [MOL] a criminal's girlfriend. "The loyalty shown by *molls* to gangsters of the 20s and 30s is rather surprising." "The *moll* was not taken in by the policeman's words." "The *moll* was really attractive." "The *moll* stuck it out with her gangster." Also "gun moll."

mollycoddle [MOLeekodul] a man or boy who is accustomed to being coddled; to coddle. "The woman made a mistake and made her son a *mollycoddle*." "The *mollycoddle* did not know how what he wanted from girls." "The dog lovers named their pet collie *Mollycoddle*." "The *mollycoddle* attended only private schools." "The *mollycoddle* was not prepared for the army." "He was a pampered *mollycoddle*, a mama's boy." Syn.: milksop.

Molotov cocktail [MOLutof KOKtayl] a makeshift incendiary grenade consisting of a bottle filled with a flammable liquid and saturated wick that is lit before throwing. "The demonstrator threw a *Molotov cocktail* at the tank." "People who throw a *Molotov cocktail* obviously have no actual weapons for use." "The crowd threw a few *Molotov cocktails* and the police fired rifles and tear gas." "The *Molotov cocktail* is not a very effective weapon." After the Soviet foreign minister V.M. Molotov (1890-1981).

momism [MOMizum] excessive dependence on maternal love, often causing a lack of maturity and independence. "The idea of *momism* has been discussed in U.S. society." "The social critic criticized *momism*." "*Momism* must be a larger problem with males." "The scholar did not learn of the term *momism* until late, at age 30."

moniker [MONukur] a name or nickname. "Her *moniker* was 'Lez,' for a rather obvious reason." "His *moniker* was 'Doc,' though he was not a doctor." "They called him 'Rudy,' though noone knew where the *moniker* came from." "Some *monikers* are used like badges to categorize and pidgeon-hole someone."

monkeyshines [MUNGkeeshihnz] a mischievous prank. "The *monkeyshines* the man played on his wife led to gentle mutual teasing." "The boy did not appreciate his friend's *monkeyshines*." "*Monkeyshines* was strictly forbidden at the security checkpoint." "The teacher reprimanded the boy for *monkeyshines*." Syn.: antic, caper, shenanigans.

Monroe Doctrine [munROH DOKtrin] a doctrine, not a law, enunciated by President James Monroe in 1823 prohibiting European intervention and further colonization in the Americas. "Although not a law, the *Monroe Doctrine* would soon be enforced because the U.S. had the power." "The *Monroe Doctrine* was invoked by some American presidents in the 19th century." "The history student studied the *Monroe Doctrine*." "The Secretary of State claimed that French backing of the Mexican presidential candidate violated the *Monroe Doctrine*."

Montezuma's revenge [montiZOOmuz...] (facetious, in Mexico) diarrhea. "Eating nothing but nachos gave him *Montezuma's revenge.*" "His *Montezuma's revenge* was effectively treated by a pill." "Having *Montezuma's revenge*, he had to keep going to the bathroom." "The phrase *Montezuma's revenge* refers to the killing of the Aztec leader Montezuma by the Spanish conquistadors."

moot [MOOT] debatable; doubtful; of little or no practical value. "The teacher's argument was *moot*, since the student withdrew from the course." "The magistrate ruled that the plaintiff's motion was *moot*." "The theory that frustration causes aggression became a little *moot* after further analysis." "Since the man was dead, the charge of slander was *moot*." Syn.: arguable, questionable, unproven.

morality play [meRALitee PLAY] an allegorical play of the 14th to 16th centuries in which characters personify good, virtue, etc. "That *morality play* was performed in 1390." "The *morality play* dramatized taboos." "The *morality play* was enacted by men, with no women." "Some people felt compelled to attend the *morality play.*"

morbid [MORbid] suggestive of disease; gruesome; suggesting poor mental health. "He had a *morbid* interest in death." "The billionaire had a *morbid* desire for money." "The physician saw some patients with hopeless *morbidity.*" "*Morbidity* refers to disease, while mortality refers to death." Syn.: grim, gruesome, macabre, unhealthy, unwholesome. Ant.: healthy, wholesome.

mordant [MORdunt] caustic, as in wit or criticism. "The newspaper issued a *mordant* editorial on the politician's large 'consulting fee.'" "The writer showed *mordant* criticism of opportunism." "The journalist's wit was obtuse and not *mordant.*" "The *mordant* review of the movie was amusing." Syn.: acerbic, acrimonious, bitter, scathing.

mores [MORayz] the fundamental ways of a society. "American *mores* place importance on fairness." "The subculture's *mores* included a heightened emphasis on male sexual prowess." "The *mores* celebrated wealth and being rich." "In sociology, *mores* are the social 'laws,' and then come folkways and usages." Syn.: customs, morals, norms, principles.

morganitic [morguNATik] pertaining to a form of marriage in which a man of means marries a woman of lesser rank, with a prenuptial agreement specifying that neither the wife nor any children inherit the man's property or title; the term can also apply to a marriage between a woman of higher, and a man of lower, rank. "The earl entered into a *morganitic* marriage." "The marriage of the actress and the count was *morganitic.*" "It was a good thing for the husband that his marriage was *morganitic*, since it did not last." "The wealthy woman insisted on a *morganitic* marriage."

morose [muROHS] gloomily melancholy. "The widower was *morose* after the death of his wife." "He felt *morose* that winter morning." "He was *morose* after his play was canceled early." "The teenage boy was often *morose.*" Syn.: glum, sullen. Ant.: amused, optimistic.

mossback [MOSbak] an extreme conservative; a rustic. "The *mossback* expressed contempt for Jews, blacks and Hispanics." "The *mossback* was adamantly opposed to women becoming a priest or preacher." "The *mossback* was in favor of 'gun rights.'" "The term *mossback* expressed both his rural outlook and political old-fogyism." Syn.: backwoodsman, provincial.

motif [mohTEEF] a recurring subject or idea in an artistic work, as a novel or musical composition. "The *motif* in Chopin's compositions is often melancholy." "The *motif* of Wagner's works is pagan Germanic mythology." "The *motif* of her paintings is rural beauty." "The *motif* of the short stories of Franz Kafka (1883-1924) is allegorical Angst." Syn.: leitmotiv, motive, theme.

mot juste [moh ZHEUST] (French) the most suitable or appropriate word. "The radical claimed that the *mot juste* for American politics is 'reaction.'" "The *mot juste* describing him is 'jerk.'" "He had to struggle to think up the *mot juste*." "The *mot juste* to describe the spirit of America may be 'business.'"

mountebank [MOUNtubangk] a quack or charlatan. "The *mountebank* lived by appealing to one's 'love of Jesus.'" "The *mountebanks* used a shill to try to encourage sales of their snake oil." "Vitamin enthusiasts are sometimes mistakenly branded as *mountebanks*." "The radical equated psychoanalysts with the *mountebank*, and even the conservative agreed that psychoanalysis is unscientific." *Mountebank* is derived from Italian.

mousy [MOUsee] quiet or noiseless: *a mousy schoolgirl.* "The new vacuum cleaner was *mousy*." "The church service was dignified and *mousy*." "He was anything but *mousy* and reticent." "The black airplane was *mousy* in flight." Syn.: timid. Ant.: garrulous, loquacious.

moxie [MOKsee] nerve or perseverance. "His *moxie* paid off with the girl, whom he married." "He showed much *moxie* by taking a poke at the bully." "What *moxie*, thought the woman." "The boy showed pluck and *moxie* in asking the girl for a date." Syn.: determination, grit, resolution. Ant.: affability, humbleness, meekness.

muckrake [MUKrayk] to search for and expose political or business corruption. "The original *muckrakers* were American journalists of the Progressive Era (about 1895 to 1914)." "The *muckraker* exposed kickbacks in city government." "Upton Sinclair (1878-1968) was a prominent *muckraker*." "The *muckraking* political scientist called attention to the practice of members of corporate boards voting themselves a huge income!" "The *muckrakers* of the Progressive era were striking at genuine wrongs."

mufti [MUFtee] civilian clothes. "The general appeared a very different man in *mufti*." "They were not allowed to be in *mufti* on the base." "His *mufti* was very neat." "The platoon dressed in *mufti* for the dance."

mugwump [MUGwump] a person who remains neutral concerning a political issue. "Regarding the death penalty, the governor remained a *mugwump*." "The candidate for state Attorney General was a *mugwump* on many issues." "Many voters are a sort of *mugwump* due to apathy." "The *mugwump* believed that nothing he could do would change the way politics would affect him." From an Algonquain Indian word.

mulatto [muLAToh] a half-white, half-black person. "In the South, *mulattos* were treated as blacks." "The practice of owners having sex with female slaves produced many *mulattos*." "The woman *mulatto* was lovely." "The *mulatto* worked as a cabaret singer."

mulct [MULKT] a fine; to obtain by fraud. "The mean teacher not only *mulcted* the student with an F, but also made a clean getaway." "The high cost of the fine, the *mulct,* made the man angry." "The *mulct* was regressive." "The mean policeman issued a *mulct* for trespassing." Syn.: cheat, chicane.

muliebrity [myooleeEBritee] the qualities of a woman; womanhood. "Some philosophers have found *muliebrity* to include, supposedly, passivity." "Her *muliebrity* was cherished by her family." "She had a tender, loving regard for herself and her own *muliebrity.*" "The French woman showed charming *muliebrity.*"

munchasaurus [munchuSARus] a fat person who constantly eats. "He had several female *munchasauruses* in his family." "She became a *munchasaurus* in her 30s." "He had to work at avoiding becoming a *munchasaurus.*" "The *munchasaurus* weighed 270 pounds." (Spears.)

munificent [myooNIFisunt] marked by great generosity. "The conservative argued that heirs are free to do what they wish with their money, and may be stingy or *munificent* as they please, since someone at some point earned the money, and thus was free to leave it to descendents." "The radical argued against the conservative view, stating that heirs are seldom *munificent,* and that the American people are opposed to inherited wealth." "Some American industrialists showed *munificence*—atleast the philanthropic kind—and some did not." "The *munificent* wealthy heiress founded an orphanage and hospital for children." Syn.: bountiful, charitable, magnanimous, unstinting. Ant.: stingy.

Muse [MYOOZ] the power regarded as inspiring a poet. "Alexander Pope (1688-1744) called upon the *Muse* for the writing of *The Rape of the Lock.*" "Apparently the *Muse* was not around for the writing of that dull poetry." "The *Muse,* or some kind of talent, helped her write hit songs." "The student was in need of the *Muse* to assist in his assignment for the composition class."

museum piece [myooZEEum PEES] something regarded as old-fashioned or broken-down. "The 1910 automobile was a *museum piece.*" "The airplane was a *museum piece* too frail to fly." "They made a tour of the rail yard, which was really a collection of old train cars, *museum pieces* seldom used." "They joked that the old wooden tennis racket she used was a *museum piece.*"

musty [MUStee] antiquated; dull; having an odor or flavor like mold. "The *musty* law prohibited shopping on Sunday." "The *musty* ordinance 'still in the books' forbade certain sexual acts." "The library was old and *musty* but still functional." "His room was *musty* and lacked sunlight and ventilation." Syn.: mildewed, moth-eaten, stale.

myrmidon [MURmidon] a loyal follower who unquestioningly executes orders. "The soldiers of most armies can be described as *myrmidons* who do not think for themselves." "The president was surrounded by a staff of *myrmidons.*" "The *myrmidon* later asserted that he was just following orders and so could not be held accountable for his actions." "The *myrmidon* had no compassion." Syn.: disciple, hanger-on, lackey.

mystagogue [MIStugog] someone who instructs persons about religious mysteries or sacraments. "After lunch they met with the *mystagogue* in a bamboo hut." "The *mystagogue* talked about rebirth and eternal life in the hereafter." "He was not qualified to be a *mystagogue* and did not make a good minister." "The *mystagogue* tried to teach them meditation but they could not concentrate."

N

nabob [NAYbob] a very wealthy person (especially one who made his fortune in India). "You cannot have several *nabobs* without many poor commoners, peasants, and share croppers." "The *nabob* believed that he owed his wealth to prudent habits and intelligence." "The *nabob* realized that concession had to be made to ascendant socialism." "The *nabob* owed his fortune to slavery." "The *nabobs* sat in a reserved section of the seating for nobles at the horse track at Ascot." Syn.: aristocrat, blue-blood, Brahmin, Croesus, noble, patrician. Ant.: commoner, worker.

naissance [NAYsuns] a birth or origination, such as that of a person, idea or movement. "Basketball had its *naissance* with the idea of James Naismith (1861-1939)." "The *naissance* of baseball is unknown." "The *naissance* of the United Nations was in international conferences of the 1940s." "The *naissance* of American ideology was the availability of a frontier where one could get rich."

naiveté [nahevTAY] the state of being naive. "When young he exhibited *naiveté* and lost some money because of it." "*Naiveté* may be a function of youth, with it being gradually lost with age." "Her *naiveté* was extreme, but she was a sweet woman." "*Naiveté* may be in for hard times in a harsh world."

namby-pamby [NAMbee PAMbee] insipid or sentimental; lacking decisiveness. "The play was *namby-pamby*, not of serious literary value." "The movie was a turkey, was *namby-pamby*." "The screenplay was *namby-pamby* and ruined the movie based on it." "The novel's characterization was *namby-pamby*." This term dates from 1726, when an English critic used it to belittle the poetry of Ambrose Philips.

narcissism [NARsisizum] a term used by the quack Sigmund Freud to refer to a psychological complex of self-aggrandizement and solipsism; in popular usage, selfishness or egotism. "In reality there is no psychological complex of '*narcissism*.'" "Americans need not fret that their society is subsiding into a slough of *narcissism*, since the term is a fiction created by psychoanalysts." "The psychoanalyst had a *narcissistic* desire to label other people as narcissists." "The selfish man was called '*narcissistic*.'"

nascent [NASunt] emerging; beginning to exist or develop. "The *nascent* nation of the 18th century rejected control by the mother country." "The *nascent* business went bankrupt." "The *nascent* marriage foundered on the issue of finance." "Masturbation, 'defilement by hand,' may represent *nascent* sexuality." "The *nascent* nation first produced notable writers and artists in its 30th year." Syn.: inceptive, inchoate, incipient. Ant.: conclusive, final, terminal.

nave [NAYV] the main part of a church, used by the congregation. "One might compare the *nave* of a church to the fuselage of an airplane." "The *nave* lies between the chancel and the entrance of the church." "The worshippers filled the *nave*." "Singing came from the *nave*."

nebbish [NEBish] (Yiddish) an ignored, insignificant person. "The *nebbish* was a groupie and not lonely." "The *nebbish* was derided as a 'nerd.'" "The *nebbish* was not good at soccer." "Socially he was a *nebbish* without influence."

nebulous [NEByulus] vague or confused. "According to the newspaper critic, the economist's bestselling books on prosperity were *nebulous*." "As it rambled on past 1,000 words, the article became *nebulous*." Syn.: obscure, unclear. Ant.: certain.

nefarious [niFAReeus] evil. "There may be no greater *nefariousness* than to wrong someone and then rub it in." "The *nefarious* criminal did not live very long." "The social critic identified as *nefarious* 'anxious self-scrutiny.'" "It can be *nefarious* to be labeled mentally ill, for example a lunatic or person 'needing help.'" Syn.: flagitious, heinous, iniquitous, recreant. Ant.: kind.

nellie [NELee] an effeminate homosexual man. "He was homosexual but by no means a *nellie*." "The *nellie* did not seem to want to remain in the 'closet' with his sexuality." "The *nellie* was promiscuous." "It was obvious he was a *nellie*."

neologism [neeOLujizum] a new word or phrase. "*Spork* is a simple example of a *neologism* ('spoon' plus 'fork.')" "Cop is a *neologism*, being coined from the copper badges the police formerly wore." "A *neologism* is also called a recent coinage." "Slang is full of *neologism*."

neophyte [NEEufiyt] a proselyte; a beginner. "The *neophyte* in golf grounded his tee shot to the left into the woods." "The *neophyte* chef burnt the steak." "He was a *neophyte* but he tried hard." "The *neophyte* would not listen to instructions." "He was a *neophyte* at public speaking, but he tried to say that wealth is socially created."

nepenthe [niPENthee] something that brings serene forgetfulness. "As yet, science has not discovered a true *nepenthe*, a happiness pill, though there are some things psychopharmacology can do along these lines." "He desperately sought some sort of *nepenthe* in many ways, but always came up empty." "Quaff this kind nepenthe and forget thy lost Lenore; Quoth the raven 'nevermore.'" (Edgar Allen Poe, "The Raven"). "A sound deep sleep can bring atleast temporary *nepenthe*." Syn.: anodyne.

nepotism [NEPutizum] favoritism based on family relationship. "*Nepotism* was involved in the man's acceptance into the university." "It was *nepotism* when the son succeeded the father in the corporation." "Government is supposed to be free of *nepotism*." "Inheriting a fortune can be seen as *nepotism*."

nescience [NESHuns] ignorance; lack of knowledge. "His *nescience* was complete, he had no idea what his wife was up to." "She found their *nescience* concerning history to be appalling." "When pressed to speak in public his *nescience* became obvious." "He was *nescient* on the subject of math." Ant.: omniscience.

nicety [NIHsitee] a fine distinction; detail. "The *niceties* of a foreign language require much effort to learn, and you cannot speak it fluently until they are learned." "He was a learned scholar, and the *niceties* of the world's body of knowledge were known to him." "The *niceties* of the sport of skiing were unknown to him." "The particulars is not a synonym for *niceties*." Syn.: subtlety.

niggle [NIGul] to find trivial fault with. "The college course was marked by *niggling* requirements." "The *niggling* assignment drew moans from the high school students." "She was a *niggling* pissant." "The *niggling* teacher forced her own fussy method on students." Syn.: carp, cavil, nitpick.

nirvana [nirVAHnu] a state of bliss; in Hinduism, salvation. "Probably noone unable to shed self-consciousness can attain *nirvana*." "She seemed to be in a state of *nirvana* or some sort of rapturous emotional intoxication." "The bride was in *nirvana*." "The culture struggled to provide the people with *nirvana*." Syn.: seventh heaven, spiritual enlightenment.

Nisei [NEESAY] an American of Japanese descent. "The *Nisei* are well-integrated into American society." "The *Nisei* was very successful." "The *Nisei* was two generations removed from Japan." "The *Nisei* sent their children to college."

nix [NIKS] to veto; to refuse. "He *nixed* the contract written by his staff." "The SEC *nixed* the big self-payouts that the corporation's board had arranged." "Would the American people *nix* the trust funds of the wealthy if they had a chance to vote on it?" "He *nixed* his wife's idea of traveling to the Orient." *Nix* is a variant of German *nichts*, which means "nothing." Syn.: cancel. Ant.: approve.

noblesse oblige [nohBLES oBLEEZH] (French) the reactionary belief that the nobility is obligated to act honorably and assist the poor. "*Noblesse oblige*, according to the radical, is paternalistic." "The elite felt no *noblesse oblige*, no duty toward the masses." "Obviously, there can be no *noblesse oblige* in a classless society." "That they owed a debt of *noblesse oblige* never occurred to that ruling class." This term means "nobility obligates" in French.

noisome [NOIsum] offensive or noxious. "A child that kicks and screams at his feeble parents is *noisome*." "The *noisome* odor clashed with the beauty of the June day." "The *noisome* smell coming from the apartment made them nauseated." "The sound of the siren was *noisome* if you were close to it." Syn.: dangerous, foul, horrible, repellent, repugnant, repulsive. Ant.: benign, pleasant.

nonage [NONij] a period of immaturity. "In the upper-class, governesses, maids, nurses and tutors watch over those in their *nonage*, with the wealthy mother being free from the continuous toil that engulfs women of lower classes." "A photo of her in *nonage* showed that she was not entirely happy." "The feminist asserted that men should help women raise children in their *nonage*." "In his *nonage* he was a nature-lover."

nonce [NONS] the present occasion. "For the *nonce* they will stay in Italy." "For the *nonce* they agreed to drop their complaint." "For the *nonce* he will continue to pay the bills." "For the *nonce* mainstream sociology is beset with unclear language."

non compos mentis [non KOMpus MENtis] (Latin) not of sound mind. "The court declared the man *non compos mentis*." "She was obsessed and *non compos mentis* during the affair." "The teacher was paranoid and *non compos mentis*." "The people in the notorious institution on Bellevue were, some but not all of them, *non compos mentis*." Syn.: crazy, daft.

nonjuror [nonJOORur] one who refuses to take an oath, as of allegiance. "*Nonjurors* have recently arisen who dislike pledging allegiance to God and country." "The radical declared himself a *nonjuror* when it comes to honoring the Pope." "It was dangerous to be a *nonjuror* in Nazi Germany." "A *nonjuror* in court would apparently be one who refuses the oath to tell the truth."

nonpareil [nonpuREL] (French) peerless, unrivaled; unique. "In his field of paleontology he was *nonpareil*." "She was *nonpareil* as an example of a scholar-athlete." "Shakespeare (1564-1616) was the *nonpareil* genius of the English Renaissance." "He was *nonpareil* in academics in his Yale law school class." Syn.: matchless, unequalled, unparalleled. Ant.: common.

nonplus [nonPLUS] utter confusion; to completely confuse. "The trigonometry quiz *nonplussed* the 12 year old." "He was *nonplussed* by his son's behavior." "The parents were *nonplussed* by their children and talked of parenting as something needing study." "The teenagers were rather *nonplussed* as to correct behavior." Syn.: bewilderment, perplexity.

non sequiter [NON SEKwitur] (Latin) a conclusion that does not follow from the previous reasoning. "It is a *non sequiter* to argue that since a man is Hispanic he must not have graduated from college." "It is a *non sequiter* to try to discredit socialism with 'far out, let's go trash the ROTC!'" "The book contained several *non sequiter's*." "The debator tried to throw his opponent off with a *non sequiter*." "In declaring him wrong, the man relied on a *non sequiter*."

non-U [nonYOO] not part of or characteristic of the upper-class, especially in Britain. "It is *non-U* to eat supper early, rather than about 7 p.m." "It is *non-U* to marry early in life." "The *non-U* family shopped at K-Mart." "The *non-U* man did not inherit a fortune."

nostrum [NOStrum] a quack remedy; a pet plan. "He had a ridiculous *nostrum* for making money through real estate." "His *nostrum* for repairing the car actually ruined it." "Psychoanalytic therapy is a *nostrum*." "She did not feel good about her husband's *nostrum*." Syn.: cure-all, panacea.

novitiate [nohVISHeeit] the period of being a novice. "His *novitiate* as a skater saw him fall on the ice often." "He quickly finished a *novitiate* as a firefighter." "The *novitiate* psychoanalyst diagnosed her with 'Electra complex' and 'penis envy.'" "It was her *novitiate* in love." Syn.: commencement, inception.

nugatory [NOOgutoree] of no actual value; futile. "Her opinion of and knowledge of the German language was *nugatory*." "The student's offense, for which he was expelled, was *nugatory*." "Her dedication to clinical psychology was *nugatory*." "His ability in racquetball is *nugatory*." Syn.: chickenshit, insignificant, negligible, niggling.

O

obdurate [OBdorit] hardhearted. "The judge was *obdurate* in the face of the defendant's insistence that he was innocent." "The *obdurate* soldiers executed their prisoners." "The *obdurate* employer paid low wages." "The *obdurate* men in planes dropped napalm." "It was a thing allowed only on account of *obdurateness*." Syn.: adamant, contumacious, merciless, pitiless, unfeeling. Ant.: amenable.

obeisance [ohBAYsuns] a gesture of deference; homage. "The junior executive paid *obeisance* to his boss." "The governing class had the *obeisance* of the masses." "Members of Congress pay *obeisance* to the corporate lobby." "She owed *obeisance* to him." Syn.: submission, tribute, veneration. Ant.: insolence.

obfuscate [OBfuskayt] to confuse. "The lawyer successfully *obfuscated* the issue in court and won an acquittal." "The issue was *obfuscated* by the many contending organizations." "*Obfuscation* helped his cause." "Race *obfuscated* the issue of the killing." Syn.: muddle. Ant.: clarify.

obiter dictum [OBitur DIKtum] an incidental remark. "In an unexplained *obiter dictum*, the sportscaster exclaimed 'welcome to Tokyo.'" "The woman said that her remark was an *obiter dictum* taken out of context." "The *obiter dictum* was offensive." "Her *obiter dictum* contained an obscenity."

objet d'art [obzhe DAR] (French) an object, especially a small one, of artistic value. "The jade *objet d'art* was worth several hundred dollars." "They had a whole roomful of *objets d'art*." "The *objet d'art* was made of ivory." "The thief stole several *objets d'art*."

objurgate [OBjurgayt] to berate. "He felt badly after *objurgating* his friend for an alleged slight." "He *objurgated* an employee for mistreating another employee." "The manager of the kitchen *objurgated* him for breaking a stack of plates." "He was teased and even *objurgated* by his teammates for striking out." Syn.: reproach, upbraid. Ant.: commend.

obloquy [OBlukwee] calumny; public censure. "The lucky heir who inherited a multi-million-dollar trust fund got away with no *obloquy*." "*Obloquy* should attach to those who do not work but consume luxuriously nevertheless."

"When her crime became known she felt humiliating *obloquy*." Syn.: abasement, aspersion, condemnation, denunciation, disapprobation, disrepute, reprimand, reproach, revilement. Ant.: credit, renown.

obscurantism [ubSKYOORuntizum] deliberate lack of clarity; opposition to advancement in knowledge and the truth. "*Obscurantism* rules in the bureaucracies of corporations and government." "Just as you cannot fight city hall, sometimes you cannot overcome *obscurantism*." "*Obscurantism* is a fine defense for those with means." "The biography showed some *obscurantism* in avoiding the question of whether the general was excessively interested in fame." "*Obscurantism* helped his cause; what Bacon said seemed to be coming true: 'The mixture of a lie doth ever add pleasure.'" "The *obscurantism* of the empire spread to its every town."

obsequence [OBsukwuns] being anxious to obey or please; the state of being obsequious. "The *obsequence* of the salesman to the bosses above him was plain to see." "The philosopher of ancient Greece seemed no wiser than other men in his *obsequence* to social norms." "He wanted to make vice-president and then executive president so badly that he fell to *obsequence*." "Americans sometimes accuse Germans of authoritarian *obsequence*, though Germans in reply say that Americans have their own type of *obsequence*."

obsequious [ubSEEkweeus] fawning. "The hammy actor was *obsequious* in front of the camera." "In social interaction he was actually neither *obsequious* nor blunt." "The president's men were *obsequious*." "He was *obsequious* to the point of begging." Syn.: cringing. Ant.: censorious.

obsequy [OBsukwee] (usually used in plural, *obsequies*) a funeral rite or ceremony. "The priest performed *obsequies* at the funeral of their mother." "The *obsequies* for the fallen soldier were very solemn." "The *obsequies* included a eulogy by the son of the woman who passed away." "The people did not seem mournful at the *obsequies*."

obstreperous [ubSTREPurus] unruly; clamorous in resistance to control. "The suspect was *obstreperous* and shouting obscenities as the police dragged him into custody." "The singer *obstreperously* resisted the audience's desire to see him leave the stage." "The *obstreperous* suspect was charged with resisting arrest." "The crowd was *obstreperous* and smashed some windows." Syn.: disorderly, disruptive, rowdy, uncontrolled, undisciplined. Ant.: calm, obedient.

obtest [ubTEST] to entreat. "The mother of the slain man *obtested* for information from the public." "She *obtested* readers to agree with her opinion." "The radical *obtested* the public with the question 'what right does the Attorney General have to lay down the law?'" "The professor *obtested* his students to think about an unkind saying: 'When a woman dies there is one less quarrel on the earth.'" Syn.: supplicate.

obtund [obTUND] to dull or blunt. "The impact of the scandal was *obtunded* by a blitz of media hype." "They had *obtunded* affects caused by permissive child rearing." "His fear of death was *obtunded* by mulling over the idea that one may look forward to the conclusion of life as one of nature's blessings." "The force of the bullet was *obtunded* by a helmet." Syn.: deaden. Ant.:

sharpen.

obvert [obVURT] to turn over; to alter appearance. "His campaign for president *obverted* all one's conventional wisdom." "*Obverting* the canoe, he found it full of holes and useless." "She *obverted* her looks with a mask." "After a failure, he *obverted* his personality, making it more subdued."

obviate [OBveeayt] to avoid problems, necessity, etc. "American police eagerly assume that their occupation *obviates* the need for an intellect." "He was told to *obviate* at all costs a confrontation with the activists." "Patient prevention *obviates* the need for pounds of cure." "They *obviated* the need to pitch to Ruth by intentionally walking him."

odious [OHdeeus] hateful, detestable. "Comparisons are *odious,* runs an old proverb." "Class society is *odious,* declared the radical." "The social critic gave an insightful, though perhaps *odious* quotation in his book: 'The death of conscience is not the death of self-consciousness.'" "Work as a mason is *odious,* believe some." Syn.: execrable, invidious, loathsome. Ant.: amorous.

Oedipus complex [EDupus KOMpleks] supposedly, a psychoanalytic complex wherein a boy desires sex with his mother and hates his father as a rival, though in reality there is no such thing. "The psychoanalytically-oriented social critic referred to unresolved '*Oedipus complex*' in the culture." "What evidence is there for an *Oedipus complex,* asked the radical?" "Some psychiatrists try to accommodate psychobabble psychoanalysts by including the '*Oedipus complex*' in their texts and diagnosis." "In reality, there is no *Oedipus complex.*"

offal [Oful] trash. "The abstract sculpture was declared *offal* by the newspaper." "The *offal* was recycled into useful products." "The wind blew the *offal* all over the street." "He searched the heap of *offal* for old beer cans." Syn.: rubbish.

officious [uFISHus] offensively offering aid or advice. "His *officiousness* was very rude and insolent." "The private *officiously* offered advice to his company commander." "The media commentator *officiously* played both ends against the middle." Syn.: interfering, meddling, presumptuous.

offish [OFish] aloof. "He was an *offish* loner and seemed to like it that way." "She was strangely *offish* the whole evening." "The schizoid man preferred being *offish,* though the result may be eating out one's heart." "The fifteen-year-old boy was sometimes *offish,* sometimes friendly." Syn.: detached, standoffish, unfriendly. Ant.: gregarious.

off-the-wall [OF...] very unusual or bizarre. "She made *off-the-wall* comments at the press conference that made people raise their eyebrows." "The college student's behavior that Saturday evening was *off-the-wall.*" "The manic talker had just about exclaimed his whole life story to the stranger in five minutes, which the latter understood but still found *off-the-wall.*" "He often regretted and even ruminated about his past *off-the-wall* behavior." Syn.: atypical, freakish, rare. Ant.: customary, normal.

ogre [OHgur] a monster; one who is especially cruel or hideous. "Noone denied that the dictator was an *ogre.*" "The *ogre* was a greedy opportunist." "The *ogre* passed as amiable in public." "The *ogre* had every reason to lie." "It was true of the *ogre* that as nature had done wrong by him, so must he do wrong by nature." Syn.: fiend, tyrant. Ant.: gentleman.

ombudsman [OMboodzman] a government official charged with hearing and acting on complaints by citizens against the government. "The woman met with an *ombudsman* to discuss child-care facilities." "Complaints about harassment in the army were referred to an *ombudsman.*" "The *ombudsman* recommended making traffic fines proportional to income." "The *ombudsman* investigated charges of rigging votes." This word is from Swedish.

omnibus [OMnubus] pertaining to numerous objects or items at once. "The Senate passed an *omnibus* bill." "The movers loaded *omnibus* goods in the truck." "The teacher taught *omnibus* subjects." "The state legislature considered the *omnibus* bill." Syn.: collection, compilation.

omnifarious [omnuFAReeus] of all kinds. "*Omnifarious* dinosaurs are found in the museum." "Societies with polygyny are *omnifarious.*" "The restaurant served *omnifarious* soups." "There are *omnifarious* heirs and heiresses in the country, but they are united in their opposition to equality." Syn.: multitudinous.

oneiric [ohNIHrik] pertaining to dreams. "His *oneiric* life was rich and imaginative." "He went several days without *oneiric* sleep." "The oracle made an *oneiric* prophecy." "He had an *oneiric* vision of his fate."

onerous [OHnurus] oppressive or troublesome. "She found her duties as chairperson *onerous.*" "His work on the auto assembly line was *onerous.*" "Being the mother of several children can be *onerous.*" "He found manual labor very *onerous.*" Syn.: arduous, burdensome, tiresome. Ant.: easy.

op-ed [OP ED] a page in a newspaper carrying editorials; an editorial therein. "The *op-ed* called attention to opponents of the war." "She wrote an *op-ed* attacking the controversial study." "The *op-ed* criticized bombing as gunboat diplomacy." "The *op-ed* assailed appeasement of criminals." This term is from the words *opposite* and *editorial* (the page in a newspaper on the opposite side of the editorial page).

opprobrium [uPROHbreeum] ignominy. "He suffered considerable *opprobrium* for committing adultery." "The *opprobrium* from the crime far outweighed its profit." "The man still felt a little *opprobrium* for mistakes made years earlier." "The prisoner was reminded of the *opprobrium* by confinement to a cell." Syn.: censure, condemnation, contempt, excoriation, scorn. Ant.: approval, commendation, decency.

oppugn [uPYOON] to dispute, call in question. "They *oppugned* the engineer's integrity." "The prosecutor *oppugned* the idea that the defendant was lawabiding." "The commission *oppugned* the witness's testimony." "The lawyer *oppugned* the reliability of the witness." Syn.: controvert. Ant.: confirm.

original sin [uRIJunul SIN] in theology, man's supposed inherent depravity or evil as arising from Adam's sin. "*Original sin* as depicted in the Bible is rather bizarre." "In ridiculing *original sin,* the radical asked, 'What is so wrong with biting an apple?'" "The priest did not like to discuss *original sin.*" "In an old school reader, *original sin* appears as 'In Adam's fall, we sinned all.'"

orison [ORuzun] a prayer. "The sick man did not believe that his *orison* was answered." "She said an *orison* for her grandmother." "You needn't say an *orison* for me, he declared to his mother." "Nymph, in thy orisons be all my sins remembered" (Shakespeare, *Hamlet*). Syn.: desire, hope, wish.

orotund [OHRutund] having a pompous manner of speaking. "The *orotund* emcee went on and on, disgusting the audience with his verboseness." "They both thought that he was rather *orotund*." "The politician was *orotund*." "The governor spoke in a way that would have been *orotund* if any one else had done it." Syn.: bombastic, long-winded, pompous, self-important. Ant.: modest.

Orwellian [orWELeeun] pertaining to or characteristic of the nightmarish dystopia in the novel *1984* by George Orwell (1903-50). "The war propaganda was *Orwellian*." "She described a social scene that was *Orwellian*." "*Orwellian* chaos disrupted the rock concert." "The play had an *Orwellian* theme."

oscillate [OSulayt] to vacillate. "In the past some politicos have *oscillated* between liberalism, radicalism and conservatism, following political trends the way others follow fashion." "His loyalty *oscillated* frequently." "He *oscillated* in giving political support, but he also noted that 'he lies like a politician.'" "The woman *oscillated* in answering his marriage proposal." Syn.: dither, swing, waver.

otherworldly [UTHurWURLDlee] like another world, as in the spiritual or imaginative realm. "The minister was not *otherworldly*, and instead liked his leisure and hiring others to do the work of mowing the church lawn, and so forth." "The Hindu mystic was *otherworldly*." "The boy's musings were *otherworldly*." "The young revolutionaries were not *otherworldly*." Syn.: eerie, inhuman, uncanny, unearthly, weird. Ant.: earthly.

otiose [OHsheohs] idle. "*Otiose* behavior is disapproved of in the U.S., though the disapprobation varies by class." "People of the leisure class are *otiose*." "His German shepherd snoozed often and was *otiose*." "The boy's *otiose* behavior was unacceptable." Syn.: inactive. Ant.: active.

out-Herod [outHERud] to exceed in extravagance or excess. "The new mansion *out-Heroded* all the homes next to it." "He did not want to *out-Herod* anything in the size of food portions." "The art work *out-Herods* all in the use of color." "The teacher's meanness was *out-Heroding*." After Herod Antipas (4 B.C.-A.D. 40), ruler of Judea.

oxymoron [oksiMOHRon] a figure of speech in which an apparent contradiction expresses a positive idea. "He expressed his tearful joy rather like an *oxymoron*." "The expression 'working hard or hardly working' resembles an *oxymoron*." "'You have to be cruel to be kind' is an *oxymoron*." "That his memories were bitter-sweet is an *oxymoron*." Syn.: contradiction, irony.

P

pablum [PABlum] banal ideas or writing. "The book on envy was *pablum*." "Liberalistic books are often *pablum*, said the radical." "The conservative attacked the '*pablum*' of liberalism." "Social studies teachers, overrelying on seatwork, manifest *pablum*, or spinelessness, according to the journalist." Syn.: dross, triteness.

pack rat [PAK RAT] a person who collects or hoards useless small items. "The wealthy celebrity was a *pack rat*." "He tried to save money by being a *pack rat*." "The *pack rat* rode the bus to save money." "The refrigerator of the *pack rat* was full of packets of ketchup and other condiments."

padrone [puDROHnee] a master; an employer who dominates his employees for the purpose of exploitation. "The *padrone* grew rich but only, a Marxist would say, by paying subsistence wages." "The *padrone* was tight with his own money." "The *padrone* drove a Mercedes." "The *padrone* tried to influence the life of his employees on and off the job." *Padrone* is an Italian word related to "patron."

paladin [PALudin] a champion of a great cause. "He was a *paladin* of atheism who pointed out the crimes of Christianity." "The conservative was a *paladin* for the sake of children being born to married parents, not out of wedlock." "The communist was a *paladin* for equality." "Admiral Hyman Rickover (1900-86) was a *paladin* for reform of American education." "An honored *paladin* emerged from the war." Syn.: crusader.

palatine [PALutihn] having royal privileges; palatial. "The corporate lawyer could afford a *palatine* house." "The Italian villa was *palatine*." "She dreamed of living in a *palatine* house." "The rooms at the dormitory were not *palatine*." Syn.: grand, opulent, regal, splendid.

palaver [puLAVur] idle chatter. "The women exchanged *palaver* over the back fence." "The *palaver* turned mean as the two friends had a falling out." "The girls' *palaver* concerned dating and relationships." "The *palaver* was trivial." Syn.: gibberish, prattle.

palimpsest [PALimpsest] a parchment or old paper from which writing has been partially or completely erased and re-used for writing, and being a source of the recovery of lost ancient literature. "The *palimpsest* had French and Greek writing on it." "A valuable *palimpsest* was discovered in the Serbian monastery." "The *palimpsest* contained a work of Virgil." "The *palimpsest* was regarded as a great find by scholars."

palinode [PALunohd] a poem containing a retraction of something the poet wrote earlier; a recantation. "The writer knew of no *palinode* by Edgar Allen Poe (1809-49)." "The literary critic catalogued *palinodes*." "The radical urged the historian, an 'apologist for Rockefeller,' to issue a *palinode*." "The writer said that his second article on the subject was no *palinode*."

Palladian [puLAdeeun] pertaining to knowledge, study or wisdom. "*Palladian* accomplishment will not be come by lightly; one may need to 'turn over the pages of the Greeks by night and by day.'" "Her *Palladian* ability was considerable, and she spoke five languages." "The television shows little of *Palladian* value." "The novel was *Palladian* and entertaining." From ancient Greece. Syn.: intellectual, scholarly.

palliative [PALeeaytiv] serving to ameliorate or mitigate. "The jury found *palliative* circumstances in the case of the man charged with manslaughter." "Nothing was *palliative* about his actions that day." "His remarks on the affair were *palliative*." "After the turmoil of the day the good night of sleep he got was *palliative*." Syn.: calming, comforting, mollifying, relaxing, soothing.

pallor [PALur] unnatural paleness; wanness. "The love-sick boy showed *pallor*." "Her *pallor* was due to a nutritional deficit." "His *pallor* spoke volumes about his knowledge of the affair." "*Pallor* can be a sign of fear, lying, anxiety or ill-health."

palmer [PALmur] a pilgrim of the Middle Ages who had made a journey to the Holy Land; a religious pilgrim. "The *palmer* visited Medina." "The woman was unusual as an American *palmer* who converted to Islam." "The *palmer* army attacked an Islamic Saracen army on the way to Jerusalem." "The *palmer* was very hopeful of finding peace of mind on his journey."

palooka [puLOOku] an athlete such as a boxer lacking ability, motivation or experience. "The *palooka* lost the bout in the second round." "He was a *palooka* in tennis, incapable even of learning the sport." "She was a *palooka* in golf but was eager to learn." "He found that at age 40 he was almost a *palooka*, incapable of performance in hockey and soccer, which he could do at 20."

palter [POLtur] to act deceitfully. "He was capable of *paltering* day after day during negotiations." "She *paltered* when honesty would have served her well." "Do not *palter* in giving your name." "The business owner *paltered* in his IRS returns." Syn.: cheat, gull, hoax, swindle.

pandemic [panDEMik] widespread, as of fear or a disease. "Ignorance of the reality of inherited wealth was *pandemic*." "Reaction was *pandemic* across the country." "AIDS is *pandemic* in Africa." "The belief that parenting is difficult was *pandemic*." Syn.: prevalent, ubiquitous. Ant.: restricted.

pandemonium [panduMOHneeum] tumult. "*Pandemonium* broke out when the basketball team lost in the final and the crowd went wild." "There was *pandemonium* in the city schools." "General *pandemonium* in a society needs a bold cure or will not be cured." "The *pandemonium* on campus was quelled by riot police." After the name of the capital of hell in *Paradise Lost,* by John Milton (1608-74). Syn.: anarchy, chaos, turmoil. Ant.: calm.

pander [PANdur] to cater to baseness; (noun) a pimp. "The 'strip poker' television show *pandered* to the most degenerate taste." "He would have *pandered* to anything to make a buck." "The *pander* controlled four prostitutes." "The rich man *pandered* to his mistress' love of money." Syn.: procure, truckle.

Pandora's box [panDORuz BOKS] a source of extensive problems and evils. "In Greek mythology, the first woman, Pandora, opened *Pandora's box,* as the gods expected, and out came all man's evils." "The war, although it resolved unemployment, opened up a *Pandora's box* for society to deal with." "Per-

missive child rearing has opened a *Pandora's box* on every level of society."
"The myth of *Pandora's box* may speak to the human condition in mass,
class society."

panegyric [paniJIRik] a eulogy; praise. "The actress was the recipient of a *pane-gyric*." "The son-in-law read the *panegyric* at her funeral." "The senator delivered a *panegyric* for his colleague at the holiday celebration." "The teacher had only *panegyric* for his French student." Syn.: acclaim, commendation. Ant.: disapprobation.

panjandrum [panJANdrum] a self-important official. "The municipal *panjandrum* insisted that registration be done his way." "The *panjandrum* was rather poorly paid." "The university was full of chancellors, vice-chancellors and other sinecure *panjandrums*." "The *panjandrum* judge laid down the law according to his own beliefs and values." *Panjandrum* was coined by an English dramatist in the 18th century.

panoply [PANuplee] a complete and resplendent array of something. "The bride wore a *panoply* of white silk and lace at her wedding." "The school room featured the *panoply* of equipment, such as microscopes, slide rulers and maps, but no comparable teaching and learning." "The magnificent home of the duke was attended by servants in a *panoply* of uniforms." "He had a *panoply* of credentials—M.D., Ph.D., FACS, and so forth."

pantheon [PANtheeon] the realm of the persons venerated by a group; a temple dedicated to all the gods; a public building housing memorials to the honored dead. "He is firmly in the *pantheon* of American football." "She is a musical giant, standing tall in the *pantheon* of pop musicians." "The *pantheon* honored veterans of World War I." "The *pantheon* was destroyed in the war."

panty raid [PANtee RAYD] college hijinks involving a raid by young men on a women's dormitory, ostensibly to obtain underwear like panties as trophies. "The man had attended four colleges but had never witnessed a *panty raid*." "The *panty raid* was halted by the police." "The college women did not appreciate the *panty raid*." "One Friday night in fall the fraternity boys got excited and staged a *panty raid*."

pantywaist [PANteewayst] a sissy. "The short, skinny boy was taunted as a *pantywaist*." "The *pantywaist* was the team's water boy." "The *pantywaist* lifted weights to grow stronger." "The commentator claimed that Jesus was 'no *pantywaist*.'"

paparazzi [pahpuRAHTsee] (singular, *paparazzo)* reporters and photographers who pursue celebrities for news material. "The actress was superficially hostile to the *paparazzi*." "The *paparazzi* were waiting for her at the boat." "The *paparazzi* pursued the celebrity using motorcycles." "The *paparazzo* got a photo of the woman sunbathing topless." The term *paparazzi* stems from a character in the Italian movie *La Dolce Vita* (1966).

paper tiger [PAYpur TIHgur] a person or thing with a fierce aspect of power but actual weakness. "Kent State proved that the national guard is no *paper tiger*." "In his dreams his problems all melted away into a *paper tiger*." "The bully was rather short but heavy-set, and put up the image of a *paper tiger* to mask his fear." "She was no *paper tiger* when it came to grading a student she did not like."

Paphian [PAYfeeun] pertaining to love or illicit sexual love. "*Paphian* traffic proceeded through the house of ill-repute." "*Paphian* intercourse, while being a wonderful expression of sexuality, may lead to broken marriages, venereal disease and unwanted pregnancy." "*Paphian* playfulness led to the working-class girl's becoming 'knocked-up.'" "The conservative denounced *Paphian* godlessness." Syn.: carnal, erotic, sensual.

papist [PAYpist] a Roman Catholic; (adj.) pertaining to the Roman Catholic Church. "The president was criticized as a *papist.*" "*Papists* were disparaged by the dominant Protestants." "The *papists* answered to Rome." "The *papists* were opposed to women becoming priests."

paralogism [puRALujizum] a violation of principles of valid reasoning. "The prosecutor committed a *paralogism.*" "His reasoning contained a *paralogism* and was circular, since he assumed what he wanted to prove." "The masses' reasoning was *paralogistic.*" "The woman was careful to avoid *paralogism.*"

pariah [puRIHu] a social outcast. "In Hawthorne's *The Scarlet Letter* (1850), a woman is chastened as a *pariah* for adultery." "The working class motorcycle gang was viewed as a *pariah.*" "He was a *pariah* for a week for having snitched." "The *pariah* sought out comfort in solitude." Syn.: outsider, reprobate, untouchable.

pari passu [PAree PASoo] (Latin) side by side; without partiality; fairly. "The radical claimed that the wealth is not distributed *pari passu.*" "The Congressman lent a hand and, *pari passu* with commoners, shoveled sand into a few bags on the levee." "Justice is supposed to be distributed *pari passu.*" "People do not inherit fortunes *pari passsu.*" Syn.: equitably, impartially. Ant.: unfairly.

parlance [PAHRluns] idiom. "The *parlance* of the underworld reflects hostile social conditions." "Their *parlance* was full of poor usage." "The men's *parlance* contained obscenities." "The *parlance* of the physicist was hard to follow." Syn.: argot, cant, lingo.

Parnassian [parNASeeun] pertaining to poetry. "Lord Byron (1788-1824), most people agree, was a *Parnassian* genius." "He had no *Parnassian* talent." "*Parnassian* ability is learned, not inherited." "His *Parnassian* writing was dull." After a mountain in Greece concerned in mythology.

paroxysm [PARuksizum] any sudden, violent outburst. "In a *paroxysm* the defendant lashed out at the prosecutor." "To control any irate *paroxysm* that might get you into trouble, Francis Bacon (1561-1626) referred to reciting the alphabet and other means." "The policeman's *paroxysm* was caught on camera." "She manifested a sort of *paroxysm* of paranoia."

parsimonious [pahrsuMOHneeus] stingy. "The wealthy in America may be *parsimonious* in some respect." "Although born very poor, he was never *parsimonious* when it came to tipping and charity." "The old man was *parsimonious*, a tight-wad." "His brother was *parsimonious,* and perhaps needed to be." Syn.: close-fisted, miserly, penurious, stingy, tight-fisted. Ant.: generous, liberal.

Parthian shot [PARtheeun SHOT] a telling comment made while departing. "As a *Parthian shot*, he referred to her obesity." "The *Parthian shot* made them laugh." "The comedian was a master of the *Parthian shot*." "He let loose with a devastating *Parthian shot*."

parti pris [partee PREE] (French) bias. "The teacher was guilty of *parti pris* in assigning grades." "Each of the jurors denied having any *parti pris*." "He had strong *parti pris* against the suspect." "Her *parti pris* was in the direction of animosity toward upstarts." Syn.: partiality, prejudice.

party animal [PARtee...] (in America) a person given to hedonistic celebration. "The *party animal* loved wine, women and song." "The favorite day of the week of the *party animal* is Saturday." "Do you know any *party animals?*" "The *party animal* is the product of an emphasis on consumption." Syn.: epicure, hedonist.

parvenu [PARvunoo] an upstart. "The middle-class *parvenu* was rejected by the city's high society." "The wealthy *parvenu* was not invited to any of the fashionable balls." "The *parvenu* appeared on television several times, apparently on an ego trip." "The *parvenu* politician wanted to abolish the Department of Education." Syn.: pretender, social climber.

pasquinade [paskwuNAYD] a lampoon or satire, especially one posted in public. "In revenge for the wrong he circulated a *pasquinade* detailing the alleged offense." "The magazine specialized in *pasquinade* of celebrities." "The *pasquinade* attacked the overpayment of celebrities." "The magazine's *pasquinade* was amusing." Syn.: travesty. Ant.: applause.

passé [paSAY] outmoded; aged. "The talk show host's comic refrain was a sensation, attracting forced laughter from all quarters, until it became *passé* in one week." "Bell-bottom jeans are now *passé*." "Disco music is *passé*, although it is sometimes played on the radio." "Eight-track tapes are *passé*." Syn.: archaic, out-of-date.

passel [PASul] a large or indeterminate group or number. "The couple had a *passel* of children." "The billionaire had a *passel* of vices." "He had a *passel* of bags in his closet." "A *passel* of U.S. presidents have been generals."

pastiche [paSTEESH] an artistic or literary work that imitates a previous artist's work, often satirically. "The *pastiche* Broadway play was a comedic hit." "The second film *To Be or Not to Be* was a turkey and *pastiche*." "The *pastiche* novel did not sell." "Most of the public did not recognize that the story was a *pastiche*." Syn.: imitation, lampoon, parody, satire, spoof, takeoff.

patina [PATunu] a glow, aura, etc., such as from age or use. "The *patina* of the mahogany was beautiful." "She had a lovely tan *patina* to her skin." "The gold watch had a lustrous *patina*." "The *patina* of the leather was black."

patois [paTWAH] a regional dialect; the substandard language of a group. "The *patois* he spoke identified him as a rural bumpkin." "She spoke the *patois* of rural Ohio." "Her *patois* had a Southern drawl." "His *patois* was learned in Brooklyn." "Their *patois* testified to provincialism." Syn.: argot, cant, jargon, lingo.

payola [payOHlu] a secret payment in return for the promotion of a product, for favorable business consideration, etc., through corrupt use of one's position; bribery or a bribe. "*Payola* may be found in one sort or another in all countries." "Certain persons involved in the 'public' television children's program may be guilty of *payola*." "The state speaker of the house denied *payola* but went to prison nevertheless." "The term *payola* does not refer merely to radio D.J.'s." From *pay* and (Victr)ola (a type of phonograph).

peccadillo [pekuDILoh] a small fault. "He, like his fellow corporate officers, regarded the manipulation of his own company's stock as a mere *peccadillo*." "As teenagers they shoplifted, but saw it as not even a *peccadillo*." "She had the *peccadillo* of biting her finger nails." "His *peccadillo* was a short attention span." Syn.: imperfection, shortcoming. Ant.: impeccability.

peccant [PEKunt] guilty, as of a sin. "The Congressman was *peccant* of adultery, but asserted the lie firmly and assiduously enough that the media and public lost interest in the story." "The *peccant* in the literature read by the class all met death for sinning." "The *peccant* priest had sodomized a girl." "The minister, himself *peccant*, attacked sinners in the hands of an angry God." Syn.: faulty, wrong. Ant.: flawless, unfailing.

pecking order [PEKing ORdur] a hierarchy in a group analogous to the dominant-subordinate relationships of chickens. "She was at the top of her clique's *pecking order*." "Class society's *pecking order* ranges from the extreme elite to the Lumpenproletariat." "As a youth he knew nothing about how a *pecking order* might affect himself." "The military academy had a mean *pecking order*."

Pecksniffian [pekSNIFeeun] hypocritically pretending to be very moral or proper. "The *Pecksniffian* woman claimed her son-in-law was lazy." "The prosecutor donned *Pecksniffian* superiority in court." "The fact that he was being *Pecksniffian* was lost on noone on the set of the television program." "The *Pecksniffian* newspaper editor identified the genocide committed by other countries but not his own." After a character in *Martin Chuzzlewit*, a novel by Charles Dickens (1812-70). Syn.: pharisaic, phony, sanctimonious.

peculate [PEKyulayt] to embezzle. "The money *peculated* by white-collar criminals far exceeds that taken by armed bank robbers." "He was in no position to *peculate* business earnings." "The executive president *peculated* from the company." "In that business it was not possible to *peculate*." Syn.: defalcate, misappropriate.

pedant [PEDunt] a person excessively adherent to rules. "The bureaucrat at the highway department was a *pedant* and stickler for the law." "But it could not be said even in her favor that she was a *pedant*." "The teacher was *pedantic* and irrational." "The county worker was mean and *pedantic*." Syn.: hairsplitter, sophist, stickler.

pederasty [PEDurastee] sex between two males, especially when one is a minor. "He had engaged in some *pederasty* as a youth, which he later renounced." "The priest was accused of *pederasty*." "The *pederast* was charged with a crime." "The *pederast* was not attracted to women." Syn.: bucklebury, Greek love. (Spears.)

peevish [PEEvish] fitfully angry; cross. "The harridan was *peevish*." "The actor had a *peevish* temper." "He was in a *peevish* mood." "Her *peevishness* was hard to bear."

pelf [PELF] money as booty. "The financier was a carpetbagger, a holder of great *pelf.*" "The petty criminal carried around part of his *pelf* in his wallet." "The opportunist's *pelf* came from inheritance, from a trust fund on which very little tax was paid." "The CEO hauled in $80 million of *pelf* a year!" Syn.: cybercash, kale, long green, lucre, mazuma, shekels, simoleon, spondulix.

pell-mell [PEL MEL] in a confused or hasty manner; (noun) confused haste. "He drove *pell-mell* to get to the airport on time." "The boy's room was a *pell-mell* mess." "The university's committee was staffed *pell-mell* by fascists." "Her *pell-mell* paranoia ran dizzily through her addled head and concluded with an accusation of threat."

penis [PEEnis] the male genital. Syn.: Aaron's rod, busk, chanticleer, ding-dong, dinger, dipstick, gooser, mad mick, schlong, torch of Cupid, whang. (Spears.)

penis machinist [PEEnis muSHEEnist] military slang for a physician who checks men for venereal disease. "Some of the waiting men looked on the '*penis machinist*' with resentment." Syn.: pecker-checker. (Spears.)

penurious [puNOOReeus] stingy. "He was *penurious* and disliked the soliciting for charity that came through the mail." "He was never rich, and adopted *penurious* habits of necessity." "The *penurious* man gave a tip of five percent." "The poor, *penurious* man could have afforded to be a little more charitable." Syn.: niggardly, parsimonious. Ant.: generous.

peon [PEEun] a peasant or lowly worker. "The Bible says that there will always be *peons.*" "He protested as *peonage* the wage offered by the business." "The boys of the working-class family were destined to be *peons.*" "The *peon* hated his life." Syn.: plebe. Ant.: aristocrat.

percipient [purSIPeeunt] discerning. "He was a shrewd little doctor of no mean *percipience.*" "The professor was *percipient.*" "The dull broadcaster lacked *percipience.*" "The ninety-year-old man was still *percipient.*" Syn.: artful, perspicacious, shrewd. Ant.: dull.

perdition [purDISHun] damnation; utter destruction or ruin. "The earthquake reduced the city to *perdition.*" "His *perdition* was being locked in prison with no possibility for parole." "Wartime bombing caused widespread *perdition.*" "The building was reduced to *perdition* by the fire." Syn.: hades, inferno.

perdurable [purDOORubul] permanent. "Alexander Pope's wit is *perdurable* and still sparkles today." "The almost *perdurable* letter went through many hands before being discarded." "The novelist made a bid for *perdurable* fame, for literary immortality." "A marble monument is nearly *perdurable.*" Syn.: imperishable. Ant.: impermanent.

peregrine [PERugrin] coming from abroad. "All societies receive *peregrine* cultural enrichment." "A particular animal was referred to as *peregrine* if it migrated a long way." "The country's alphabet was *peregrine.*" "The bird was *peregrine.*" Syn.: alien, foreign. Ant.: domestic, native.

peremptory [puREMPturee] imperative; dictatorial. "The army's message to the surrounded fort was *peremptory*—surrender or die." "The corporation's rule was *peremptory*—relocate or lose your job." "The worker finds life *peremptory,* and must take a job or go hungry and shelterless." "A gun pointed at you is *peremptory.*" Syn.: arbitrary, authoritative, despotic, dogmatic, imperious, unconditional. Ant.: negotiable.

perfervid [purFURvid] zealous. "Tocqueville (1805-59) found the pursuit of wealth to be everywhere *perfervid* in the new republic." "The *perfervid* miners sought gold in great quantity." "The politician was *perfervid* about the greatness of his country." "The *perfervid* individualism was both a celebration and annihilation of it." Syn.: fanatical. Ant.: calm, serene.

perfidious [purFIDeeus] treacherous. "The most dangerous military opponent is a cleverly *perfidious* soldier." "His nephew was *perfidious* in putting him down." "His dreams turned into nightmares of *perfidious* persons." "The snowy ice was *perfidious*." Syn.: unscrupulous. Ant.: honest, upright.

perforce [purFORS] of necessity. "Parents must *perforce* raise their children." "Tourists in Paris visit *perforce* the Eifel Tower." "Where there is smoke there is *perforce* fire." "Overeating causes *perforce* weight gain." Syn.: inescapably, unavoidably.

peripatetic [perupuTETik] walking or traveling about; itinerant. "The drifter never gave up his *peripatetic* ways." "The *peripatetic* salesman traveled often." "The *peripatetic* soccer team traveled the world." "The *peripatetic* policeman walked the beat."

periphrasis [puRIFrusis] circumlocution. "Her *periphrasis* frustrated the ability of people to understand her." "She would talk in *periphrasis* on the phone and never quite finish a sentence." "Both sisters talked in *periphrasis*." "*Periphrasis* has been facetiously called beating around the bush." Syn.: indirection, indirectness, roundaboutness, verbiage. Ant.: compactness.

perorate [PERurayt] to speak at length. "The lecturer *perorated* for half the day on Chinese history." "The man *perorated* to the court on his suffering at the hands of the defendant." "The president *perorated* to the luncheon crowd." "The commencement speaker's *peroration* lasted two hours." Syn.: orate.

perquisite [PURkwizit] a gratuity; something received as a privilege. "The *perquisites* of high social station include freedom from work." "As a *perquisite* he got use of the company car." "The *perquisites* of a university sinecure include much free time." "A *perquisite* of working at the cafeteria was half-price food." Syn.: bonus, freebie, perk, reward.

persnickety [purSNIKitee] fastidious. "You must be *persnickety* regarding details when preparing a manuscript." "She was mean and *persnickety* when she drank." "The actress was *persnickety* about her dress." "He was *persnickety* when it came to how to treat his dogs." Syn.: choosy, finicky, fussy, meticulous, nitpicking, particular, punctilious. Ant.: slapdash.

perspicacious [purspuKAYshus] discerning. "The Spanish teacher was a very *perspicacious* woman." "One of his golf friends was very *perspicacious*." "The presidential aide was very *perspicacious*, as shrewd as the dickens." "The *perspicacious* man was not deceived." Syn.: astute, percipient. Ant.: dull, witless.

perspicuous [purSPIKyoous] discerning; lucid. "The short story 'The Man of the Crowd' shows Edgar Allen Poe's *perspicuous* power of observation." "The doctor was a *perspicuous* little man." "Women are said to be emotionally *perspicuous*, as men see far and women see deep." Syn.: clear, unequivocal.

peruse [puROOZ] to read carefully. "She *perused* several parent-training manuals but still felt inadequate as a mother." "*Peruse* that book but do not let it intoxicate you!" "The college student *perused* the text on German." "He browsed the dictionary but did not *peruse* it." Syn.: examine.

petitio principii [puTISHioh prinSIPee] a fallacy in logic in which that which is to be proved is presumed at the outset.; begging the question. "A classic case of *petitio principii* is to argue that one is paranoid because he has a persecution complex, and has a persecution complex because he is paranoid." "The speaker stumbled into a *petitio principii*." "The man was angry that his opponent's *petitio principii* was not recognized." "The writer was careful to avoid *petitio principii*."

pettifog [PETeefog] to quibble over trivia; to engage in chicanery. "They *pettifogged* for an hour over who was to get how much of the winnings." "The *pettifogging* debate was not worth listening to." "The group of friends fell into *pettifogging* teasing and bickering." "The right-wing consistently *pettifogs*, avoiding the real issue of equality raised by the left-wing." Syn.: dissemble, machinate, prevaricate, tergiversate.

phantasmagoria [fantazmuGOHReeu] a series of specters or apparitions. "He described a *phantasmagoria* in which his car ran over a man who had run into his path." "He wrote a short story about a *phantasmagoria* in which he becomes obsessed with confessing a murder." "The *phantasmagoria* caused a nightmare." "The emotionally-ill woman was troubled by repeated *phantasmagorias*." Syn.: chimera.

Pharisaism [fariSAYizm] sanctimoniousness. "The belligerent *Pharisaism* of the pastor was too much for some to bear." "The *Pharisaism* of the attorney general appalled the observer, who asked what right he had to lay down the law for others." "The governor was *pharisaic*." "The *pharisaic* priest did not observe the Golden Rule." Pharisaism was an ancient Jewish sect strictly adhering to traditional ritual. Syn.: self-righteousness.

pharisee [FARisee] a sanctimonious, hypocritical person. "He was a *pharisee* when it came to practicing what you preach." "The *pharisee* did not want to hear the opinion of others." "The *pharisee* said one thing and did another." "The *pharisee* was given an award for humanism."

pheromone [FERumohn] substances secreted by a person or animal which waft through the air and sexually arouse another person or animal of the opposite sex. "Human semen is a very powerful *pheromone*." "Moths have astonishing perception for tiny amounts of *pheromone*." "The human female also gives off *pheromones*." "The libertine tried to make use of *pheromone* by putting in his breast pocket a handkerchief wiped on the scrotum."

Philadelphia lawyer [filuDELfeeu...] a lawyer skilled in fine aspects of the law. "The upper-class family hired a *Philadelphia lawyer* when their son got into criminal trouble." "The *Philadelphia lawyer* went to court on behalf of the corporation." "The plumber could not afford to hire a *Philadelphia lawyer*." "The *Philadelphia lawyer* got his client out of jail."

philippic [fiLIPik] a speech of vehement denunciation. "The man's *philippic* against established education at the PTA meeting was not well received."

"The dictator gave a *philippic.*" "The schizophrenic thought out a *philippic,* but it was all in her head." "Giving a *philippic* in front of millions of people is only possible for a few." Syn.: diatribe, harangue, screed, tirade.

philistine [FIListeen] "an ignorant, narrow-minded person, devoid of culture and indifferent to art" (*Funk & Wagnall's*). "He went through a phase of accusing many people of being a *philistine.*" "The *philistine* principal did not wish to hear that his actions had a chilling effect on teacher morale." "Philistine must have originally meant, in the mind of those who invented the nickname, a strong, dogged, unenlightened opponent of the chosen people, of the children of light" (Matthew Arnold). "The *philistine* never read books or went to the museum." Syn.: barbarian, boor. Ant.: aesthete.

philter [FIltur] a love potion. "Though there may be no true love potion, literature is replete with *philters,* such as Goethe's *Faust.*" "The drink acted like a *philter* on him, as he suddenly came to life and felt attracted to the girl next to him." "The *philter* that the man concocted did not work." "The man tried to slip her a *philter* by spiking her drink." In German, philter is *Liebesgetrank,* literally "love drink."

phlegmatic [flegMATik] unemotional. "In comparison to the vivacious Latins, Americans are rather *phlegmatic.*" "He had a *phlegmatic* attitude toward life." "His reaction to the movie was *phlegmatic.*" "Their father was *phlegmatic* and not easily moved." Syn.: apathetic, inexcitable, languid, sluggish, stolid. Ant.: lively.

phrenic [FRENik] pertaining to mental activity. "The drug valproic acid has a *phrenic* or psychotropic effect." "The university student's *phrenic* exertion in cramming proved inadequate." "Some vitamins are therapeutically *phrenic.*" "*Phrenic* behavior cannot be localized to or isolated in one part of the brain."

phylactery [fuLAKturee] an amulet, charm or safeguard. "She wore a *phylactery* on a necklace as a souvenir from Europe." "The tribal man had a *phylactery* around his neck to ward off evil spirits." "Formal *phylacteries* are not as common in the West." "The girl wore a necklace full of *phylacteries.*" "He kept in his pocket a *phylactery* of special sentimental value."

piacular [pihAKyulur] atoning; blameworthy. "The priests made a *piacular* sacrifice to their gods." "The court's judgment was *piacular.*" "He knew which man was *piacular* in the fight." "The scandal was not her doing, she was not *piacular.*"

picaresque [pikuRESK] pertaining to rogues; a Spanish literary form featuring rogues as heroes. "As a boy in school he had a *picaresque* reputation, for he rallied his class in contests against rival classes." "The *picaresque* drifter was always in search of money for a drink." "The play involved a *picaresque* group of friends out for fun." "The family had *picaresque* fun at the theme park." Syn.: mischievous, villainous.

picaroon [pikuROON] a rogue, thief or pirate. "The *picaroon* raided the employee pension fund." "The psychopath was a vicious *picaroon.*" "The *picaroons* stormed the ship." "The *picaroon* was a cutthroat."

picayune [pikeeYOON] small; petty. "The amount of money he gave the boy for chasing tennis balls was *picayune.*" "The pizza deliverer earned a *picayune* sum." "The money spent on public housing is *picayune*." Syn.: puny, trifling. Ant.: generous, liberal.

pickaninny [PIKuninee] (offensive*)* a black child. "As a *pickaninny*, the adopted child felt out of place in the white family." "He hated the term *pickaninny* when applied to himself." "The *pickaninny* was thin." "The *pickaninny* raided the cookie jar."

Pickwickian [pikWIKeeun] simple, endearing or otherwise like Mr. Pickwick, protagonist of Charles Dicken's novel *The Pickwick Papers* (1837). "He took *Pickwickian* delight in befriending his sidekick." "Jimmy Stewart in the movie *Harvey* is a good example of *Pickwickian*." "She was a gentle old *Pickwickian* woman." "The *Pickwickian* Jewish doctor was kind but naive."

piker [PIHkur] a contemptible miser. "The *piker* paid his sister five dollars for five days of babysitting her nephew and niece." "The *piker* was as stingy as he was mean." "Scrooge was a *piker*." "The *piker* regarded his wife and children but as bills of fare." Syn.: cheapskate, niggard, skinflint, tightwad.

pillory [PILuree] to expose to public ridicule. "The state politician tried to *pillory* his opponent as inexperienced and childish." "All he had to do was mention 'liberal' and his opponent was *pilloried*." "She *pilloried* her own mother as fat." "The conservative *pilloried* the injustice of sending a person to 20 years in prison for possessing a small amount of cocaine." A pillory was originally a wooden device for immobilizing a person in public as punishment. Syn.: brand, deride, humiliate, scorn. Ant.: praise.

pin money [PIN MUnee] an allowance or small sum of money set aside for personal expenditure, as from a husband to a wife. "He gave his children *pin money* each week." "The girl spent all her *pin money* in one day on jewelry and cosmetics." "The idle rich get whopping *pin money* indeed!" "The niggard did not give his wife any *pin money*."

pipe dream [PIHP DREEM] a baseless hope. "Her Hollywood plans were naught but a *pipe dream*." "His *pipe dream* was to get rich from a fantastic invention." "His methods of finding a wife were *pipe dreams*." "The worker longed to get away to a beautiful tropical setting, but that was rather a *pipe dream*." This term comes from the imaginative desires induced by smoking a pipe of opium, whereby an onlooker might suppose that the smoker perceives a fancy, a dream induced by the pipe.

piquant [PEkunt] appealingly provocative. "His grandpa had a *piquant* gift for telling family legends." "Her dress and make-up were *piquant*." "She had a *piquant* wit." "She wrote a *piquant* 'dear John letter' to her boyfriend." Syn.: enticing, incisive, trenchant. Ant.: dull, numb, stupefied.

pique [PEEK] to irritate or wound, as someone's pride; to excite or provoke, as interest or curiosity. "His stare *piqued* her resentment." "The woman's rebuff of his advance *piqued* his pride." "The cave *piqued* his interest." "The old coin *piqued* her fascination." Syn.: affront, gall, irk, rile, roil. Ant.: assuage, please.

pissant [PISant] a niggling person. "The prim social worker's insistence on regulations earned him a reputation as a *pissant*." "The stubborn teacher was a *pissant* mindlessly insisting on her own way." "The foreign-language *pissant* shoved down students' throats the idea that teaching grammar was a waste of time." "The *pissant* was not a happy person."

pithy [PITHee] succinctly clear. "A *pithy* English saying asserts that 'virtue is the only nobility.'" "The general's reply to the appeal to surrender was *pithy*— 'nuts.'" "The book was vague and tedious rather than *pithy*." "The *'pithy'* expression 'so it goes' quickly became trite." Syn.: laconic, terse. Ant.: verbose.

pizzle [PIzul] the penis of an animal. "The dog directed his *pizzle* at a bush to urinate." "The bear's *pizzle* was erect."

placable [PLAKubul] tolerant. "The justice system is not *placable* with regard to the poor." "He was not a *placable* man." "The *placable* man did not mind that his radio was stolen." "His rage was not *placable* or capable of being appeased." Syn.: lenient, temperate. Ant.: austere, implacable, relentless.

plaintive [PLAYNtiv] melancholy. "Many of Tschaikovsky's compositions are *plaintive*." "She sang a *plaintive* song of difficulty with love." "His poem was *plaintive*." "The gray February day was *plaintive*." Syn.: chapfallen, doleful, funereal, lugubrious, somber, woe-begone. Ant.: cheerful, gay, mirthful.

plangent [PLANjunt] pertaining to the sound of bells; plaintive. "He wrote a *plangent* poem." "The *plangent* clang from the belfry resounded in his mind." "November is a *plangent* month in New England." "He felt *plangent* after losing his job." Syn.: rueful, sorrowful.

platitude [PLATitood] a banal remark. "American political campaigns—the ballyhoo of swell guys—are the triumph of the *platitude* and glittering generality." "He mouthed several *platitudes*, and his speech moved noone." "The conservative referred to the supposed *platitudes* of radicals." "The country song was replete with *platitudes*." Syn.: cliché, commonplace. Ant.: aphorism, axiom.

plaudit [PLOdit] (*often* plaudits) enthusiastic praise. "Charles Lindbergh, one of the last reluctant celebrities, did not know what to do with the *plaudits* bestowed on him." "The actress received *plaudits* from all over for her stage performance." "*I Pagliacci* by Leon-Cavallo (1858-1919) received widespread *plaudits*." "The book was honored with *plaudits* and the Pulitzer Prize." Syn.: acclaim, applause, recognition. Ant.: blame, obloquy.

plebeian [pliBEEun] pertaining to a commoner. "She was *plebeian* and did not mix with aristocrats." "Driving a Ford or Toyota paints one as *plebeian*, so indicative of class is the expense of a car." "The *plebeian* could work at the country club but not join it." "The *plebeian* did not inherit a lightly-taxed, multi-million-dollar trust fund." Syn.: ill-bred, proletarian, unrefined. Ant.: aristocratic, noble, patrician.

plenary [PLEnuree] full or absolute. "The American police have *plenary* authority when pulling over a motorist." "The first *plenary* session of parliament was contentious." "His health was *plenary* for the football game." "The army's armaments were *plenary*." Syn.: supreme, unrestricted. Ant.: limited.

plethora [PLETHuru] a superabundance. "Sinecures, such as university deanships, offer a *plethora* of spare time." "The heir had a *plethora* of money and leisure." "Supposedly it is not good to have a *plethora* of time on your hands." "The celebrity had a *plethora* of money." Syn.: plenitude. Ant.: scarcity.

plinth [PLINTH] a slab or stone block at the base of a statue, column or pedestal. "The *plinth* was made of marble." "The *plinth* supported a statue of a French king." "On the top of the steps of the museum were *plinths*." "On top of the *plinth* was a pedestal, and on that was a statue of a Roman god."

plugugly [PLUGuglee] a tough. "The department store security man was a *plugugly*." "The *plugugly* had no compassion." "The *plugugly* and the tall political activist wound up in a fight." "The *plugugly* ate and drank too much." The origin of "plugugly" is unknown. Syn.: hood, hooligan, ruffian, thug.

pluvial [PLOOveeul] pertaining to rain. "The *pluvial* weather continued for five days." "*Pluvial* is reminiscent of French *pleuvoir*, 'to rain.'" "The plant responded to *pluvial* weather." "The *pluvial* storm brought three centimeters of rain."

Podunk [POHdungk] a small, unimportant town. "The town had the reputation of a provincial redneck *Podunk*." "The *Podunk* did not have even a bank." "The *Podunk* was not on the highway." "The *Podunk* was not on the maps."

pogrom [pohGRUM] an organized massacre, especially of a minority like Jews. "The Nazi *pogrom* was relentless." "The Saint Bartholomew's Day *pogrom* claimed the lives of about 3,000 Huguenots in 1572 in France." "Fortunately, not counting wars with the Indians, American history is not stained with many *pogroms*." "The Ministry of Propaganda instigated a *pogrom*." Syn.: persecution, slaughter.

politesse [poliTES] politeness. "She learned *politesse* and 'culture' at an elite Swiss boarding school." "His *politesse* in such situations was not affected." "*Politesse* may work where severity won't, or, according to Bacon, 'Severity breedeth fear, but roughness breedeth hate.'" "*Politesse* is not out of place in court." Syn.: manners.

polity [POLitee] the system of government. "The *polity* of Nazi Germany was fascist." "The modern *polity* is full of bureaucratic insensitivity." "The *polity* of the warring nation was a dictatorship." "The leaders of the *polity* were all rich." Syn.: establishment, governance, political entity.

Pollyanna [poleeANu] a mindlessly optimistic person. "*Pollyannas* might succeed in life because they are trustworthy and evoke no displeasure." "He soon realized the limits of being a *Pollyanna*." "It was a *Pollyanna* who blew the whistle." "One should keep a positive outlook on life but perhaps not become a *Pollyanna*." "She was a *Pollyanna* who never thought ill of anyone." Pollyanna is a heroine in a work by the American writer Eleanor Porter (1868-1920). Syn.: Dr. Pangloss, optimist. Ant.: pessimist.

poltergeist [POHLturgihst] a ghost supposedly manifest in noises. "A medium was brought in to investigate the house's *poltergeist*." "The 'noise ghost,' the *poltergeist*, scared everyone." "The supposed *poltergeist* turned out to be a canard." "The girl did not believe in a *poltergeist*." This word comes from German, literally meaning "noise ghost."

poltroon [polTROON] a contemptible coward. "The *poltroon* emptied the trusting old woman's savings account." "The *poltroon* abandoned his girlfriend and two children." "The *poltroon* stole ten dollars from the man as a prank." "The *poltroon* violated the thirteen-year-old girl." Syn.: craven, milquetoast.

polyglot [POLeeglot] (adj.) speaking several languages; a person who speaks several languages. "The *polyglot* Oxford graduate spoke six languages." "The writer was a *polyglot* who liked studying languages." "The American Secretary of State is seldom a *polyglot*, though that would be helpful in such a position." "The Jewish physician was very-well educated and a *polyglot* who spoke five languages." "Europe is *polyglot*, with some 30 languages." "The *polyglot* teacher spoke four languages—English, Spanish, French and German." Syn.: multilingual.

polymath [POLeemath] a person of great or varied learning. "He was a *polymath*, spoke five languages and had graduated from Cambridge University." "The physicist was a *polymath*." "The Spanish physician was a *polymath*." "The conservative was a self-educated *polymath*." Syn.: Renaissance man, scholar.

pontificate [ponTIFikayt] to speak pompously. "Maybe asking whether he is Catholic can be replaced by 'does the pontiff *pontificate?*'" "Supposedly he *pontificated,* but he did not see it that way." "Be an assertive lecturer but do not *pontificate!*" "Persons in high places may speak in a manner that would be *pontificating* for a normal person." Syn.: declaim, inveigh, preach.

popinjay [POPinjay] a vain person given to empty chatter. "The *popinjay* was much in demand at middle-class parties." "He was a flighty *popinjay*." "The *popinjay* paid close attention to his wardrobe." "He was a short, thin *popinjay*."

pork barrel [PORK...] government spending on local projects designed to ingratiate legislators with their constituents. "The senator fought to keep the air force base open, which was actually a *pork barrel* action." "The *pork barrel* military contract cost billions." "The radical asked, 'Who really profits from *pork barrel* laws, the people in a given Congressional district or the families which own defense corporations?'" "The county *pork barrel* had a contractor repaving roads again and again, though they did not need it."

portentous [porTENtus] foreboding. "The storm which nearly ripped off the roof of their cabin was a *portentous* start to their vacation." "It was a *portentous* moment which they will never forget." "The scene was *portentous*, something was in the air." "The game had a *portentous* start when the pitcher walked in a run in the first inning." Syn.: fateful, momentous, ominous, significant. Ant.: propitious.

portly [POHRTlee] rather fat; stout. "The actor was *portly* and needed to go on a diet." "The woman was a little *portly* but otherwise lovely." "The *portly* boy had a fat father." "The man's mother, aunt, niece and sister were all *portly*." Syn.: corpulent, obese, overweight.

portmanteau word [pohrtmanTOH] a word formed by combining parts of two words. "Smog, from 'smoke' and 'fog,' is a *portmanteau word*." "Spork, from 'spoon and fork,' is a *portmanteau word*." "The *portmanteau word* filled a need in the language." "Slithy, from 'lithe' and 'slimy,' is a *portman-*

teau word."

poseur [pohZUR] one who affects an attitude. "The high school actor tried to approach the art as a *poseur*, in that he sort of donned an attitude to enhance his acting ability." "The *poseur* at the party was all too apparent." "She was a genuine diamond in the rough, no *poseur*." "The morning weatherman affected extreme enthusiasm and optimism, and was an unctuous *poseur*." Syn.: charlatan, fop, prig.

positivism [POZitivizum] a philosophy devoted to gaining knowledge through observation and experiment and rejecting the metaphysical and theological approach. "The graduate student studied *positivism*." "*Positivism* is part of the sociology developed by Auguste Comte (1798-1857), a French philosopher." "The social scientists were *positivists*." "The philosopher rejected *positivism* in favor of existentialism."

postiche [poSTEESH] counterfeit or sham. "The unused books on the elegant shelves were a *postiche* of knowledge." "The money launderer had the habit of saying 'bogus,' *postiche,* seemingly in every other sentence." "The painting was *postiche*, not worth much." "The *pastiche* knowledge of the teacher-teachers reformulated the obvious as make work." Syn.: bogus, faux. Ant.: authentic.

potboiler [POTboilur] an inferior literary or artistic work intended merely for financial benefit. "The simpering romance novel was a *potboiler*." "The *potboiler* motive is seldom very far beneath American pulp fiction." "He produced one *potboiler* painting after another, which the critics tore into but the public ate up." "The *potboiler* was crude sentimentality." This term is from boiling the pot for a meal, the idea thus being providing money for meals and a living.

potentate [POHTuntayt] a sovereign, monarch or ruler. "The word Caesar yielded two other *potentate* names—Kaiser and czar." "The African *potentate* resigned and fled the country." "The oppressive *potentate* was assassinated." "The *potentate* and his wife threw a party for the elite."

pother [POTHur] a commotion or uproar. "The *pother* in the theater disturbed the play." "Everyone left the classroom to see what the *pother* was." "The false alarm caused a *pother*." "The trifling incident caused a *pother* in the media." Syn.: disturbance, fracas, fuss, rumpus, tumult, turmoil.

potluck [POTluk] food that is already available and requires no additional preparation. "Their *potluck* picnic consisted of beans and potato salad." "They took *potluck* to the ballgame." "The women held a *potluck* party to celebrate the nurse's retirement." "The *potluck* of chicken salad and nachos was delicious."

potpourri [pohpooREE] dried flowers and spices kept in a jar for their fragrance. "The woman liked to keep *potpourri* going in her office and home." "The *potpourri* smelled of vanilla." "The *potpourri* lost its fragrance after three weeks." "His favorite *potpourri* was cherry."

pot-valiant [POTvalyunt] brave only as a result of being drunk. "He got *pot-valiant* almost every evening and would start talking abusively about everyone who appeared on the television." "In redneck country *pot-valiant* entails picking a fight." "The wife resented the time when her husband got *pot-valiant* and zulued." "He became more uninhibited and daring when *pot-valiant*."

prandial [PRANdeeul] pertaining to a meal. "The medication was to be taken post-*prandial*." "He got *prandial* heartburn." "He felt *prandial* mellowness, as if the dinner had caused it." "The woman missed the al fresco *prandial* get-togethers with her friends."

prate [PRAYT] to babble. "The fifth-graders were still *prating* as they went to bed." "The boy *prated* into the girl's ear." "The twin girls were *prating* to each other." "Infants like to *prate*, which is practice for true speech." Syn.: blather, gibber, jabber.

pratfall [PRATfal] a fall backwards onto one's butt. "The actor did a skillful *pratfall*." "The movie ended with a 'nuclear pratfall.'" "She did more of a *pratfall* into third base rather than a slide." "While backpeddling to retrieve a lob, he lost his balance and did a *pratfall* on the tennis court."

preachify [PREEchufih] (derogatory) to preach in a tedious or didactic manner. "The writer was once accused of *preachifying*." "The minister *preachified* and went on and on about trivia." "The teacher was *preachifying*, but atleast he taught." "*Preachifying* in and of itself is not so bad, thought the radical." Syn.: sermonize.

preadamite [preeADumiht] a person supposed to have existed before Adam. "Anthropologists necessarily believe in *preadamites*." "Unless you believe in the tomfoolery of the Bible, said the radical, you must admit there were *preadamites*." "Apparently no clergyman admits that there were *pread-amites*." "*Preadamites* are the subject of the discipline of prehistory."

prebend [PREBund] a stipend given to a clergyman. "Some critics say that a *prebend* allows a preacher to live off the labor of others." "The priest was eager to receive as large a *prebend* as possible." "The *prebend* was substantial for the minister of the suburban church." "The minister saw his *prebend* as a means to do good deeds."

preciosity [presheeOSitee] overrefinement. "The aspiring writer spoke with *preciosity*, with too much sophistication, but she was earnest." "*Preciosity* kills spontaneity." "His *preciosity* and airs were almost too much to bear." "The films were marked by *preciosity*." Syn.: fastidiousness. Ant.: neglect.

précis [praySEE] a summary. "He sent in a *précis* of his employment qualifications." "A *précis* preceded the body of the book's text." "A *précis* is also called an abstract." "Every medical article should have a *précis*."

preen [PREEN] to primp; to dress oneself up. "She *preened* in front of a mirror for so long and with such fuss that it was grotesque." "The women *preened* in the ladies room before entering the auditorium." "The birds' *preening* seemed grotesque to him." "The student was in need of more *preening* in his bathroom." Syn.: doll up.

prelibation [preeliBAYshun] a foretaste. "The coastal bombardment gave a *prelibation* of the invasion to come." "The television gave a *prelibation* of the show's next episode." "The winery gave a free *prelibation* of its vintage." "The book's cover was an accurate *prelibation* of its contents."

premonitory [priMONitoree] serving to warn beforehand. "The large black bird was *premonitory.*" "The oracle's prediction was also *premonitory.*" "Her bad feeling was *premonitory.*" "It seemed to be in the air, the accident was *premonitory.*" Syn.: ominous.

prepossessing [preepuZESing] impressing favorably. "At age 20 she was a *prepossessing* beauty, with brown hair and well-set brown eyes." "The blonde teenage girl was *prepossessing.*" "The *prepossessing* woman got the acting part." "Far from being amiable or *prepossessing*, the reclusive actor was sullen." Syn.: attractive, winsome. Ant.: repellant.

PreRaphaelite [preeRAFeeuliht] one of a group of English artists about 1850 who wished to revive Italian art before the time of Raphael (1483-1520). "The *PreRaphaelite* poured over a book on Italian painting." "The *PreRaphaelites* included Dante Gabriel Rossetti (1828-82) and John Everett Millais (1829-96), and the famed art critic John Ruskin (1819-1900) was a staunch supporter of the group." "The *PreRaphaelites* published romantic poetry." "The social critic referred to an idea of the *PreRaphaelites.*"

prescind [priSIND] to consider individually; to remove. "The lawyer *prescinds* his criminal law practice case by case." "The teacher *prescinded* each student's merits." "The coach *prescinded* the small boy from the football team." "The patient was *prescinded* from the hospital."

preternatural [preeturNACHurul] abnormal or supernatural. "Depth psychology (Freudian nonsense) is supposedly based on human *preternatural* instinct." "The *preternatural* is but fit only for talk by the fireside in winter." "He was a scientist who rejected the idea of *preternatural* influence." "There was nothing *preternatural* about the Missouri minister who burned down his own church for the insurance money." Syn.: extraordinary, unusual. Ant.: ordinary.

prevaricate [priVARikayt] to equivocate, speak misleadingly. "He was a mooch, a liar, and a wastrel who *prevaricated* with ingenuity." "He urged his father not to *prevaricate* when administering advice or criticism." "His aunt could spend hours on the phone *prevaricating* on and on about nothing." "The lawyer was a great *prevaricator.*" Syn.: dissemble, dither, evade, fudge, hedge, misstate, quibble.

prevision [priVIZHun] prescience or foresight. "The army's commander countered the enemy's moves with what seemed like *prevision.*" "The manager showed *prevision*, he could see the delay coming." "The palm reader's *prevision* was not so good." "The psychic claimed to have *prevision.*"

prig [PRIG] a prudish person. "The girls suspected the school's *prig* of snitching on them for smoking." "The French visitor found the women to be *priggish* and rather inhibited." "The *priggish* couple disapproved of the bikini she wore." Syn.: pedant.

prim [PRIM] affectedly proper. "He was stiff and *prim* at his job interview." "The twin girls were well-behaved though a little *prim.*" "He noticed that the working-class woman acted very *prim* in the presence of middle-class people." "The religious couple was *prim.*" Syn.: prissy, straitlaced. Ant.: artless, broadminded.

prima facie [PRIMuh FAYshee] (Latin) immediately obvious; legally sufficient. "There was no *prima facie* evidence that he did the killing." *"Prima facie* evidence was needed." "The prosecution made a *prima facie* case for murder." "Some people say there is *prima facie* evidence for a God, and some disagree." Syn.: apparent, clear-cut, obvious, unambiguous.

primal [PRIHmul] original; primeval; fundamental. "A *primal* fact of mass society is that people cannot live without moral prejudices." "A *primal* 'law' of society is who defers to whom." "Classes are *primal* to state societies." "The conservative asserted that inequality is *primal* and normal." *Primal* is related to Latin *primus*, "first." Syn.: aboriginal, ancient, prehistoric, primitive, primordial.

primp [PRIMP] to dress or groom oneself carefully. "She compulsively *primps* in front of a mirror every morning." "He puts on a suit and *primps* before heading for work." "Women seem to *primp* more than men." "He *primped* hard before his date." Syn.: fussy up, preen.

primogeniture [prihmiJENichur] inheritance or succession by the first-born male. *"Primogeniture* was very important in feudal Europe." *"Primogeniture* was less important in America, which had no feudalism." *"Primogeniture* meant that the eldest son inherited the family business." *"Primogeniture* did not include females."

prink [PRINK] to dress for show; to primp. "They *prinked* before going to church." "She *prinked* in front of the mirror prior to her date." "He nervously *prinked* prior to the job interview." "He *prinked* and did his toilette every morning before work."

probabilism [PROBubilizum] the philosophical doctrine that certainty is impossible and that probability is sufficient for faith and practice. "The educated scientist had faith in *probabilism*." "The philosophy student studied *probabilism*." "She wrote a treatise on *probabilism*." *"Probabilism* stems from the Scottish philosopher David Hume (1711-76)."

procrustean [proKRUSTeeun] ruthless or dictatorial. "The *procrustean* regime dictated economic policy." "The peasants refused to acquiesce to the *procrustean* demands of the prince." "Work with the New Deal programs was stringent and often *procrustean*." "Army barracks life was *procrustean*." *Procrustean* comes from classical mythology; Procrustes was a thief who warped the bodies of his victims to fit his bed.

prodigal [PRODigul] wastefully extravagant. "Wealthy heirs and heiresses are *prodigal* with money they did not earn." "He was too generous and *prodigal* with gifts." "The nouveau-riche man spent *prodigally*." "The economy was *prodigal* and produced frivolous goods and commodities that noone needed." Syn.: lavish, profligate. Ant.: niggardly.

profane [prohFAYN] characterized by irreverence for God; heathen. "The ritual they performed outdoors was *profane*." "The man said that the carol they sang was *profane*." "She used *profanity* to denounce her ex-husband." "His *profane* language shocked those who heard it." Syn.: blasphemous, disrespectful, sacrilegious. Ant.: sacred.

proffer [PROFur] to tender. "In his will Shakespeare *proffered* to his wife his second-best bed." "The brilliant young student in the math class *proffered* an explanation of the azimuth." "The disgraced teacher *proffered* his resignation." "The student, to the utter surprise of the professor, correctly *proffered* the answer to the question about the Roman emperor-philosopher." Syn.: offer, submit. Ant.: withdraw.

profligate [PROFligayt] completely immoral or dissolute; wasteful. "Socialists believe that class society is *profligate*." "She was *profligate* with her father's credit card." "They taught their children not to be *profligate*." "In America *profligate* things are not necessarily taboo." Syn.: intemperate, reckless, spendthrift, wanton.. Ant.: sparing.

prolepsis [prohLEPsis] a rhetorical method of anticipating objections in order to answer them in advance. "He used *prolepsis* in the debates held by the college." "The sociologist wrote *prolepsis* into his book." "The polemical book featured the author's *prolepsis*." "She was good at *prolepsis*."

prolix [PROHliks] verbose. "The *prolix* shock-jock was criticized as a 'demoralized degenerate.'" "The television talk show was *prolix* and insubstantial, as it never got to the heart of its subject." "His novels are criticized as *prolix*." "The vague essay was *prolix*." Syn.: loquacious, wordy. Ant.: reticent.

pronunciamento [prununseeuMENtoh] a pronouncement or manifesto. "The dictator issued a *pronunciamento* denouncing foreign attempts to intervene in his country." "President Franklin Roosevelt (1882-1945) issued a *pronunciamento* closing banks for a 'bank holiday.'" "The philosopher's *pronunciamento* declared that God is dead." "The *pronunciamento* declared that the family is sacred."

propinquity [pruPINGkwitee] proximity. "The *propinquity* in the car of the teenage girl to the boy excited furtive feelings of love in him." "The *propinquity* of the candy store to his home was to figure in the decline of his health." "She believed that the *propinquity* of the chemical plant and its pollution led to her husband's cancer." "The *propinquity* of the frozen custard shop was bad for her diet." Syn.: closeness, nearness.

propitiate [prohPISHeeayt] to appease. "It is probably a mistake to *propitiate* a warlike country." "The teacher was not about to be *propitiated* by kind remarks from the student." "Her paranoia could not be *propitiated*." "The editor would not be *propitiated*." Syn.: mollify. Ant.: antagonize.

propitious [pruPISHus] appearing to be favorable; auspicious. "The weather was *propitious* for baseball." "The early election results were *propitious* for their candidate." "All indications were *propitious* for the rocket launch." "The day looked *propitious* for a picnic." Syn.: promising.

propound [pruPOUND] to set forth. "The father and mother confidently *propounded* through their actions the proper behavior for their children." "The Declaration of Independence went beyond politics and *propounded* some human rights." "Marx *propounded* the reasons for the supposed inevitable collapse of capitalism." "The social critic *propounded* the theory of a dying culture." Syn.: proffer.

proprietary [pruPRIHiteree] pertaining to property or ownership. "The drug was a *proprietary* medicine." "She opened a chain of *proprietary* shops." "The

formula was *proprietary*, was patented." "The shop had a *proprietary* logo."
prosaic [prohZAYik] commonplace, dull, unimaginative. "The frightful *prosaic*
truth is that they were all the same." "The *prosaic* college did not have high
standards." "The town's culture was *prosaic*." "The modern mystery novel is
prosaic and not imaginative." Syn.: matter-of-fact, pedestrian, plain.
proscenium [prohSEEneeum] the arch that separates a stage from the auditorium. "Workers added a *proscenium* to the theater." "The *proscenium* framed
the spectacle playing on the stage." "The play's director put in a second *proscenium* to the theater." "The *proscenium* was a dramatic structure."
proscribe [prohSKRIHB] to prohibit. "To say *proscribe* in German you refer to
something as *verboten*." "Smoking in restaurants was *proscribed* by state
law." "Racial discrimination was formally *proscribed* by civil rights laws."
"Discussing inherited wealth in the media was *proscribed* as a taboo." Syn.:
ban, disallow, enjoin, interdict. Ant.: allow.
proselyte [PROSuliht] a new convert. "Roman catacombs are intriguing sites
because, among other things, early Christian *proselytes* would gather in them
for forbidden worship." "*Proselytes* to Greek fraternities must needs be cautious." "The *proselytes* were ruthlessly hazed." "The *proselytes* were inte-
grated into the association." Syn.: follower.
prosody [PROSudee] poetic meter and versification. "Their spoken language
had a distinct *prosody*." "The poet's *prosody* was involved." "The poem had
a unique *prosody*." "The dramatist's *prosody* was blank verse."
protean [PROHteeun] readily versatile. "He was a *protean* artist—actor, director,
writer and stunt performer." "The third baseman was *protean*, as he hit for
power, stole bases and defended brilliantly." "The woman was *protean*, as
she held down a job and was wife and mother at the same time." "The television station's corruption was *protean*."
pro tempore [PROH TEMpohree] for the time being. "She was named ambassador *pro tempore*." "He took control of the business *pro tempore*." "He became *pro tempore* Speaker of the House." "He needed to take a job *pro tempore*." Sometimes abbreviated *pro tem*.
provenance [PROVununs] place of origin; source. "The *provenance* of his fortune was Africa." "Her *provenance* was Australia and New Jersey." "The
provenance of his earnings was a restaurant where he was a dishwasher."
"The *provenance* of the countess was Russia." Syn.: derivation.
provender [PROVundur] provisions. "*Provender* for the rich, claimed the radical, is coercively taken from workers." "*Provender* first goes to the prince
(from Latin *primus*, first), before being mass distributed." "The military
needed much *provender*." "The family fearing a third world war put *provender* in a bomb shelter."
provincial [pruVINshul] culturally backward; lacking intellectual and esthetic
refinement. "The city was so *provincial* that its television station announced
every night, 'It's 10pm, do you know where your children are?'" "There are
few who would not rather be taken in adultery than *provincialism*." "Mark
Twain hated American *provincialism*." "The conservative claimed that *provincialism* stems from poorly-educated masses." Syn.: illiberal, narrow-

minded, parochial, rustic, unsophisticated. Ant.: cosmopolitan.

prurient [PROOReeunt] suggestive of or tending toward erotic desire or behavior. *"Prurient* behavior in public is frowned on." "He had to suppress a *prurient* urge evoked by his female coworker." "He never felt *prurient* toward another male." "The magazine was *prurient.*" Syn.: concupiscent, lecherous, risqué, salacious, unchaste.

psychedelic [sihkiDELik] pertaining to a mental state of intense perception and sometimes sensory distortion and hallucination. "The philosopher tried LSD in a *psychedelic* effort to transcend reality." *"Psychedelic* sometimes refers to psychotic perception." "Hippies were into the *psychedelic.*" "The young woman sank into emotional illness and the *psychedelic* hearing of voices." Syn.: hallucinogenic, intoxicating, mind-expanding.

public domain [PUBlik dohMAYN] the status of literary works and inventions whose copyright or patent has expired and thus may be used or reproduced by anyone without paying a fee. "The book, written in 1920, under American law is in the *public domain,* its copyright having expired." "The invention passed into the *public domain* so that one family could no longer profit from it." "Everything written by Mark Twain (1835-1910) is in the *public domain.*" "The woman renewed the copyright on her late father's novel so that it would not enter the *public domain.*"

pudency [PYOODnsee] modesty; bashfulness. "His *pudency* was a burden to a social life." "Their love was marred by *pudency.*" *"Pudency* had nothing to do with it, he declared regarding an act that brought him praise." *"Pudency* may be a vice." From a Latin word meaning "to be ashamed." Syn.: coldness, coyness, timidity. Ant.: audacity, lechery, venery.

puerile [PYOORul] childish. "One might occasionally shed his wise maturity for a little *puerile* fun." "They had trouble maturing and at heart were always *puerile.*" "The woman was embarrassed by her husband's *puerile* behavior." "The men and women at the party adopted *puerile* behavior." Syn.: immature. Ant.: serious.

pugnacious [pugNAYshus] quarrelsome. "Society, said Hobbes, is a war of everyone against everyone due to man's inherently *pugnacious* nature." "He was *pugnacious* and got into fights frequently." "His *pugnacity* included fighting another man for a parking space." "He was a *pugnacious* hockey player." Syn.: belligerent, combative, truculent. Ant.: amiable.

puissant [PWISunt] powerful. "Bacon noted that while new nobility stems from *puissance,* established nobility owes its position to time." "The *puissant* are wealthy, and vice-versa." "He is *puissant* but uneducated." "The CEO was *puissant.*" Syn.: potent. Ant.: impotent.

pulchritude [PULkritood] physical beauty. "A woman's *pulchritude* will fade, as is said in French, as the leaf falls to the ground." "Most of a woman's *pulchritude* is in the setting of the eyes." "The *pulchritude* of the woman brought her many suitors." "Helen of Troy possessed fabled *pulchritude.*" Syn.: handsomeness, loveliness. Ant.: ugliness.

pulpit [PULpit] the platform from which a clergyman preaches; the clerical profession; clergymen. "The American *pulpit* seems to have no notion of criticizing greed." "The American *pulpit*, claimed the conservative, is given over to money." "The *pulpit* was so demoralized that it ceased to preach." "The *pulpit* is sometimes responsible for establishing what became great universities."

punctilio [pungkTILeeoh] a fine point of conduct or etiquette. "*Punctilio* required that he precede her into the building." "*Punctilio* regulated all aspects of the society ball." "The French observe *punctilio* between the sexes." "Their disagreement was a matter of *punctilio* and nothing more."

purblind [PURblihnd] slow-witted; slow to perceive. "Justice is sometimes *purblind*." "She was *purblind* to her husband's infidelity." "The *purblind* student needed special instruction." "The big young woman was *purblind*."

Puritan [PYOORitun] a morally-rigid person austere about sex. "The people were liberated from most sexual taboos, but still were *Puritanical* in some respects." "The conservative seemed to advocate *Puritanism*." "The teachers were *Puritanical*." "The Republican senator's position left him open to the charge of *Puritanism*."

purlieu [PURLyoo] environ; one's haunt or neighborhood. "Until recent times a man's lifetime *purlieu* might be restricted to a town or village and a few fields nearby, and he would never see anything of the greater world." "His *purlieu* was the Bronx." "He entered his rival's *purlieu* seeking revenge." "His business was in his own *purlieu*."

purlieus [PURloo] outskirts; environs. "They set up their business on the *purlieus* of Paris." "The army bombarded the city from its *purlieus*." "A castle was built on the river's *purlieus*." "Her home was on the *purlieus* of the city." The origin of *purlieus* is uncertain.

purview [PURvyoo] the range of a subject or concern; comprehension. "Animal behavior is not in the *purview* of sociology." "Murder is not usually in the *purview* of the federal government." "Ability in foreign languages was not in the *purview* of the Arkansas man." "Computer literacy was not in the *purview* of the elderly couple." Syn.: scope.

pusillanimous [pyoosuLANumus] cowardly. "When his soldiers showed some *pusillanimity* in the face of the enemy army, Frederick the Great exhorted them with the words 'do you want to live forever?'" "It is proverbial that the *pusillanimous* man dies a thousand deaths." "Only *pusillanimity* prevented him from divulging the truth." "His witnesses were *pusillanimous* and easily cowered." Syn.: faint-hearted, fearful, lily-livered, spineless. Ant.: brave, courageous.

putative [PYOOtutiv] reputed. "He was the *putative* crime boss of New York." "*Putatively* they had no compassion." "The report put the blame for the disaster on the *putative* alcoholism of the captain." "*Putatively* women should observe silence among men." Syn.: alleged, presumed, supposed.

Putsch [POOCH] (German) a sudden revolt or coup. "Hitler's beer hall *Putsch* was an attempt to take control of Weimar-governed Munich." "The *Putsch* to oust the new chancellor failed." "The men behind the *Putsch* lacked arms." "The tottering government inspired more than one *Putsch*." Syn.: intrigue, plot.

pyrrhic victory [PIRik VIKturee] a victory gained at great cost. "After the army's *pyrrhic victory*, the row upon row of the dead was a dreadful sight." "Obviously the *pyrrhic victory* of the First World War was not enough to deter further wars." "It would be a *pyrrhic victory* to gain fortune at the cost of an honest reputation." "The creases on his brow spoke of a *pyrrhic victory*." After a King Pyrrhus of Epirus (in ancient Greece).

Q

quacksalver [KWAKsalvur] a quack doctor. "The psychoanalyst was a *quacksalver*." "The *quacksalver* offered to crook a person's back." "Modern medicine often discovers that some of the remedies of *quacksalvers* from prior centuries had a sound basis in physiology, though they may have been only marginally effective." "The nutritional therapist was mistakenly accused of being a *quacksalver*." Syn.: charlatan, fraud, mountebank.

quash [KWOSH] to quell; to make null or set aside in a legal action. "The court *quashed* the man's request for an injunction without even allowing him to call a witness." "The queen sent a duke to *quash* the hungry peasants' rebellion." "The U.S. *quashed* the Japanese attempt to take Australia." "The judge felt some satisfaction in *quashing* the suit of the 'tree huggers.'" Syn.: suppress.

querulous [KWERulus] peevish. "Seeing a *querulous* customer at a restaurant fussing over trivia reminded him of the German word for 'to complain'–*beklagen* (as though it expressed in English *beclog*)." "She was *querulous*, and not an amiable companion for a man." "He reacted *querulously* to the citation for speeding." "He was *querulous* in protecting his sports car." Syn.: cantankerous, cranky, whining. Ant.: agreeable

quiddity [KWIDitee] the true essence of something. "The *quiddity* of the extremist is opposing extreme inequality." "The *quiddity* of fairness is that each person have a democratic say in the makeup of things." "The *quiddity* of democracy is not merely the franchise." "The *quiddity* of his argument was that man is not biologically adjusted to mass society." Syn.: quintessence. Ant.: nonsense.

quidnunc [KWIDnungk] a busybody. "He was a sort of *quidnunc*, with a stake in everyone's opinion of himself." "The *quidnunc* could never pass up an opportunity to gossip." "She was an amiable *quidnunc*." "The *quidnunc* this time had an important piece of gossip." Syn.: gossip, kibitzer, meddler, talebearer.

quid pro quo [kwidprohKWOH] (Latin) an equal exchange or substitution. "The terrorists demanded a *quid pro quo* for release of the hostages." "The boy angled for a *quid pro quo* at the restaurant where he worked." "The lawyer arranged a *quid pro quo* for his client." "The man entered an illegal *quid pro quo* in a business deal." This term means "something for something" in Latin.

quiescent [kwihESunt] dormant. "The *quiescent* volcano suddenly erupted." "There was nothing *quiescent* or restrained about his temper tantrums." "A streak of rage, though temporarily *quiescent*, was nevertheless visible in his gaze." "The old man had *quiescent* ability in tennis." Syn.: inactive, inert, latent. Ant.: active.

quietism [KWIHitizum] a form of religious mysticism; a state of repose or passivity. "The man wished to meditate and attain *quietism*." "The *quietist* extinguished desire." "The youth spent time meditating but could not achieve true *quietism*." "The Indian mystic practiced *quietism*."

quietus [kwihEEtus] something that causes an end; release from life. "He wanted some sort of *quietus*, but he was not suicidal." "The *quietus* in his life was to be an antidepressant." "For who would bear the whips and scorns of time, the oppressor's wrong, the proud man's contumely, the pangs of disprized love, the law's delay...when he himself might his quietus make with a bare bodkin?" (Shakespeare, *Hamlet*.) "The terminal cancer patient wanted *quietus*."

quintessence [kwinTESuns] the most typical instance. "The *quintessence* of being extremely rich is symbolic violence, the successful manipulation of cultural symbols." "The *quintessence* of evil, he thought, is to do a wrong and then rub it in." "The *quintessence* of sloth is to sleep half the day." "The *quintessence* of psychiatric illness, whatever the diagnosis, is emotional pain." Syn.: embodiment.

Quis custodiet custodes? [KWIS...] (Latin) "Who will guard the guardians?" Juvenal. "With regard to the leaders of class society, it is reasonable to ask, '*Quis custodiet custodes?*'" "*Quis custodiet custodes?* raises the issue that every governing class acts in its own interest, rather than the interest of the nation as a whole." "*Quis custodiet custodes?* asked the candidate for the senate." "The sociologist pondered the idea of *Quis custodiet custodes?*"

quisling [KWIZling] a traitor. "The major *quislings* were executed after the fall of the enemy occupation." "Pierre Laval was a French *quisling* executed for collaboration with the Nazis." "She was considered a *quisling* for being the mistress of an enemy officer." "The *quisling* tried to flee the country." This term comes from the name of Vidkun Quisling (1887-1945), the principal Norwegian collaborator with the Nazis. Syn.: collaborator, deserter, turncoat. Ant.: loyalist.

quixotic [kwikSOTik] impractically chivalrous or romantic. "The young man for a time was a *quixotic* dreamer." "She was very practical and never *quixotic*." "The romance novel described a pair of teenagers *quixotically* in love." "The young woman became *quixotically* attached to a man, but love between them was not to be." "The man accused his daughter of *quixotically* choosing a man to marry." Syn.: unrealistic. Ant.: practical.

quotidian [kwohTIDeeun] recurring daily. "The *quotidian* ringing of church bells is a serene tintinnabulation in a European village." "He took his *quotid-*

ian shower at ten a.m." "The *quotidian* violence in the streets was a national blight." "The retiree took his *quotidian* walk through the subdivision." Syn.: diurnal.

R

rabble [RABul] the vulgar commoners. "The *rabble* contrasts socially with the ruling elite—the one overwhelmed by toil, the other blessed with class privilege." "He was born to the middle class and was more at home with the more polite people than the *rabble*." "The *'rabble,'* as she called them, marched down the street she lived in." "The *rabble* were not revolutionary." Syn.: canaille, hoi polloi, mob, proletariat, riffraff.

rackrent [RAKrent] exorbitant rent; (verb) to exact exorbitant rent from. "The miser demanded *rackrent* to the sum of $9000." "The poor family was the victim of *rackrent*." "The young man could not afford the *rackrent*." "*Rackrent* was common in the district."

raconteur [rakonTEUR] a skilled story teller. "When drunk he made an amusing *raconteur*." "The old *raconteur* had trouble remembering facts." "The *raconteur* did not like to be interrupted in his story." "The *raconteur* related interesting anecdotes about his experience in the war."

raffish [RAFish] vulgar; low-class; rakish. "The carnival was full of *raffish* people." "The *raffish* people attended the blood-letting in the Roman coliseum." "Shakespeare referred to *raffish* people as 'tagrag.'" "The masses of men and women may be *raffish,* but they are part of common humanity." Syn.: coarse, inelegant, offensive, plebeian, uncouth, ungenteel.

ragamuffin [RAGumufin] a ragged, unkempt child. "The *ragamuffin* was the product of a broken home." "The *ragamuffin* was an orphan." "A *ragamuffin* was the hero of the novella." "Through pluck the *ragamuffin* succeeded in life." From the poem *Piers Plowman* (1393). Syn.: tatterdemalion.

raillery [RAYluree] banter. "Just as Bacon advised mixing 'jest' and 'earnest,' a little *raillery* is not improper in almost any situation." "The *raillery* among the group of pals became mean at times." "The couple did engage in *raillery* but still professed to be in love." Syn.: badinage, persiflage.

rakish [RAYkish] smart or dashing. "He always wears *rakish* suits to impress the ladies." "The *rakish* young man settled down to a family life in middle-age." "He was fat and dowdy rather than *rakish*." "In his youth he was a *rakish* boulevardier." Syn.: dapper, debonair, jaunty, stylish. Ant.: bland.

ramshackle [RAMshakul] rickety and dilapidated. "Many *ramshackle* buildings in the city desperately need to be demolished." "The homeless man lived in a *ramshackle* hut under the highway." "The man was sad to learn that his boyhood home became *ramshackle.*" "The train station was reduced to a *ramshackle* state." Syn.: derelict, tumble-down.

rancor [RANGkur] malice. "The heavy-drinking man felt such *rancor* toward his wife that he beat her." "The *rancor* between the two men flared into a fist fight." "The soldier felt no *rancor* toward the enemy soldiers he killed." "The *rancor* between them was extreme." Syn.: animosity, bitterness, spite, venom, vindictiveness. Ant.: amiability.

randy [RANdee] lustful. "The *randy* ambassador had a reputation as a womanizer." "He was *randy* but lacked the ability to charm a woman into bed." "The *randy* teen knew what he wanted." "His *randy* ways got him into trouble." Syn.: lascivious, libidinous.

rankle [RANGkul] to keenly annoy. "Subservience to his supervisor *rankled* the factory worker." "Someone must have *rankled* the premier, since he appeared horn-mad." "The social critic *rankled* people with his book." "He was *rankled* by the F arbitrarily dished out by a paranoid teacher." Syn.: exasperate, irk, nettle. Ant.: pacify.

rapacious [ruPAYshus] predatory. "The defeated retreating army *rapaciously* gouged everything in its path." "He *rapaciously* pursued money." "He wanted this and he wanted that—his desires were *rapacious.*" "The radical claimed that possession of multi-millions of dollars is *ipso facto* proof of *rapacity.*" Syn.: greedy, ravenous, voracious.

rapine [RAPin] plunder. "Aztec *rapine* included vanquished people for human sacrifice." "The conquistadors searched for *rapine* of gold and silver." "The *rapine,* you might say, of high status is a high income." "The *rapine* was shipped back to Europe."

rapport [ruPOHR] (French) a harmonious relationship. "Some young men establish a *rapport* with a girl with but one lascivious goal in mind." "The *rapport* of the two stars of the movie made it a hit." "The excellent teacher failed to establish a *rapport* with the other teachers." "*Rapport* is important in the military." Syn.: camaraderie, fellowship. Ant.: friction.

rapprochement [rahproshMAHN] (French) reconciliation, especially between two nations. "The American *rapprochement* with postwar Germany and Japan was intended to counter the influence of Communist Russia." "President Nixon initiated American *rapprochement* with China." "The two countries could not establish a *rapprochement.*" "The peace negotiations went well and a *rapprochement* seemed near." Syn.: accord, entente.

rapscallion [rapSKALyun] a rogue or rascal. "The *rapscallion* informed on the group." "The *rapscallion* was careless with cigarettes and almost started a fire." "The *rapscallion* stole the coat from the man's locker." "The *rapscallion* was guilty of shoplifting." The word *rapscallion* is based on "rascal." Syn.: blackguard, knave, scoundrel.

rara avis [RARu AYvis] (Latin) a rare person or thing. "A country trying itself for war crimes is a *rara avis.*" "It was a *rara avis* to see her in a swim suit." "A beautiful happy moment in his life was a *rara avis.*" "The father's absence in the family was not a *rara avis.*" In Latin *rara avis* means a "rare bird."

rarefy [RARufih] to refine. "A poor man may *rarefy* his spiritual life as compensation for not being wealthy." "He was chastised into a more modest lifestyle by his search for *rarefied* pleasure." "His *rarefied* intellect contrasted with his lack of means." "The book on education was *rarefied*." Syn.: purify.

ratiocination [rasheeosuNAYshun] the process of logical reasoning. "Sherlock Holmes used *ratiocination*." "The man's *ratiocination* was bizarre and pathological." "The schizophrenic's *ratiocination* was poor." "*Ratiocination* led her to reject the idea."

rat race [RAT RAYS] a constant and exhausting activity or routine; the jungle. "The woman threw herself into the *rat race* at 17 as a secretary in the corporation, and moved up the hierarchy to a nice position in middle management." "Because American society is very competitive, *rat race* is a common expression." "The elderly man was glad to retire and get out of the *rat race*." "The artist refused to be a part of the *rat race*."

rattlebrained [RATulbraynd] scatterbrained. "She was a *rattlebrained*, artless young woman." "The skinny little boy was *rattlebrained*." "Because the man was *rattlebrained* they could not understand him." "The mentally retarded youth was *rattlebrained*." Syn.: harebrained. Ant.: bright.

Realpolitik [rayALpohliteek] (German) the politics of national self-interest. "*Realpolitik* in all ages has consisted of imperialism and propaganda." "The administration sought to steer a course of *Realpolitik*." "The country's *Realpolitik* pursued resources like coal, oil and crops." "Niccolò Machiavelli (1469-1527), author of *The Prince,* was the advocate of *Realpolitik par excellence.*"

recalcitrant [riKALsitrunt] resisting control; hard to deal with. "The *recalcitrant* prisoner refused to take the medicine." "The *recalcitrant* suspect was beaten by police." "'Damn right I'm going to be *recalcitrant,*' exclaimed the man arrested for allegedly disturbing the peace." "The screaming *recalcitrant* child refused to eat what was served." Syn.: disobedient, headstrong, intractable, obstinate, refractory, unruly. Ant.: cooperative, docile.

réchauffé [rayshohFAY] (French) revived, overworked material, as in the arts. "The movie *History of the World* is a *réchauffé* turkey." "The museum contained some abstract, *réchauffé* works of 'art.'" "The theme of the novel was a little *réchauffé*." "Private detective stories are a *réchauffé* theme."

recherché [rusherSHAY] (French) rare; exquisite; overrefined. "Milton's works are to some critics *recherché* to the point of obscuring language." "The editor declared the essay *recherché* and would not publish it." "The art piece was *recherché* and valuable." "The furnishings of the society woman were *recherché*." Syn.: extraordinary. Ant.: ordinary.

recidivism [riSIDuvizum] behavioral backsliding, as in repeating a crime. "The alcoholic had a hard time avoiding *recidivism* and staying on the wagon." "The rate of *recidivism* was high for high school dropouts." "Much time and effort went into preventing *recidivism*." "*Recidivism* was high when the prognosis was guarded, as in schizophrenia." Syn.: recession, regression, relapse, reversion.

reclame [rayKLAM] (French) publicity; hunger for publicity. "His desire for *reclame* exceeded all bounds." "The political race was a contest for *reclame*." "His *reclame* was out-Heroding." "He never outgrew *reclame*." Syn.: fame.

recondite [riKONdiht] abstruse or esoteric. "Knowledge of a classic language like Greek or Sanskrit is *recondite*." "The scholar dealt with very *recondite* facts." "The outsider had difficulty understanding the expert's *recondite* jargon." "His ability at math was *recondite*." Syn.: complex, enigmatic. Ant.: clear, exoteric, facile.

recreant [REKreeunt] a coward; a disloyal person. "A *recreant* tells a lie that sinks in." "A *recreant* in his definition was anyone worth more than $10 million." "He was a *recreant,* since he refused to come forward and tell the truth." "The *recreant* betrayed him to the police." Syn.: base, dastardly, pusillanimous.

rectitude [REKtitood] moral uprightness. "He was loathsome, having no *rectitude* at all." "Social perception of *rectitude* can be bought." "You should not attribute much *rectitude* to the man who pulled that prank." "His *rectitude* did not cover believing his nephew." Syn.: integrity, probity, righteousness.

recusant [REKyoozunt] refusing to submit or comply; (noun) a person who is recusant. "It is not easy being a *recusant* in prison." "The draft dodger was a kind of *recusant*." "The *recusant* refused to take an oath of allegiance." "With regard to the need to diet she was *recusant*." Syn.: disobedient.

red-letter [RED LETur] memorable; denoting a holiday. "The origin of *red-letter* days is evident in the word *holiday*, which comes from the combination of 'holy' and 'day.'" "Christmas 1980 was a *red-letter* day he will never forget." "His mother went out of her way to make the *red-letter* day special." "Nineteen-eighty-one was not *red-letter* for him, instead being a year he would rather forget."

redneck [REDnek] an ignorant country bumpkin. "The *redneck* was uneducated." "The *rednecks* liked boats, fishing and pick-up trucks." "The *redneck* fought with his neighbor." "The whole county was *redneck*." "The *redneck* lived in a shabby home." Syn.: hoosier, oakie, rube, yokel.

redolent [REDulunt] odorous; suggestive. "A profusion of butterflies is *redolent* of the end of summer." "The restaurant was *redolent* of seafood." "The air was *redolent* of a dead skunk." "The odor was *redolent* of flowers in spring." "To him the smoke of the fireworks was *redolent* of past Independence Days." Syn.: aromatic, reminiscent.

redress [riDRES] to set right. "The poor man finds *redress* of his grievances in court impossible." "He was not in a position to *redress* the injustice." "*Redress* your complaints in the real world, not in your imagination, was his advice." "The revolutionaries sought *redress* of their grievances." Syn.: rectify, remedy. Ant.: aggravate.

reductio ad absurdum [ridukTEEoh AD...] (Latin) "reduction to an absurdity": a demonstration of the invalidity of an argument by showing its conclusion to be absurd. "The radical showed that the conservative's argument amounted to a *reductio ad absurdum*." "The economist tried to discredit equality with a *reductio ad absurdum*." "His *reductio ad absurdum* did not make sense." "Her *reductio ad absurdum* was an attempt to ridicule evolution science."

refulgent [riFOOLjunt] radiant. "Fifteen years had sufficed to steal the *refulgent* glow of youth from her cheeks." "The woman looked *refulgent* and beautiful at her wedding." "At age 45 she was no longer *refulgent*." "The Christmas tree had a beautiful *refulgent* beam." Syn.: brilliant, glittering, lustrous, sparkling.

regale [riGAYL] to delight through entertainment. "The wedding reception for the 'socialite' was an expensive *regaling*." "He *regaled* them with stories about his college days." "Scheherazade *regaled* her husband every night." "They *regaled* each other with sentimental talk about the old days." Syn.: amuse, divert, entertain.

reify [REEufih] to treat an abstraction as if it were concrete. "Sartre asserted that the opposite of *reification* in human affairs—turning people into an abstraction—is the source of evil." "The sociologist claimed that the writer in his book *reified* society." "It is not always easy to understand the way the word *reify* is used." "People attempt to *reify* social institutions." Syn.: objectify.

reliquary [RELukweree] a receptacle for storing sacred relics. "Several valuable antiques were found in the *reliquary*." "Something was stolen from the *reliquary*." "The *reliquary* contained objects of sentimental value to the family." "Below the cellar, where the family had never gone, a treasured *reliquary* was discovered." "The *reliquary* contained nothing of commercial value."

remiss [riMIS] negligent. "The fathers were *remiss* in not playing a role in the life of their family." "The education of the successful corporate president was *remiss*." "She felt *remiss* and unable to provide emotionally for her children." "He was *remiss* in not treating her better." Syn.: careless, derelict, dilatory, lax, negligent, slack, slothful, thoughtless.

remonstrate [riMONstrayt] to protest. "The dishwasher *remonstrated* that the penurious sub-minimum wage he was getting was unfairly far below the wage of the waiters and waitresses." "The radical *remonstrated* that the system crushes the poor, and rich men rule the system." "He *remonstrated* against nuclear weapons." "Martin Luther *remonstrated* that the church was corrupt." Syn.: argue, expostulate, object.

remunerate [riMYOOnurayt] to compensate for. "Marx's principle of surplus value states that the source of profit lies in *remuneration* of labor at less than full value." "The novelist felt that her *remuneration* was inadequate." "The house painter hated his job, thought the *remuneration* was too little and referred to it as a 'grind.'" "CEOs, asserted the radical, receive excessive *remuneration*." "The conservative asserted that one's *remuneration* is generally exactly what it should be." Syn.: compensate, pay, tender.

rentier [ranTYAY] (French) a person with a fixed income, as from rent or bonds. "Being a *rentier*, she did not work for a living." "The family made a handsome living as *rentiers*." "The rent established by *rentiers* was exorbitant." "The conservative found no reason to find fault with idle *rentiers*."

repertoire [REPurtwar] the body of works of an artist or company. "The *repertoire* of the theatre was stock sentimentality." "He had a whole *repertoire* of famous songs." "His *repertoire* included an ideology as a creative artist." "The *repertoire* of the circus included a lion-tamer." Syn.: repertory.

repine [riPIHN] to fret or complain; to yearn for. "He *repined* for his teenaged love." "The old woman *repined* for the happiness of youth." "He *repined* that their house was undistinguished." "The man *repined* that he did not have enough money." Syn.: grieve.

reprobate [REPrubayt] a wicked person. "The Congressman declared that only a *reprobate* would wish to raise the inheritance tax." "The convicted 'child molester' was seen as a *reprobate*." "The *reprobate* teased the man he had just assaulted." "The sociologist was considered a *reprobate* for calling attention to society's taboos." Syn.: blackguard, scoundrel, villain. Ant.: angel, saint.

reprove [riPROOV] to scold or rebuke. "The family was *reproved* for allowing their three-year-old daughter to loll on the beach topless." "The city's wealthiest family was *reproved* for not giving to charity." "The woman *reproved* her children for 'taking the Lord's name in vain.'" "The woman *reproved* her daughter for calling too often for mother." "The boy was *reproved* for satirizing the sweet mentally-retarded girl." Syn.: admonish, censure, chide.

requiem [REKweeum] a musical service or dirge for the dead. "The *requiem* for the victims of the accident was moving." "The pastor performed a *requiem* for the fallen hero." "Still wouldst thou sing, and I have ears in vain—To thy high requiem become a sod." (John Keats, *Ode to a Nightingale*.) "A *requiem* was held for the victims of the bombing." Syn.: funeral, mass.

requite [riKWIHT] to repay; to avenge. "She was well *requited* for the love of the rather unusual man." "The boy's love for the fifteen-year-old girl was not *requited*." "He never had a chance to *requite* his uncle for the kindness." "He *requited* the man who did him wrong." Syn.: compensate, recompense, reimburse, repay.

reticent [RETisunt] habitually silent. "His coworkers seemed determined to prick it out of him, since he was *reticent*." "The *reticent* man married a shy woman." "The class would not allow the bashful boy to remain *reticent*." "She was *reticent* and pretty." Syn.: taciturn. Ant.: garrulous, loquacious, talkative, voluble.

retrench [riTRENCH] to reduce; to economize. "Congress' continual economic *retrenchment* never seems to fail to mean gutting the budget for social needs." "The student without means was forced to *retrench* his spending habit." "*Retrenchment* for the family meant 'belt-tightening,' which appears to refer to losing weight due to less money for meals." "*Retrenchment* meant less money for entertainment." Syn.: curtail. Ant.: lavish.

revanche [riVANCH] (also *revanchism*) the policy of a country to retake lost territory. "The country's reckless *revanche* led to war." "The nation's leaders were committed to *revanche*." "European history is littered with *revanche*." "*Revanche* caused much conflict." Syn.: irredentism.

reverie [REVuree] daydreaming. "During the slow tedium of the economics class, the student had to try hard to not get lost in *reverie*." "When her life became dull she turned to *reverie*." "Debussey composed *reverie* music." "The girl was lost in a romantic *reverie*." Syn.: musing, wool-gathering.

rialto [reeALtoh] a marketplace. "They sold their wares at the *rialto*." "She shopped at the *rialto* in Florence." "The *rialto* was busiest on Friday." "No aristocrats appeared at the *rialto*." After the rialto in Venice, Italy.

ribald [RIBuld] lewd; abusive. "The girl was showered with *ribald* exclamations as she walked past the group of men." "The *ribald* denunciation could not be repeated in court." "After a while the *ribaldry* from mean coworkers did not affect him." "The boxer was *ribald* and mean." Syn.: bawdy, coarse.

rickshaw [RIKsha] in Asia, a two-wheeled passenger vehicle pulled by a man. "The *rickshaw* took the man to the marketplace." "The man was weary of pulling a *rickshaw* for a living." "There were dozens of *rickshaws* waiting for a passenger at the airport." "*Rickshaws* were to be found all over the city."

Riemannian geometry [reeMANeeun...] nonEuclidean geometry wherein parallel lines intersect. "The mathematician studied *Riemannian geometry*." "The student did not understand how *Riemannian geometry* was applied." "*Riemannian geometry* seemed contrary to common sense to the college student." "The engineer used *Riemannian geometry* in her calculations."

riposte [riPOHST] a quick retort in speech or action; a counterstroke. "His effective *riposte* made his opponent cringe." "The comedian was known for his quick *riposte*." "The argument ended with a *riposte* by the husband." "The attacking army met with a solid *riposte* by the enemy." Syn.: rejoinder, reply.

risible [RIZubul] laughable; pertaining to laughter. "The young man's attempt at a handstand was *risible*." "The comedian evoked *risible* applause." "The pupil's art work was *risible*." "The lyrics of the song were *risible*." Syn.: humorous, ludicrous. Ant.: serious.

Risorgimento [reesorjeeMENto] the movement for Italian liberation and unification; the period of this movement, 1750-1870. "The *Risorgimento* finally succeeded." "The *Risorgimento* fought foreign control of Italy." "The *Risorgimento* needed a leader." "The history student wrote his dissertation on the *Risorgimento*."

risqué [risKAY] almost indecent. "He enjoyed telling *risqué* jokes at their family get-togethers." "*Risqué* words like 'ass' and 'crap' can now be said on television." "Her occupation was *risqué*—exotic dancer." "Her bikini was *risqué*." Syn.: bawdy, indelicate, lewd, naughty, ribald, salacious, suggestive, smutty. Ant.: decent, decorous.

ritz [RITS] ostentatiousness; a pretension of wealth or luxury. "The wealthy couple was 'putting on the *ritz*.'" "He desired *ritz* but was poor." "There is a popular song with the phrase 'putting on the *ritz*.'" "The Rosenkranz family was accustomed to *ritz*." Syn.: opulence, prosperity.

rococo [ruKOHkoh] an elegant and ornately refined style of architecture beginning in France about 1720, that evolved from baroque. "The tourists got an idea of the power of the palace's erstwhile prince by touring the *rococo* residence." "*Rococo* is more refined than baroque." "The *rococo* palace was magnificent." "Commoners did not live in *rococo* residences."

rodomontade [rodumonTAYD] bluster or empty bragging; vainglorious boasting. "He was 'sick and tired' of hearing his nephew's *rodomontade*." "He got away with *rodomontade* at school." "The general's *rodomontade* did not help win the war." "His *rodomontade* was meant to deter bullying by bigger boys." "His *rodomontade* of war stories was nevertheless interesting conversation." Syn.: braggadocio, bravado, magniloquence, swagger. Ant.: diffidence, humility, timidity.

roil [ROIL] to disturb. "The thought of her son in the hospital *roiled* her evening." "He was *roiled* by the price of the car." "The illness *roiled* him." "The news *roiled* his sleep." Syn.: disquiet, fret. Ant.: calm, pacify, soothe, tranquilize.

roister [ROIstur] to act in an uproarious manner. "The college students partied and *roistered* through the night." "They got sauced and *roistered* in town." "He cut off his *roistering* when the bus arrived at school." "The six friends had fun *roistering*." Syn.: carouse, party, revel.

roman à clef [roMA naKLAY] (French) a novel about actual persons and events, though disguised. "The writer of academic books tried his hand at a *roman à clef*." "Her *roman à clef* was a bestseller." "The *roman à clef* spilled some scandalous secrets." "The French writer's *roman à clef* was worth reading."

Roman holiday [ROHmun HOLiday] a time of debauchery or violent or sadistic enjoyment. "The two dictionaries gave different definitions of *Roman holiday*." "The crowd spilled out of the auditorium and went on a *Roman holiday*." "The sixth-grade boys played hookie and went on a *Roman holiday*." "The anthropologist studying leisure delved into the *Roman holiday*." This term comes from the sadistic gladiatorial contests of ancient Rome.

rose-colored glasses [ROHZ...] an optimistic view of life and the world. "The sociologists analyzed society with *rose-colored glasses* and ignored conflict." "The Pollyanna seemed to wear *rose-colored glasses*." "One need not wear *rose-colored glasses*, but it is wise to keep a positive outlook." "Children seem to wear *rose-colored glasses*."

roué [rooAY] (French) a debauchee or libertine. "The *roué* never worked." "A female *roué*, for example a prostitute, is very stigmatized." "The *roué* was sentenced to 20 years imprisonment for putting child pornography on the Internet." "The *roué* attempted to coit with girls, not adult females." Syn.: libertine.

rueful [ROOful] causing sorrow; mournful. "Upon the death of her fiancé, the *rueful* woman vowed to live as a spinster." "He was very *rueful* when his dog died." "They did not appear very *rueful* when their mother died." "The boy was *rueful* when the family had to move and he lost his friends." Syn.: doleful, pitiable. Ant.: cheerful, gay, mirthful.

ruffian [RUFeeun] a hoodlum. "The party's *ruffians* intimidated voters at the polls." "The *ruffians* met at a predetermined site and rumbled." "Many of the fans at the soccer game were *ruffians*." "The *ruffians* tore up the restaurant." Syn.: rowdy, thug.

rumpus [RUMpus] a commotion; an uproar. "The children's *rumpus* woke up the parents." "A *rumpus* broke out in which one card player charged another with cheating." "The *rumpus* disturbed the college dormitory." "They were good friends, but went through several *rumpuses*." Syn.: disturbance, tumult.

rustic [RUStik] rural; boorish. "The European visitor finds some American cities *rustic*." "He was a *rustic* fool." "Jobs are scarce in many *rustic* areas." "The *rustic* family lead a mean life in the woodlands." Syn.: backwoods, provincial, unsophisticated. Ant.: cosmopolitan, cultured, worldly.

ruth [ROOTH] compassion; sorrow. "He felt *ruth* after beating up his best friend." "They have no *ruth*, claimed the historian after studying the society." "Whether they have or have not *ruth* is a great, valid question." "They had nothing but *ruth* for the girl suffering from spina bifida." Syn.: commiseration, condolence, mercy.

S

saccharine [SAKurin] excessively sweet. "The television show had actors exchanging *saccharine* comments and unctuous looks." "Their grandmother was *saccharine* with the kids, who sometimes misbehaved." "The man liked being *saccharine* to his girlfriend." "The family showered *saccharine* love on their dog." Syn.: cloying, mawkish, treacly.

sacerdotalism [sasurDOHTulizum] the system of the priesthood. "*Sacerdotalism* traditionally involved poverty." "Ostensibly *sacerdotalism* is about brotherly love." "Their *sacerdotalism* emphasized the Bible." "Although there were women ministers, *sacerdotalism* did not allow women priests."

sachem [SAYchum] a chief of a North American Indian tribe. "The *sachem* tried to bring peace to the Indian tribes of the Plains." "The *sachem* was not an elected official." "The *sachem* was warlike." "The Navaho *sachem* was peaceable."

sacred cow [SAYkrid KOU] something considered exempt from criticism. "Inherited wealth is America's *sacred cow*." "The writer asserted that every society has *sacred cows*." "The university's *sacred cow* was football." "The original *sacred cow* refers to an Indian practice."

sacrilege [SAKrulij] the violation or profanation of something held to be sacred. "The youths professing to be Christian were *sacrilegious*, wearing T-shirts and sandals to church." "The man appeared in church and committed *sacrilege* by glowering disinterestedly at the altar." "It is *sacrilege* to be money-hungry in the name of God." "The writer came across an amusing sentence in a French textbook that hints of *sacrilege*: 'Which is more scandalous, the Bible or the magazine *Oui*?'" Syn.: blasphemy, desecration, profanity.

sacrosanct [SAKrohsangkt] inviolable. "The environ of justice is *sacrosanct*; and as Bacon noted, 'the place of justice is a hallowed place.'" "The grave site was supposed to be *sacrosanct*." "His promise was *sacrosanct*: He never violated it." "Marriage should be *sacrosanct*." Syn.: revered, sacred, venerable. Ant.: debauched, defiled, impure, shameless.

sagacious [suGAYshus] wise. "Solomon of the Bible was reputedly *sagacious*." "Mix some light-hearted folly with your *sagaciousness*." "His marriage tested his *sagaciousness*." "For some reason the *sage* Francis Bacon (1561-1626) is considered mean." Ant.: benighted, fatuous, foolish.

salacious [suLAYshus] lascivious. "An escort service is quite a *salacious* place." "He was not attracted to the *salacious* girl." "The neighborhood was *salacious*, if there can be such a thing." "The magazine *Hustler* is *salacious*." Syn.: lewd, libidinous, wanton. Ant.: chaste.

salient [SAYleeunt] outstanding or prominent. "The *salient* fault with permissive child rearing is a lack of firmness." "The *salience* of the big-city mayor made him the target of a criminal investigation." "He was a *salient* high school football player." "The *salient* track star made the Olympic team." Syn.: conspicuous, prominent, striking. Ant.: commonplace.

salmagundi [salmuGUNdee] any mixture of things. "The salad was fortified with a *salmagundi* of food." "The drawer was called a 'junk drawer,' as it contained a *salmagundi*." "He took a *salmagundi* of courses at the university." "His recent life had been a *salmagundi* of mistakes." Syn.: conglomeration, gallimaufry, hodgepodge, medley.

salubrious [suLOObreeus] conducive to good health. "The Germans regard hot baths at such places as Baden-Baden as very *salubrious*." "The air in the country was *salubrious*." "Moderate daily exercise seems to be *salubrious*, whereas strenuous exercise may shorten life." "Polluted city air is not *salubrious*." Syn.: healthful, prophylactic, sanative. Ant.: insalubrious, morbid, vitiated.

samizdat [SAMizdat] an underground press. "Copies of the sexually-explicit novel were circulated for years in the *samizdat*." "The *samizdat* published anti-government tracts." "The *samizdat* kept alive forbidden literature." "Where there is much censorship there is likely to be a *samizdat*." This term comes from Russia.

sanctimonious [sangktuMOHneeus] affecting self-righteousness. "The police acted *sanctimoniously* during their arrest of the suspect." "The man hated *sanctimony*." "What a display of *sanctimony* the high school principal put on!" "The minister preaching the gospel of money was *sanctimonious*." Syn.: holier-than-thou, pious. Ant.: artless, candid, ingenuous, unassuming.

sang-froid [SANFRWA] (French) calmness, cool; in French, literally "cold blood." "The burglar stealthily carried out the crime with *sang-froid*." "It took considerable *sang-froid* to win the tennis match." "The police believed that the murderer had *sang-froid*." "The actor played his roles with *sang-froid*."

sanguinary [SANGgwuneree] blood-thirsty; pertaining to bloodshed. "The American Civil War was very *sanguinary*." "They wanted no part of *sanguinary* actions." "The D-Day invasion was *sanguinary*, as Allied troops were pinned on the beach and exposed to machine-gun fire." "The battle was tragically *sanguinary*." Syn.: gory.

sanguine [SANGgwin] cheerful or hopeful. "The diplomat was quite *sanguine* in his belief that there would be no more use of nuclear weapons." "Americans are *sanguine*, though that attitude may not be very deep." "He was *sanguine* about his prospect for finding a job." "The economist was *sanguine* about the economy." Syn.: buoyant, optimistic, positive, upbeat. Ant.: despondent, heavy-hearted, somber, sullen.

sans souci [SAN sooSEE] (French) carefree. "His *sans souci* performance as a right-fielder belied his excellent defensive ability." "She was a little disturbed rather than *sans souci*." "He longed for the *sans souci* days of youth." "Life at the rustic college was *sans souci*." "The old man lived *sans souci*." Syn.: lighthearted.

sapient [SAYpeeunt] wise. "The man was reputed to be *sapient*." "Whether the queen was *sapient* was open to question." "It is *sapient* to not say the first thing that comes to mind." "It may or may not be *sapient* to avoid extremes." Syn.: sagacious.

sardonic [sarDONik] bitterly derisive. "She *sardonically* described that her brother had paid her the equivalent of 12 cents an hour for watching his children while he worked." "The conservative *sardonically* reviewed the liberal's book." "He *sardonically* mentioned the low wages he made as a dishwasher." "She was *sardonic* about how her husband treated her." Syn.: caustic, scornful. Ant.: commendatory, laudatory.

saturnalia [saturNAYleeu] unrestrained celebration. "The life of the leisure class is fairly much continual *saturnalia*." "The tourists loved the *saturnalia* of the Italian town." "The people seemed incapable of enjoying *saturnalia* and really letting themselves go." "Many got drunk during the town's *saturnalia*." "In the West Saturday is the day of *saturnalia*." Syn.: festivity, jubilation, revelry. Ant.: dejection, solemnity.

saturnine [SATurnihn] morose; sluggish and gloomy. "The *saturnine* outlook of workers is due to their class position." "His marital difficulty left him *saturnine*." "She was *saturnine* when people left her party early." "He was prescribed a serotonin-increasing antidepressant for his *saturnine* mood, which was believed to involve a chemical imbalance." Syn.: disconsolate, doleful, glum. Ant.: blithe, genial.

satyr [SAYtur] a lecher; a man afflicted with satyriasis (excessive sexual desire in the male). "One of the unfortunate things of the *satyr* is that, according to a Greek myth, woman enjoys nine-tenths and man one-tenth of the pleasure of sex." "The *satyr* was compelled to free himself from thoughts of sex." "He was a 'dirty old man,' a *satyr*, and he sought out girls for pleasure." "The *satyr* did not consider masturbation an alternative." Syn.: erotomaniac, goat.

savoir-faire [SAVwar FER] (French) skill in social situations; moral tact. "The French, as opposed to American informality, insist on a sort of diplomatic *savoir-faire*, on formal, polite manners." "She was dignified and possessed of wonderful *savoir-faire*." "Early in his life he was in need of more *savoir-faire*, and suffered because of it." "He was a fool who lacked *savoir-faire*." Syn.: adroitness. Ant.: gaucherie, tactlessness.

scalawag [SKALuwag] a reprobate or rascal. "The *scalawag* insisted on being honest and turning in the wallet." "The *scalawag* underpaid his employees." "The *scalawag* had double the pleasure in tricking the trickster, as the proverb goes." "The *scalawag* slept until noon." Syn.: blackguard, knave, rapscallion, scoundrel.

scamp [SKAMP] a rogue or rascal. "The youngster was a *scamp* given to playing mean tricks on neighbors." "The *scamp* needed a sound spanking." "The *scamp* ate the whole chocolate cake." "The *scamp* stole from his grandmother." Syn.: knave, rapscallion.

Scaramouch [SKARumoosh] a cowardly braggart. "A character named Falstaff was a *Scaramouch* in two of Shakespeare's plays." "The *Scaramouch* told of his exploits." "The *Scaramouch* held forth at the inn." "What the *Scaramouch* said could not be trusted."

scarify [SKARufih] to harm by harsh criticism. "The man *scarified* his wife when in anger he called her a bad mother." "His friends turned on him and *scarified* him." "He accidently *scarified* his own father." "He was *scarified* by the newspaper article." Syn.: terrify.

Schadenfreude [SHAHdenfroyde] (German) pleasure derived from seeing others harmed. "*Schadenfreude* is one of those essential iniquities of human nature, being found in all societies and throughout history." "*Schadenfreude* was her motive, as it were, in refusing to admit the visitor." "The spectators in the Coliseum erupted in gleeful *Schadenfreude* as the lion jumped on the condemned man." "The radical referred to *Schadenfreude* as an example of human malevolence." In German, *schaden* means to "harm" and *Freude* means "pleasure." Syn.: ill-will. Ant.: commiseration, compassion, empathy.

Scheherazade [shuheruZAdu] a character in *The Arabian Nights* (a 10th century collection of Eastern folktales), and the wife of the sultan of India, who tells such interesting tales each night that the sultan spares her life to hear the continuation of them. "*Scheherazade* feared for her life." "*Scheherazade* was a legendary queen of Samarkand." "*Scheherazade* related the tale of 'Sinbad the Sailor.'" "The life of *Scheherazade* was finally spared after 1,000 nights."

schizophrenia [skitsuFRENeeu] a common psychosis marked by emotional withdrawal, and sometimes delusions, the hallmark of the disease being hearing voices (auditory hallucinations). "The *schizophrenic* was treated with a 'neuroleptic,' also called a major tranquilizer." "The radical argued that neuroleptics are not a 'chemical straight jacket,' and that *schizophrenics* are much better off taking them." "The chief biological trait of *schizophrenia* is excessive activity of the neurotransmitter dopamine, though that is not to say it is the cause." "The *schizophrenic* recovered after realizing that the 'voices' were not real."

schlepp [SHLEP] (Yiddish) to carry or lug something. "He practically *schlepped* his wife to the football game." "The defendant was *schlepped* out of the courtroom." "The screaming woman *schlepped* her crying son up the shoulder of the road and into the car." "The man *schlepped* a briefcase all around campus."

schlock [SHLOK] (Yiddish) (adj.) very inferior in quality; (noun) very bad taste;

a cheap article. "The producers and directors made violent films with bloody gore and realized a handsome profit from the *schlock*." "The radical claimed that violent *schlock* in movies promotes imitative and suggestive violence in 'real life.'" "The rummage sale was full of *schlock*." "The conservative decried the sentimental *schlock* on television." Syn.: junk.

schmaltz [SHMALTS] (Yiddish) excessive sentimentality, as in the arts. "The *schmaltz* of that musical was too much for him to bear." "Television tends to gloss over the past with *schmaltz*." "'*Schmaltz* has no place in politics,' said the radical." "*Schmaltz* is another word for treacle." Syn.: mawkishness. Ant.: realism.

schmo [SHMOH] (Yiddish) a stupid person or jerk. "She had much self-respect but was still known as a *schmo* by classmates." "The *schmo* had to put up with a lot of derision." "The teacher was no *schmo*." "A real *schmo* is like Moe, Larry and Curly." Syn.: cretin, idiot, imbecile.

schnorrer [SHNOHRur] (Yiddish) a parasite or sponger. "The *schnorrer* was always trying to borrow money from people." "He was a mooch and *schnorrer* who would eat food from the line in the cafeteria." "The *schnorrer* asked his grandmother for money." "The radical claimed that the true *schnorrer* is an heir who lives off society's labor." Syn.: scrounge.

scintilla [sinTILu] a small trace. "There was not a *scintilla* of evidence that he committed murder." "There was not even a *scintilla* of evidence that the psychiatrist's theory was true." "There was a *scintilla* of odor in the hat." "The bloodhound picked up a *scintilla* of the substance in the student locker." Syn.: iota, jot, speck.

sciolism [SIHulizum] superficial knowledge. "Rejection of Marx as dogmatic may show *sciolism*." "The height of *sciolism* is the everyone knows argument, in which an inarticulate appeal is made to commonly held 'facts.'" "His testimony at the hearing was at the same time witness to his *sciolism*." "The radical did not assert that acceptance of psychoanalysis is *sciolism*." Syn.: bewilderment, dilettantism, smattering. Ant.: enlightenment, erudition, worldliness.

screed [SKREED] a diatribe. "Partisan political agenda, went the *screed* of the radio station producer, who refused to let the political scientist on the air." "Frustrated with his inability to get on a broadcast, he issued a *screed* attacking and analyzing access to the media." "He distributed a *screed* on campus to vent his frustration." "The dictator declaimed a *screed* before the crowd." Syn.: declamation, harangue, rant, tirade. Ant.: appeal, plea.

scurrilous [SKURulus] foul-mouthed. "In their spare time the *scurrilous* workers sat around and listlessly exchanged joking obscenities." "The fight was preceded by *scurrilous* words and threats." "'There's no need to get *scurrilous*,' declared the man as he tried to make peace." "The group of men *scurrilously* reviled the attractive woman walking down the street." Syn.: coarse, opprobrious, vituperative. Ant.: affable, gracious.

sea change [SEE CHAYNG] a remarkable change, as in appearance. "The formerly fat woman lost 90 pounds and effected a *sea change* in her personality." "The emotional crisis produced a *sea change* in the writer." "The psy-

chologist studied people who had undergone a *sea change*." "Paroxetine, an
antidepressant, caused a *sea change* in the depressed man."

sedulous [SEJulus] diligent or persevering. "American teachers *sedulously*
pass—despite boredom, indifference or lack of work—anyone who shows up
for class; that is the unwritten rule that everyone passes." "He made it his job
to *sedulously* criticize all forms of sentimentality, thereby, he thought, contributing to culture." "She was a *sedulous* scholar, and often lucubrated in her
room." "He *sedulously* ignored the harassment." Syn.: steadfast, unfailing,
unflagging. Ant.: overcome, resigned, stultified, vanquished.

self-abuse [SELF uBYOOS] masturbation. "*Self-abuse* is a mean manner of
referring to spanking the monkey." "*Self-abuse* is inferior to sex." "*Self-
abuse* in females is called touching yourself." "Female *self-abuse* is much
less considered self-defilement compared to the male act." Syn.: arming the
cannon, burping the worm, choking the chicken, jacking off, jilling off.

self-abnegation [SELF abnuGAYshun] self-denial. "Religious ascetics practice
self-abnegation, spurning material goods and the 'good life' hurriedly pursued by everyone else." "I have normal desires, so why should I believe in
self-abnegation? thought the writer." "For some people *self-abnegation* with
regard to food is very difficult." "*Self-abnegation* regarding sleep is not possible past a certain point." Syn.: abstemiousness, asceticism, austerity. Ant.:
hedonism, indulgence, luxuriance, sensuality, sensuousness, voluptuousness.

self-effacing [SELF eFAYSing] given to humility. "The *self-effacing* wife dis-
claimed any credit for the success of her husband as an engineer." "The financial titan was not *self-effacing*." "She was *self-effacing*, not boastful."
"Judging by his appearances on television, the football linebacker was not
self-effacing." Syn.: modest, reserved. Ant.: brash.

semblance [SEMbluns] outward appearance. "Many animals assume a *semblance* of being much larger when threatened, as by a hunched back and erect
hair, or in the case of some butterflies by large 'eyes' (spots on the wings)."
"Although conservatives said justice was done, the left-wing criticized a
'*semblance* of justice.'" "The *semblance* of the house was a well-maintained
lawn and neatness." "The *semblance* is not always the reality." Syn.: air,
guise, presence. Ant.: dissimilarity, unlikeness.

seminal [SEMunul] outstanding and original, as of a study. "Werner von Braun
(1912-77) performed *seminal* work in rocket science, first with the Nazis and
then with NASA after 1945." "The book presented *seminal* research on the
psychology of the gaze." "Was the publication on culture and personality a
seminal work?" "The social critic wrote a *seminal* work on inauthenticity."
Syn.: far-reaching, ground-breaking. Ant.: degenerate, desultory.

sempiternal [sempiTURnul] (literary) everlasting. "The idea of a *sempiternal*
summer was referred to by Shakespeare in one of his sonnets: 'But thy eternal summer shall not fade.'" "Two hours can seem *sempiternal* when watching a bad movie." "Their wait seemed *sempiternal*, like an eternity." "The
work of digging ditches with a shovel seemed *sempiternal*." Syn.: eternal,
forever. Ant.: ephemeral.

sententious [senTENshus] having pithy sayings; of the nature of a maxim. "Bacon's *Essays* excels in *sententiousness*." "Ben Franklin (1706-90) invented *sententious* advice in his almanac." "The article was vague and not *sententious*." "He cited a *sententious* quotation: 'He who knows not how to dissemble knows not how to live.'" Syn.: laconic, succinct, terse. Ant.: vague.

sentient [SENshunt] marked by sensation; conscious. "The supposedly paranoid man was at this time *sentient* of being followed." "The worker was *sentient* of being exploited." "The man suffered from being excessively *sentient*." "She was *sentient* of being a victim of inequality." Syn.: alert, aware.

seraglio [siRALyoh] a harem. "Brigham Young (1801-77) had a *seraglio* of wives and fathered some 57 children." "Though a *seraglio* may be rather rare, polygamy is not." "It is very prestigious to have a *seraglio* or multiple wives." "The sultan enjoyed his *seraglio*."

serendipity [serunDIPitee] being accidently fortunate; coming upon favorable things unintentionally. "He could hardly believe the *serendipity* of finding a wallet full of money on the street." "Through her job she experienced the *serendipity* of meeting her future husband." "Maintain a positive outlook and *serendipity* will come along some time or other." Horace Walpole (1717-97), an English novelist and essayist, coined the term *serendipity* in reference to a Persian fairy tale, *The Three Princes of Serendip*. Syn.: auspiciousness. Ant.: calamity, inauspiciousness.

serotonin [seruTOHnin] a very important neurotransmitter, chemical name 5-HT, involved in numerous functions such as eating and sleeping, and the most important neurotransmitter to consider in depression. "The psychiatrist used tryptophan, an amino-acid and precursor of *serotonin*, to treat insomnia." "The depressed adolescent found psychotherapy useless but found boosting *serotonin* very helpful." "Too little *serotonin* can cause psychiatric illness, while too much *serotonin*, caused by modern antidepressants, is also a possibility." "*Serotonin* neurons are especially found in an area of the brain called the raphe nucleus." "*Serotonin* is crucial for analgesia and enjoyment of life."

seventh heaven [SEVunth...] a state of bliss. "After receiving his multi-million-dollar commission, he was in *seventh heaven*." "The youth was depressed, but then took the antidepressant fluoxetine and re-ordered his life, and found himself in *seventh heaven*." "The teacher was in *seventh heaven* during summer." "The teenagers were in *seventh heaven* cruising the hamburger stand."

Seven Wonders of the World [SEV...] the seven most remarkable structures of the ancient world: the Egyptian pyramids, the Mausoleum at Halicarnassus, the Temple of Artemis at Ephesus, the Hanging Gardens of Babylon, the Colossus of Rhodes, the statue of Zeus at Olympia, and the lighthouse of Alexandria. "The historian longed to visit what is left of the *Seven Wonders of the World*." "The Egyptian pyramids are the most impressive of the *Seven Wonders of the World*." "The boy dreamed of finding the ruins of one of the *Seven Wonders of the World*." "The tour took people to the *Seven Wonders of the World*, or what was left of them."

severally [SEVurulee] separately or respectively. "The five siblings all left home *severally* and moved to other cities." "His happiest year was 1980, when he, in the summer and September *severally,* traveled to Europe and started a new job." "They *severally* drove to work on the highway in a personal automobile." "The wives *severally* left off their children at the swim club."

shaman [SHAMun] a medicine man or spiritual healer in tribal society. "The *shaman* was called in to treat a man prostrated with fever." "The *shaman* seemed to have cured the manic-depressive man." "The *shaman* learned his craft from an older *shaman* in a neighboring village." "A *shaman* was summoned to rally the spirits in the tribe's war." "The *shaman* tried to make the barren woman fertile."

shamus [SHAYmus] a policeman. "The *shamus* stopped a drunk driver." "The *shamus* who had a college degree made detective." "The American *shamus* had Irish ancestry." "The *shamus* checked the handles of locked doors."

Shangri-la [SHANGgrula] an earthly paradise. "The 19th century explorers thought they had found a *Shangri-la* on the African island." "The writer stated that no *Shangri-la* or hidden paradise exists." "The radical believed that *Shangri-la* is mainly in a calm, contented mind." "The name *Shangri-la* is much better known than the title of the book it comes from." After a hidden paradise in the novel *Lost Horizon* (1933), by James Hilton (1900-54).

shibbolith [SHIBulith] the distinctive behavioral or linguistic features of a class of people; a slogan. "The *shibboleths,* or the giveaways, of class are multitudinous." "People are constantly using *shibboleths* for moral judgment, though not necessarily consciously." "Money is an accurate *shibboleth* for class." "An apartment, trailer or shack is a *shibbolith* for working class." This word comes from the Bible, in the book *Judges.* Syn.: catchword, motto.

shiftless [SHIFTlis] unresourceful and lacking in motivation. "The poor of the city were seen as *shiftless.*" "There was a point in the man's life when he was *shiftless.*" "The conservative argued that *shiftless* people deserve what they have." "The poor man was the opposite of *shiftless,* and hoped to go from rags to riches." Syn.: improvident, unenterprising. Ant.: enterprising, resourceful, thrifty.

shilly-shally [SHILee SHALee] to vacillate. "The early feminist movement *shilly-shallied* over whether to seek outright liberation or just the suffrage." "With the phone in his hand, he *shilly-shallied* over whether to call his friend." "*Shilly-shallying* on the highway can be dangerous." "She *shilly-shallied* over whether to seek the office." Syn.: falter, hesitate, procrastinate.

shindy [SHINdee] an uproar. "A *shindy* followed when the john refused to pay for her service." "A *shindy* broke out in the home when the children were denied ice cream." "A *shindy* broke out in the crowded tavern." "A *shindy* disturbed the campus on a Saturday night." *Shindy* is a variant of *shindig.* Syn.: commotion, row, ruckus, tumult.

shrew [SHROO] a nagging, vicious woman. "From the male point of view, a *shrewish* wife is grounds for divorce." "There are many words for *shrew* but no words for a male equivalent." "The *shrew* held forth in the kitchen and yelled out orders to her children." "*The Taming of the Shrew* by Shakespeare suggests how men view a scold." Syn.: fishwife, henpecker, scold, termagant, virago, vixen.

shrinking violet [SHRINKing VIHlet] a shy, modest person. "The scholar was not a *shrinking violet*, but some people thought so." "The *shrinking violet* was skinny and still a maiden at 30." "The *shrinking violet* worked as a file clerk." "He was a *shrinking violet* when it came to interacting with people."

Shylock [SHIHlok] a usurer. "The *Shylock* charged 20 percent interest on the short-term 'payday' loan." "The *Shylock* was ruthless about money." "The *Shylock* grew rich." "The bank was in the hands of a *Shylock*." After a Jewish character in Shakespeare's comedy *The Merchant of Venice*.

shyster [SHIHster] a lawyer who uses unprofessional conduct to gain money. "The *shyster* charged people $500 for a retainer." "The *shysters* got one-third of the award of a personal injury case." "The *shyster* law firm charged corporate clients $1,000 an hour." "*Shyster* law firms do nothing for the poor and only act when paid."

sidereal [sihDEEReeul] pertaining to or determined by the stars. "U.S. time is *sidereal*, calculated astronomically." "Our sun is *sidereal*, a star." "The anthropology student studied cross-cultural use of *sidereal* facts." "Calendars other than *sidereal* are possible."

silver-tongued [SILvur TONGD] persuasive or eloquent. "The *silver-tongued* orator had the people clapping and cheering." "The college student was not *silver-tongued*, but good enough to pass a public-speaking course." "The poet was *silver-tongued*." "The social critic was *silver-tongued*, not to all the critics, but atleast to the radical." Syn.: conclusive, convincing, decisive. Ant.: unconvincing, vague.

simile [SIMulee] a figure of speech using a comparison. "The *simile* comparing the country's president to an orangutan was not a diplomatic one." "The *simile* was a bad one, mixing two different classes, said the critic." "The *simile* was not well-received by the persons it referred to." "A *simile* contrasts with a metaphor."

Simon Legree [SIHmun liGREE] a brutish overseer. "When has there not been in recorded history a *Simon Legree* who bosses the poor?" "The *Simon Legree* whipped into action the slaves of the Roman galley." "The cafeteria had its own *Simon Legree* in the person of a mean supervisor of the dish crew." "The *Simon Legree* kept the workers busy." This term comes from the novel *Uncle Tom's Cabin* (1852) by Harriet Beecher Stowe (1811-96).

simon-pure [SIHmun PYOOR] genuine. "Her Southern drawl was *simon-pure*." "His business was *simon-pure*, not a con game." "His heart of gold was *simon-pure*." "His concern for his friend was *simon-pure* and not affected." *Simon-pure* is derived from a play of the 19th century. Syn.: authentic, bona fide, naturalistic, unadulterated. Ant.: artificial, faux, inauthentic, phony.

simony [SIHmunee] sinful traffic in ecclesiastical emoluments. "*Simony* includes the well-known sale of indulgences." "Martin Luther attacked *simony*." "The *simony* of purchasing 'salvation' seems a little laughable." "Someone raided the church for *simony*." This term comes from the Bible, in the book *Acts*.

simulacrum [simyooLAYkrum] a false appearance; a sham. "All too many once beautiful actresses cling to a *simulacrum* of beauty, fortified with a ton of makeup and the uncritical media." "It was only a *simulacrum* and not the real thing." "The junta held elections to establish a *simulacrum* of democracy." "Preachers offer a *simulacrum* of salvation that they tie to certain actions, the main one being sending in a check." Syn.: dissimulation, façade, humbug. Ant.: authenticity.

sinecure [SIHnukyoor] a well-paying job with few duties. "Examples of *sinecures* include college deans, school administrators, members of corporate boards and church officials." "He held a *sinecure* position but tried to stay busy at work." "Professors have it very easy—few hours to teach and much spare time—but perhaps their employment is not an actual *sinecure*." "She grew modestly wealthy from her *sinecure*." The word *sinecure* stems from ecclesiastical practice and the Latin term *sine cura* ("without cure"), indicating a religious functionary who performed no service.

sire [SIHur] to beget as the father. "The priest *sired* several children." "The man was anxious to *sire* a son or daughter before he became too old." "The king *sired* no sons, only daughters." "The mikado wanted to *sire* a son desperately."

Sisyphean [sisuFEEun] endlessly monotonous or unavailing. "To some the housewife's work is *Sisyphean*." "The radical declared his hatred of *Sisyphean* manual labor." "The word *Sisyphean* is from a Greek myth involving Sisyphus." "The writer could think of many types of *Sisyphean* work." From an ancient Greek myth.

skin game [SKIN GAYM] a dishonest or fraudulent scheme or business; a swindle. "The men's *skin game* brought in $65,000." "The *skin game* involved franchising." "Their *skin game* targeted the unemployed." "The *skin game* moved from city to city and state to state." Syn.: bunco, graft.

skulduggery [skulDUGeree] mean trickery. "'What *skulduggery* is going on here?' asked the woman as she opened the door." "The man was uncomfortable in the inner-city neighborhood, and it seemed like *skulduggery* lurked on every street corner." "The two no-good men were up to *skulduggery*." "What the boys were doing was *skulduggery*, not clean fun." "He disliked the *skulduggery* of the salesman." "Many students complain of the *skulduggery* of teachers who grade frivolously according to their emotions." *Skulduggery* is an American variation of a Scottish obscenity. Syn.: artifice, chicanery, machination, sharp practice.

skulk [SKULK] to sneak; to hide as if for some malign purpose. "At feeding time the German shepherd, when done with his own food, *skulked* around the corner waiting to see if the other dog left any chow in her dish." "The burglar *skulked* around the neighborhood furtively casing homes." "He *skulked* around at night looking for an easy mark." "The two adulterers felt shamed in having to *skulk* so as not to be noticed." "The journalist *skulked* around the house looking for information." Syn.: cower, creep, prowl, steal.

slant-eyed [SLANTihd] having "slanty" eyes, or epicanthic folds, such as the Chinese and Japanese. "The *slant-eyed* immigrants faced discrimination at first in the U.S." "The *slant-eyed* people such as the Nisei faced a negative stigma." "He was somewhat *slant-eyed*, but not enough to cause a stigma." "The *slant-eyed* American seemed to deal with the stereotype of foreignism with a reactionary demeanor."

slapdash [SLAPdash] in a hasty, careless manner. "Detesting manual labor, the writer did a *slapdash* paint job in his room." "He jerry-rigged a *slapdash* phone jack to his desk." "The text on prehistory was a *slapdash* work." "The brick house was a *slapdash* bit of construction." Syn.: shoddy.

slather [SLATHur] to spread on thickly; to spread lavishly. "The newly-rich singer *slathered* money on her relatives." "He *slathered* butter on his corn on the cob." "The millionaire *slathered* the tips to waiters and waitresses." "They *slathered* on the cheerfulness." The origin of *slather* is unknown.

slattern [SLATurn] a slut. "The homeless bag woman was stigmatized as a *slattern*." "The lovely actress was playing a *slattern* and was not, of course, a harlot in real life." "The clothes of the *slattern* were horrifying." "The home of the *slattern* was small and dingy." The origin of this word is uncertain. Syn.: sloven.

sloth [SLOTH] indolence. "In German, the graphic word for 'lazy' is *faul*, which, because of its cognate in English, seems to indicate a negative view of *sloth*." "The writer found ways to avoid *sloth*." "*Sloth* is truly a vice, but care should be taken not to give it a class bias by saying it does not apply to the idle rich." "The leisure class is *sloth*." Syn.: apathy, languor, laziness, lethargy, sluggishness. Ant.: liveliness.

slovenly [SLUVunlee] unkempt; habitually untidy; slipshod. "The patient's *slovenly* appearance did not improve the psychiatrist's diagnosis for him." "What a cardinal error it would be to show up *slovenly* at a job interview!" "Although poor, he was never *slovenly*." "The *slovenly* man had B.O." Syn.: slatternly, tacky. Ant.: orderly.

slugabed [SLUGubed] a lazy person who is in bed too much. "The *slugabed* would miss school too often." "He yearned to be a *slugabed* and sleep late, but had to get up for work." "The *slugabed* was reprimanded by his father." "Society sternly disapproved of the *slugabed*." Syn.: lazybones, sluggard.

slurb [SLURB] a rundown, ill-planned suburban area. "He lived in an ugly *slurb* where property values were declining." "Crime in the *slurb* was on the increase." "Lower-middle-class houses in the *slurb* deteriorated into upper-lower-class ones." "Well-off people moved from the *slurb* to better suburbs." *Slurb* is a combination of "slum" and "suburb."

slush fund [SLUSH FUND] money used for a corrupt purpose, as for buying influence or bribing a politician. "The corporation had a *slush fund* for contributing to political campaigns." "The political caucus had a *slush fund* for advertisements in favor of its causes." "The conservative claimed that *slush funds* are harmless because people with money have a right to express their opinion." "A *slush fund* seems to be a part of the idea of assigning votes based on the number of dollars one has."

sobriety [suBRIHitee] solemnity; alcoholic abstinence. "The *sobriety* of the church congregation before the service impressed Ralph Waldo Emerson as better than any preaching." "He practiced *sobriety* on weekdays but on Saturday he got sauced." "She worked hard at *sobriety* but fell off the wagon again." "The police set up a *sobriety* checkpoint." Syn.: reverence. Ant.: frivolousness, levity, unimportance.

sobriquet [SOHbrukay] a nickname. "Her apt *sobriquet* was Fanny." "They knew him by the *sobriquet* Leo." "Ty Cobb's *sobriquet* was The Georgia Peach." "His *sobriquet* was Sammy." "He did not like the *sobriquet* the other boys attached to him." Syn.: appellation, moniker.

sob sister [SOB SIStur] a journalist, usually a woman, who writes newspaper articles devoted mainly to human-interest stories (sob stories). "The *sob sister* in her column advised the woman against divorce." "The *sob sister* attacked sex before marriage as immoral." "The *sob sister* warned the girl that her boyfriend may have been after sex, and nothing but sex." "His letter to a *sob sister* was published in the newspaper, his name having been omitted though."

social contract [SOHshul KONtrakt] a supposed voluntary agreement among members of society by which the state is granted the right to regulate social organization for the general welfare. "The philosophers Thomas Hobbes (1588-1679), John Locke (1632-1704), and Jean-Jacques Rousseau (1712-78) all formulated a *social contract*." "People are not, of course, aware of a *social contract* that guides their behavior." "The sociologist asserted that a *social contract* makes for smooth patterns of consensual behavior." "The radical criticized *social contract* theory as unable to account for conflict."

Socratic irony [SOH...] feigned ignorance, like Socrates practiced. "The radical often pretended not to know, used *Socratic irony*, when interviewing his subjects." "*Socratic irony* allowed her to better know her friends." "One may learn deep secrets through *Socratic irony*." "The college debater employed *Socratic irony* very effectively at times."

sodality [sohDALitee] comradeship. "*Sodality* is more important to men than women." "The *sodality* of people in the neighborhood was important." "*Sodality* in the military, or esprit de corps, keeps morale high." "The Roman legions' *sodality* was carefully watched."

sojourn [SOHjurn] a temporary stay. "Her *sojourn* in the hospital for appendicitis was unpleasant." "Except for a *sojourn* in Rome they saw little of the country." "They stopped their tour for a *sojourn* in the South of France." "They had a *sojourn* in Acapulco." "He had a *sojourn* at a conference at Harvard but is not a graduate of the university." Syn.: stopover, visit.

solecism [SOLisizum] an informal usage of language; an impropriety. "A strange *solecism* is the pronunciation of *height* as 'heighth,' as if there were an extra *h* on the end." "He did not engage in anything that could be called a *solecism*." "The *solecism* of the sordid affair was when he propositioned her." "*Going* is a *solecism* for 'will.'" Syn.: blunder, faux pas, gaffe.

soliloquy [suLILukwee] the act of talking aloud to oneself. "Shakespeare (1564-1616) made good use of the *soliloquy*." "Hamlet's *soliloquy* begins 'to be or not to be.'" "The *soliloquy* is important because the audience cannot exactly read a character's mind." "Silent *soliloquy*, or the habit of silently keeping up a conversation, is a bad habit!"

solipsism [SOLipsizum] the idea that only the self exists. "His *solipsism* held that one can not verify the existence of others." "The writer used the word *solipsism* to indicate a kind of selfishness." "Her philosophical *solipsism* postulated that only consciousness proves one's existence." "The psychology student researched *solipsism*."

sop [SOP] a bribe to pacify or quiet. "As a *sop* to the howling toddlers, an extra hour of television was granted." "His affected kindness was intended as a *sop* to the teacher who would grade his work." "The business accepted a closed shop, but *sops* to individual workers were allowed." "*Sops* to the poor were not evenly distributed." Syn.: propitiation.

sophomoric [sofuMORik] immature. "Her Ph.D. dissertation on a method of primary education was *sophomoric*." "His attempt at using a sophisticated word and thereby showing intelligence was *sophomoric*." "His essay was *sophomoric*." "Looking back on it, he had to admit that his action in getting revenge was *sophomoric*." In its Greek root, the word *sophomoric* means "wise" and "foolish." Syn.: callow, foolish, inane.

soporific [sopuRIFik] causing or tending to cause sleep. "The antihistamine is *soporific*." "Opium may or may not be *soporific*." "The neuroleptics— antipsychotic drugs like Clozaril—are *soporific*." "The brain hormone melatonin is *soporific*." Syn.: hypnotic.

sorites [sohRIHteez] a syllogistic form of logical argumentation. "The philosopher's *sorites* on consciousness was brilliant." "Most philosophy is not in the form of *sorites*." "The *sorites* attacked the conservative view of class conflict." "The *sorites* explored the formation of attitudes."

sou [SOO] a very small amount of money. "She inherited not a *sou* from her father." "He had not a *sou* in the bank." "He did not give his niece a *sou* for Christmas." "The wealthy banker gave hardly a *sou* to charity."

soubrette [sooBRET] a kind of stage actress; a flirtatious woman. "The *soubrette* got more than she bargained for when her boss expected a sexual favor for her promotion." "He fell in love with the *soubrette* whom he found broke and on the street." "The *soubrette* was spotted by a television producer." "The *soubrette* was afraid of an emotional commitment." Syn.: coquette.

sour grapes [SOUur GRAYPS] a show of dislike for something one cannot obtain. "The poor sometimes express *sour grapes* about their lack of success." "The actor was merely guilty of *sour grapes* in saying he did not want the role in the movie." "The carpenter, when in the interview he talked about being wealthy, showed that his 'rejection' of money was *sour grapes*." "'I'd rather eat at White Castle, said the working-class man, though obviously it was *sour grapes*, especially in that he never dined at a ritzy restaurant, to say nothing of the implied idea that he would rather be poor than rich." From Aesop's fable in which a fox describes as sour the grapes he cannot reach.

Spartan [SPARtun] austere; disciplined. "He ate a *Spartan* breakfast of oatmeal and an apple." "The accommodations at the hotel were *Spartan*." "Life in the military was *Spartan*." "The poor necessarily lead a *Spartan* life." From the ancient Greek city-state of Sparta. Syn.: ascetic, frugal, severe, stark, stoic.

specious [SPEEshus] deceptively appealing and untrue. "It is *specious* to argue that because 'everyone' believes in it, the idea must be true." "Using *specious* reasoning, she said that they could not take her on the picnic since it always rained when they did." "'They're all the same' is not a *specious* suggestion." "The television commercial of the political candidate was *specious*." Syn.: casuistic, insincere. Ant.: forthright, logical.

sphinx [SFINGKS] a mysterious person or thing. "He was a *sphinx* to everyone but his one good friend." "The effect of the moon on behavior is a *sphinx*, as science cannot explain it yet." "Ultimate reality is the greatest *sphinx* to unravel." "The mysterious stranger was a *sphinx*." Syn.: conundrum, enigma, perplexity.

spirituel [spirichooEL] pertaining to a refined and cultured mind. "He loved Chopin, Keats, Fragonard, but what really made him *spirituel* was virtuous living." "They were provincial, even as they did business with the rest of the world, and hardly *spirituel*." "Being the daughter of a biologist and art critic, she received an early education, learned four languages and was *spirituel* in her teens." Syn.: polished, well-bred, well-educated. Ant.: coarse, philistine.

splenetic [spliNETik] irritable. "The three-year-old girl threw a *splenetic* fit each time she did not get her way." "He became *splenetic* when tired." "He was morose and *splenetic* often, and anything could set him off." "The drunken father vented his *spleen* on his son." Syn.: cranky, cross, disagreeable, irascible, testy. Ant.: good-natured.

Sprachgefühl [SHPRAKHgufuel] (German) a feeling for language. "Edgar Allen Poe (1809-49) had an ingenious *Sprachgefühl*." "Those without a *Sprachgefühl* probably should not write poetry." "The conservative cultivated a *Sprachgefühl*." "He struggled in English composition and had no *Sprachgefühl*."

spry [SPRIH] active or nimble. "She was *spry* and talkative on television, but that may have concealed a deeper side of her character." "The old widow was still *spry* at 85." "The autistic boy was *spry*, but he did not speak." "The forty-year-old teacher was no longer *spry*." Syn.: animated, pert, vivacious. Ant.: dejected, demoralized.

spurious [SPYOOReeus] not genuine. "The rumor that he was gravely ill was *spurious*." "His whole behavior was *spurious*, inauthentic, fake." "The painting was not an original, but was *spurious*." "The letter was *spurious*, not the real Mccoy." Syn.: apocryphal, inauthentic. Ant.: authenticated, certified.

squib [SKWIB] a short, witty or sarcastic saying. "He wrote a *squib* ridiculing his rival." "The *squib* traveled around town as a rumor." "He denied inventing the *squib*." "The *squib* alluded to her sexual deficiency." Syn.: apothegm, epigram, witticism.

stage whisper [STAYJ WISpur] a loud whisper, as by a performer on stage. "In a *stage whisper*, she told her friend that her husband did business with the prominent industrialist." "In a *stage whisper*, the paranoid patient said that a certain orderly had threatened her." "He indicated in a *stage whisper* that he had received the award for information about the suspect." "The actress spoke a *stage whisper* in the play."

staid [STED] pertaining to a sedate nature. "He was *staid*, and did not get worked up over much." "The family was 'old school,' *staid* and socially conservative." "When the going gets difficult, remember to remain calm and *staid*." "His direction of the team was *staid*." Syn.: inexcitable. Ant.: irascible.

Stakhanovism [stuKAnuvizum] in the Soviet Union, a method of increasing production by rewarding a worker's individual initiative. "The American economist studied *Stakhanovism*." "The factory's *Stakhanovism* did increase output." "The *Stakhanovite* received a little extra pay." "The radical asked whether *Stakhanovism* increased inequality in the communist country."

stalking horse [STOking HORS] a pretext; a decoy; a political candidate put forth to draw votes from a rival candidate. "Two black candidates—one perhaps a *stalking horse*—ran for the mayoralty, and the white candidate became mayor of the city." "The television commercial run by the business was a *stalking horse*, part of the scam to cheat job hunters out of $150." "*Stalking horses* in political elections are common." "The supervisor used a *stalking horse* to fire the employee." "The man used a girlfriend as a kind of *stalking horse* to conceal his homosexuality."

stalwart [STOLwurt] having a robust build; resolutely or uncompromisingly partisan. "He was one of the party's *stalwart* hardliners." "He was a tall *stalwart* fellow who played rugby." "He was not allowed on the television news program because he was deemed to have a *stalwart* political agenda." "The *stalwart* politicians voted against a tax on high incomes." Syn.: staunch, steadfast, vigorous.

statutory [STACHootoree] pertaining to or regulated by a statute (a legislative enactment). "*Statutory* rape is sex with a girl legally considered a minor." "The *statute* forbade hauling in money by robbing a bank, but not hauling in money by inheritance, robbing the people." "The state *statute* restricted abortion rights." "The ban against embezzlement was *statutory*."

stele [STEElee] an upright slab of stone with an inscription or design used as a monument or at the base of a building to commemorate something. "The *stele* on the library read A.D. 1926." "The *stele* marked the battle site." "At the base of the statue was a *stele* with a date and dedication." "The *stele* in the cemetery was for a wealthy woman." "The *stele* marked the spot in the cemetery where the family graves were."

stentorian [stenTOReeun] extremely loud. "He had a *stentorian* voice well-suited to his employment as an emcee." "The explosion was *stentorian* and heard for miles around." "The motorcycle made *stentorian* noise that irritated people in its path." "The *stentorian* explosion shook the windows." Syn.: booming, ear-splitting, thunderous.

stereotype [STEReeutihp] a rigid, standardized image of a person or people held by another person and involving, for example, race, occupation, character, etc. "The high school students buzzed about with *stereotypes* of each other, such as 'brain,' 'jock,' and 'burnout.'" "The *stereotype* portrayed the race as prone to crime." "She was *stereotyped* as 'sweet.'" "As a sort of badge of the man, *stereotyping* reached an extreme in the culture." *Stereotype* comes from the craft of printing. Syn.: pigeonhole, typecast.

sterling [STURling] very worthy or excellent. "Fragonard's art is *sterling* beauty." "Her compositions were *sterling*." "The museum held nothing but *sterling* art." "His reputation is *sterling*." Syn.: estimable, first-rate, preeminent. Ant.: despicable.

stirps [STURPS] a line of descent; the branch of a family. "The Huxley *stirps* has several distinguished members." "The Roosevelt *stirps* furnished two presidents." "The man's *stirps* had both short and tall members." "Their *stirps* was free of inherited diseases."

stoic [STOHik] impassive; an adherent of the ancient Greek philosophy, founded by Zeno, that taught indifference to passion and emotion and resignation to one's fate. "Marcus Aurelius (121-80) was a Roman emperor and *stoic* philosopher." "From forty to fifty a man is at heart either a stoic or a satyr." (Sir Arthur Pinero.) "It is hard to be *stoic* in a world that offers such comforts for the flesh." "He was *stoic* in that he bore imprisonment with dignity." Syn.: ascetic, long-suffering, self-controlled. Ant.: excitable, impassioned.

stool pigeon [STOOL PIjun] a person acting as a decoy or informer for the police. "The *stool pigeon* 'sang.'" "The bank robbery was prevented thanks to a *stool pigeon*." "A *stool pigeon* informed the police about the drug smuggling." "The *stool pigeon* risked his life by infiltrating the criminal gang." Syn.: mole, squealer, stoolie.

straitlaced [STRAYTlayst] very strict in behavior or morality; prudish. "His family was *straitlaced* and religious." "She was so *straitlaced* that she disapproved of the bikini." "His parents were *straitlaced* but provided a good home." "His beliefs were *straitlaced* and a little behind the times." Syn.: hidebound, prim, puritanical. Ant.: Bohemian.

stricture [STRIKchur] censure; a limitation. "The *strictures* of society limit the ability of a man to communicate a taboo idea to the public, no matter how legitimate and legal it might be." "Legal *strictures* made it very difficult for the independent candidate to get on the ballot." "Teachers are in effect regulated by the *strictures* of public opinion." Syn.: animadversion, castigation, rebuke, reprehension, reprimand. Ant.: approbation, commendation, encomium.

strumpet [STRUMpit] a prostitute. "The *strumpet* did not enjoy sex with strangers." "The *strumpet* worked with a pimp." "The *strumpet's* work was dangerous." "The *strumpet* dressed in red." Syn.: harlot, whore.

stultify [STULtufih] to make one appear foolish or ineffectual. "He was so frustrated and emotionally constricted that his every movement or utterance was *stultifying*." "The desert heat was *stultifying*." "The high school basketball team was baffled and *stultified* by the opposing team." "The teacher's stuttering was *stultifying*." Syn.: debase, enfeeble, undermine. Ant.: empower, enable.

subaltern [subOLturn] lower in rank. "The *subaltern* employees made less money than their bosses." "The janitor was *subaltern* compared to the teachers." "The nurse's aids were *subaltern* in relation to the registered nurses." "The poor are *subaltern*, being subordinate to the middle and upper classes."

sublimate [SUBlumayt] to express an impulse in a socially or intellectually higher form. "Psychoanalysis speaks much of *sublimation*, but it is unscientific." "The poem was *sublimated* aggression." "The soccer match had its *sublimated* side and its lower side." "What is and is not *sublimation* is hard to determine."

sublime [suBLIHM] impressive and elevated, as in thought or language; inspiring awe. "The poetry of John Keats (1795-1821) is said to be *sublime*, such as 'Ode on a Grecian Urn' and 'To One Who Has Been Long in City Pent.'" "The view from the mountainside was *sublime*." "The Florida beach, with its white sand and blue-green ocean, was *sublime*." "The month of June is *sublime* in some places in the northern hemisphere." Syn.: magnificent, majestic, superb. Ant.: dismal.

suborn [suBORN] to induce someone to commit a crime. "*Subornation* may be common, but prosecution for perjury is not." "The agent-provocateur committed a crime while *suborning* one among radicals." "The defense lawyer was careful not to *suborn* perjury but got around the restriction nevertheless." "The defendant was accused of *suborning* perjury." "*Subornation* is one thing, but when a prosecutor lies in court, it is called prosecutorial discretion, and when a defendant lies in court, it is called perjury."

sub rosa [SUB ROHzu] (Latin) confidentially or secretly. "The man agreed with his father *sub rosa* that only his girlfriend and he would know that they were not actually married." "The KKK met *sub rosa* in a clearing in the woods." "They plotted *sub rosa* to kill the czar." "The lovers departed *sub rosa* to enjoy the solitude of the waterfall in the tropical forest."

subterfuge [SUBturfyooj] a means of hiding a fact or evading a rule or policy; a dishonest expedient. "The college instructor used *subterfuge* to get his book adopted as the course's text." "The absence of a sense of class privilege in the American elite may be *subterfuge*." "The sociologist theorized that the belief that ideology is gone may represent *subterfuge*." "It would have been *subterfuge* to let her believe that." Syn.: artifice, pretext, ruse, stratagem. Ant.: artlessness.

succèss d'estime [suksedesTEEM] (French) critical or artistic success rather than commercial success. "The writer said that *succèss d'estime* is nice but it does not pay the bills." "The opera *I Pagliacci* by Ruggiero Leon-Cavallo (1858-1919) was a popular success and a *succèss d'estime*." "His novel analyzing social norms was a *succèss d'estime*." "The movie garnered some *succèss d'estime* but failed at the box office."

succor [SUKur] aid or relief. "Congress, being swayed by the corporate lobby, doles out large sums for the *succor* of business." "The lonely man desired feminine *succor*." "Instead of being *succor*, the philanthropic foundation was actually a tax dodge." "The town devastated by the flood needed *succor*." Syn.: consolation, solace. Ant.: hindrance.

sully [SULee] to tarnish or stain, as a reputation. "The actress' reputation was so *sullied* that she would not be permitted endorsement deals." "The World Series was *sullied* by people claiming that baseball is a bore." "His life became *sullied*, listless, and dull due to thoughts crowding out emotional experience." "Her reputation was *sullied* by the affair." Syn.: blemish, mar, soil, stigmatize. Ant.: venerate.

summum bonum [SOOMoom BOHnoom] (Latin) the principal good. "The best is the enemy of the *summum bonum*, said Voltaire." "Governments claim to rule for the *summum bonum*." "The idea of *summum bonum* is important for social control." "The radical rejected the idea of governmental *summum bonum*."

sumptuary [SUMPchooeree] referring to or regulating expenditure. "In past centuries, *sumptuary* laws were precise in regulating how a person in a given social class could dress." "The middle-class husband and wife both made the *sumptuary* decisions in the family." "The advertising industry had sway over families' *sumptuary* practices." "The *sumptuary* law forbade women to dress beyond their social station."

sunder [SUNdur] to part or divide. "The bathing beauty *sundered* her locks down the middle." "God supposedly *sundered* the Red Sea." "The river *sundered* the state in two." "The two women *sundered* their late mother's money." Syn.: dissever.

sundry [SUNdree] diverse. "He ordered a *sundry* list of goods from the store." "She stole *sundry* goods from the department store." "He had a list of *sundry* complaints against his employer." "He possessed *sundry* skills." "The newspaper listed *sundry* homes for sale." Syn.: miscellaneous, various.

superannuate [soopurANyooayt] to allow to retire due to age or infirmity; to grow or become obsolete. "In American society elderly employees are often *superannuated* before they have actual diminished work capacity." "Lacking formal employment, he felt *superannuated* at the age of 45." "The automobile quickly becomes *superannuated*." "The home seemed to be *superannuated*." Syn.: outmoded, out-of-date.

supercilious [soopurSILeeus] haughtily disdainful. "The tanned, slender, zaftig girl walked with her dog past the man, declining to reply to his 'hello' and seeming *supercilious*." "The upper-class woman was *supercilious*." "He was fair and equable, never *supercilious*." "The celebrity was *supercilious*." Syn.: arrogant, conceited, hoity-toity, snobbish. Ant.: unassuming.

supererogatory [soopuruROGutohree] exceeding what duty requires. "He is a superpatriot, his conformity being *supererogatory*." "The workers never did anything *supererogatory* on the job." "He had a sort of phobia about doing something *supererogatory*." "The contractor for the federal building was hardly *supererogatory*, and did everything on the cheap." Syn.: overmuch, superfluous.

supervene [soopurVEEN] to occur as extraneous; to ensue. "The baseball game was canceled after a *supervening* thunderstorm." "A fight *supervened* after heated words were exchanged." "The *supervening* competition was murderous." "The old man's death *supervened*."

supplicate [SUPlukayt] to ask for humbly and earnestly. "The union *supplicated* the corporation for a living wage, but scabs were brought in during a strike." "His *supplication* to the government for attention to the harassment was completely ignored." "The poor man *supplicated* the policeman but was given a crushing traffic ticket nevertheless." "The homeless woman *supplicated* the church for a place to sleep but was denied." Syn.: beseech, entreat.

Ant.: exact, levy.

supposititious [supoziTISHus] spurious; hypothetical; suppositious. "His suspicions were merely *supposititious*." "His reputation as a golf pro was *supposititious*." "His discovery was merely *supposititious*." "Their gold mine was *supposititious*."

surcease [surSEES] (mainly poetic) cessation; end. "Did his troubles *surcease*?" "The life of the plaintive lover *surceased* through suicide." "His hope of recovery *surceased*." "He returned home when his stream of income *surceased*." "Eagerly I wished the morrow; vainly I had sought to borrow, From my books surcease of sorrow—sorrow for the lost Lenore, For the rare and radiant maiden whom the angels name Lenore, Nameless here for evermore." (Edgar Allen Poe, "The Raven.")

surfeit [SURfit] excess; overindulgence. "The celebrity experienced no *surfeit* of desire for money, and hauled in $20 million for every movie made." "The motto of the Medici—power to get money, and money to protect power—expresses no *surfeit* of love of wealth." "After his *surfeit* of food he felt fat and nauseated." "After several visits to the ice cream store, he had had a *surfeit* of strawberry sundaes." Syn.: glut, overabundance, surplus.

surly [SURlee] malignly bad-tempered. "He was *surly* that evening." "He had to consciously tell himself not to be *surly* with his mother." "His stepfather became very *surly* after drinking." "The teacher was sometimes *surly*." Syn.: churlish, gruff, morose, sullen, uncivil. Ant.: courteous, polite.

surname [SURnaym] one's family name. "Torquemada, de Sade and Hitler are *surnames* one may wish to avoid." "Many *surnames* come from occupations, like Smith and Schmidt." "His *surname* spoke of wealth—Rockefeller." "Most *surnames* are gramatically masculine rather than feminine."

surreptitious [surupTIshus] obtained or done with stealth. "The meeting of devil worshipers in the woods was *surreptitious*." "In Poe's 'The Cask of Amontillado' a man *surreptitiously* entombs and chains up his enemy and leaves him to perish." "Great wealth is inherited by heirs and heiresses rather *surreptitiously*." "All alone in her bed at night, the young woman *surreptitiously* interfered with herself." "The Congressional committee held its hearing almost *surreptitiously*, behind closed doors." Syn.: clandestine, concealed, covert, furtive, hidden. Ant.: public.

suttee [SUTee] a Hindu practice, now banned, in which a widowed woman was burned to death on her husband's funeral pyre. "From an anthropological perspective, *suttee* was part of the belief that women should serve men, the wife should exist to serve the husband." "Whatever its justification, *suttee* is a mean practice." "Several instances of *suttee* occurred in modern times." "The anthropology student studied *suttee*." From a Sanskrit word meaning "virtuous wife."

suzerain [SOOzurin] a state which politically controls a dependent state. "The U.S. is the *suzerain* of Puerto Rico." "Ancient Rome was the *suzerain* of Britain." "England of 1700 was the *suzerain* of the American colonies." "The *suzerain* ordered a crackdown on the independence movement in its colony." Syn.: sovereign. Ant.: colony.

svelte [SVELT] slender. "She always had an exquisite *svelte* figure." "In his 30s he lost his narrow waist and *svelte* outline." "To remain *svelte* a woman must eat very sparingly." "She had a *svelte* figure even in her 50s." Syn.: gracile, thin. Ant.: fat, plump.

swain [SWAYN] a lover or country lad. "The *swain* was in love with a girl from the neighboring hamlet." "The *swain* worked on a farm." "The *swain* was proud of his country origin." "The *swain* had not a sou but was free."

swank [SWANGK] very stylish. "The *swank* resort where the president stayed was labeled 'up-scale' by the press." "The hotel in which they spent their honeymoon was *swank*." "The home of the producer was 'posh,' *swank*." "The flea-bag motel they stayed in was not exactly *swank*." The origin of *swank* is unknown. Syn.: posh, ritzy. Ant.: cheap, seedy, shabby, sleazy, tawdry.

swan song [SWON SONG] a final work, appearance, utterance, etc., as of a person, group, or period. "The tenor's *swan song* came at Carnegie Hall." "The man's *swan song* was an attempt at lasting fame." "His *swan song* was a critical success after his death." "The *swan song* of Thomas Hobbes (1588-1679) was his utterance, 'I am about to go on my final journey, a great leap in the dark.'" From the myth that a swan sings while dying.

swarthy [SWORthee] having a dark complexion. "She grew *swarthy* through sun bathing." "Native Americans are rather *swarthy*." "The woman from India was *swarthy*." "One summer he grew uncharacteristically *swarthy*." Syn.: olive-skinned, tanned, tawny.

sybarite [SIBuriht] a person given to luxury and self-indulgence. "The still-stern American work ethic does not seem to apply to the *sybarites* in the leisure class." "He was as *sybaritic* as a member of the working-class could be." "To be a *sybarite* seems to require a certain amount of free time and money." "The upper-class *sybarite* belonged to a number of leisure clubs." Syn.: hedonist, voluptuary. Ant.: ascetic.

sycophant [SIKufunt] a servile, self-seeking flatterer. "The conservative laid on thick the flattery in his *sycophantic* interview of another conservative, the 'Connecticut Squire.'" "The student refused to be a *sycophant* to the instructor who was to grade his work." "*Sycophancy* inevitably invades the relationship between a superior and his lower-status friend." "His review of the book was *sycophantic*." Syn.: bootlicker, fawner, minion, toady, truckler, yes-man. Ant.: opponent.

sylph [SILF] a slender and graceful woman. "The actor married a lovely *sylph*, a ballerina from the Bolshoi ballet." "The *sylph* could not defend herself against the larger man." "She was an educated *sylph* with an air of aristocratic dignity." "She was a *sylph* who liked to play soccer." "She is a *sylph* who carefully watches everything she eats and drinks."

sylvan [SILvun] pertaining to the woods. "The poet wrote of pristine *sylvan* settings and *Waldeinsamkeit*." "The writer was not attracted to *sylvan* places." "The *sylvan* areas of the Midwest can be dreary." "Behind their home began *sylvan* acres."

T

tabula rasa [TAByulu RAYsu] (Latin) the state of the mind prior to experience. "The philosopher pondered the *tabula rasa*." "The biologist believed that there can be no *tabula rasa*, since learning can even take place in the womb." "The novelist explored the implications of a *tabula rasa*." "Ultimately the *tabula rasa* may be unknowable."

taciturn [TASiturn] habitually silent. "The bashful woman was *taciturn*." "The working-class wife was *taciturn*." "He was a *taciturn* man but spoke enough to function socially." "The *taciturn* student spoke up in class." Syn.: reticent. Ant.: garrulous.

talion [TALeeun] lex talionis, the principle that the punishment should fit the crime. "The convicted murderer received *talion*, as it were, and was executed." "The conservative believed in *talion*." "In his case *talion* could not be literally applied, as his crime was hacking a person to death." "*Talion* is revenge to some people."

talisman [TALismun] an amulet or charm. "The *talisman* of occult power finds its peak in the tribal form of society, where a variety of objects are used as such an amulet." "In the 1970s he had a *talisman* in the form of a 'mood ring.'" "The hippie had a string of beads as a *talisman*." "The native American sold *talismans* to tourists."

tangential [tanJENshul] digressive. "Her story went off *tangentially* when she came to explain her role in the accident." "The teacher's diatribe against communism was woefully *tangential*." "His account of his nightmare was *tangential*." "The obsessed man spoke *tangentially*, being unable to stay on the same subject."

tantamount [TANtumount] equivalent. "Being born into the lower-class is *tantamount* to failure." "What he did was almost *tantamount* to murder." "Inheriting a fortune is *tantamount* to a crime." "What the heiress Barbara Hutton did was *tantamount* to robbing a bank."

tautology [toTOLujee] redundant words, as in "wealthy millionaire"; in logic, a redundant statement which is true regardless of outcome: for example, *he will either lose the match or win the match*. "The prophecies of the oracles were *tautological*." "In a *tautology*, he 'predicted' that a great empire would be lost in the war." "It is almost *tautological* to claim that 'your mother was pro-life.'" "The *tautology* 'the team might win' was fatuous."

tawdry [TAWdree] cheap, tacky; pertaining to showy poor taste. "The ornaments in the office were *tawdry*." "All over the walls and desks were *tawdry* notes and signs like 'enthusiasm is infectious.'" "The backyards of the lower-middle-class homes were full of *tawdry* birdbaths, gnomes and boats." "His room was ratty and *tawdry*." Syn.: garish, gimcrack. Ant.: esthetic.

temerity [tuMERitee] reckless boldness; audacity. "His *temerity* even extended to publicly calling for personal assistance from the country's president." "In a fit of foolish *temerity* he asked his uncle for money." "Do you have the *temerity* to marry a person of a different race?" "He had the *temerity* to try to jump across the gap between the buildings." Syn.: gall, impudence, nerve, rashness. Ant.: deliberateness.

temperate [TEMpurit] moderate; not excessive; moderate with regard to drinking alcohol. "Writers should strive for a *temperate* tone." "The former alcoholic remained *temperate* for years." "The city's climate was *temperate*." "Her speed on the highway was *temperate*." Syn.: continent. Ant.: intemperate.

tempestuous [temPESchoous] violently stormy; tumultuous. "Their short marriage was *tempestuous*." "A *tempest* destroyed the remainder of the Spanish fleet." "The celebration after the high school football game was *tempestuous*." "The bombing caused *tempestuous* confusion in the city." "The North Atlantic is *tempestuous* and cold." Syn.: furious. Ant.: calm.

temporal [TEMpurul] pertaining to time; short-lived. "As Horace said, our *temporal* lives do not permit undertaking extensive projects." "The life of flies and mosquitos is *temporal*." "*Temporal* humanity but limns the water and writes in dust." "The fly had a *temporal* cycle of one day." Syn.: ephemeral, evanescent. Ant.: intransient, long-standing.

temporize [TEMpurihz] to hesitate in order to gain time or delay acting. "The manager *temporized* so the relief pitcher could warm up." "The marshal *temporized* so his army could prepare for battle." "The man *temporized* so that he would be really hungry at dinner." "The student *temporized* to give himself time to prepare for the test."

tendentious [tenDENshus] biased; promoting a particular view rather than being objective. "The news on television is very *tendentious*." "*The New York Times*, as objective studies have shown, is *tendentious*, and not liberal." "Which do you believe is more *tendentious*, *Pravda* or *Time* magazine?" "Although professing to be objective, the sociologists were *tendentious*." Syn.: partial, partisan, prejudicial. Ant.: dispassionate, unbiased.

tenderloin [TENdurloin] a district of a U.S. city noted for corruption. "Many city workers were on the take in the *tenderloin*." "The *tenderloin* was working-class." "The brothel was located in the *tenderloin*." "He had a job in the *tenderloin*."

tenebrous [TENubrus] dark; gloomy; obscure. "The cellar was musty and *tenebrous*." "The February day was cold, rainy and *tenebrous*." "The prose of *The Divided Heaven* is *tenebrous*." "The inside of the big old house was *tenebrous* and poorly maintained."

tenet [TENit] any belief held to be true. "The author's *tenet* of 'paternalism without father' is that the father has effectively abandoned his family." "The conservative's *tenet* was that higher education should remain elitist." "The radical's *tenet* is that inequality breeds injustice." "The *tenet* of American society is that anyone can get rich." Syn.: creed, precept, principle.

tenuous [TENyoous] weak; poorly supported. "The archeologist's theory was *tenuous.*" "He provided copious footnotes so his theory would not seem *tenuous.*" "The psychotic man had only a *tenuous* grip on reality." "His fame was rickety and *tenuous.*" Syn.: unsubstantial. Ant.: substantial.

tergiversate [TURjivursayt] to equivocate; to abandon one's faith, as in a religion or cause. "The left-wingers of the 60s who *tergiversated* and joined the right in the 80s may have merely had superficial beliefs to begin with." "The radical regarded *tergiversated* 'born-again' devotees as phony." "The Congresswoman *tergiversated* on the tax question." "Senator McCarthy *tergiversated* as to how many communists were in the state department." Syn.: apostatize.

testy [TEStee] irritable. "He was *testy* when it came to his own fussy method of doing things." "The puppy was *testy* and liked to bite hands." "Manual work made him *testy.*" "His *testy* comments came at a press conference." Syn.: cross, ornery, petulant. Ant.: staid.

thanatos [THANutos] death as a personification; an alleged death wish. "The quack Sigmund Freud (1856-1939) elaborated on *thanatos.*" "The social scientist did not believe that everyone harbored *thanatos.*" "The will to live and believe may be stronger than *thanatos.*" "Suicide victims perhaps indeed harbor *thanatos.*" *Thanatos* is Greek for "death."

thaumaturgy [THOmuturjee] the working of miracles; magic. "The *thaumaturgy* in the Bible is not supported by evidence." "The teacher dabbled in *thaumaturgy.*" "The magician's apparent *thaumaturgy* impressed the audience." "The magician revealed the secrets of the *thaumaturgy* of his fellow magicians."

theocracy [theeOKrusee] a government consisting of religious leaders. "The Vatican is a *theocracy.*" "It is doubtful whether there have been many *theocracies* in history." "The chiefdom was organized into a *theocracy.*" "The *theocracy* collapsed and was conquered."

theodicy [theeODisee] a vindication of God's goodness in the face of evil. "Gottfried von Leibniz (1646-1716) expounded a *theodicy.*" "A modern *theodicy* would not be an easy task." "The *theodicy* was ambiguous." "The *theodicy* stated that man is half-good and half-evil."

thimblerig [THIMbulrig] to cheat through sleight of hand. "The thief *thimblerigged* the man's wallet." "He *thimblerigged* at poker." "It was hard to *thimblerig* at the casino." "He *thimblerigged* in the shell game."

thrall [THROL] a bondman or slave; thralldom. "The peasant of the Middle Ages was in *thrall* to his master or lord." "The radical reminded people of how hard it would have been to be a *thrall.*" "The social critic was in *thrall* to Freud for some unstated reason." "The woman was in *thrall* to food and chocolate."

threadbare [THREDbayr] hackneyed. "The right-wing constantly brings up the *threadbare* argument of burning down the ROTC, a straw-man logic, whereas actually radicals advocate equality, which right-wingers so seldomly address." "The argument for school prayer was *threadbare.*" "The conservative stumbled on the *threadbare* attack which maintained that the poor will always be around." "The high school's choice of a play to stage was *thread-*

bare." Syn.: banal, commonplace, trite.

threnody [THRENudee] a song or poem of lamentation. "Bacon wrote a great *threnody* expressing weariness with life: 'What then remains, but that we still should cry, Not to be born, or being born to die.'" "The *threnody* was read in a chapel on the cemetery grounds." "The *threnodist*, as he were, Edgar Allen Poe (1809-49), wrote, 'a dirge for her, the doubly-dead, in that she died so young.'" "His *threnody* bewailed the brevity of life." Syn.: dirge, elegy, requiem.

throes [THROHZ] an attack of pain or agony. "The nursing home patient was in her death *throes.*" "The *throes* of poverty was very great during the 1930s." "The *throes* of economic depression convince some that socialism is the answer." "The cancer patient suffered *throes.*" Syn.: affliction, pang, throb. Ant.: anodyne, balm, salve.

tiff [TIF] a spat; a bit of anger. "The slow service at the restaurant had the couple in a *tiff.*" "He was in a *tiff* because someone, a relative, had opened his mail." "The coach was in a *tiff* because his team ran the wrong play." "The man was in a *tiff* because his dinner was late." Syn.: altercation, quarrel, squabble, wrangle. Ant.: sanguineness.

timocracy [tihMOKrusee] a form of government in which office holders must own a given amount of property. "The colonial American government was a *timocracy.*" "A *timocracy* is not an egalitarian form of government." "The *timocracy* was corrupt." "*Timocracy* can also refer to a government of meritorious rulers."

tinhorn [TINhorn] a phony; (adj.) cheap and showy. "He was castigated as a *tinhorn* leader, but in his own country he had great power." "The do-nothing teacher was like a *tinhorn.*" "The *tinhorn* decorations were jarring." "The *tinhorn* doctor was under investigation." Syn.: charlatan, faker, imposter, mountebank. Ant.: real McCoy.

tirade [TIHrayd] a diatribe. "His *tirade* against 'drug-and-surgery' medicine at the convention antagonized the audience, and afterward noone would talk with him." "She learned to resist doing a *tirade* in her head." "Presley had a bad temper and a *tirade* by him was not out of the question." "He went into a *tirade* on the television news show." Syn.: harangue, invective, philippic, screed. Ant.: encomium.

titan [TIHTun] something enormous, as in size or influence. "The adult male elephant has a *titanic* penis." "The ship was *titanic*, like the one which sank on its maiden voyage." "The Wall Street banker had *titanic* economic influence, and no small amount of political influence." "He was a *titan* among novelists." Syn.: colossus. Ant.: tiny.

titter [TITur] to laugh when inappropriate in a self-conscious or nervous manner. "The woman *tittered* when she saw the naked man." "The man in the automobile with three other carpoolers *tittered* when he heard the man on the radio refer to 'joking off.'" "The two teenage girls *tittered* at the idea of milking the teets of a cow." "The man could not help *tittering* in church when something amusing struck him."

toady [TOHdee] a sycophant. "He was a *toady*, a yes man, in the company, and he never questioned authority." "The writer rejected being *toady*, since he thought that the potential gain was outweighed by the subservience." "The *toady* did not accept the idea that his country was wrong to wage war." "The *toady* could not break free of the social and emotional bonds that held him." From the word *toad* (the amphibian). Syn.: bootlicker, fawner, truckler. Ant.: insurgent.

tomfoolery [tomFOOluree] foolish behavior; a silly thing. "The customer refused to put up any longer with the used-car salesman's *tomfoolery*." "He showed *tomfoolery* in joining the games of children." "After dwelling on his past, he vowed to do away with *tomfoolery*." "The kids' father did not stand for *tomfoolery*." Syn.: folly, monkeyshines, shenanigans, silliness. Ant.: astuteness.

tope [TOHP] to drink alcohol to excess. "They snuck out of the house on summer nights and *toped* until thoroughly hooched, absolutely zulued." "They *toped* beer while floating the river." "The young man refused to *tope* with his friends." "He was never warned not to *tope* and drive." Syn.: booze. Ant.: teetotal.

torpid [TORpid] inactive; lethargic. "A *torpid* intellect was generally to be found on the teaching staff." "She grew *torpid* with excessive time on her hands." "The desert was hot and *torpid*." "He knew better than to grow *torpid* and slothful." Syn.: apathetic, listless, slothful. Ant.: active, vivacious.

tour de force [TOOR DU FORS] a great achievement. "The magician's show was a *tour de force*, as he seemingly made a woman disappear." "His novel on the Civil War was a *tour de force*." "The neoclassical building was the architect's *tour de force*." "The woman's *tour de force* in life was being master of her own emotions and passions."

tovarich [tuVARish] (Russian) comrade. "The Russians say *tovarich*, and the Americans say 'my fellow Americans.'" "The use of *tovarich* expressed their esprit-de-corps." "Russian *tovarich* is *Genosse* in German."

tractable [TRAKtubul] easily swayed. "The people of the bygone society were said to be *tractable* to money; that is, they were corrupt." "She was not *tractable* to becoming intimate with him." "The heiress was not *tractable* to hasty offers of marriage." "She was *tractable* to a romantic appeal." Syn.: compliant, docile, manageable, manipulable, pliant, yielding. Ant.: intractable.

trade-last [TRAYDlast] a flattering remark about the person to whom it is told, this person then relaying something flattering about the person who told it. "An unintentional *trade-last* can be embarassing." "The *trade-last* was about his mother." "The two friends exchanged a *trade-last*."

traduce [truDOOS] to slander; to malign. "The radical was *traduced* by the newspaper." "The tabloid regularly *traduced* famous people." "Authors must be careful not to *traduce* anyone." "The *traducement* by the townspeople concerned the young woman's affair and who got her pregnant." Syn.: calumniate, libel.

traipse [TRAYPS] to walk about aimlessly or idly. "They *traipsed* all over the park looking for the playground." "They *traipsed* the theme park all day." "The little girl *traipsed* to school." "The soldier *traipsed* into a mine field."

trammel [TRAMul] something that hinders one's freedom. "The *trammels* of poverty are hard to endure." "The *trammels* of breast cancer in women and prostate cancer in men sometimes end in death." "The greatest *trammel* in his life was his own cognition, oppressive thoughts." Syn.: constraint, curb, hindrance, restriction.

transfix [transFIKS] to hold in awe. "The crowd at the ballpark was *transfixed* by the streaking woman." "She was *transfixed* by his gaze." "The sight of the body *transfixed* him." "He was *transfixed* by the vista in the Himalayas." Syn.: engross, fascinate, hypnotize, mesmerize.

transmogrify [transMOGrufih] to change into a different or bizarre form. "In Kafka's 'The Metamorphosis,' a man is *transmogrified* into a creature resembling a giant dung beetle." "She *transmogrified* the suit he wore into a 'tuxedo.'" "The $50 he lent him was *transmogrified* into $1,000." *Transmogrify* is a recent coinage. Syn.: metamorphose, transfigure.

transom [TRANsum] a window above a door. "The *transom* is found in older buildings." "The *transom* was not opened much." "A *transom* was above the door to the kindergarten." "The *transom* was green and opaque."

transpontine [transPONtin] across or beyond a bridge. "The army fought its way *transpontine*." "The route to downtown was *transpontine*." "The parade proceeded *transpontine*." "In the city's center were several *transpontine* roads."

travail [truVAYL] painful experience or hardship. "The *travail* of working at minimum wage should shame the rich, but it does not." "The boy grew up accustomed to *travail*." "English *travail* is reminiscent of the French word for to 'work,' *travailler*." "Some jobs, like digging ditches and tuckpointing, are *travail*." Syn.: adversity. Ant. life of Riley.

treacle [TREEkul] excessive sentimentality. "The television show layed the *treacle* on thick." "Some of the polite jokes in the family magazine were *treacle*." "*Treacle* sometimes sells in that culture." "The radical claimed that *treacle* masks some problem or evil in society." "European critics have accused Disneyland of *treacle*." Syn.: mawkishness, schmaltz.

trenchant [TRENchunt] caustic; vigorous or effective. "The anthropologist had *trenchant* criticism of the idea of democracy." "H.L. Mencken (1880-1956) was a *trenchant* observer of the American scene." "Mark Twain (1835-1910) had *trenchant* criticism for the dollar-crazed devotees of the gospel of wealth." Syn.: acrimonious, mordant. Ant.: commendatory.

trencherman [TRENchurmun] a hearty eater. "With those *trenchermen* at the table there was no danger of food going to waste." "The German is a *trencherman*, while the Frenchman is a gourmet." "The buffet restaurant was a favorite of *trenchermen*." "The *trenchermen* of the family devoured the woman's cooking."

trepidation [trepiDAYshun] nervous apprehension. "As Virgil (70-19 B.C.) said, *trepidation*, fear, lent wings to his feet." "*Trepidation* seemed to physically age him, causing dry skin, gray hair, and so forth." "The speaker felt *trepidation* as he waited to address the audience." "The burglar felt *trepidation* during his crime." Syn.: affright, alarm, dread. Ant.: insouciance.

tribulation [tribyuLAYshun] severe adversity. "He overcame the *tribulation* and learned from it, but as the Bible said, 'in much wisdom is much grief.'" "The family experienced *tribulation* when the father died and had to move to the city." "The *tribulation* figured prominently in his novel." "The man encountered *tribulation* in trying to pass the rigorous academic program leading to a license." Syn.: hardship, misfortune, ordeal, suffering.

troglodyte [TROGludiht] a cave man; a person considered to be like a cave man. "He was labeled a *troglodyte* due to his habit of working in his room." "The old *troglodyte* culture was investigated by anthropologists in the caves in the south of France." "The *troglodytes* drew animals on the wall of the caves." "The *troglodyte* was a Neanderthal."

Trojan Horse [TROHjun HORS] a person or group that attempts to subvert or destroy from within. "The communists were accused of being a *Trojan Horse* in government, of trying to infiltrate key positions and bring it down." "The CIA often manages a *Trojan Horse*." "Their *Trojan Horse* trick did not work." "The enemy brought the *Trojan Horse* inside the city gates, unaware that Greek soldiers inside it would open the gates to let the Greek army in." After an event in a classical myth involving the war between Troy and the Greeks.

trollop [TROLup] a slovenly woman; a prostitute. "It seemed that everyone in town realized that the woman was a *trollop* 'for sale,' you might say." "The *trollop* was in a dangerous occupation." "The *trollop* was not attractive." "The *trollop* was poorly paid." Syn.: harlot, hussy, slattern, whore.

troth [TROTH] a promise to marry (betrothal). "He reneged on his *troth* and did not marry her." "She remembered his *troth* and faithfully waited for him." "Their mutual *troth* was fulfilled, as they married a year later." "The teenager gave his girlfriend *troth*."

truckle [TRUKul] to be servile or submissive. "The commoners *truckled* to the patrician senator." "The salesmen *truckled* to the sales manager." "The feminist asserted that women *truckle* to men sometimes." "The teachers *truckled* to the principal." Syn.: cringe.

truculent [TRUKyulunt] fierce and cruel; scathing. "The Congressional candidate issued a *truculent* denial that he had had extramarital sex with a woman on his staff." "He was a *truculent* football player." "The commission's report was tentative rather than *truculent*." "He had a *truculent* disregard for etiquette." Syn.: militant, vitriolic. Ant.: amiable, likeable, obliging.

truism [TROOizum] a self-evident truth. "The radical regarded it as a *truism* that the poor are trampled underfoot by impersonal institutions." "That people prefer wealth to being poor is a *truism*." "To some it is, or was, a *truism* that all men are created equal." "It may be merely a partial *truism* that all politics is local."

trull [TRUL] a prostitute. "*Trulls* are not respectable people." "The *trull* carried on business in a mobile home." "The *trull* tried to avoid getting venereal disease." "The *trull* was becoming overaged." Syn.: call girl, harlot, hooker, whore.

trumpery [TRUMpuree] something without use or value; nonsense. "He drove around buying *trumpery* at garage sales." "The thrift store sold some things that were *trumpery*." "What he said on the phone was *trumpery*." "The comic strip dealt in *trumpery*."

tryst [TRIST] an appointment to meet at a specified time and place, especially for lovers. "Their *tryst* was planned for midnight in the cemetery." "Their *tryst* was spoiled by the arrival of his mother." "His *tryst* with his beloved excited his imagination." "She met as usual at their *tryst* but the thrill was gone." Syn.: assignation.

tu quoque [TOO KWOkwe] (Latin) thou also; you too have the same fault or guilt. This renowned phrase is based on the similarity of human cultures and the people who make them up. Obviously, there are differences of class, sex, culture and age, but still many similarities exist. *Tu quoque* says that one's opponent or debater has the same failing, can be reproached for the same reason. Thou also, my friend, are the same way. "He criticized his cousin for wanting fame and fortune, but anyone could have said to him, '*tu quoque!*'" "*Tu quoque*, the great 'thou also,' signifies the essential similarity of humanity." "'*Tu quoque*,' said the television commentator." "The writer noted that although each person is unique, everyone is subject to the same charge, *tu quoque*."

turncoat [TURNkoht] a person who switches allegiance, joins an opposing faction, etc.; a traitor. "The most famous *turncoat* in American history is Benedict Arnold (1741-1801), who betrayed to the British the defense of West Point." "She was an unrepentant *turncoat*." "The priest was a *turncoat* who abandoned his faith and became a born-again atheist." "The *turncoat* was caught by his former army and executed." Syn.: Quisling.

turpitude [TURpitood] depravity; a depraved act. "The *turpitude* and greed of the CEO went uncriticized in the media." "He hated to listen to the *turpitude* of the shock jock." "The morning television news seemed flippant and full of *turpitude*." "The newspapers did not report the *turpitude* of the idle rich." Syn.: baseness, degeneracy, degradation, vileness. Ant.: incorruptibility, probity, rectitude.

tutelary [TOOTuleree] pertaining to a guardian or guardianship. "In the will the youth's uncle was made his *tutelary*." "Her older sister had *tutelary* authority over her." "He was a *tutelary* to his grandniece." "The oldest brother was made executor and *tutelary*."

twaddle [TWODul] trivial or silly talk or writing. "The mother-daughter kaffeeklatsch was full of *twaddle*." "The girls were *twaddling* all day." "The movie was marred by scenes of self-conscious *twaddle*." "Left to themselves the pupils would only *twaddle* and get no work done." Syn.: chatter, palaver.

twerp [TWURP] a despised or insignificant person. "The *twerp* had but few friends." "He was a *twerp* and a runt who was careful to avoid fights, since all the boys were bigger." "The *twerp* saw a doctor for a hormone to make him taller." The origin (etymology) of *twerp* is unknown.

U

ubiquitous [yooBIKwitus] present everywhere. "Opportunism is *ubiquitous* in class society." "Social promotion was *ubiquitous* in the schools." "Crime was *ubiquitous* in that time and place." "Playing baseball became *ubiquitous*." Syn.: pervasive. Ant.: rare.

ukase [YOOkays] an authoritarian edict. "The czar issued a *ukase*." "The *ukase* declared martial law and set a curfew." "The *ukase* was the response to the attempt to assassinate the leader." "The *ukase* was not well received."

ululate [YOOyulayt] to howl like a dog; to wail. "The dog *ululated* when struck by his master's hand." "He let out a *ululation* when he got the bad news." "The woman giving birth *ululated*." "The country yahoo drove up and down the county route *ululating*."

umbrage [UMbrij] offense or annoyance. "Her *umbrage* at not being invited to the party would not be assuaged." "He took a little *umbrage* when his neighbor walked past without seeming to notice him." "The policeman felt *umbrage* when the man refused to keep his hands out of his pockets." "His small stature made him *umbrageous*." Syn.: affront, pique, slight. Ant.: gratitude.

Uncle Tom [UNGkul TOM] a black felt to be excessively deferential to whites. "He was accused of being an *Uncle Tom* in order to gain white political support." "The radical remarked that some blacks are Republicans, but that some blacks are also an *Uncle Tom*." "The *Uncle Tom* was deferent because he needed a job." "The policeman was an *Uncle Tom*." After a slave in *Uncle Tom's Cabin*, a novel by Harriet Beecher Stowe (1811-1896).

unconscionable [unKONshunubul] unscrupulous. "It is *unconscionable* to steal but that word needs a redefinition." "How *unconscionable* it is for the rich not to give to charity." "The behavior of the outlaw was *unconscionable*." "The 'jokes' played upon him were *unconscionable*." Syn.: malicious, unprincipled. Ant.: conscientious.

uncouth [unKOOTH] socially awkward. "The behavior of the teenager was *uncouth*." "The tourist was *uncouth* when he strayed from the usual tourist traps." "They were *uncouth* together, not a happy couple." "Their father would not hear of *uncouth* behavior." "He was so bashful and *uncouth* that he sometimes avoided being social." "Her bad breath makes her unintentionally *uncouth*." Syn.: gauche. Ant.: befitting.

unctuous [UNGKchoous] marked by affected or exaggerated earnestness. "The television show was so bad that one critic referred to its '*unctuous* spoon feeding to the audience.'" "He could not help acting *unctuous* when the police questioned him." "The quarterback made for an *unctuous* actor." "The man was *unctuous* with the girl he wished to date." Syn.: simpering.

unequivocal [uniKWIVukul] unambiguous. "'It's *unequivocal*, the witness lies like a politician,' claimed the defendant." "His determination to lose weight was *unequivocal*." "She made an *unequivocal* mistake that cost her dearly." "Her love for the prisoner was *unequivocal*." Syn.: certain, explicit, indisputable, undeniable. Ant.: vague.

unexceptionable [unikSEPshunubul] beyond criticism. "His school work was *unexceptionable*, although he did not participate in sports or extracurricular activities." "Her mastery of the piano was *unexceptionable*." "Dvorak's music is *unexceptionable*." "His belief in equality was *unexceptionable*." Syn.: faultless, inoffensive, unobjectionable.

unregenerate [unriJENurit] unreconstructed; not renewed spiritually. "The 'liberal-left' entertainer was considered an *unregenerate* collaborator by the right-wing." "The *unregenerate* comedian ridiculed sacred institutions." "The *unregenerate* parents could not stop the screaming and crying of their son, who did not wish to go to bed." "The morning radio-DJ was cynical and *unregenerate*." Syn.: demoralized, depraved. Ant.: reclaimed, redeemed.

untoward [unTORD] unfavorable; improper. "He was *untowardly* flirtatious with another man's wife at the celebration." "By age 25 his skin had become *untowardly* dry." "The bus made an *untoward* stop to let a woman use a bathroom." "It is *untowardly* nasty to have to scrub toilets at minimum wage." Syn.: indecorous, unbecoming. Ant.: befitting, seemly.

unwonted [unWONtid] rare. "He was an *unwonted* visitor at the library." "Radicals in American broadcasting are very *unwonted* if not altogether absent." "It was *unwonted* of him not to tell his wife where he was going." "It is an *unwonted* worker indeed who does not want more money." Syn.: scarce, uncommon, unusual. Ant.: ordinary, prevalent.

upbraid [upBRAYD] to censure. "The scold *upbraided* her children." "A teacher had her students write about sex and was *upbraided* for it." "The radical *upbraided* cultural damnation." "The social critic *upbraided* various figures in the counterculture." Syn.: chastise, rebuke, reprimand.

uppishness [UPishnes] arrogance; snobbishness. "The déclassé middle-class family was considered *uppish* by its neighbors." "*Uppishness* contains a little aggression." "She was *uppish* because she had money." "*Uppishness* varies by class." "It was easy enough for a wealthy heir to proclaim, 'ask not what your country can do for you,' for with no admission of his own debt of gratitude it was like *uppishness*." Syn.: haughtiness. Ant.: humbleness, humility, meekness.

urbane [urBAYN] sophisticated; having the polish of a large city. "The social critic thought that, far from being *urbane*, the telejournalist had a shallow intellect." "Shakespeare, rather than being *urbane*, is said to have been like a craftsman." "The *urbane* writer denounced provincialism." "An *urbane* man would not accept such an excuse, said the radical." Syn.: cultured, genteel, polished.

usury [YOOzhuree] an exorbitant rate of interest; the practice of lending at an exorbitant rate of interest. "Payday and quick-loan shops, which were popping up all over town, practice *usury*." "The writer knew that *usury* was associated with Jews, but he did not know if this association were justified." "Some forms of *usury* are outlawed." "The radical asserted that the banks are allowed to practice *usury* in how and to whom they lend." Syn.: loan shark-ing.

utilitarian [yootiliTAReeun] concerned with usefulness rather than esthetic qualities. "The *utilitarian* philosophy of John Stuart Mill (1806-73) advo-cated the greatest good for the greatest number." "Art is not normally *utilita-rain.*" "Only a philistine is entirely consumed with the *utilitarian*, claimed the conservative." "His dealings in the business of art were *utilitarian*." Syn.: practical, serviceable.

uxorious [ukSOHReeus] excessively devoted or submissive to one's wife. "He enjoys a very happy marriage, though he might be a little *uxorious*." "He was *uxorious*, she wore the pants in the family." "The gift he bought for his wife was so generous that it made him rather *uxorious* in presenting it." "The timid man was rather *uxorious*."

V

vacillate [VASulayt] to waver in decision or opinion. "The president's *vacilla-tion* in campaigning cost him re-election." "The general could not afford to *vacillate*." "*Vacillation* cost the soldiers their life." "The writer often paused, trying to think, causing *vacillation*." Syn.: falter, shilly-shally.

vacuous [VAKyoous] empty; devoid of a certain quality, as intelligence or skill. "The *vacuous* curriculum at public high schools includes P.E., shop, study hall, and home economics." "The intellect of the people was *vacuous* and underdeveloped." "The class of the teacher of French was mind-draining and *vacuous*, with a Halloween party in October and a Christmas party in De-cember." Syn.: inane. Ant.: fortified.

vagary [vuGARee] an unanticipated or capricious occurrence; an unusual idea. "The *vagaries* of being a traveling salesman may make the job not worth the trouble." "Life's *vagaries* had been hard on him." "She hatched the *vagary* of directly phoning him for a reply to the charge." Syn.: quirk, whim. Ant.: normalcy.

vainglory [VAYNglohree] empty or fancied honor or greatness. "Bacon said, with respect to *vainglory*, that 'the arch flatterer, with whom all petty flatter-ers have intelligence, is a man's self.'" "The president was so full of *vain-glory* and affectation that he was far removed from reality." "*Vainglory* is folly, and the remedy is a friend to disabuse you of *vainglorious* ideas." Syn.: conceit, vanity. Ant.: affability, humility.

vamoose [vaMOOS] to leave in a hurry. "*Vamoose!* she cried, and everyone hurriedly headed for the door." "He yelled *vamoose*, and an encouragement to the team." "In the middle of their closely-contested tennis match, he shouted *vamoose*, 'I'm going to put you away!'" "They *vamoosed* after hearing the siren." This word is from Spanish *"vamos,"* which means "let's go."

vamp [VAMP] an unscrupulous, seductive woman. "One famous example of a *vamp* is the fictional character Lolita, from a novel of the same name by Vladimir Nabokov." "She was reputed to have been a *vamp* in her youth." "The *vamp* stole a married man from his wife, thereby breaking up the family." "The *vamp* was from a broken home." *Vamp* is a shortening of the word *vampire.* Syn.: jezebel. Ant.: angel.

vapid [VAPid] insipid or dull. "The movie about John Dillinger was *vapid*, and featured more bullet holes than any other film." "The book was a *vapid* disappointment, as it merely contained mindless violence." "The radical discussed life in the suburbs, claiming it was *vapid* for several reasons." "The museum's avante-garde art collection is *vapid*." Syn.: inane, jejune, prosaic, tasteless. Ant.: titillating.

vaticinate [vuTISunayt] to prophecy. "The oracle's *vaticination* did not come true." "She could hardly believe the *vaticination*." "His *vaticination* called for the end of the world." "The prophet's *vaticinations* were vaguely worded."

velleity [vuLEEitee] a wish without an accompanying effort to obtain it. "Her *velleity* was that her mother-in-law go away." "He hated to wait for anything, but that was a *velliety*, since it was sometimes necessary." "The man's *velleity* was to be free of oppressive thoughts." "She wanted to die, but that was a *velleity*, and she did not kill herself."

venal [VEENul] open to bribery; subject to purchase even though not rightfully: *venal sex with a prostitute.* "The *venal* federal prosecutor was caught taking a bribe and went to prison." "The *venal* woman was arrested in a raid, but not her johns." "The radical claimed that one's labor should not be *venal*." "The people were *venal* and acted as though they were commodities." "The radical asserted that people on corporate boards are *self-venal*, so to speak, since they award themselves a huge income." Syn.: bribable, corrupt. Ant.: honest.

veneer [vuNEER] a superficial character trait, such as friendliness. "His *veneer* of cheerfulness was not convincing." "The athlete had a *veneer* of rage which was suppressed but sometimes came to the surface." "Her *veneer* of happiness told a lie." "The people were full of a *veneer* of friendliness that may or may be an accurate reflection of character." Syn.: appearance, façade, guise, semblance.

venial [VEEneeul] excusable or pardonable. "The historian's biography of John D. Rockefeller 1 seemed to present his actions as *venial*, thus being an apologist for the industrialist who declared that God had given him his money." "His faults were *venial*, as he was a kind, honorable man, and had suffered more wrong than he had committed." "His sin was *venial*, not mortal." "Although his mistake was *venial*, he was very embarrassed by it." Syn.: exculpatory, justifiable, trifling. Ant.: grave, indefensible, mortal, trifling.

venue [VENyoo] the scene of an event; the place where a trial is held. "The *venue* greatly affected the outcome of the murder trial." "The *venue* of the libel was complicated, since the broadcast was seen around the world." "The *venue* of his heartbreak was Rouen, France, where he met a charming, artless girl and succumbed to *Liebeskummer*." "The lawyer asked for a change of *venue*." Syn.: locale, location, setting.

verbatim [vurBAYtim] word for word. "During the interview the actor quoted *verbatim* almost a whole scene from *Macbeth*." "He quoted *verbatim* the heated words that preceded the altercation." "He knew *verbatim* the words of the poem." "She repeated *verbatim* the man's obscenities."

verbose [vurBOHS] wordy. "The novelist had a *verbose* style and shunned sententiousness." "A good writer is able to work out his treatment of a subject without being *verbose*." "Her statement at the press conference was *verbose*, lasting 25 minutes." "Henry James (1843-1916) may have been a little *verbose*." Syn.: loquacious, prolix. Ant.: laconic, succinct.

verisimilitude [verisiMILitood] likelihood; the mere appearance of truth. "The *verisimilitude* of politics is obscured in uncertain plausibility." "The *verisimilitude* of his denial of an extramarital affair was questionable." "The *verisimilitude* was very deceptive, especially to those who do little thinking." "The *verisimilitude* of how others see us is fraught with irrationality." Syn.: façade, image.

verism [VERizum] realism in art and literature. "The *veristic* artists sought to portray class struggle in their murals." "Their brand of *verism* was dismal." "The *veristic* painting depicted a dreary urban scene." "The *veristic* novel impeached inequality."

verity [VERitee] the state of being true. "The 'Camelot' of President Kennedy's administration was not a *verity*." "Poets have made much of the *verity* that life is short." "The radical declared a *verity* that the poor struggle against the rich." "He suggested a *verity* that the media are the servants of power." "It is a *verity* that people obey authority without thinking." Syn.: truism.

vestige [VEStij] a sign of something that no longer exists. "*Vestiges* of the former kingdom are hard to locate." "There are still *vestiges* of chivalry to be found in modern European societies." "*Vestiges* of the doomed airplane were found scattered over miles." "Some embryonic parts of the human fetus are *vestigial*." Syn.: relic.

vesuvian [vuSOOveeun] given to often violent tantrums. "The defendant was *vesuvian* and had a history of violence." "In one of his *vesuvian* fits he attacked his wife, forcing her to the hospital for treatment." "He had a *vesuvian* nature, and no more so than when he got tanked." "She had a *vesuvian* nature." Named for Mount Vesuvius in Italy. Syn.: enraged, wrathful. Ant.: equable, pacific.

viaticum [vihATukum] money or supplies for a journey. "As *viaticum* he carried a credit card." "The crusaders packed *viaticum* into a line of wagons." "The group's *viaticum* was lost while trying to ford a river." "The most convenient form of modern *viaticum* is to be able to draw on 'cybercash.'" Syn.: funds, means, resources.

vilify [VILufih] to defame. "Their neighbor was *vilified* as a child molester but was actually innocent of the hysterical charge." "The *vilification* proceeded to the point that an affable man was pictured as diabolic." "The woman who came forward to charge the politician with adultery was *vilified* as a loose woman and deceitful tramp by the media." "The *vilification* by the tabloid resulted in a libel suit." Syn.: blacken, calumniate, defile, revile, sully, traduce. Ant.: acclaim, extol.

vilipend [VILupend] to vilify; to regard as worthless. "The radical *vilipended* the premier as a fascist." "She *vilipended* his 'art' collection." "The politician was *vilipended* by the newspaper." "He *vilipended* the amateur's painting." Syn.: calumniate, revile. Ant.: glorify, laud, praise.

vindicate [VINdukayt] to justify; to clear from blame. "The autopsy *vindicated* the suspect." "The ends should not *vindicate* the means." "The publicity *vindicated* the writer of the charge of paranoia." "The discovery of the knife *vindicated* the man who was thought to have murdered the woman." Syn.: acquit, exculpate, exonerate. Ant.: incriminate.

virago [viRAYgoh] a shrew. "The *virago* was much tamer when her husband arrived home from work." "The *virago* was an unpleasant woman." Syn.: battle-ax, fishwife, scold, termagant, vixen.

virile [VIRul] having thoroughly masculine characteristics. "He was very *virile,* he himself imagined, since he had fathered children with six women." "The actor who seemed so *virile* in the movies was actually homosexual." "With a tall and muscular body, he seemed *virile*." "*Virility*, people seem to think, lies in making a child." Syn.: manly, potent. Ant.: effeminate.

virtuoso [vurchooOHsoh] a person who has exceptional skill in a given field. "The piano *virtuoso* had the audience enraptured with Rachmaninov." "She was a *virtuoso* with the violin." "He was a *virtuoso* in six languages." "Arthur Conan Doyle (1859-1930) created a memorable *virtuoso* in the character of Sherlock Holmes." Syn.: maestro.

virulent [VIRulunt] very poisonous; malicious. "The snake's venom was not *virulent*." "The newspaper's review of the play *42nd Street* was *virulent*." "The *virulent* spokesman destroyed a life in trying to salvage his client's reputation." "The conservative *virulently* denounced socialism." Syn.: malignant, venomous. Ant.: benign.

visage [VIZij] the countenance, face. "A narrowing of eyes on one's *visage* indicates anger." "The beauty of her *visage* was due to the setting of her eyes." "A good book on discerning character based on *visage* is *Reading Faces* (L. Bellak)." "The radical believed that the *visage* betrays the liar."

vitiate [VISHeeayt] to debase. "Humaneness is *vitiated* in mass society by impersonal institutions." "His health was *vitiated* by a habit of eating fastfood." "The war effort was not *vitiated* by the peace movement." "The norm of sociability *vitiates* the private life." Syn.: adulterate, degrade. Ant.: consecrate, dignify.

vitriolic [vitreeOLik] very harsh, as criticism; scathing. "The actor's *vitriolic* lines clashed with the general temper of the play." "He unleashed *vitriolic* wrath." "She was guilty of *vitriolic* control of her children." "The tone of the letter was *vitriolic*." "His humor was *vitriolic*." "The columnist's criticism was *vitriolic*." "The woman *vitriolically* yelled at her daughter for spilling her milk." Syn.: acrimonious, brutal. Ant.: gentle.

vituperate [viTOOpurayt] to berate. "The cantankerous mother *vituperated* against her daughter for being a 'cry baby.'" "The supervisor *vituperated* against his fellow employee for going on break without permission." "*Vituperation* there was, and nothing could have justified it." "For wrecking the car, the young man was administered *vituperation* by his father." Syn.: censure, objurgate, tongue-lash, upbraid, vilify. Ant.: praise.

vivify [VIVufih] to bring to life; to enliven. "The crowd was *vivified* when a zaftig woman dashed naked across the ball field." "He felt *vivified* by the new woman in his life." "What would it take to *vivify* your marriage after 15 or 20 years?" "He felt *vivified* by the cool weather." Syn.: invigorate. Ant.: smother.

vociferous [vohSIFurus] clamorous. "The crowd's *vociferous* booing spurred on the home team." "The classroom was *vociferous*." "The children were *vociferous* in their demand for candy." "The protest became *vociferous*." Syn.: noisy, obstreperous, raucous, strident.

vogue [VOHG] popularity; the period when something is in fashion. "Noone has determined the origin of the word *bikini,* but it came into *vogue* just after World War ll." "The model was in *vogue,* appearing in many ads and magazines, until she became 'old' at 35." "The name Laurie for girls was in *vogue* in the 60s." Syn.: convention, rage, taste. Ant.: old-fashioned, outmoded.

volitive [VOlitiv] pertaining to volition or the will. "The beating was *volitive,* an act of willfulness." "The new wealthy were an act of *volition,* of aggressive will." "Since his bad habits were *volitive,* he reasoned, they could be consciously reversed." "The philosopher claimed that all behavior is *volitive* and not determined." Syn.: discretionary, purposive. Ant.: ineluctable, inexorable.

voluble [VOLyubul] fluent in speaking; talkative. "Women are seen as more *voluble* than men." "She was *voluble* and a little loquacious, yet she still gave thought to her words." "The television news readers were necessarily *voluble*." "He was a reticent man, but when he opened up he was surprisingly *voluble*." Syn.: garrulous, glib, verbose. Ant.: halting.

voluptuary [vuLUPchooeree] a sensualist; (adj.) pertaining to indulgence in pleasure. "In philosophy, an Epicure, although a *voluptuary* enjoying the carnal and gustatory pleasures of the world, is not to be confused with an abject libertine." "The radical realized that his culture abhorred *voluptuaries*." "He was a *voluptuary,* a hog in the sty of Epicure." "The super-rich television producer was a *voluptuary* with a passel of magnificent homes around the world." "She was a middle-aged *voluptuary* who liked meditation, baths, reading, and swimming." Syn.: hedonist. Ant.: ascetic, Puritan.

votary [VOHturee] a monk or nun; a fervent devotee of some cause or organization. "The organization marshaled its *votaries* to vote against the proposition." "The *votaries* lived in seclusion in a monastery nestled atop an isolated bluff in Greece." "It was a *votary,* Gregor Mendel (1822-84), who discovered the basic laws of heredity." "The *votary* mainly prayed and worshiped God." Syn.: aficionado, enthusiast, fanatic.

votive [VOHtiv] offered or dedicated in accordance with a vow. "*Votive* celibacy is not part of being a Protestant minister." "The priests did not partake of *votive* poverty." "His ambition was *votive*, for he had sworn to avenge himself for early poverty." "He lit a *votive* candle in the cathedral." Syn.: prayerful, ritual.

vouchsafe [vouchSAYF] to grant condescendingly; to deign. "The woman *vouchsafed* to clean the kitchen." "He *vouchsafed* the correctness of her opinion." "He *vouchsafed* to clean the toilet." "She *vouchsafed* that women are more emotional than men."

vox populi [VOKS POPyulih] (Latin) the voice of the people; popular opinion. "*Vox populi* in America is probably against inherited wealth." "*Vox populi* disparaged politicians." "Media propaganda—basically found in all countries—has a strong role in forming *vox populi*." "*Vox populi* is not the same as the outlook of news broadcasts."

vulgate [VULgit] (adj.) common; (noun) informal or substandard speech. "The people's *vulgate* contained many graphic idioms." "Writing ought to be more acceptable than *vulgate*." "The working-class uses *vulgate*." "That type of sandal is *vulgate*."

W

wag [WAG] a mischievous person. "The *wag* went too far when he told a joke about a recently-deceased man." "The *wag* told a sexual joke." "The *wag* was not funny."

wall-eyed [WOLihd] marked by an agitated stare, as in rage or fear. "Walleyed wrath and staring rage" (Shakespeare). "He was *wall-eyed* and horn-mad." "Hitler turned red and *wall-eyed*." "The man became *wall-eyed* just before he took to his heels and ran." "The *wall-eyed* woman could hardly believe her eyes."

wan [WAN] pale as if ill; lacking in forcefulness. "The *wan* effort to ban handguns fell short." "Why so pale and wan, fond lover? Prithee, why so pale? Will, when looking well can't move her, looking ill prevail?" (Sir John Suckling [17th century].) "The *wan* attempt to raise the minimum wage was defeated by the business lobby." Syn.: bloodless, pallid. Ant.: sanguine.

Wanderlust [VAHNderloost] (German) a desire to travel. "*Wanderlust* is difficult to fulfill if you have little or no money." "*Wanderlust* led him to Italy." "The retired couple, feeling *Wanderlust*, traveled the world." "The professor was suddenly smitten with *Wanderlust*." Because all nouns in German are capitalized, this word should likewise be capitalized in English.

wangle [WANGgul] to bring about through devious means. "He went to court and *wangled* his way out of a speeding ticket." "The college student *wangled* his way out of an F by complaining to the departmental chairperson." "He *wangled* out of the contract he rashly signed." "He landed the job through some *wangling*." Syn.: finagle, machinate.

wanton [WONtun] willful; malicious and unjustifiable; sexually permissive. "He regarded the slight as a *wanton* act of aggression." "The two teenagers had *wanton* sex." "It was a *wanton* act of defiance." "The Spanish teacher never graded *wantonly*." Syn.: dissolute, licentious. Ant.: intentional.

war horse [WORHORS] a person who is the veteran of many fights or battles, as a war veteran or a politician. "The old reporter was a *war horse* who had covered everything from murder to civil war." "The *war horse* retired from the army as a colonel." "The *war horse* retired from the senate at age 69." "The old fisherman was a sort of *war horse* of the sea, since he had fished it and traveled it for 55 years."

warmed-over [WORMDohvur] unimaginatively reworked, as a literary or artistic work. "The novel was *warmed-over* F. Scott Fitzgerald." "The *warmed-over* 'sculpture' was salvage-yard reject." "The critic called the play '*warmed-over* bosh.'" "The radical referred to the comic's routine as '*warmed-over*' *Gilligan's Island*."

war of nerves [WOR...] a conflict in which psychological harassment is prominent, as in the attempt to erode the enemy's morale. "The White House and the press were in a *war of nerves*." "The bickering spouses were in a *war of nerves*." "The contending football teams were in a *war of nerves*." "The *war of nerves* between the two groups of children had them saying things like 'get off our property' and 'we'll sue you!'"

wastrel [WAYstrul] a spendthrift; a loafer. "The conservative labeled as '*wastrels*' those on welfare, on public aid." "He dropped out of high school—there being no teaching or learning there anyway, he thought—and in his late teens was a sort of *wastrel*." "*Wastrels* are stigmatized, perhaps or perhaps not justifiably." "The *wastrel* lived from paycheck to paycheck." Syn.: idler, lotus-eater, sluggard. Ant.: drudge, toiler.

wean [WEEN] to free someone from an undesirable thing. "It was hard, but she was eventually *weaned* of her vice of gambling." "He was *weaned* of his habit of stealing." "She was *weaned* of prodigal spending." "The twin boys were *weaned* of their pugnaciousness." Syn.: deter, discourage, dissuade.

weasel words [WEEzul WORDZ] ambiguous, misleading or indirect language. "The Pentagon spokesman digressed and started using *weasel words*." "The cheating girlfriend's *weasel words* dismayed her boyfriend." "The report of the presidential commission employed *weasel words*." "Bureaucratic officialdom is drawn to *weasel words* and abhors plain language."

welsh [WELSH] to renege; to fail to fulfill an obligation. "He *welshed* on paying the dentist's bill." "Because she *welshed* on some bills, she had many collection agencies hounding her." "He *welshed* on his promise to pay back the loan." "He was unfaithful and *welshed* on his wedding vow."

Weltanschauung [VELTanshauung] (German) literally, outlook on the world; one's philosophy on questions like the human condition and the cosmos. "He read almost never, continually watched television, and had no *Weltan-schauung,* inarticulate or otherwise, to speak of." "He was not an intellectual and had no *Weltanschauung,* but he knew a social taboo on confronting it." "The conservative's *Weltanschauung* was for tradition and family, but apparently not for equality." "The liberal political *Weltanschauung* was bankrupt." Syn.: ethos, viewpoint.

welter [WELtur] confusion; a state of turmoil. "Rome was thrown into *welter* when the Roman army was defeated by the 'barbarians.'" "The American defense and scientific establishment was thrust into *welter* by the success of Sputnik (a Soviet satellite that was the first to orbit the earth)." "*Welter* made the woman change her mind about helping the man." "The *welter* at the office lay on his mind." Syn.: commotion, disorder, hubbub. Ant.: serenity.

Weltschmerz [VELTshmerts] (German) pessimism or sadness over the condition of the world, especially a rather romantic one. "With their collection of mechanical tripe and salvage-yard sculptures, 20th century abstract artists seemed to be declaring the reign of *Weltschmerz.*" "He rejected *Weltschmerz* and insisted to himself that he had to maintain a positive outlook." "The boast of the state legislator appeared to issue straight from hard-won *Weltschmerz*: 'When I go after the things I believe in, I also recognize that with that is going to come some howitzers and small arms fire.'" "The people of the declining civilization were full of *Weltschmerz.*"

wench [WENCH] a girl or young woman. "The *wench* had flaxen hair." "The *wench* studied art at the university." "The *wench* sat in the Louvre copying the painting of a great master." "The *wench* was a straight-A student." Syn.: damsel, maiden.

wergeld [WERgeld] (also *wirgeld*) money paid to the family of a murdered person. "The *wer* of *wergeld* means 'man,' and the *geld* means 'money.'" "The civil court ordered the man to pay *wergeld.*" "The tribal leaders met to decide on *wergeld.*" "The anthropologist studied *wergeld.*"

wetback [WETbak] (derogatory) a Mexican immigrant worker in the U.S. illegally. "The *wetbacks* joined the demonstrations in favor of immigrant rights." "The *wetbacks* earned just pennies a bushel for working in the fields." "The *wetbacks* did work that noone else wanted to do." "The *wetbacks* were poor."

wet blanket [WET BLANGket] a person who spoils enjoyment. "The young man entered the house where the party was and almost instantly acted like a *wet blanket.*" "The *wet blanket* talked about how skiing and ski resorts destroyed the environment." "The group regarded her as a *wet blanket* because she refused to smoke marijuana." "The *wet blanket* said something that demoralized the others." Syn.: kill-joy. Ant.: enthusiast.

wheedle [WEEdul] to try to influence someone through guile or flattery. "He *wheedled* her into bed with a vague promise of love." "He *wheedled* $500 out of his father." "She *wheedled* her parents into buying the dolls." "He was *wheedled* into selling the house." Syn.: cajole.

whirlygigs [HWURleegigz] the testacles. "'That really hurt my *whirlygigs*,' said the man who jumped onto the horse." "'She is as ugly as the back of my *whirlygigs,*' cried the man." "'Please be gentle with the *whirlygigs,*' said the man to the doctor who was examining him." Syn.: baubles, kanakas, nuts, rollies.

widow's mite [WIDohz MIHT] a relatively generous contribution of money by a poor person. "The working-class woman contributed a *widow's mite,* $50, to charity." "His contribution was a *widow's mite,* but more donations from people like him were needed." "The old man gave a *widow's mite* to the Red Cross." "The charity received many a *widow's mite.*" This term comes from the Bible.

wile [WIHL] cunning; deceit as a stratagem. "She used all her *wiles* to snare the wealthy heir as a husband." "The fox's *wile* tricked the hounds." "The artless girl had no *wiles.*" Syn.: trickery. Ant.: honesty.

wing-ding [WING DING] a lively or noisy party or celebration. "The *wing-ding* lasted until 3 a.m." "The revelers at the *wing-ding* were afraid that there might be a better party somewhere." "The upper-class persons threw rival *wing-dings* on New Year's Eve." "The flapper loved *wing-dings* and high living." Syn.: festivity, fête, soiree.

windfall [WINDfol] an unexpected benefit or good fortune. "The oil *windfall* tax was defeated in Congress." "She reaped a *windfall* in endorsement deals." "The death of their mother brought a *windfall.*" "He felt good about the *windfall.*" This term comes from something blown down by the wind, especially ripe fruit from a tree.

winsome [WINsum] winning or charming. "Her beauty and *winsome* ways attracted many suitors." "His little friend was *winsome.*" "The hood was not exactly *winsome.*" "The French girl was *winsome.*" Syn.: captivating, endearing. Ant.: repulsive.

wiseacre [WIHZaykur] a wise guy; a person who pretends to be very wise. "The *wiseacre* pretended to know better than the rest of them." "The *wiseacre* was not actually wise." "Better to use Socratic irony and know nothing than to know everything as *wiseacre.*" "The *wiseacre* tried to tell the group that it would rain that day."

wistful [WISTful] full of sad yearning. "The unfulfilled man was *wistful* and pensive." "He was always *wistful* during Christmas." "The widower was *wistful* and melancholy." "It is alright to be *wistful,* but as Francis Bacon (1561-1626) advised, do not eat your heart out." Syn.: languishing, longing, wishful. Ant.: cheerful.

wont [WUNT] accustomed. "He was *wont* to skip classes." "She was *wont* to fall asleep on the couch." "Their son was *wont* to be lazy." "His father was *wont* to drink too much." Syn.: habituated, inclined, used.

wraith [RAYTH] an apparition of a living person; a ghost. "A *wraith* haunted the man's dreams." "The *wraith* supposedly portended his death." "She believed she saw a *wraith* representing her mother." "Ostensibly the *wraith* appeared and disappeared quickly." The origin of *wraith* is unknown. Syn.: phantom, specter.

X, Y, Z

Xanthippe [zanTIPee] a shrew. "The *Xanthippe* was hard to get along with." "She was a *Xanthippe* whether or not in the house or out in public." "The *Xanthippe* had rigid views on proper behavior." "There was an epidemic of *Xanthippes*." This word is from the name of Socrates' wife, who was reputedly a shrew. Syn.: battle-ax, fishwife, scold, termagant, virago, vixen.

xenophobia [zenuFOHbeeu] an unreasonable dislike or fear of strangers or foreigners. "*Xenophobia* is a trait of provincialism." "The nation of immigrants was *xenophobic*." "A certain amount of patriotic *xenophobia* is normal in all cultures." "*Xenophobia* is rampant in that society." Syn.: chauvinism. Ant. tolerance.

Yahweh [YAwe] (also *Jehovah*) the Jewish God. "*Yahweh*, as expressed in the Bible, is very strict about personal vice." "*Yahweh* was said to disapprove of their conduct." "Their prayers to *Yahweh* went unanswered." "*Yahweh* makes his sun to shine on the just and unjust alike."

yammer [YAMur] to whine; to utter complainingly. "The children *yammered* during the whole car ride." "His *yammering* got him nowhere." "She *yammered* for sweets." "He never stopped *yammering* on the vacation." Syn.: bewail, grumble, remonstrate.

yen [YEN] a desire or craving. "Having a *yen* to travel, the salesman flew to Spain to take in the sights." "The addict had a *yen* for heroine." "She had a *yen* to write." "His *yen* was for a certain kind of music." Syn.: hankering, longing, yearning.

yore [YOR] time past. "He was much happier in days of *yore*." "Helen, thy beauty is to me, Like those Nicean barks of *yore*" (Edgar Allen Poe). "The two friends sat around talking about their days of *yore*." "In years of *yore* he had loved school."

zaftig [ZAFtik] (Yiddish) having large breasts; full-bosomed. "Most actresses must be *zaftig* to succeed." "The models in the magazine were *zaftig*." "She was both *zaftig* and beautiful." "The *zaftig* woman was proud of her 'size.'" "The pornographic actress was *zaftig*." "Boys were drawn to the *zaftig* girl." "Men prefer *zaftig* women." "Women obviously wish to be *zaftig*, as demonstrated by the popularity of breast implants." In German, *zaftig* literally means "juicy." Syn.: buxom. Ant.: boyish, flat.

Zeitgeist [TSIHTgihst] (German) the spirit of the times, or the cultural attitude of a period. "The *Zeitgeist* of the 60s was radical, with the booming economy and the Vietnam War having allowed challenging the norms." "The romantic *Zeitgeist* of the 19th century was partly a reaction to the French Revolution." "Can you describe your ideal *Zeitgeist*?" "For women the *Zeit-*

geist of the 1920s was expressed as the flapper." "The *Zeitgeist* of 1790 France was revolutionary."

Appendix A:
Select Proverbs and Quotations

La belle dame sans merci. "The beautiful lady without pity." Title of a poem by John Keats.

Bene qui latuit, bene vixit. He has lived a good life who has remained unknown.

Das Weib sieht tief; der Mann sieht weit. Woman sees deep, man sees far.

Veniam petimusque damusque vicissim. We beg pardon and give it in return.

Tout comprendre c'est tout pardonner. To understand everything is to pardon everything.—Madame de Stael.

Tempus omnia revelat. Time reveals all things.

Scelere velandum est scelus. One crime has to be concealed by another.—Seneca.

Rien de plus eloquent que l'argent comptant. Nothing is more eloquent than cash.

Qui timide rogat, docet negare. He who asks timidly makes denial easy.—Seneca.

Quel che pare burla, ben sovent èvero. What seems a joke is very often true; many a true word is spoken in jest.

Die Probe eines Genusses ist seine Erinnerung. The test of a pleasure is the remembrance of it.—Jean Paul Richter.

Nemo propheta acceptus est in patria sua. No prophet is accepted in his own country.

Le mieux est l'ennemi du bien. The best is the enemy of the good. Leave well enough alone.

Lo que no se puede remediar se ha de aguantar. What can't be cured must be endured.

Locos y ninos dicen la verdad. Madmen and children speak the truth.

Lauda la moglie e tienti donzello. Praise a wife but stay a bachelor.

In nocte consilium. Night brings counsel.

Il vaut mieux employer notre esprit à supporter les infortunes qui nous arrivent qu'à prevoir celles qui nous peuvent arriver. It is much better to set our minds to bearing present ills than to foreseeing those that may befall us.—La Rochefoucauld.

Honores mutant mores. Honors change manners. It is not unusual for those who rise in the world to kick down the ladder by which they ascended.

Forsan et haec olim meminisse juvabit. Perhaps it will be pleasant to remember these hardships someday.—Vergil.

Ex vitio alterius sapiens emendat suum. A wise man corrects his faults when seeing another's.—Publilius Syrus.

Et semel emissum volat irrevocabile verbum. The word once uttered cannot be recalled.—Horace.

Es kann der Frömmste nicht im Frieden bleiben, Wenn es dem bösen Nachbar nicht gefällt. The gentlest man cannot live in peace, if it does not please his wicked neighbor.—Friedrich Schiller.

Deus est in pectore nostro. There is a divinity in our hearts.—Ovid.

Corruptissima in republica plurimae leges. The more corrupt the state, the more numerous the laws.—Tacitus.

Avant que de desirer fortement une chose, il faut examiner quel est le bonheur de celui qui la possède. Before desiring something passionately, one should inquire into the happiness of the man who possesses it.—La Rochefoucauld.

Die Alten zum Rat, die Jungen zur Tat. The old for advice, the young for action.

Parturient montes, nascetur ridiculus mus. Mountains will be in labor, and the birth will be an absurd little mouse.—Horace.

Nunc scio quid sit Amor. At last I know what love is really like.—Virgil.

Bis dat qui cito dat. He gives twice who gives promptly.—Publilius Syrus.

Appendix B: Latin Roots, Prefixes and Suffixes

a, ab, abs from, away from
acer sharp, acrid, acrimony
ad to
aedes building (edifice, edify)
age *used mainly in forming abstract nouns*
ager field
ago I act (action, agent, agitate)
al *used in forming action words*
alo I nourish (aliment, alimentary)
alter another (alternate, alteration)
altus high (altitude, exalt)
am, ambi about, around
amo I love (amorous, amiable)
anima breath, life (animal, animate)
animus mind (unanimous, magnanimity)
annus year (annual, anniversary)
ant *denoting an agent*
ante before
antiquus ancient (antique, antiquity)
appello I call (appeal, appellation)
aqua water (aquatic, aqueduct)
arbor tree (arboreal, arborage)
arcus bow (arcade, archer)
ars art (artist, artisan)
ary *denoting a thing belonging to*
ate *denoting an office or function*
audio I hear (audible, audience, auditory)
augeo I increase (auction, augment)
barba beard (barber)
bellum war (bellicose, belligerent)
bi, bis twice
brevis short (brevity, abbreviate)
cado I fall (accident, decadence)
canis dog (canine)
cano I sing (canticle, chant)
cavus hollow (cave, cavity, excavate)
cedo I go, yield (cede, accede, precede)
cito I call, summon (cite, recite, citation)

civis citizen (civil, civilian, civic)
clamo I cry out (exclaim, proclamation)
clarus clear (clarify, clarion, declare)
claudo I shut (exclude, seclusion)
cle, cule *denoting diminution*
clino I bend (incline, decline)
coelum heaven (celestial)
colo I tell (cultivate, culture)
com with, together
contra against
cor heart (cordial, courage)
corona crown (coronet, coronation)
credo I believe (creed, credible, incredulous)
cresco I grow (increase, decrease, crescent)
crux cross (crucify, crucifix, cruciform)
culpa fault (culprit, culpable)
cura care (curate, accurate)
de down
decem ten (decimal, decimate, December)
dens tooth (dental, dentist, indent)
dexter right-handed (dexterity, dexterous)
dico I say (dictation, verdict, diction)
dies day (diurnal, diary)
dignus worthy (dignity, indignity, dignify)
dis apart
doceo I teach (docile, doctrine)
domus house (domicile, domestic)
duco I lead (induct, educate, ductile)
durus hard, lasting (durable, duration, endure)
ego I (egoist, egotism)
emo I buy (redeem, exemption, pre-emption)
erro I wander (errant, error, aberration)
ess *denoting the feminine of*
esse to be (essence, essential)
et, ette *denoting diminution*
ex out of, from, off
extra beyond
facilis easy (facile, facilitate, facility)
fames hunger (famine, famish)
felix happy (felicity, felicitous)

femina woman (feminine, effeminate)
fido I trust (confide, fidelity, confident)
finis end (finite, infinite, finish)
fluo flow (flux, fluid, fluent)
folium leaf (foliage, portfolio)
fortis strong (fortify, fortress, fortitude)
frango I break (fragile, fraction)
frater brother (fraternal, fraternity, friar)
frons forehead (front, frontal, frontier)
fumus smoke (fumigate, fumigation)
fundus bottom (foundation, founder, profound)
gelu frost (gelid, congeal, gelatin)
gens race, people (gentile, generation, gender)
gradus step (grade, gradient, degrade)
gravis heavy (grave, gravity, grieve)
grex flock, herd (aggregate, congregate, gregarious)
habeo I have (habit, habitual, inhabit)
haereo I stick (adhere, cohere, cohesion)
halo I breathe (inhale, exhale)
homo man (homage, human, homicide)
hostis enemy (hostile, hostility)
humus earth, soil (humble, exhume)
ice, ise *denoting quality, condition, act*
ignis fire (ignite, ignition, igneous)
impero I command (empire, imperial, imperative)
in in, into
in not
ine *denoting feminine*
insula island (insular, peninsula)
inter between, within
ion, tion, sion *used in forming abstract nouns*
ira anger (irate, ire)
judex judge (judicial, judiciary)
jungo I join (juncture, junction)
jus right (justice, jurisdiction)
lapis stone (lapidary, dilapidated)
laus praise (laudable, laudation)
lavo I wash (lave, lavatory)
laxus loose (lax, laxity, relax)
lego I gather, read (collect, lecture, legible)

lego I send (legate, delegate)
lex law (legal, legitimate)
liber free (liberty, liberate, liberal)
liber book (library, librarian)
libra balance (librate, equilibrium)
lignum wood (ligneous, lignite, lignify)
ligo I bind (ligament, liable, religion)
litera letter (literal, literary, literature)
locus place (local, location, allocate)
loquor I speak (elocution, eloquent, loquacious)
lumen light (luminary, luminous, illuminate)
luna moon (lunacy, lunatic, lunar)
luo I wash (ablution, dilute)
lux light (lucid, lucidity, elucidate)
macula spot, stain (immaculate, maculate)
magnus great (magnify, magnitude, magnificent)
male bad, ill
malus bad, evil (malevolent, malady)
manus hand (manual, manufacture, manuscript)
mare sea (marine, maritime, mariner)
Mars god of war (martial, Martian)
medius middle (median, medium, intermediate)
memor mindful (memory, memorial)
mens mind (mental, mentality)
ment instrument of, act
mergo I dip (emerge, immersion)
miles soldier (military, militant, militia)
miror I admire (miracle, admirable)
mitto I send (commit, remit, mission)
moneo I warn (monitor, monition)
mons mountain (ultramontane, promontory)
mony instrument or means of
mors death (mortal, immortal, mortify)
moveo I move (motion, motive, motor)
multus many (multitude, multiply)
munus gift (munificent, remunerate)
murus wall (immure, mural)
muto I change (mutable, transmute)
narro I relate (narration, narrative)
nascor to be born (nascent, natal, native)
navis ship (navy, naval, navigation)

nihil nothing (annihilate, nihilist)
noceo I injure (noxious, innocent, innocuous)
nomen name (nominal, nomination, cognomen)
non not
norma rule (normal, abnormal, enormous)
novus new (novel, renovate, novice)
nox night (nocturnal, equinox)
nudus nude (denude)
nuntio I declare (announce, denounce)
ob against, in the way of
octo eight (octave, octagon, October)
oculus eye (ocular, oculist)
odi I hate (odium, odious)
omnis all (omnipotent, omniscience, omnibus)
on, oon *denoting increase or augmentation*
onus burden (onerous, exonerate)
226
opus work (operation, cooperate)
orno I adorn (adorn, ornament)
oro I speak (orator, oration)
ory place where
ovum egg (ovate, oval)
pando I spread (expand, expanse, compass)
pareo I appear (apparent, appearance, apparition)
paro I prepare (preparation, repair)
pars part (partial, partition, partner)
paseo I feed (pastor, pasture, repast)
patior I suffer (patient, passive, passion)
pax peace (pacific, pacify)
pecco I sin (peccable, peccant)
pecunia money (pecuniary, impecunious)
pello I drive (compel, repel, compulsive)
pendeo I hang (pendant, suspend, suspense)
per through
pleo I fill (complete, complement, supplement)
poena punishment (penal, penalty, penance)
pons bridge (transpontine, pontiff, pontifical)
porto I carry (export, report, deportment)
post after
pre before
primus first (primary, primitive, primrose)

pro before, in front of, forward, for, in behalf of
probo I prove (probable, approve, improve)
proprius one's own (proper, property, appropriate)
pungo I prick (puncture, pungent, expunge)
puto I reckon (compute, count)
quaero I ask (query, inquire, require)
quartus fourth (quart, quarter, quartet)
radix root (radical, eradicate)
rapio I seize (rapine, rapture)
re back, again
rego I rule (regent, regular, rector)
retro backward
rex king (regal, royal)
rideo I laugh (ridicule, deride, risible)
rodo I gnaw (rodent, corrode)
rogo I ask (interrogation, derogatory)
rota wheel (rotary, rotate, around)
rumpo I break (rupture, disruption, eruption)
rus country (rustic, rusticate)
sacer sacred (sacrament, sacrilege, sacristan)
sanctus holy (sanctify, sanctuary, saint)
sanguis blood (sanguinary, sanguineous)
sanus sound (sane, insane, sanity)
sapio I taste (sapid, insipid)
scio I know (science, omniscience)
scribo I write (scribe, scribble, scripture)
se aside, apart
semi half
senex old (senior, senile, senator)
sentio I feel (sense, sentiment, sensual)
septem seven (septennial, September)
sequor I follow (sequel, sequence, consequence)
servio I serve (servant, service, sergeant)
signum sign (signal, significant, designate)
socius companion (social, socialist, society)
sol sun (parasol, solar, solstice)
specio I see (inspect, circumspect, spectator)
spero I hope (desperate, despair)
spiro I breathe (aspire, inspire, conspire)
struo I build (structure, construct, construe)
suadeo I advise (persuade, dissuade)

sub under
sumo I take (assume, consume, assumption)
super over, above
tango I touch (contact, tangible, contagious)
tempus time (temporal, contemporary)
teneo I hold (tenet, tenant, tendril)
terminus boundary (terminal, terminate, term)
terra earth (terrestrial, subterranean)
terreo I frighten (terrible, terrify, terror)
timeo I fear (timid, timidity, timorous)
traho I draw (tract, traction, contraction)
trans beyond, through, across
tude *used in forming nouns*
tumeo I swell (tumor, tumid, tumult)
ty quality, state, condition
ultra beyond
umbra shadow (umbrella, umbrage)
un, uni one
unus one (unit, unite, union)
urbs city (urban, urbane, suburban)
ure action, result of
valeo I am strong (valiant, valid, invalid)
venio I come (convene, venture, advent)
verbum word (verbal, verbiage, proverb)
verto I turn (convert, divert, versatile)
verus true (verity, verify, veracious)
vestis garment (vestment, vesture, invest)
vice in the place of
video I see (vision, visit, evident)
vinco I conquer (victor, victory, convince)
vivo I live (vivid, survive, revive)
voco I call (vocal, vocalist)
volo I will (volition, voluntary, benevolence)
vox voice (vocal, vocalist)
vulgus common (vulgar, vulgate, divulge)
vulnus wound (vulnerable, invulnerable)

Appendix C: Greek Roots,
Prefixes and Suffixes

a, an not, without
aer air (aeroplane, aeronaut, aerostat)
agon contest (agony, antagonist)
allos another (allopathy, allegory)
amphi on both sides
ana back, again, up
angelos messenger (angel, evangelist)
anthos flower (anthology, anthologist)
anthropos man (philanthropy, misanthropy)
anti opposite, against
ap, apo from, away from
arch, archi chief
arche rule, beginning (archbishop, monarch, archaic)
aristos best (aristocracy, aristocrat)
aster, astron star (astronomy, astrology, asteroid)
atmos vapor (atmosphere)
autos self (autocrat, autograph, automobile)
ballo I throw (symbol, hyperbole)
bapto I dip (baptize, baptism)
biblos, biblion book (Bible, bibliography)
bios life (biology, biography, amphibious)
cat, cata down
cheir hand (chiropodist, chiropractor)
chromos time (chronicle, chronic)
daklulos finger (dactyl, dactylography)
deka ten (decade, decalogue)
demos people (democracy, demagogue, epidemic)
dendron tree (rhododendron, dendrology)
di, dis twice
dia through
doxa opinion (doxology, dogma, orthodox)
dunamis power (dynamite, dynamics)
dys ill
ec out of
eidos form (kaleidoscope, spheroid)
eikon image (icon, iconoclast)
electron amber (electric, electricity)
en, el, em in

endo in
ep, epi upon
ergon work (energy)
eu well (euphony, eucharist)
gamos marriage (polygamy, monogamy)
gaster stomach (gastric, gastronomy)
ge earth (geography, geology, geometry)
glossa tongue (glottis, glossary)
gramma letter (monogram, diagram, grammar)
grapho I write (biography, telegraph)
gyne woman (gynecology, misogyny)
haima blood (hemorrhage, hemorrhoid)
helios sun (heliography, heliotrope)
hemi half
hepta seven (heptarchy, heptagon)
hieros sacred (hieroglyphic, hierarchy)
hippos horse (hippopotamus, hippodrome)
hodos way (method, exodus, period)
homos same (homogenous, homologous)
hydor water (hydraulics, hydrogen)
hyp, hypo under
hyper over, above
ic pertaining to
ichthus fish (ichthyology, ichthyophagy)
isk denotes diminution
ism act, state, condition
isos equal (isotherm, isosceles)
ist agent (psychiatrist, novelist)
kakos bad, evil (cacophony, cacogenic)
kardia heart (cardiac, carditis)
kosmos world, order (cosmology, cosmopolitan)
krino I judge (critic, criterion, hypocrite)
kyklos circle, ring (cycle, cyclone)
kyon dog (cynic, cynicism)
lithos stone (lithograph, monolith)
logos word, discourse (monologue, dialogue, trilogy)
met, meta after, over
methon measure (diameter, barometer, thermometer)
mikros small (microscope, microcosm)
misos hatred (misogyny, misanthrope)
mon, mono alone, one, single
monos alone (monologue, monosyllable)
morphe shape (amorphous, metamorphosis)
mythos fable (myth, mythical, mythology)
naus ship (nautical, navigation, argonaut)
nekros dead, dead body (necropolis, necrology, necromancy)

neos new (neophyte, neologism)
neuron nerve (neuritis, neuralgia)
nomos law (autonomy, astronomy)
nosos disease (nosology)
oide song (ode, prosody, palinode)
oikos house (economy, ecology)
onoma, onyma name (synonym, patronymic, anonymous)
orthos right (orthodox, orthography)
pais child (pedagogue, pediatrics)
pan all (pandemic, panoply, panoramic)
par, para beside
pathos feeling (pathetic, sympathy, apathy)
pente five (pentagon, pentarchy)
peri round, around
petra rock (petrify, petrography)
phaino I show (phantom, phenomenon)
philos loving (philosophy, philanthropy)
phobos fear, dread (hydrophobia, claustrophobia)
phone sound (microphone, telephone)
phos light (phosphorescent, photography)
physis nature (physiology, physician)
poieo I make (poem, poet, pharmacopoeia)
polis city (politics, police)
polys many, much (polygamy, polygon)
pous foot (podiatrist, antipodes)
potamos river (hippopotamus, transpotamian)
pro before
pros towards
protos first (prototype, protoplasm, protocol)
pseudes false (pseudonym, pseudoscientific)
psyche soul, mind (psychology, psychotropic)
pyr fire (pyrotechnics, pyromaniac)
rheo flow (rhetoric, catarrh)
sis, sy state, condition, action
skopeo I see (microscope, telescope)
sophia wisdom (sophist, philosophy)
sphaira sphere (hemisphere, atmosphere)
stello I send (apostle, epistle)
stratos army (stratagem, strategy)
strepho I turn (catastrophe, apostrophe)
sy, syn with, along with
techne art, skill (technician, technical)
tele afar, distant (telegraph, telescope)
theos God (atheist, theocracy)
therme heat (thermometer, thermal)
topos place (topical, topography)

treis three (tripod, triangle)
trepo I turn (heliotrope, tropic)
typos mark, impression (stereotype, typewriter)
y *used in forming abstract nouns*
zoon animal (zoology, zoo)

Appendix D:
Words Pertaining to Class—Being a List for Social Scientists, and a Demonstration of the Importance of Class

aristocrat
arriviste
artisan
badly off
baron
beast of burden
beau monde
blue blood
blue collar
born to the manor
born to the purple
born with a silver spoon in the mouth
bourgeois
Brahman
caste
clan
clout
comfortable
commoner
count
cracker
Croesus
déclassé
degree
dowager
duke
earl
establishment
estate
exalted
fag
filthy rich

financially embarrassed
flush with money
full of piss and vinegar
grandee
hard up
haut monde
high born
high bred
high society
hourly worker
idle rich
ignoble
ill-assorted marriage
ill-off
impecunious
in reduced circumstances
lace curtain
leisure class
liege
loaded
lord
lower class
magnifico
margrave
mechanic
mésalliance
moneyed
net worth
noble
nobody
non-U
nouveau riche
opulent
parvenue
patrician
peasant
peer
peon
pinched
poor

poorly off
poor relation
poverty
powerful
prestige
privileged
proletarian
prosperous
rank
rentier
rich
ruling class
serf
SES (socio-economic status)
short of money
silk stocking
slave
social climber
socialite
society
somebody
standing
straitened
untouchable
upper class
upper-cruster
uppish
uppity
upscale
vile
viscount
wage earner
wealthy
well-off
well provided for
well-situated
well-to-do
white collar
worker
working class

236
working stiff
wrong side of the tracks

Bibliography

Chapman, Robert L., ed., *Roget A to Z* (New York: HarperCollins, 1994).

Cohen, J.M. and M.J. Cohen, *The Penguin Dictionary of Quotations* (Middlesex, England: Penguin Books, 1960).

Morris, William, ed., *The American Heritage Dictionary,* 4th ed. (Boston: Houghton Mifflin, 2002).

Room, Adrian, *Cassell's Foreign Words and Phrases* (London: Cassell, 2000).

Spears, Richard A., *Slang and Euphemism*, 3rd ed. (New York: Signet, 2001).

Funk & Wagnalls Standard Dictionary, 2nd ed. (New York: HarperPaperbacks, 1993).

About the Author

Born in 1965, John Fleming earned a B.A. in sociology (with a minor in German) from the University of Missouri, St. Louis, in 1989. His first book is entitled *The War of All Against All: An Analysis of Conflict in Society* and was published in 2000. In it he analyzes the idea of classlessness, man's primeval evolution in hunting-gathering bands and the effect of territorial crowding. Fleming also develops an original concept of the following as the basis of social power (the rich have larger followings). In addition, he has written articles that were published on the Internet. His scholarly interests include linguistics, pharmacology, vitamins, political sociology, English and American literature, and prehistory, and he speaks four languages (German, French, Spanish and native English).